GLOBALISATION, HUMAN RIGHTS AND LABOUR LAW
IN PACIFIC ASIA

Anthony Woodiwiss's pathbreaking book is the first substantive contribution to a sociology of human rights. In it, he takes up the critical question of whether so-called Asian values are compatible with discourses of human rights, and argues against those who see human rights issues as the major obstacle to global cooperation in the post Cold War world. Dr Woodiwiss's sociological and post-structuralist approach to the concept of rights, and his incorporation of trans-nationalism into sociological theory, enable him to demonstrate how, on the one hand, the global human rights regime can accommodate Asian 'patriarchialism' (to use Weber's term), while on the other hand, Pacific Asia is itself adapting through the emergence of what he calls 'enforceable benevolence'. His comparative studies of Hong Kong, the Philippines, Malaysia and Singapore highlight similarities between Pacific-Asian and Western societies and show the importance for the level of respect accorded human rights of the particular character of the local patriarchalism and the balance of social forces in play.

ANTHONY WOODIWISS teaches in the Department of Sociology, at the University of Essex. He has also held visiting positions at the Universities of Hong Kong and SUNY at Stonybrook, at the National University of Singapore, Griffith University, the University of the Philippines, and at Hitotsubashi University in Japan. His previous book publications include *Postmodernity U.S.A.: On the Crisis of Social Modernism in Postwar America* (1993), *Law, Labour and Society in Japan: From Repression to Reluctant Recognition* (1992), and *Rights v. Conspiracy: A Sociological Essay on the History of Labour Law in the United States* (1990).

CAMBRIDGE STUDIES IN LAW AND SOCIETY

Series editors

Chris Arup, Martin Chanock, Pat O'Malley
School of Law and Legal Studies, La Trobe University
Sally Engle Merry, Susan Silbey
Departments of Anthropology and Sociology, Wellesley College

Editorial board

Richard Abel, Harry Arthurs, Sandra Burman, Peter Fitzpatrick,
Marc Galanter, Yash Ghai, Nicola Lacey, Boaventura da Sousa Santos,
Sol Picciotto, Jonathan Simon, Frank Snyder

The broad area of law and society has become a remarkably rich and dynamic field of study. At the same time, the social sciences have increasingly engaged with questions of law. In this process, the borders between legal scholarship and the social, political and cultural sciences have been transcended, and the result is a time of fundamental re-thinking both within and about law. In this vital period, Cambridge Studies in Law and Society provides a significant new book series with an international focus and a concern with the global transformation of the legal arena. The series aims to publish the best scholarly work on legal discourse and practice in social context combining theoretical insights and empirical research.

Forthcoming titles include

Mariana Valverde, *Diseases of the will*

GLOBALISATION, HUMAN RIGHTS AND LABOUR LAW IN PACIFIC ASIA

Anthony Woodiwiss

PUBLISHED BY THE PRESS SYNDICATE OF THE UNIVERSITY OF CAMBRIDGE
The Pitt Building, Trumpington Steet, Cambridge CB2 1RP, United Kingdom

CAMBRIDGE UNIVERSITY PRESS
The Edinburgh Building, Cambridge CB2 2RU, United Kingdom
40 West 20th Street, New York, NY 10011–4211, USA
10 Stamford Road, Oakleigh, Melbourne 3166, Australia

First published 1998

Printed in the United Kingdom at the University Press, Cambridge

Typeset in 11/13 pt Goudy [WV]

A catalogue record for this book is available from the British Library

Library of Congress cataloguing in publication data
Woodiwiss, Anthony
    Globalisation, human rights, and labour law in Pacific Asia
/ Anthony Woodiwiss
      p.   cm. – (Cambridge studies in law and society)
    Includes bibliographical references (p.   ) and index.
    ISBN 0 521 62144 5. – ISBN 0 521 62883 0 (pbk.)
    1. Human rights – Asia, Southeastern. 2. Social values – Asia,
Southeastern. 3. Labor laws and legislation – Asia, Southeastern.
I. Title. II. Series.
JC599.A785W66 1998
303.3'72'095 – dc21   97–25650 CIP

ISBN 0 521 62144 5 hardback
ISBN 0 521 62883 0 paperback

To Kathianne with love

Give as much as you take, all shall be very well

Maori proverb

CONTENTS

FIGURES

ACKNOWLEDGEMENTS

I am very grateful for financial support from the British Academy, the Japan Society for the Promotion of Science and, in particular, the Fuller Fund of the Department of Sociology at the University of Essex. Because of wordage limits, my acknowledgements of my intellectual debts also have to be far more peremptory than I am happy with. They remain heartfelt none the less. Thus I wish to thank: in Japan, Watanabe Masao, Fuwa Kazuhiko and Harada Katsu; in Malaysia, Raymond Lee, Dunstan Ayadurai and Chandra Muzaffar; in Singapore, Kwok Ken-Woon, Chua Beng-Huat, James Jesudason and Hing Ai-un; in the Philippines, Froilan Bacungan and Marie Aganon; in Taiwan, Shieh G.-S., and Liou C.-P.; in Hong Kong, David Levin, Ng Sek Hong, Rod Broadhurst, Daniel Han, Wong Siu-Lun, Ng C.-H., Harold Traver, Carol Jones, Thomas Wong, Benjamin Leung, Cindy Chu, and Quah K.-E.; in the United States, John Miller, Richard Price, and Christine Harrington, Sally Merry and all my other colleagues in Conglass II and III; in the UK, Richard Wilson, Ian Neary, Kevin Boyle, Ted Benton and Michael Freeman; in Australia, Colin Mercer, Norma Chalmers, Jeff Minson, Jacques Bierling, Gary Wickham and Bryan Turner; in the Netherlands, Marcel van der Linden; and in Brazil, Michael Hall. Wordage limit or not, two of my chums must be singled out for special thanks: Frank Pearce for his continuing intellectual effervescence which makes him the most refreshing person I know, and Kathianne Hingwan who accompanied and supported me on all the adventures reported on herein.

Various large and small fragments of the present study have appeared elsewhere (Woodiwiss, 1992b, 1997b) and I would like to thank the following journals for their permissions to include this material in the present text: *Social and Legal Studies*, *Citizenship Studies*.

Finally, I would like to thank Cambridge University Press for permission to reprint Figure 1.1 from Michael Mann's *The Sources of Social Power* (1986), vol. 1.

CONVENTIONS

Throughout the book Pacific-Asian names appear in the style of the region; that is, with the exception of the Philippines and those individuals who use Western first names, with surname first and given name second.

THE 'CLASH OF CIVILISATIONS' AND THE PROBLEM OF HUMAN RIGHTS

One of the few benefits of the Cold War was the creation of a compendium of human rights that appeared to be capable of commanding the assent of peoples across the globe. Thanks to the insistence of the Soviet Union and its allies, and using Sir Isaiah Berlin's (1969) terminology, the 'positive' social and economic rights associated with the socialist tradition were added to the largely 'negative' civil and political rights of the liberal tradition when the 1966 United Nations Covenants were formulated (Cassese, 1990). Apart from hugely broadening the array of human rights, the bargained nature of this outcome meant that the two traditions ceased to be mutually exclusive in the sense that their adherents now accepted, at least formally and pending ratification, that their human rights records should be judged against each other's standards. One might have expected, therefore, that with the ending of the Cold War, the scene was indeed set for the establishment of a New World Order premised on universal respect for human rights.

PATRIARCHALISM AND THE POSSIBILITY OF ENFORCEABLE BENEVOLENCE

This has not turned out to be the case and this study is intended to offer both a contribution to the explanation of this state of affairs and a suggestion as to how a revival of the human rights project on a more equal civilisational basis that, because it assumes the hybrid nature of all societies (Bhahba, 1994), is neither Occidentialist (Carrier, 1992) nor Orientalist (Said, 1978) might yet become possible (see also, Wilson, 1996; Merry, 1996 and the ongoing discussion in *Human Rights Dialogue*). Central to the pursuit of both aims will be an acknowledgement of the fact that the coincidence of the ending of the Cold War with the maturation of the economic take-off in Pacific Asia has meant the eruption within global society of an ideological/cultural third force, in addition to liberalism and socialism, namely patriarchalism in its diverse forms.

1

For Max Weber, patriarchalism was one of the elementary forms of traditional authority:

> [It] is the situation where, within a group (household) which is usually organised on both an economic and kinship basis, a particular individual governs who is designated by a definite rule of inheritance. *The decisive characteristic ... is the belief of the members that domination, even though it is an inherent traditional right of the master, must definitely be exercised as a joint right in the interests of all members and is thus not freely appropriated by the incumbent.* In order that this shall be maintained, it is crucial that in both cases there is a complete absence of a personal (patrimonial) staff. Hence the master is still largely dependent upon the willingness of the members to comply with his orders since he has no machinery to enforce them. Therefore the members are not yet really subjects.
>
> (Weber, 1972, p. 231, emphasis added)

For Weber, then, patriarchalism was a strictly hierachical political structure justified by a familialist discourse and resting on an economy structured in part by kinship relations. Clearly, given the nature of contemporary state and economic forms, patriarchalism no longer has a political or economic referent outside of some relatively self-subsistent indigenous communities with which this study will not be concerned. However, it seems to me that the belief that is the 'decisive characteristic' does still have a referent in the wider societies within which such communities are related. Thus I will use patriarchalism to signify a familialist discourse that, regardless of institutional context, both assumes the naturalness of inequalities in the social relations between people and justifies these by reference to the respect due to a benevolent father or father-figure who exercises a 'joint right'.

Perhaps the best way to bring out the analytical significance of the term 'patriarchalism' is to explain why it has been preferred over 'patriarchy' and 'paternalism'. Patriarchy refers only to male domination over females, whereas patriarchalism may be used to refer to male/male relations as well, and therefore to any mode of domination that rests on familialist principles. Where the ruler is a woman, the term 'matriarchy' may be used to refer to an otherwise identical set of relationships and claims. The possibility of the latter situation suggests that patriarchalism is perhaps not as inimical to male/female equality as is often thought (Othman, 1997; Stivens, 1996). In the absence of its associated political and economic conditions of existence, ruling can all too easily become an exercise in absolutism and so 'freely appropriated by the incumbent' rather than the exercise of a joint right. This is because, given the bureaucratic state and the separation of the majority from property in the means of production that is intrinsic to capitalist economic relations, group members are no longer free to decide whether to comply or not.

Paternalism is the term most often used to refer to such a state of affairs in the West (Sartorius, 1983). However, it lacks the strongly familialist connotations of 'patriarchalism' and so would not accurately describe the discourses that I am concerned with. In Pacific Asia, the exercise of even such untrammelled discretion is always, rather than sometimes as in the West, justified by invoking a familialist discourse. Moreover, to use 'paternalism' in referring to the 'claims' made within Pacific-Asian discourses of rule would be to deprive oneself of the critical possibilities created by the implicit claim to the presence of Weber's 'decisive characteristic' that is carried by such a discourse. This is because, where the latter is supposed to be present, rule 'must definitely be organised as a joint right in the interests of all members'. Where discretion is not in fact exercised on such a basis one must of course use the term paternalism, but its connotations will be even more negative than they are when the term is used in the West since it suggests a dereliction as well as an asymmetrical variety of gift-giving – 'the unreciprocated gift . . . makes the person who has accepted it inferior . . . Charity is . . . wounding for him who has accepted it' (Mauss, 1990, p. 65).

Much of what follows is devoted to making these critical possibilities clear in the hope of releasing their reformative potential by descrying the possibility of an emergent new patriarchalism specified as a regime of 'enforceable benevolence'. The latter is a mode of governance where, whilst social relations remain distinctly hierarchical, the content of benevolence is democratically decided and its delivery legally enforced. Although such a regime would remain from my point of view a regrettably inegalitarian and no doubt sexist one, it could at least claim to be authentically patriarchalist rather than merely and at best paternalistic. This is because democracy, as instanced by national electoral and workplace participative structures, and the rule of law must be present as the structural equivalents of kinship and 'joint right' respectively, if Pacific-Asian and indeed Southern discourses of rule more generally are to be regarded as authentically patriarchalist. In a world of subjects and capitalism as opposed to kin relations, people's mutual dependencies and responsibilities as well as their respect for one another are institutionalised through the forms and practices of liberal democracy, whilst the rule of law prevents incumbents from simply

3

appropriating all benefits to themselves. More importantly, the social embeddedness of a human rights regime constructed on such a basis could mean that such a regime could prove to be more effective in Pacific Asia than one premised on the individualistic or social-democratic means of qualifying inequality that Westerners have resort to. In what follows I will indicate the degree to which a particular patriarchalist discourse projects such a model by the term I combine with patriarchalism. Thus I will refer, in ascending order of approval, to a 'mendicant patriarchalism' in the Philippines, an 'authoritarian patri-archalism' in Malaysia, a 'patriarchalist individualism' in Hong Kong and an 'active patriarchalism' in Singapore. The fact that the positions of the Philippines and Singapore in this hierachy of approval are the reverse of what they are according to the most widely used of human rights indices, that produced by Charles Humana (1992), is suggestive of both the difference that taking a sociological approach can make and the justificatory burden that one incurs as a consequence of taking it up.

PATRIARCHALISM AND THE PROBLEM OF HUMAN RIGHTS

Quite suddenly, then, 'traditional' bodies of thought such as Confu-cianism, Islam, Buddhism, or better their associated 'invented traditions' (Hobsbawm and Ranger, 1984), have regained a global presence that would have been unthinkable even five years ago. One result is that these days many Pacific-Asian governments are taking up a much more ambivalent stance towards what they sometimes refer to as the 'Western concept' of human rights than was the case during the Cold War (Christie, 1995; Freeman, 1995; Halliday, 1995). They point out that whereas the developed countries of the West are very critical of the records of Asian governments with respect to civil and political rights, they refuse to recognise the achievements of Asian governments in the areas of social, economic and cultural rights. With varying degrees of good faith (Chan, 1995; Ghai, 1995), some Pacific-Asian governments then go on to give one or more of three main reasons for the unbalanced judgements of their critics (Gabelleno-Anthony, 1995). First, Western governments refuse to acknowledge fully their responsibility for the late development of the region and the consequent continuing impoverish-ment of much of its population. Second, Western governments refuse to recognise that many of the social pathologies, supposed or otherwise, confronting them – pre-marital sex, divorce, single-parent families, crime, drug abuse, and, above all, stagnating economies – owe something to what are regarded as their excessively individualistic cultures. And finally, Western governments refuse to recognise even the possibility of the lesser pertinence and indeed lesser value of individual rights in non-individualistic cultures.

Like those of some of their Asian equivalents, the responses of some Western governments are also characterised by varying degrees of good faith (Muzaffar, 1993a), and not simply because of their refusals to take the counter-arguments and charges of their critics seriously. Two particularly problematic aspects of the position that some of them adopt are: first, it is founded on a refusal to recognise both the inadequacy and the unevenness of the protection offered human rights in their own societies (for an account of Britain's failures with respect to labour rights, see Ewing, 1994); and second, it is associated with an unwillingness even to contemplate that there might be other ways to secure respect for human rights than those that exist in their own societies.

Perhaps the most succinct instance of the insurgent patriarchalism of concern here is an old text, but perhaps also a particularly appropriate one in view of Japan's archetypal status within contemporary Pacific Asia. This text is the *Imperial Rescript on Education* of 1890 with its stress on the necessity of maintaining the 'five relationships' central to Confucianism – ruler/ruled, parents/children, husbands/wives, brothers/sisters and friendship – if Japan was to retain its distinctive cultural identity and indeed humanity as it developed economically:

> Know ye, our subjects
>
> Our imperial ancestors have founded our empire on a basis broad and everlasting and have deeply and firmly implanted virtue; our subjects, ever united in loyalty and filial piety, have from generation to generation illustrated the beauty thereof.
>
> This is the glory of the fundamental character of our empire, and therein also lies the sources of education.
>
> Ye, our subjects, be filial to your parents, affectionate to your brothers and sisters; as husbands and wives be harmonious, as friends true; bear yourselves in modesty and moderation; extend your benevolence to all; pursue learning and cultivate art, thereby develop your intellectual faculties and perfect your moral powers; furthermore, advance the public good and promote common interests; always respect the constitution and observe the law; should any emergency arise, offer yourselves courageously to the state; and thus guard and maintain the prosperity of our imperial throne, coeval with heaven and earth. So shall ye not only be our good and faithful subjects, but render illustrious the best traditions of our forefathers.

> The way set forth is indeed the teaching bequeathed by our Imperial ancestors, to be observed alike by their descendants and subjects, infallible for all ages and true in all places. It is our wish to lay it to heart in all reverence, in common with you, our subjects, that we may all thus attain to the same virtue.

An equally succinct instance of the defensive response that commitment to such values leads when critical questions are raised with respect to the human rights records of Pacific-Asian governments is that voiced by the Singaporean government official, Kishore Mahbubani:

> from the viewpoint of many Third World citizens, human rights campaigns often have a bizarre quality. For many of them it looks something like this: they are like hungry and diseased passengers on a leaky, overcrowded boat that is about to drift into treacherous waters, in which many of them will perish. The captain of the boat is often harsh, sometimes fairly, sometimes not. On the river banks stand a group of affluent, well-fed, well-intentioned onlookers. As soon as these onlookers witness a passenger being flogged or imprisoned or even deprived of his right to speak, they board the ship to intervene, protecting the passengers from the captain. But those passengers remain hungry and diseased. As soon as they try to swim to the banks into the arms of their benefactors, they are firmly returned to the boat, their primary sufferings unabated. This is no abstract analysis. It is exactly how Haitians feel.
>
> (Mahbubani, 1992, p. 10)

Neatly instancing as it does both a strong sense of 'Western hypocrisy' and an equally strong awareness of the patriarchalist nature of social relations in many Pacific-Asian societies (the nautical metaphor), such responses have become politically significant statements – witness their confident repetition in the *Bangkok Governmental Declaration* of 1993, at the subsequent United Nations Conference on Human Rights in Vienna (Boyle, 1995; Loh, 1995), and in the continuing World Trade Authority (WTO) discussions over the 'social clause' (Ago, 1995; Compa and Diamond, 1996; Siegel, 1994; Sengenberger and Campbell, 1994).

On the basis of a reading of such texts, and putting to one side the accusation of hypocrisy, the sociologically most interesting justifications given for the criticisms they contain may be reduced to two variants of the sovereignty theme: (1) the cultural unacceptability of individualist and universalistic norms within patriarchalist and particularistic social formations wherein heteronomy is apparently preferred to autonomy as a base value – most obviously exemplified with respect to gender relations; and (2) the cultural unacceptability of an enhanced role for the 'cold' techniques of the law within the 'warmth' of flexible and 'homo-functional' (Murakami, 1987) patriarchalist social relations (see also the Chinese director Zhang Yimou's recent film *Qiu Ju*). Although the first of these justifications is the most obviously difficult for Westerners to accept, the second is equally disturbing. As will be suggested below, there *are* ways of conceptualising rights that are not entirely individualistic, although they must, of course, necessarily always be universalistic. However, in my view and at the margins, which is generally where individuals are most at risk, there is no reliable or effective means of enforcing respect for any rights, no matter how conceptualised, in the absence of the rule of law.[1]

But how, *in addition to insisting upon the necessity of the rule of law*, should Western human rights advocates respond to the challenge coming from Pacific Asia? One response is to briskly reject it as self-serving casuistry in the absolutist manner of Lady Thatcher and the North American political scientists Rhoda Howard and Jack Donnelly (1986). As reported in the *New Straits Times* (4 September 1993), Lady Thatcher said during a visit to Malaysia: 'One hears talk of something called human rights imperialism. This is nonsense.' Far more sophisticatedly, Howard and Donnelly (1986, p. 813) make the same point when they argue that:

> communitarianism [socialism or patriarchalism, for example] . . . is structurally, ideologically, and philosophically incompatible with human rights. The view of human dignity found in all communitarian societies is that the individual realizes himself as part of a group by unquestioningly filling his social role or being loyal to the state . . . At the core of this incompatibility is the denial of social value to personal autonomy and privacy . . . the state (or traditional authorities) . . . must control family life, religion, education, and all other potentially independent aspects of life . . . the rule of law and procedural due process are obviously incompatible with such regimes . . . In communitarian regimes, one is entitled to the protection of the laws . . . only to the extent that one fits within certain substantive, ideologically defined categories.

Another response is a regretful deference to the Asian challenge in the name of an economic and political 'realism' which is sometimes given a relativist or multiculturalist gloss.

It seems to me that neither response is adequate and, interestingly, for the same reasons. First, both assume that authoritarian and antinomian interpretations of patriarchalist belief systems are the only possible ones. This is difficult to square not just with the existence of radical, pro-rights positions that also have regional cultural/religious support such as that exemplified by the Asian NGO's response to the 1993 *Bangkok Governmental Declaration* (see also, An-Na'im, 1990; Du and Song, 1995; Hsiung, 1985; Rouner, 1988; Welch and Leary, 1990), but also with the actual rights regimes in many Pacific-Asian societies. Second, both responses are strongly coloured by Orientalist or, in Asia itself, Reverse Orientalist assumptions which lead to the exaggeration or even absolutisation of the difference between East and West (Carrier, 1992; Minear, 1980; Said, 1978). These assumptions are equally suspect regardless of whether they emanate from the East or the West. And this is not simply because of their shared colonialist and racist genealogies, but also because they are falsified by Japan's postwar experience in particular since it demonstrates that patriarchalism, the rule of law and therefore respect for human rights may be made compatible with one another. These, then, are also the reasons that prompted my search for a more defensible response to the current patriarchalist challenge to the discourse of human rights.

The new prominence, pro and con, accorded to the discourse of human rights and patriarchalism are but two of many current intimations as to the increasingly obvious globalisation of social life. Also, for good and for ill, the global context within which we now have to think about human rights is one marked not only by the ending of the Cold War, but also by an ongoing shift in the planet's economic and cultural centre of gravity from the North Atlantic to the North Pacific. More concretely, this means that if we are to understand the fate of the discourse of human rights, let alone contribute to a positive outcome, we have to think transnationally and with full cognisance of what is happening in Pacific Asia. Given this context, then, the aims of this study are threefold:

(1) to advance our theoretical understanding of transnational sociality and the consequent porosity of national boundaries in general, as well as of the varying legal forms that enforceable human rights may take in particular;

(2) to contribute to our substantive understanding of the interrelationships between transnational processes, economic and social development, and variations in the form of, and the level of respect afforded to, human rights in the theoretically and politically critical Pacific-Asian region.

(3) to contribute to the construction of a non-Eurocentric basis upon

which increased efforts may be made to enhance respect for human rights in the wider world in addition to Pacific Asia.

HUMAN RIGHTS AND THE PERTINENCE OF THE SOCIOLOGY OF LABOUR LAW

In seeking to contribute to the long overdue creation of the sociology of human rights that Ted Benton (1993) and Bryan Turner (1993) have recently so eloquently initiated with their stress on bodily frailty as the *raison d'être* of rights, this study will say very little about the doctrinal or formal side of the texts and mechanisms at the heart of the global labour standards and human rights regimes. These aspects have been extensively and expertly described and analysed by many other scholars, notably Cassesse (1990) Dorman (1992) and Elwell (1995). Instead, this study focuses on a segment of what might be termed the 'social undergrowth' of the global regime and investigates the extent to which the tangled social-structural forms found there either protect or smother the growth of respect for human rights. Specifically, it focuses on those rights most directly pertinent to labour: first, the civil and political right to freedom of association, which like Sheldon Leader (1992, ch. 3) I regard as an independent and not a derivative right; and second, the social and economic rights to work, 'just and favourable conditions', trade union membership, collective bargaining and a living wage. I have chosen this focus for five reasons.

(1) Freedom of association is critical to the enforceability of all conceivable human rights regimes (Wiseberg, 1990).

(2) The tensions intrinsic to industrial relations in developing economies are one of the principal causes of human rights violations. This is because, as attested by the content of the core human rights texts, the greatest social-structural challenge to any sort of rights regime in the employment sphere is the capitalist economic system, since it requires precisely the inequality and differential treatment that the discourse of human rights rejects.

(3) Apart from forming and participating in political parties and/or social movements of one kind or another, independent trade unions are almost the only means available to ordinary people to assert any sort of countervailing collective power *vis-à-vis* the intrinsically collective entities instanced by companies and governments. As T. H. Marshall (1962) put it in the early 1960s, provided there are

9

no legal impediments, independent trade unions provide ordinary people with what he termed a 'secondary industrial citizenship' through which they can exert a continuous surrogate political power sufficient to ensure that their other rights are respected.

(4) The human rights that pertain to labour are amongst the most deeply entrenched of all such rights. They feature in the United Nations' Universal Declaration of Human Rights (1948) and are reinforced by the long-standing conventions of the International Labour Organization (ILO), as well as by the more recent United Nations International Covenants on Civil and Political Rights, and Economic, Social and Cultural Rights (1966). Moreover, they are enforced by the (admittedly rather weak) reporting systems of the ILO and the UN (Cassese, 1990; Hannum, 1992), and are also very often repeated in state constitutions and labour laws with the result that they supposedly already enjoy legal protection at the national level too. In addition, even if they do not often appear in the dockets of international juridical institutions, their observance is also monitored and sometimes more effectively enforced on a daily basis by the largest and best-organised set of NGOs in the world, the national and international trade union organisations. Finally, and somewhat surprisingly, they have recently gained the only slightly qualified imprimatur of the World Bank (1995, pt. 3) as critical to the achievement of balanced economic development.

(5) The Pacific-Asian people to whom labour law is directly pertinent are often considered to be amongst the more 'privileged' members of their societies, compared to the vast numbers of 'unprotected workers' (Cox, 1987; Harrod, 1987). Thus, the current labour rights situation may be suggestive of future developments with respect to the human rights of the population at large.

In sum, I have chosen to focus on labour rights because of their intrinsic importance, the opportunity they provide for the precise investigation of the relations between civil and political rights and economic and social rights, and because, finally, in studying them one may be, so to speak, closer to the future. Moreover, by examining them within a Pacific-Asian context I hope to demonstrate both something about the variety of legal forms that labour and human rights can take, as well as the variability of the social-structural contexts within which respect for human rights is possible. Finally, it seems to me that, as will be clear by the end of the study, because of their differences as well as their similarities, a detailed comparative study of the conditions obtaining in the Philippines, Hong Kong, Malaysia and Singapore provides a good framework within which to examine these diverse forms, unravel their complex relationships with their national and transnational social contexts, and explain their diverse consequences for the institutionalisation of human rights.

AN OUTLINE OF THE ARGUMENT

The main body of what follows is divided into two parts. The first part sets out the theoretical and methodological framework to be deployed within the second part. It then goes on to outline the pertinent features of the regional transnational context within which the labour law systems of Pacific Asia subsist, paying particular attention to the development of the highly influential discourse on the proper role for labour in Pacific capitalism that crystallised in the course of a still ongoing conference series organised by the Japan Institute of Labour. The second part provides support for the study's theoretically generated propositions by sociologically explaining the development and current effectiveness of the labour and human rights regimes to be found in the four case studies.

Chapter 1 outlines the theoretical moves necessary if sociology is to be capable of appreciating the newly apparent transnational character of sociality in general and in the spheres of law, human rights and labour relations in particular. It concludes with the presentation of a positivist and disaggregated concept of rights. I use the term 'positivist' in the sense of legal positivism because for me human rights should not be seen as any sort of natural moral entity but simply as socially constructed discursive entities that either have or do not have the social effects that are claimed for them. Thus, much as I am attracted by Turner's effort to provide sociological support for the discourse of human rights by deploying on its behalf what sociologists have had to say about the social significance of our bodily frailty, I regard such an effort as instancing ethical rather than properly sociological discourse. For me, the sociology of human rights is concerned not with debates over their universality or otherwise (see instead Nickel, 1987), but rather with understanding and explaining the extent to which, as discursive entities, they have the social effects that are hoped for. Such knowledge does of course have some ethical and political relevance and I will not be shy of pointing out what I think this is in what follows. However, given that I am going to argue that embeddedness is critical to enforcement, I will try very hard when specifying such relevance to limit my comments to arguing for changes that have some extant social-structural support rather than merely a presence on my own personal wish-list. I use the term 'disaggregated' because this acknowledges that there are different ways of giving discursive form to rights, according to how they combine and which they stress of 'liberties', 'immunities', 'powers', and 'claims' (see below, pp. 47–49). Such disaggregation makes it possible to escape from the Western and especially American privileging of liberty as the principal component of all rights without resorting to the antinomianism that currently and correctly engenders so much suspicion of any talk of alternative human rights regimes. More specifically, it allows for the possibility that rights may be as well written and secured through stressing a requirement to recognise and satisfy social and economic 'claims' against the state and the powerful more generally as through stressing the 'liberties' of the less powerful to oppose the more powerful.

Thus, not only does the constructed hybridity of rights discourse exemplified by the coexistence of the two UN Covenants allow one to be sensitive to differences without being in any way relativistic, but so too does a more sophisticated understanding of the formal structure of rights. This is because, as a matter of positive international law, both Covenants have equal validity and cannot be used to cancel each other out. As a result, for example, labour's discursive entitlement is always double, always has a civil/political component and an economic/social one, and therefore always includes, for example, an element of economic security and an element of freedom of association. However, the relative weight of these elements may and indeed ought to vary greatly in different social structural conditions. This is not so much because in all likelihood courts would permit such variation (Merrils, 1988), as because rights only stand a chance of enforcement if they are congruent with or embedded within the larger structures of social life and their associated practices – witness the tragic irrelevance of so many imitatively individualistic Bills of Rights under the patriarchalist conditions obtaining in Latin America wherein patron–client systems tend to deliver 'justice' according to one's location within these systems and/or the outcomes of the struggles between them rather than according to one's individual entitlement.

Because Pacific Asia, then, represents the source of much contemporary criticism of the discourse of human rights, and moreover promises/threatens to provide models of social organisation that may soon become directly pertinent to the West, what follows focuses on that region. Thus Chapter 2 uses the theoretical position outlined in Chapter 1 to justify the demarcation of Pacific Asia as a distinctive regional social formation. After outlining the nature and structure of this social formation in general terms, it discusses the domestic labour law systems of the United States and Japan, the two most influential powers in the region. The chapter then focuses on the displacement of the American New Deal model by the Japanese model as part of the emergence of a post-colonial discourse on labour for 'Pacific capitalism'. It discusses in detail the emergence of a new discourse of industrial governance in the form of an 'export version' of the 'Japanese Employment System' (JES) which stresses the importance of enterprise unionism instead of the lifetime employment central to the 'domestic version'. In so far as enterprise unionism is contrasted to political or militant unionism, what it connotes is above all a disciplined labour force. Thus even enterprise unionism is recommended not so much as a necessary component of an effective industrial relations system as the preferred form when unions of some kind are unavoidable.

The chapter ends, however, by suggesting that, as in the case of the 'domestic version' of the JES, the best strategy for ensuring the effectiveness of labour and human rights regimes in Pacific Asia is likely to be one that seeks to articulate indigenous patriarchalist discourses with the rule of law and so reintroduce elements of internal critique and substantive mutuality into such discourses. In other words, the political hope is that in this way patriarchalism, and, in particular, the legally enforceable 'claims' against the powerful that may be derived from the lure of virtue and the claim of benevolence, may come to play the role of the critical moral and legal trump much as individualism and 'liberties' to oppose the powerful did in the West.

I will now set the context within which I propose to support this hope by outlining my argument with respect to labour rights in somewhat more detail. During Western capital's triumphant heyday in the latter half of the nineteenth century, parties to contracts were legally and culturally allowed to seek the best possible terms for themselves without concern for the consequences for each other. Under such circumstances it was eventually widely recognised that a just labour law system was one where freedom of association sanctioned a wide variety of further 'liberties' or, in Britain, 'immunities' with respect to acts of dispute on labour's part so as to ensure that contracts were not unduly affected by the asymmetrical balances of power created by the difference between labour's inevitably individual mode of embodiment and capital's necessarily collective one. Gradually, as the economically disruptive consequences of this expanded conception of freedom of contract became apparent, the 'liberties' or 'immunities' of both parties to the employment contract were constrained by legislation and judicial decisions. However, alongside this constraint came compensations. Thus 'liberties' or 'immunities' were exchanged for enforceable 'claims' on employers and the state, or welfare capitalism in its varying forms.

By contrast, in the newly post-colonial East the constraints on contracting parties inherited as part of the various postwar and independence settlements were both uncompensated for and elided with indigenous patriarchalist social relations. The result was that neither the local state nor capital thought back to freedom of contract and therefore was not mindful of the exchange that legitimated the constraints. Instead, it assumed both the subordination of labour and the moral superiority of its own emergent form of capitalism. Labour's structural problem, then, was that it often lacked much in the way of 'liberties' or 'immunities' that could be bargained away as well as indigenous cultural resources that could be used to legitimate its demands. However, it was Japanese labour's good fortune that, just when almost everything appeared to be lost as a result of the successful assault on the militant unions of the 1950s, the Supreme Court began to take the claim to moral superiority seriously and invented its own orientalised version of the unknown or forgotten liberal or social-democratic bargain. Thus in postwar Japan a just labour law system came to be seen as one wherein employee loyalty and cooperation had to be rewarded, albeit more by employer benevolence, specifically in the form of lifetime employment, than state welfare. In other words, labour's disadvantages under capitalist conditions gained recognition and protection not so much on the basis of legislation and therefore democratic citizenship as in the West, but primarily on the basis of the ideological and therefore judicial recognition of the obligation engendered by loyal service. The sociological and political question that this study therefore sets out to answer is, 'Does this alternative rationale for industrial justice, which I term "enforceable benevolence", provide a plausible template for effective labour and human rights regimes throughout Pacific Asia?'

This question is answered in a largely positive manner in the second part of the study. In each of the case studies the social genealogy and nature of the locally dominant form of patriarchalism is outlined and related to the development and coverage of the labour law system as an instance of human rights discourse. The discussion of the Philippines emphasises the 'mendicant' character of the local patriarchalism that was the result of a dependence on the United States that continued long after the formal granting of independence. This dependence accounts for both the alien nature of much of Philippine legal discourse and, relatedly, the refusal of Filipino capital to be bound by the rule of law. With respect to labour law, emphasis is given to two features: first, the lack of fit between the American-derived positive 'liberties' upon which the postwar system was based and the patriarchalist social-structural context within which they subsisted; and second, especially given the mendicant character of the local patriarchalism, the difficulty of maintaining these 'liberties' even when, as in the pre- and post-Marcos periods, unions or employees possessed certain additional quasi-corporatist 'powers' relative to companies and the state.

The discussion of Hong Kong emphasises the syncretic and reserved character of the local patriarchalism. This, it is argued, was the result of the colonial state belatedly taking on the patriarchal duties formerly performed by the better employers but within an ideological and social context wherein individualism had become both an approved value and, because of the growth of the middle class, a possible way of life. With respect to labour law, attention is paid to the British-derived 'voluntarism' of the early postwar system with its immunity-based conception of rights. Also, the minimalist industrial as well as wider social consequences of such a mode of governance in a patriarchalist social context are specified, as are the equally minimalist but, suggestively, far more widely supported and effectively enforced compensatory measures with respect to the individual employment contract and social rights belatedly taken by the colonial state. Finally, the robustness of the resulting rights regime is assessed in the light of Hong Kong's return to Chinese sovereignty.

The discussion of Malaysia emphasises the authoritarian character of the local patriarchalism that is the result of the effectiveness of claims on Malay loyalty in a context where Malays, as contrasted to the Chinese and Indian communities, are an economically disadvantaged but constitutionally privileged indigenous majority. With respect to labour law, attention is again paid to the failure of both the initial, British-inspired immunity-based system and the later Northern European and Australian influenced arbitration and therefore powers-based system to provide labour with much leverage. In this case, however, because of, surprisingly, an American-style economically modernistic (Woodiwiss, 1993, ch. 3) reinvention of patriarchalism that stresses loyalty over benevolence and restricts the latter to a combination of economic growth and benign neglect, there is little sign of the presence let alone effectiveness of an alternative rationale for industrial justice let alone human rights.

Finally, the discussion of Singapore emphasises the social democratic roots of the local patriarchalism and the survival of the resulting egalitarian policy commitments despite recent attempts to orientalise the discourse of rule. Thus, although employee and trade union 'liberties' have undoubtedly been restricted, employees have gained both certain quasi-corporatist 'powers' through their unions and, because of the strongly embedded character of these 'powers', the possibility if not yet the actuality of enforceable 'claims' on government and employers – to education, housing and prosperity, if not to 'lifetime employment', training and welfare, or the co-ownership that was promised in the 1960s.

In the Conclusion I step back from the detailed argumentation provided in the preceding chapters in order to make clear its significance for the possibility that 'enforceable benevolence' might represent the basis of an alternative human rights regime to those projected by and in the names of liberalism and social democracy. On the one hand, it is emphasised against those who would identify human rights with liberalism, that liberal rights would seem to be irrelevant and unenforceable in patriarchalist societies, not least because of the weakness and deference of their bearers. On the other hand, two points are stressed against the cruder advocates of the disciplinary effectiveness of so-called 'Asian values'. The first is that patriarchalism in its contemporary forms is very varied and by no means purely Asian with respect to its component elements. In fact, it represents so many instances of hybridity in that it is always an admixture of indigenous patriarchalist ideas with Western ones such as nationalism, democracy, modernisation and social democracy. Each of the latter in one way or another projects a broader sense of community than the individual patriarchal unit and so, again, suggests the need for a broader discourse of legitimate governance than simple familialism. The second is that, whereas patriarchalism is by no means intrinsically antipathetic to human rights, its effectiveness on their behalf depends not only upon the nature of the admixture, but also and critically upon the state and the powerful being prepared or made to live by their own values. The latter is something that largely depends upon the state of the social-structural power balances. Thus it implies that the powerful have to accept not just democracy and the rule of law but also that the less powerful should continue to possess certain irreducible, if perhaps in Western eyes minimal, liberties so as to be able to enforce such a disciplining. In sum, although a socially embedded rationale for human rights in Pacific Asia may have to have distinctively patriarchalist elements that differentiate it from those mobilised in the West, many of its additional elements will be the same. Moreover, it should not be forgotten that in the West too, especially in Western Europe, patriarchalist discourse was and still is mobilised on behalf of labour and human rights by christian democrats, including British 'One Nation' Conservatives, as well as by, in a transformed way, social democrats (Woodiwiss, 1998).

What follows is a highly fallible but I hope corrigible report on a thought experiment conducted in order to discover what grounds there may be for supporting the claims of those who might want to argue that patriarchalism can provide the basis for an alternative human rights regime. Finally, it has to be said that this was an experiment undertaken somewhat against my own better judgement, since I too distrust the motives of those who are behind the present assault on the current, Western-dominated version of human rights discourse. However, not only are individual human motives discounted as the ultimate determinants of social development by the structuralist mode of analysis deployed in this text, but also the question arises as to what practical as opposed to purely intellectual use Sociology has if it does not allow us to conduct such experiments despite the discomfort they may cause us ethically and politically? I agree with those (Christie, 1995, for example) who point out that it is the very success of some Pacific-Asian governments in achieving the economic development they prioritise which has undermined traditional normative structures rather than 'Western individualism' *per se*. However, I do not subscribe to the Modernisationist convergence thesis according to which similar technologically generated problems require let alone engender similar normative solutions, upon which many such arguments depend. Whether one likes it or not, Pacific-Asian societies are and most likely will remain culturally and therefore in many other ways too very different from those in the West. And this to the degree that, even under conditions of 'perfect' democracy, labour and human rights would have to be configured and enforced differently. It is for this reason, then, that I have approached the issue by thinking through Japan as well as by thinking through the United States and Europe. More immediately, if what I will outline represents an at all plausible basis for an alternative human rights regime, it seems to be more important that those who live in societies that claim to be patriarchalist should have a means of calling the moral bluff of those that rule them, than that we in the West should be untroubled in our ethical certainties.

Most contemporary commentary blames the forces summarised by the unlovely term globalisation for the current worldwide deterioration in labour's position. Although I do not disagree with such analyses, I would also like to suggest that globalisation may also have a positive dimension. This is the positivity that arises because of the increased possibilities of, as well as the necessity for, mutual learning created by our occupancy of what in some aspects at least is becoming a single global space (Robertson, 1990). As I hope to demonstrate, such possibilities include that of the North learning from the South, and so may indicate the commencement of that 'voyage in' that Edward Said (1993) has spoken of as a prerequisite for the arrival of a truly post-colonial world. In sum, then, what is provided below is a study undertaken to discover if there might be a way of naturalising the discourse of human rights in Pacific Asia and so preventing it from becoming a flash point in what some commentators see as a developing 'clash of civilisations' (Huntington, 1997).

PART ONE

AGAINST ABSOLUTISM AND RELATIVISM: TOWARDS A GLOBALLY ENFORCEABLE CONCEPT OF HUMAN RIGHTS

CHAPTER ONE

TRANSNATIONAL SOCIALITY, SOCIOLOGICAL THEORY AND HUMAN RIGHTS

These are anxious as well as exciting times in the social sciences, just as they are in the world at large. Disciplinary blocs and the relative security they brought with them are collapsing as fast in the social sciences as they are in the world which they seek to understand. However, it would be most unwise to dissolve the blocs within which intellectuals are organised as quickly as the nations of the world have dissolved the geo-political blocs into which they were so recently organised. This is because, at first sight paradoxically, a critical condition of the possibility of knowledge is acceptance of disciplinarily imposed limits to what can be known. That is, to paraphrase Michel Foucault (1974), it is the abstraction from the real produced by the operation of the pertinent 'rules of formation' of disciplines that results in the differentiation of knowledge from non-knowledge. This said, provided that the term 'inter-disciplinary' is taken literally and not as legitimating an intellect-ual cafeteria, social scientists are nevertheless in some ways more free than nation states to take advantage of the opportunities created by the present state of flux and so overcome the intellectual blindspots resulting from years of thinking in blinkered mono-disciplinary terms. For these reasons, then, I will trespass below on the territory of many other disciplines – History, Law and Asian Studies, in particular – but I will do so strictly and only as a sociologist interested in the macro-sociology of law and human rights.

DURKHEIM, MAUSS AND THE INDEXICAL NATURE OF LAW

Until recently, one of the more disappointing characteristics of the socio-logy of law and indeed of socio-legal studies more generally was its focus on the criminal law and the criminal justice system. I regard such a focus as surprising for two main reasons. First, other areas of public law and especially the private law necessarily and directly affect far more people than the criminal law. That is, far more people buy things, make con-tracts, seek redress for various civil injuries and undertake paid employ-ment than either commit or are the victims of crimes. Moreover and although this is not reflected in levels of media interest, far more legis-lative and judicial time is concerned with debating and administering these other areas of law than is spent on the criminal law. Second, the classical sociologists also paid far more attention to the private than the criminal law. This was because, as Emile Durkheim made explicit in his *Division of Labour* (1896), they regarded the law as a 'visible index' of otherwise invisible sets of social relations which were far more extensive than those bespoken by the criminal law alone.

That said, it may also be the case that a misreading of Durkheim's use of this index is in part responsible for the skewing of sociological interest that I consider to have been so disappointing. Specifically, outside the specialist literature (Hunt, A., 1978; Pearce, 1989) Durkheim is too often casually taken to have spoken of a general move from repressive to restitutive sanctions as an indicator of the transition from mechanical to organic solidarity. However, he in fact emphasised that this reflected an increase in the importance of the private law relative to the criminal law rather than an overall change in all aspects of the legal system (Durk-heim, 1984 [1896], p. 69). In sum, then, whereas an accurate reading of Durkheim would have directed sociologists to the study of the private law, an inaccurate reading may have helped to fix their sights on the criminal law and its transformations. Not the least of the reasons for regretting such a fixing of our gaze is the narrowing of the indexical potential of the law that it represents.

For Durkheim, the increased importance of the private law provided an index for and indeed instanced the approach of a new and 'organic' form of social solidarity wherein both the 'forced' and the 'anomic' forms of the division of labour might be overcome with the result that work was both justly assigned and socially rather than simply economically productive (Durkheim, 1896, pp. 353–95). Again for Durkheim and even more so for Marcel Mauss (1990) and Georges Bataille (1988), the main lineaments of this new form of social solidarity could be imagined and even acted upon although they were invisible. Hence Durkheim's enthusiasm for a particular variant of corporatism, Mauss' welcoming of the first signs of the welfare state and Bataille's more diffuse and far more eccentric anti-utilitarian celebration of excess. In sum, what all of them had in common was an appreciation of sociology's capacity to read, so to speak, the social unconscious.

When the Durkheimians spoke of a social unconscious, it is important to understand that they did not mean the same as Karl Jung, for example, meant by a similar term. Instead of some kind of collective psyche, what they were referring to was what Mauss called a 'total social fact' or the idea that in reality the different dimensions and aspects of sociality that we can distinguish analytically are not simply imbricated with one another but are also consubstantial with one another:

> In these 'total' social phenomena, as we propose calling them, all kinds of institutions are given expression *at one and the same time* – religious, juridical, and moral, which relate to both politics and the family; likewise economic ones, which suppose special forms of production and consumption, or rather, of performing total services and of distribution.
>
> (Mauss, 1990 [1924], p. 3, emphasis added)

Although Mauss was mainly concerned with the gift relationship or what 'compels the gift that has been received to be obligatorily reciprocated' (ibid.) in what he termed 'archaic' societies, he added that:

> this morality and organisation still function in our own societies, in unchanging fashion and, so to speak, hidden, below the surface, and as we believe that in this we have found one of the human foundations on which our societies are built, we shall be able to deduce a few moral conclusions concerning certain problems posed by the crisis in our own law and economic organisation. (Ibid., p. 4)

The consubstantiality of determinate combinations of social facts means that their presences are mutually implicatory. Thus with the help of the sociological imagination what is visible can tell us something about what else is present and has or could have operant effects and yet remains for the time being invisible. More particularly, Mauss tells us that the alternative to 'performing total services', as exemplified by the excesses of generosity in potlatch ceremonies, is alienation and internal conflict. For Bataille (1988) any unexpended or hoarded surplus represented an 'accursed share' which he regarded as the origin of war. More encouragingly, Mauss (1924, p. 67) also tells us that:

> All our social insurance legislation . . . is inspired by the following principle: the worker has given his life and labour . . . to the collectivity . . . and . . . to his employers. Although the worker has to contribute to his insurance, those who have benefitted from his services have not discharged their debt to him through the payment of wages. The state itself, representing the community, owes him, as do his employers, together with some assistance from himself, a certain security in life, against unemployment, sickness, old age, and death.

What is visible has implications for what is 'immanent in the population', to use a phrase of Foucault's (1991, p. 100) that through both of its main terms reminds us of his Durkheimian milieu, especially as mediated through Bataille. This, then, suggests something of the potential of an indexical investigation and therefore what may be lost if the index is constructed or read upon too narrow a basis. More specifically, what I would like to suggest is that something of the mutuality intrinsic to the gift relationship that Mauss wrote so suggestively about might be present not simply in the welfare systems that are currently under attack in the North but also in the patriarchalist familialism that has historically informed many labour law systems throughout the world (Woodiwiss, 1998) and which has recently so strongly reasserted itself in Pacific Asia. In sum, my suggestion will be that this discursive alternative to liberalism and socialism, which in Pacific Asia moreover is social-structurally far closer to the social facts of which Mauss and Bataille wrote, might yet be made into a resource for reinvigorating the current of social reciprocity, especially given the context of the newly apparent 'total social fact' instanced by globalisation. This was the current that, prior to the appearance of the welfare state, which is denounced by today's accursed band of neo-liberals, was all but cut off by the rise of, to use Mauss and Bataille's adjectives, the 'utilitarian' and 'restricted' economy of capitalism and its 'homogenous' society (see also, the discussion of the 'moral economy' in pre-capitalist societies in Scott, 1976 and Thompson, 1993).

Most likely, the greater sociological interest in criminal rather than private law is explainable by a combination of the political centrality of 'law and order', which is itself a sign of the presence of the 'accursed share', the related local hegemony of criminology with respect to the sociology of law, the fearsome technicality of private law, and the silences produced by the broader hegemony of 'utilitarian' capitalism. Interestingly, support for the last of these three suggestions is provided by the fact that, minimal though it too has been, the area of non-criminal law that has received more sociological attention than any other has been that where, prompted by the suppressed necessity for reciprocity, the latter hegemony has been most directly challenged, namely the always public/private but these days only sometimes criminal one of labour law (see Edelman, 1980; Kahn-Freund, 1981; Pritt, 1970; Renner, 1949; Selznick, 1980; and Strinati, 1982). By the same token, it should not be surprising that, aside from the Durkheimian work of Maurice Halbwachs (1958, pp. 79ff.) most of the work done in the area has been broadly Marxist in character.

Although like those who have preceded me in this field my approach is also broadly Marxist, it rejects the economic essentialism with respect to social causation and the instrumentalism with respect to the state and law that most often marks earlier Marxist work. As I now see it and thinking about the sociology of law specifically, the main reason for these rejections is that such theoretical commitments pre-judge the indexicality of law (the law necessarily and uniformly reflects capital's dominance) and so deprive us of a most valuable means for understanding the complex nature of the power balances between social-structural entities as well as for identifying some perhaps less obvious means for redressing them to labour's advantage. Moreover, these rejections should make it easier to articulate what remain basically Marxist categories with the Durkheimian problematic of the 'total social fact'. However, the simple rejection of pre-emptive presuppositions is obviously insufficient for the realisation of the indexical potential of law. Re-theorisation is required, particularly so as to make a start on unravelling the complexities of the relationships between law and other sets of social relations.

TOWARDS A SOCIOLOGY OF GOVERNANCE

In the sphere of governance within which law and rights most narrowly subsist, all that once appeared to be so solid seems to be melting into the air with particular rapidity. Simply keeping track of all the changes is an enormous task. The fading of old boundaries, the supercession of established jurisdictions, and the inscription in their place of a new but still indistinct regulatory cartography have led many to focus on the representable aspects of the current transformations. This is a focus that chimes very well with the leading-edge but unfortunately currently anti-sociological emphasis on governmentality (the hows rather than whys of public and private governance) to be found in the post-Foucaultian literature (vide, Burchell et al., 1991; Hunt and Wickham, 1994) – perhaps too well. In my view, there is a danger that once one has provided a reasonably detailed account of the pertinent 'deliberations, strategies, tactics, and devices' (Rose, 1996, p. 328) that comprise governmentality, or what David Owen in conversation has termed the 'techne' of governance, one might think that one has fully explained the phenomena involved.

Although I will incorporate several of its insights into what follows, I have three problems with the governmentality literature as it stands. The first is that it is difficult to square its empiricism with its claims to the Foucaultian mantle, indeed to be 'the Foucault effect'. Here the point is less the general difficulty of forgetting Foucault's almost constant, and far from straightforwardly inductivist, theorising than the particular difficulty of failing to acknowledge the resemblance between the terminology of 'deliberations, strategies, tactics, and devices' and that deployed in his most sustained effort at theorisation, *The Archaeology of Knowledge* (for a mediating text see the discussion of the 'intrinsic technology' or 'economy' of discourse in Foucault, 1979, p. 92). By and large, the partisans of governmentality correctly reject both the epistemological anti-rationalism of the postmodernist epigoni and the rationalism of the latter's structural-marxist predecessors. Nevertheless, they still share a privileging of vision and the visible, an ocularcentrism (Levin, 1993) therefore, with both of these positions. The result is that they eschew any attempt to create a new visuality, in the sense of a theoretical structure which could make a new way of seeing possible, and which therefore could throw light on the hitherto invisible and thus deepen our understanding of the pertinent causal mechanisms. In the absence of such an attempt, explanations or accounts of governance will remain limited to those made possible by the governmentalists' narrow reading of Foucault's original formulation, and so continue to operate with tacit assumptions as to the necessary effectivity of governmental techniques and therefore the necessarily incremental character of social change, both of which rather surprisingly call to mind very traditional modes of liberal historiography.

My second problem with the governmentality literature is that an anti-sociological and technicist reading of Foucault's theses on governmentality is an impoverished reading of the pertinent texts. In his essay entitled 'Governmentality' Foucault states that:

> The art of government . . . is essentially concerned with answering the question of how to introduce economy – that is to say, the correct manner of managing individuals, goods and wealth within the family (which a good father is expected to do in relation to his wife, children and servants) and of making the family fortunes prosper – how to introduce this meticulous attention of the father towards his family into the managment of the state.
> (Burchell et al., 1991, p. 92)

He then goes on to argue in a very Durkheimian way that the critical event *explaining* the shift away from the simple sovereign/familialist mode of governance was an extra-governmental and indeed in part an extra-discursive occurrence, namely 'the emergence of the problem of population' (Burchell et al., 1991, p. 99), or 'the perception of the specific problems of the population' (ibid.), or in still other words that 'population has *its own* regularities, its own rate of deaths and diseases, its cycles of scarcity, etc.'(ibid., emphasis added). As a consequence, 'the means that the government uses to attain these ends are themselves all in some sense *immanent in* the population' (ibid., p. 100, emphasis added). What points such as these suggest to me is that, although Foucault indeed defines governmentality as 'the ensemble formed by the institutions, procedures, analyses and reflections . . . calculations and tactics . . .' (ibid., p. 102), this in no way denies that the problems of populations and indeed populations themselves have a life, so to speak, that it is analytically prior, and not reducible, to their status as objects of governance (compare Foucault's discussion of the rules of formation of the objects of discursive formations in the *Archaeology*). This is the life that such governmentalist *savoirs* as economics and sociology were/are intended to elucidate – indeed, as Foucault says, the first form of governmentalist knowledge was 'political economy' (ibid.).

Thus, the third of my problems with the governmentality literature is that, when it is combined with the idealist reading of poststructuralism that is postmodernism, it adds up to an intellectual conjuncture which may cause us to miss the opportunity to create the new sociological visuality that I regard as implicit in what many would regard as a transgressive, realist reading of poststructuralism in general and Foucault's work in particular (Woodiwiss, 1990b). For this reason I will be at pains in what follows to point out two things. First, the continuing pertinence to the study of governance of such in themselves invisible aspects of the social life of populations as those entities that have come to be known as 'capitalism' and its 'classes'. With respect to the social relations to which they refer, this pertinence is that in addition to making new things visible they also make it possible to understand both some instances of the ineffectiveness of, and sudden changes in, systems of governance, as well as their far more common social 'directionality' (Purvis and Hunt, 1993) in favour of the already powerful. Second, the particular pertinence to the future of governance worldwide of the forms taken by capitalism, class and patriarchalism in postwar Japan and Pacific Asia more generally and so already immanent in large sections of the world's population.

GLOBALISATION AND ITS CHALLENGE TO SOCIOLOGY

The globalisation of economic relations represents a challenge, threat, or even stimulus (Mann, 1993, p. 118; Hirst and Thompson, 1996) to national systems of governance *per se* and not simply to those aspects of them that regulate economies. However, the meaning of globalisation varies according to what sort of economic relations are at issue. Roland Robertson's (1990) is the most useful definition of 'globalisation' known to me – 'the making of the world into a single place'. The main reason for preferring it to that to be found in the work of Anthony Giddens (1990), for example, is that it does not identify globalisation with 'Westernisation' and therefore pre-specify the nature of the single place that is to come (Woodiwiss, 1996). Indeed, Robertson makes it clear in his work that this place will be a hybridised one. This difference is especially important in the current context since anything but 'Westernisation' is going on with respect to employment relations. Looking back over the past twenty years, so far from employment relations converging on Western forms what one may observe is a remarkably consistent effort to seek out and to maintain those local differences that secure the inequality between capital and labour and so to make the world safer (i.e. more profitable) for one type of economic entity in particular – the transnational corporation. As it happens, in so far as the principal site in which such pertinent differences have been discovered is Pacific Asia, these differences represent instances of precisely the patriarchalism that Foucault refers to as the earliest model for governance.[1]

Moreover, as Phedon Nicolaides (1987) has said with unusual frankness concerning competition between nations, given the 'law of comparative advantage' that is central to the international perspective of the ruling neo-liberal economic orthodoxy, all efforts to establish fair trade ought to fail, since 'complete equality defeats the purpose of trade'. In sum, when one talks of the globalisation of economic relations, and whether one is talking about the regulatory activities of the General Agreement on Tariffs and Trade (GATT) now known as the World Trade Organisation (WTO), the World Bank, the International Monetary Fund (IMF), the International Labour Organisation (ILO), or the UN, one is talking about a contested concept. On the one hand, there are those who read these activities as setting new rules for the governance and therefore enrichment of the whole of the world's population. On the other, there are those who read them as involving the creation of a literally transnational or what Japanese commentators like to call a 'borderless' and ostensibly rule-less, low-risk environment for those entities that can take advantage of it, principally transnational corporations and some of their dependent sub-contractors (Ohmae, 1990). This said, what I wish to argue in this study is not so much that the first conception is superior to the second, I take that for granted, but rather two other points. First, that the second conception is every bit as governmentalist as the first in that it is informed by a particular conception of the proper management of populations, which is patriarchalist. And second, counterintuitively, that thinking about the nature of this patriarchalism may yet prove to be the means whereby the conflict between the two models may be overcome.

The remainder of this chapter is divided into two parts. The first begins by critically outlining previous attempts to think about transnational sociality. The second presents my own attempt at such theorising, and so contributes, I hope, to the solution of what was long ago identified as the 'levels of analysis problem in International Relations' (Singer, 1969), namely how to understand the interrelationships between the national and international realms.

TOWARDS A THEORY OF TRANSNATIONAL SOCIALITY

Several of the principal blindspots which have for so long impaired the vision of the social sciences are summarised by the term we use to refer to the principal instance and/or field of governance, the 'nation state' (Mann, 1986, ch. 1; Woodiwiss, 1990b, pp. 185–9). Although, for example, none of the founding figures of sociology formally identified their object of study with the nation state, just such an identification none the less characterised much of their work. This was hardly surprising given both the founders' own practical political involvements and the fact that they were writing in the 'age of nationalism', when the drawing and defending of boundaries was a major preoccupation of governmental powers. Nor was it surprising that their successors should so seldom question this identification, given that they were writing in the context of the formation of an inter-*national* system whose rivalries had such cataclysmic consequences. These consequences included, moreover, the successive eclipses of each of the principal instances of transnational and international organisation which many had hoped would have prevented the cataclysms: free trade, international working-class solidarity and the League of Nations (Murphy, 1994). Nor, finally, is it surprising that today there should be so much talk of 'sovereignty at bay', when there is only one superpower, when multinational corporations appear to be the new 'lords of human kind', when nations are ceding some of their powers of governance to supranational bodies, and when the United Nations is more and more often asked to make peace rather than simply to maintain it.

For reasons that were alluded to above, and despite their theoretical insights to the contrary, sociologists have until recently remained myopically entrapped by the representational dominance of the nation state. The result has been that the study of transnational relations and processes has been left to the denizens of International Relations. However, again until recently, and as their disciplinary label indicates, inter-*national* relations scholars too have been entrapped by the same representational dominance of the nation state. The result is that our understanding of the transnational domain remains both partial and superficial. All this has now begun to change, as international relations specialists have sought to come to terms with the rapidly changing international economic and geopolitical conditions. Within International Relations the results have already been dramatic (Gill and Law, 1988). The hitherto prevailing and very state-centred Realist School (Morgenthau, 1960) has been challenged from two directions. First, by a revived liberalism with its Hayekian stress on the transnational dimension given to markets by the logic of 'comparative advantage'. And second, by a similarly resuscitated Marxism which deploys such concepts as hegemony (Gramsci, 1971), the international division of labour (Frobel et al., 1980) and the world system (Wallerstein, 1979). The upshot is a very diverse, new international political economy, which either mixes its inherited realism with ideas drawn from one or other of the challengers (for example: Calleo, 1982, 1987; Gilpin, 1987; Keohane, 1984; Keohane and Nye, 1977; Murphy, 1994), or ostensibly eschews realism altogether and pursues one of the challengers more wholeheartedly (Cox, 1987; Pettman, 1979; for a complementary development within a pertinent area of sociology see the 'new international labour studies' discussed and exemplified by Cohen, 1991 and Munck, 1988).

Dramatic as the changes in International Relations and indeed sociological labour studies may have been, they do not yet seem sufficient to enable us to gain the analytical purchase we require if we are to gain a full understanding of the nature and forms of transnational sociality. In part this is not surprising since neither body of work has made the gaining of such an understanding its priority. However, it is also not surprising because in the absence of any sort of linguistic or poststructuralist 'turn' within them, neither body of work exhibits much interest in either the discursive dimension in general or the possibility of a non-representationalist social science in particular. I will not repeat here the elaborate argumentation I have deployed elsewhere (Woodiwiss, 1990) in favour of both bringing discourse back in and a non-representationalist social science. Suffice it to say that the aim is to provide wholly non-humanist (or 'structuralist' if that term better conveys my meaning) concepts which may be both combined so as to specify non-economically reductionist causal mechanisms and made to refer to empirical material. In the absence of such a sociology, even the most sophisticated of current approaches to the understanding of transnational processes in general, if not all of those relating to the Pacific Rim (see Appelbaum and Henderson, 1992, pp. 15-17, for an exception) remain not only representationalist but also economically reductionist (Boyne, 1990). At best, economically based groups of people as nationally organised producers, consumers and/or classes are simply substituted for states as the chief actors on the international stage (Cohen, 1991; Munck, 1988). Once again, *inter-national* relations (but now within regional and global organisations and between groups of producers, consumers or classes) are substituted for specifically transnational forms and processes as the object of study (cf. Ruccio et al., 1991).

Before outlining how I think that the continuation of this reductionism may best be avoided, I must also define my position *vis-à-vis* another influential and pertinent body of literature, that which is variously known as the 'New Dependency Theory' (Jesudason, 1989, pp. 6ff.), 'political structuralism' (Crane, 1990, p. 13) or 'statism' (Jessop, 1990, ch. 10). This is a body of theory that in some cases originates in, and in others draws support from, Theda Skocpol's (1978, 1985) critique of Marxism's economic and class reductionism. For Skocpol, political or state-centred relations, in particular those that revolve around the 'autonomy' and 'capacity' of 'state managers', are as, or most often more, important than economic and class relations as the determinants of social developments. The best-known application of such ideas in a developmental context is Peter Evans' (1979) study of Brazil, which has been widely influential amongst younger American or American-educated scholars specialising in the study of Pacific Asia (see, for example, Hawes, 1987, as well as the works by Crane and Jesudason cited above). Drawing on Skocpol, but complementing and developing the earlier work of Ernesto Laclau (1979), Guillermo O'Donnell (1973) and Fernando Cardoso and Enzo Falleto (1979), Evans argues that what was missing from, and so vitiated, much of the work in the 'dependency' tradition associated with such as Andre Gunder Frank (1969) was any appreciation of the autonomously determinative power of the nation state in relation to the direction and fate of efforts at development. There is an obvious reason why this critique proved to be so attractive to students of Pacific Asia. This was because, not only were some of the countries of the region (specifically Korea, Hong Kong, Taiwan and Singapore) amongst those that, like Brazil, had achieved a significant degree of development despite their 'peripheral' status (as Bill Warren had first pointed out in his influential article of 1973), but also each of them appeared to owe their success to state initiatives of one kind or another.

The problem with this response, especially where it has been combined with neglect of the earlier and more theoretically complex work pointing in the same direction, is that it mistakes an insight for a theory with the result that all too often a political essentialism is substituted for an economic one (for his recent and stunningly well-executed retreat from political essentialism, see Evans, 1995). What is more, to develop a point that Bob Jessop (1990, pp. 287–8) has emphasised, this is a substitution that regrettably once again reinforces the representational dominance of the nation state in so far as it depends upon an implausibly sharp dichotomy between the state and society as real structures.

THE PRIMACY OF THE TRANSNATIONAL

Turning now to sociology, the scholar who has been in the forefront of the recent efforts to make manifest the hitherto latent transnational sociology that would render anachronistic any privileging of the nation state is Michael Mann (see also Hall, 1986; Vogler, 1985). As he says in the introduction to his seminal book *The Sources of Social Power*: 'In practice, most accounts . . . take polities, or *states*, as their "society", their total unit for analysis . . . There is no one master concept or basic unit of 'society'. It may seem an odd position for a sociologist to adopt; but if I could, I would abolish the concept of "society" altogether' (Mann, 1986, I, p. 2). In other words, Mann's starting point is his refusal to identify sociality with the nation state. Instead, he identifies it with four, universal sources or 'media' of power (namely control over ideological, economic, political and military resources) and the relations created by this control. One very important but by no means the only consequence of the interaction between these sets of relations is the production of those spatially demarcated and bounded entities that we term nation states. Another consequence of such interactions are the regional clusters of such states whose effects on their component states are both continuous and cannot be entirely controlled by the component states (ibid., p. 30). All this said, the most important consequence of assigning ontological primacy to transnational over national and international social processes is that the former processes are never exhausted by the latter. Thus, for Mann (ibid., p. 29), the transnational precedes, exceeds and succeeds the national, the regional and indeed the international. All this is summarised in Figure 1.1.

For reasons that I will not elaborate upon here, I remain convinced of the utility of the classical Marxist specification of the basic dimensions of sociality as politics, discourse/ideology and economics and therefore doubt both Mann's fundamentally humanist and Weberian categorisation of them as types of power and therefore his designation of military relations as a fourth dimension. Nevertheless, Mann's insights as to what Althusser might have termed the 'eternal' nature of transnational processes, as well as to their continuing significance at the national, regional and international levels are of critical significance. Of course, the strength of these transnational processes varies according to the degree to which they are institutionalised in transnational companies, trade agreements, political structures, information networks, and military alliances, etc., but it does not depend totally upon such institutionalisation. Thus, for example, technological, managerial, commercial, political, ideological and military events or innovations will have effects throughout the world irrespective of where they originate, their modes of transmission, and the nature of any formal barriers that may have been constructed – a moment's thought on the effects of the micro-electronic revolution and the fall of the Soviet Union should be sufficient to make the point.

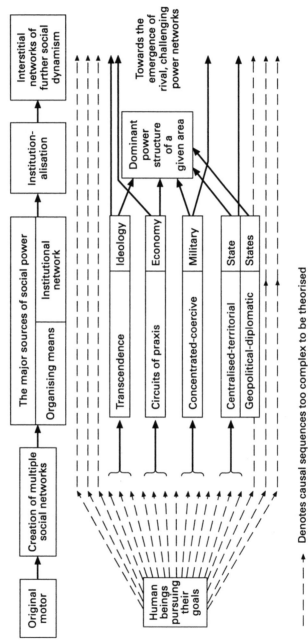

Figure 1.1 Causal IEMP model of organised power

THE FORMS OF GLOBALISATION

Although transnational forces can have effects within nation states irrespective of their levels of institutionalisation, for good or for ill these effects are nevertheless greatly amplified once global institutions are in place, since these reinforce and broaden the conduits through which the 'external' becomes the 'internal' (for descriptions of these conduits, see Murphy, 1994; Scholte, 1993). The most developed sociological approach to the study of the formation of such institutions, or globalisation, is to be found in the work of Roland Robertson. What seems to me to be particularly valuable about Robertson's work is his differentiation of the specifically globalising forces (that is, the ones that define the globe as a single social entity) from the welter of simply international or trans-national ones (Robertson, 1990, pp. 22ff). He lists the following as the most important globalising forces: (1) the diffusion of the idea of the 'nation'; (2) the spread of the idea of the 'international'; (3) the general-isation of the idea that individuals are 'citizens'; and (4) the widespread acceptance of the idea that humankind has interests in common. In sum, over the past hundred or so years and thanks to these forces, humankind has been organised into a specifically global entity that has an identi-fiable institutional structure and even an emergent ideological dimen-sion in the form of the discourse of human rights (ibid., pp. 26–7).

Strangely absent from Robertson's account of 'the actual form' taken by globalising forces are two that many scholars, and not simply Marx-ists, consider to be at least as, if not even more, important than those he mentions (see Sklair, 1996, for example). These are the now American dominated system of military alliances that underpins and so to some extent determines the activities of the UN, and the rise of what has been termed successively the multinational, the transnational and, most recently, the global corporation. Because of its far greater pertinence in the present context I will only comment on the second of these 'actual forms'. Although the rise of the global corporation obviously does not on its own explain the four developments that Robertson lists, it would nevertheless appear to be strongly associated with them. For, whatever other significance the developments listed by Robertson may have had, one undoubted consequence of their occurrence is that they have made the world a safer place for capitalist enterprises – a point whose cogency I would suggest is confirmed by another moment's thought about the importance of the legal dimension, and specifically the protection of private property rights, to each of the developments listed by Robertson (see Murphy, 1994 for the detail). The general significance of the new corporations is twofold. First, their presence in a region both indicates and intensifies the spread of a consumerism which some have argued may be seen as the harbinger of a global culture (Featherstone, 1990, 1991; Lee, 1994; Sklair, 1996). Second, and again more pertinently in the present context, they add an additional, 'private' dimension to the structure of the economic links – the producer and buyer-driven 'commodity chains'[2] – that in part explains both the emergence of common features in regional forms of economic organisation, and the positions of nations and regions in the global economic hierarchy. This 'private' dimension is what Stuart Holland (1975) has referred to as the 'meso-structure' of the international economy in that the attendant internalisation of what would formerly have been international economic relations means that some global economic flows escape governmental regulation because of how corporations may decide to price the components that circulate within them and where, sometimes relatedly, they may decide to declare their profits. For these reasons, then, the particular significance of transnational corporations in the present context is that their presence gives an additional complexity to the context within which the determinants of respect for labour and human rights have to be understood.

Robertson is certainly not in any sense a 'global village' romantic, since he stresses that globalisation is a process which may engender very negative reactions. However, it does seem to me that his neglect of the capitalist dimension to globalisation reduces his capacity to anticipate both the variety of possible scenarios which might produce such reactions and their political content. More importantly, Robertson's neglect of the corporate or capitalist dimension means that he is prevented from taking full sociological advantage of the possibilities for understanding the nature of transnational sociality opened up by Mann. These are possibilities that seem particularly exciting to the present author in the area of class analysis, where the way is now open to advance beyond the theoretically regressive, nation-centred notion of international class alliances (see above, p. 31) as well as the highly implausible notion of a global capitalist class put forward by Sklair (1996). However, as was indicated above, this way may only be followed if the representationalism that has hitherto limited the theoretical and research imaginations of social scientists is first cast aside and the significatory and non-humanist approaches associated with poststructuralism are taken up. This is not a step that either of the scholars whose work I have just outlined has been prepared to take. Thus in what follows I will be transforming the significance of their work and not simply using it. It is therefore only fair to add that this is something that they may, quite understandably, feel more than a little unhappy about. This said, perhaps wickedly, I feel particularly comfortable about so distorting Mann's work because of the opening he provides in the diagram reprinted above (Figure 1.1) where he states that the links between 'human beings pursuing their goals' and the 'creation of multiple social networks' denote 'causal sequences too complex to be theorized' – why not, then, approach the understanding of such networks simply by theoretically positing the existence of a pertinent set of *sui generis* social entities and processes?

THE NATION STATE, SPACE AND TRANSNATIONAL SOCIALITY

In spelling out the significance of this transnational orientation for how one should understand the nation state, I depend upon the metatheoretically compatible work of Bob Jessop (1982, 1990) and those he has influenced. Thus far the most productive application of Jessop's as well as Mann's ideas to the concerns of International Relations scholars is that of Fred Halliday (1987, 1989, 1994). In a series of articles, and most recently a book, Halliday has sought to overcome the impasse that he considers the discipline faces because of the incommensurability of the proliferating schools of thought within it by taking further than others (see, for example, Buzan, 1983, ch. 2) the disaggregation of its fundamental unit of analysis, namely the nation state (cf. Jessop, 1990, pp. 365–7). His first move is to substitute what he terms a sociological concept of the state as a specific set of apparatuses for the traditional, cartographic concept depended upon by International Relations specialists, and according to which the state is simply the 'social-territorial totality' that participates in international relations. Because the various apparatuses that comprise the state relate differentially to the national and transnational processes and forces with which they interact, a much more complex account of international relations is made possible. According to this account: (1) states' relations to their citizens need no longer be considered to be necessarily benign; (2) states may be understood to be the product of 'external' as well as 'internal' forces (vide the Japanese Meiji and indeed postwar state, for example); (3) states may be understood to make as well as to represent 'societies' (through their trade policies, for example); and, finally (4) state sovereignty may be understood as inherently limited, especially in relation to what Mann regards as the more 'extensive' and 'diffuse' sources of social power, namely those arising from control over ideological and economic resources. In sum, then, by insisting on what might be termed the 'porosity' of the nation state, a transnationally oriented sociology provides International Relations with a way of combining the insights generated by its competing schools and so producing an enriched understanding of the history and present state of 'the international' at both the regional and global levels.

If I have a problem with these ideas of Halliday's, it is with what seems to me to be the taken-for-granted nature of the concept of space with which he works. In other words, despite his concern to overturn the conception of the state as a 'social-territorial totality', he still works with a rather definite conception of what is *spatially* internal and external to a particular state, even though he successfully calls into question the distinction between what is *socially* internal and external to it. Here it seems to me that his conceptual efforts need to be supplemented by those of such as Edward Soja (1989), David Harvey (1973) and Reinhart Kosselleck (1985), who are responsible for restoring space as a dimension of sociality to its rightful place in the social theory from which it was excluded in the course of the nineteenth century. As Soja (1989, p. 6) says: 'We must be insistently aware of how space can be made to hide consequences from us, how relations of power and discipline are inscribed into the apparently innocent spatiality of social life, how human geographies become filled with politics and ideology.' It seems to me that such an awareness of the semiotic dimension of space, especially of its capacity both to suggest that certain social relations are stronger than they actually are – vide, the use currently made of the term 'Asian values' – and to occlude others, is particularly necessary in the pursuit of an understanding of transnational sociality. For nothing makes transnational forms and processes harder to conceive, let alone perceive, than the apparent spatial separation of nation states and the claims to sovereignty that are made in their name.

Thus, if one wishes to take further Mann and Halliday's scepticism as to the actual extent of any state's sovereign power, and yet still preserve a concept of the state that retains some analytical purchase despite the ongoing globalisation of the world, one needs a concept that does not identify the state too strongly with its institutional apparatuses. This it seems to me is what has recently been provided by Jessop, thanks to his addition of the idea of 'state projects' to his theory and his consequent recognition of the state's discursive/ideological dimension (see also, Buzan's (1983, ch. 2) concept of the 'idea of the state'). As Jessop (1990, p. 9) says in summarising his current position:

> There is never a point when *the* state is finally built within a given territory and thereafter operates, so to speak, on automatic pilot according to its own definite, fixed and inevitable laws . . . Whether, how and to what extent one can talk in definite terms about the state actually depends on the contingent and provisional outcome of struggles to realize more or less specific 'state projects' . . . Nor do national boundaries as such constitute a fixed horizon for emergent state projects: there is no more reason to rule out strategies aiming to build multi- and transnational networks and circuits of state power than there is to exclude local or regional state projects. These reflections suggest that state actions should not be attributed to *the* state as an originating subject but should be understood as the emergent, unintended and complex resultant of what rival 'states within the state' have done and are doing on a complex strategic terrain.

CLASS AND TRANSNATIONAL SOCIALITY

The most pertinent larger set of social relations when it comes to understanding the nature of employment relations are, of course, class relations. Reflecting my rejection of humanism and representationalism, what is most distinctive about my approach to class is that it is premissed upon the view that in taking individuals and/or groups as the units of class analysis most previous theories (Marxist as well as Weberian) have been mistaken. In my view, to attempt either to construct or apply a concept of class by trying to draw lines around groups of people is to embark upon a mistaken and anyway impossible task (*vide* the proliferating intermediary sub-classes to be found within the class schema of such as John Goldthorpe (1980) and Erik Olin Wright (1985), whose negative consequences are especially apparent when one tries to understand transnational class relations).

It seems to me that individual people are always both too unpredictable and, where transnational class relations are concerned, geographically too immobile to be ever usefully categorised in this way and so provide any sort of firm basis for sociological reasoning. The unpredictability may in fact only be elucidated by recourse to psychology, whilst simple economics and visa requirements explain the immobility. As I have argued elsewhere (Woodiwiss,1990b, pt. 4), the classes of capitalist societies are not in the first instance collectivities of people but rather things in their own right; that is, they are particular and non-exhaustive ensembles of economic, political and discursive/ideological structural positions, which are held together by the forces produced by capital's appropriation of surplus labour.[3] Classes as things are, of course, in part embodied by people and corporate entities such as companies and trade unions, but not necessarily by them as whole entities. Thus in some of their beliefs and behaviours, and whether they are acting inside or outside of the sphere of production, both people and corporate entities may embody capital whilst in other beliefs and behaviours they may also embody the working class. Finally, in the absence of additional modes of production, there are only two classes in capitalist social formations: capital and labour.

Thus, what my rejection of all humanist and unitised conceptions of class has led me to is the deconstruction and reconstruction of the pertinent parts of Marxist theory (that is, the concepts of surplus value, production and law) so as to be able to reconstruct the concept of class. This I have done in such a way that the political and discursive dimensions of sociality as well as non-class social phenomena are given their proper place and weight without resorting to what Derrida would term the 'dangerous supplement' of the individual. More specifically, previous generations of Marxists, Critical Theorists and indeed Weberians have sought to overcome the causal strait-jacket represented by economic determinism by reasserting the self-generated determinative power of the individual and/or the collectivity with the result that classes tend to be decomposed into fragments or to be disappeared altogether. By contrast, I have sought to overcome economic essentialism by arguing for the imbricated co-presence of 'race', ethnicity and gender-affected economic (possessory relations), political (control relations) and discursive relations (proprietary relations) as the constitutive, irreducible and mutually determining elements of the class structure.[4] The outcome is a theory of class which accommodates the complexity of real class relations whilst retaining the explanatory power that was the product of the simplicity of Marx's original two-class model.

The processes that constitute the capitalist class as an entity that is irreducible to human beings and economic relations are those reciprocal constraints that make capital's economic possession of means of production, political control over production, and discursive title to property in the means of production the mutually entailed set of positions or conditions of existence that they have to be for the capitalist class to exist. None of these positions would hold if the others did not, and the production and appropriation of surplus labour therefore depends upon their co-presence. In the absence of any one of them not only would the ensemble cease to exist, but so too would its positioning effects on subjects, since there would be nothing to constrain or discipline them on capital's behalf; for example, no capitalist title can long survive in the absence of possession and/or control. In sum, then, it is the co-presence of capital's possession of the means of production, control over their use, and title to them and any surplus produced that produces the structural ensemble that is the capitalist class.

As regards the working class, the reciprocally interpenetrative positions that comprise it are necessarily the mirror image of those that produce the capitalist class. They are therefore those that explain its incapacity, qua structural ensemble, to prevent either the existence of a difference between necessary and surplus labour or capital's appropriation of this difference. Thus the processes that constitute the working class are those reciprocal constraints that make lack of economic possession of the means of production, political subservience to capital's control, and discursive exclusion from any right to title a mutually entailed set of positions or conditions of existence. As with the capitalist class, none of these positions would hold if the others did not and only the requirements that the working class should interfere neither with the production of a difference between necessary and surplus labour nor its appropriation by the capitalist class ensures their co-presence. In sum, then, it is in this case the co-presence of separation from the means of production, lack of control over their use and lack of title to them and any surplus produced that produces the structural ensemble that is the working class.

The result of thinking about class in this way is that one need no longer think, as the hitherto theoretically determinant humanist metaphor of 'class struggle' has for so long directed, in terms of two or more armies confronting one another in an 'arena' or on a field ('terrain'). Rather, one may think of the class structure of capitalist society as a genuinely structural entity which is divided into two varyingly balanced segments as a consequence of the interaction between the economic, political and discursive relations which constitute it. And the boundary between the two classes, populated by the so-called 'middle classes', may be understood to gain or lose definition as well as move up and down the organisational hierarchy as a result of changes in its constitutive relations and interactive consequences.

One result of the increased quantum and complexity of the labour

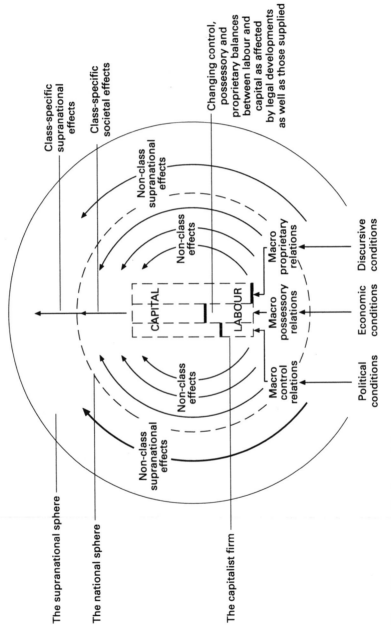

Figure 1.2   A structuralist theory of class

demanded of the occupants of the 'middle-class' positionings that populate the boundary zone is that the role of crude 'class background' as a determinant of the life-chances of individuals has been considerably reduced and partially displaced by other, although by no means unrelated, largely discursive sources of positionings such as education, gender, religion, 'race' and 'company loyalty'. As against the likes of Daniel Bell (1973), however, it is important to emphasise that this reduction should in no way be taken as being indicative of the disappearance of capitalist class relations. The continued existence of the latter is utterly indifferent to the manner in which the positionings derived from it come to be embodied by particular human subjects or groups thereof. What this reduction does indicate, however, is the occurrence of an undermining of some at least of the commonalties which in the past have provided the bases upon which solidarities have been constructed between the embodiments of labour power and, indeed, capital. To be more specific, some of the human embodiments of both classes have been separated out on the grounds of one or other non-class criteria and rewarded relatively highly, so that as the members of a supposed 'middle class' they may perform some of the labour necessary to the assembly, deployment and utilisation of capital.

Although many of the tasks performed by the embodiments of contradictory positionings may exist because of a restructuring of the tasks performed by embodiments of the proletariat and/or may involve them in exercising control over the same group, any increase in the number of such positionings nevertheless also represents a change in the balances between the classes and a potential weakening of capital. This is because, in order to procure their loyalty, payments must be made to the contradictorily positioned which exceed the value of their labour power. Thus, not only does any increase in the size of the contradictorily positioned labour force make capital's continuing appropriation of surplus labour potentially subject to the political and discursive wishes of those so positioned, but also it reduces the quantum of capital's revenues available for investment and therefore for its own expanded reproduction.

Shorn of all its additional supportive argumentation, the analytical consequences of thinking of class in this way may be summarised in seven core propositions:

(1) In the absence of other modes of production, there are only two classes in capitalist societies.

(2) These classes are not collectivities of individuals, but rather synthetic ensembles drawing on but not exhausting 'race', ethnicity and gender-affected economic, political and discursive structures.

(3) As things in their own right, classes in capitalist societies are those sets of positions, in the sense of structural regularities, which are defined by particular relations of economic possession, particular disciplinary or political relations of control, and particular significatory or discursive relations of title, the result of whose mutual determination is capital's appropriation of surplus labour.

(4) Individuals are not only or *the* only class subjects (individuals may also be 'racialised', gendered and idiosyncratic subjects, whilst corporate bodies such as companies and trade unions may also be class subjects).

(5) Not all individuals or corporate bodies are positioned by class relations.

(6) If and when individuals and corporate bodies do serve as, and therefore sometimes act as, class subjects, it is as often because of *some* of the things they say and do as it is because of everything they say and do (thus, for example, at some times in her day's work and by some of her actions an individual may embody the working class, whilst at other times and in some other of her actions the same individual may embody capital).

(7) Embodying such contradictory class positionings does not make one a member of a middle class so much as it aids the reproduction of the two classes.

In sum, for me, people do not have class positions and so are not members of classes but classes sometimes 'have' people or parts of them, and so, because of the sharedness of some of the positionings that result, create the possibility of solidarities between them. And, whilst for this reason (and many others) people and corporate bodies may often be engaged in struggles with one another, classes themselves never engage in struggle but exist instead as always conjoint elements within *causal mechanisms* which sometimes prompts such conflicts.

The net result of all of this for the understanding of the inherently reciprocal significance of class relations for extra-class phenomena such as the discursive and legal developments of interest here is that it changes the nature of the questions one asks. Specifically, one no longer asks the traditional questions about the effects of class locations on the producers of discursive or legal developments or of the latter on the size, composition and morale of the contending class armies. Rather, one asks questions about the effects of reciprocal conditions of existence: first, the effects produced by class forces on political, economic and ideological or legal developments; and second, those produced by any such developments on the strength of the specific forces that separate and bind the two classes economically, politically and discursively, and which explain the balances between the two classes and therefore the ease or difficulty of capital's appropriation of surplus labour. The critical points here are again twofold. First, this is how economic determinism may best be overcome. This is not so much because one can specify the contribution of non-economic determinants to class relations (this has always been a feature of Marxist analysis), but because the economic need no longer be regarded as necessarily either the source of the most important developments affecting the class balances or the most important site of their effects within the class structure. Second, this approach provides a means whereby one can acknowledge the domestic affects of international and transnational developments since these too are constitutive of the class structure's economic, political and discursive conditions of existence in the sense that they affect circumstances under which possession, control and title are sought and the techniques available for their achievement (cf. Ruccio et al., 1991).

LAW, RIGHTS AND TRANSNATIONAL SOCIALITY

The final concepts of significance in the present context are those of law and rights. To repeat more or less verbatim what I have written in other places (Woodiwiss, 1990a, pp. 9–10; 1990b, ch. 5), the theory of law upon which I depend is broadly Marxist. However, it of course involves a rejection of one of the central substantive tenets of traditional Marxist theory, namely the belief that the law in capitalist societies is irremediably and/or only an instrument for the protection of capitalist private property. Rather, it argues that, like the state, the law in democratic capitalist societies is characterised by a certain autonomy in the relations between it and the class structure; a relative autonomy that is understood to inhere in the particularities of its discourse and, in a more general sociological sense, to be a product of its role in democratic capitalist societies as a critical nexus of various governmentalities. In any event, it seems to me that only once one is prepared to grant the law the autonomy which is inherent in its nature as in part a discourse does it become possible to explain why and how what is generally the fair

application of the law nevertheless only sometimes favours those positioned by the subject classes whilst it generally favours those positioned
by the dominant ones. Given such an acknowledgement, democratic
capitalist law may be defined in morphological terms as: a set of state-
enunciated and enforced discourses which interpellates the subjects it
addresses in such a way that they will be law-abiding, provided that the
same subjects do not successfully resist this disciplining because of prior
or other interpellations originating in counter-discourses and articulated
with suitably empowering political, economic and/or class-structural
positionings.

The principal means by which, when so understood, the law may be
understood to affect the wider society are twofold. First, the law in
democratic capitalist societies produces a background 'ideology-effect'
in that, provided it is universalistically applied and fairly administered, it
reinforces and so helps to maintain the patterns of social relationships
that comprise the social formation of which it is a part. Second, and more
innovatively within the Marxist tradition, once the law is understood as
a set of discourses it is possible to specify how the law produces this
'ideology-effect'. This is because it is the principal mechanism for
transpositioning subjects within and between discourses and institutions. More elaborately, the law achieves its effects by intermittently
and, in the normal course of events, irresistibly reordering the relational
balances between the human and non-human entities which are known
to it in terms of rights and duties. This it does on the basis of a discursive
practice whose guiding methodological principle *must* be 'consistency'.
Thus, for example, owners can be made into sellers, employees may be
sacked or reinstated, pickets may be forced to reduce their number, and
free individuals may be imprisoned. Quite apart from any concerns about
legitimacy, such activities must be carried out on a basis that strives for
consistency since otherwise the law would become a source of disorder
rather than order.

The foundational and constitutive role of the methodological requirement for 'consistency' in the democratic capitalist law upon which the
legal systems of the Pacific-Asian states are based is therefore what gives
legal discourse its possibility of autonomy there as elsewhere. However,
'consistency' is never either a sufficient or a self-subsisting sign in legal
or in any other form of discourse. The methodology of consistency must
therefore always be a means of ensuring that any substantive principle
applies equally to all, to those that enunciate the law as well as those to
whom it is perhaps more directly addressed. It therefore cannot be

mobilised against but must always be articulated with such substantive principles – for example, 'liberty', 'equality' and 'patriarchalism' in their multiple specifications and combinations – before it can have an effect. In sum, contrary to Western prejudice, the rule of law is not to be identified with a particular political philosophy, liberalism, but rather with a social-structural effect, namely the reduction of arbitrariness (Unger, 1976; Woodiwiss, 1990b, pt. III). Thus, whether or not any substantive as opposed to merely formal consistency and juridical autonomy exists, and so how the law can operate as a defence of human rights must vary, and vary quite markedly, according to the more general social-structural background with which it is necessarily imbricated. This, then, is why, first, law must be congruent with and in this sense embedded within the wider discourses, structures and practices of a society if it is to have a disciplinary effect, as well as why, second, judicial particularism and/or inactivity rather than lack of concern for liberty should be taken as the principal sign that the rule of law may be under threat.

A POSITIVIST AND DISAGGREGATED CONCEPT OF RIGHTS

In order to take full advantage of the possibilities opened up by this way of thinking about law for developing a strategy for embedding respect for human rights within the social structures of Pacific-Asian societies, three additional theoretical moves are necessary. As was indicated in the Introduction, the first is to reject the humanist, essentialist and Eurocentric – in a word liberal – conception of human rights as the natural rights of individuals and to replace it with a decidedly more mundane but theoretically liberating legal positivist conception of rights as simply discursive entities which serve 'certain socially determined policy objectives and interests' (Hirst, 1979, p. 104). The second and related move is to recognise with William MacNeil (1992, 1995) that to view rights as discursive entities immediately raises questions as to whether and how rights are actually 'connected' with the agents, human or otherwise, that are their supposed bearers. In what follows, I will refer to this problem of connection with the term 'attachment' and I will be particularly concerned to specify the social conditions that either favour or undermine the 'attaching' of rights to their bearers.

The third theoretical move is to reject the conventional differentiation of positive and negative rights which underpins all the UN's central texts, and which, in the Anglo-American world at least, continues to evoke the liberalistic preference for the latter that was so famously expressed by Sir Isaiah Berlin (1969, ch. 3). Here what I have in mind is that one should instead follow Carl Wellman's (1989) lead and extend to human rights Wesley Hohfeld's anti-naturalistic and pluralistic conception of 'jural' or legal relations, but with this difference: that the term 'right' be used to refer to jural relations as a whole rather than to one particular type of such relation.[5] Thus rights may be understood as discursively defined clusters of: 'liberties' to perform certain actions; 'claims' or expectations *vis-à-vis* specified others; 'powers' that allow legal subjects to assume certain specified roles and change certain social relations; and 'immunities' against prosecution and/or civil suit in the proper execution of any of the foregoing.

What I wish to suggest, then, is that human rights may be effective policy instruments despite their uneven development along one or more of Hohfeld's dimensions and their lack of 'attachment' with respect to the less developed of these dimensions. That is, given their mutually implicatory character, and although 'liberties', etc. are ultimately irreducible to one another, the more, so to speak, there is of one, the less need there is for the others. In other words, if 'liberties' are clearly and broadly defined, there is less need for their implications in terms of immunities or whatever to be spelt out, since, no matter how they are specified, the purpose of rights is to protect the same conditions of being. Likewise, if 'claims', for example, are clearly and broadly defined, there is no need for their implications in terms of 'liberties' or whatever to be spelt out, since acceptance of the existence of 'claims' against one or indeed the state implies acceptance of another's 'liberty' to require their satisfaction. The behaviours thereby protected will not necessarily be the same as those protected as 'liberties' – for example attending a mediatory hearing rather than striking – but the effect of protection should nevertheless be a similarly balancing one as regards the asymmetrical social relations within which concerns as to respect for human rights arise. This is because the protection of 'claims' behaviours represents a limitation on the freedom of the more powerful *vis-à-vis* the less powerful; a limitation and therefore a mode of 'attachment' that may be much more strongly supported, given particular cultural and social-structural circumstances, than might be the case where what is at stake is one of the less powerful's 'liberties'.

Because it opens the way for the development of a non-Eurocentric concept of human rights, this is an argument that has both sociological and political significance. I will reserve a discussion of its political significance to the conclusions of the case studies and to the Conclusion of the study as a whole. Sociologically, it specifies far more concretely than has hitherto been the case what is involved in the task of investigating the social embeddedness of human rights. That is, the discursive gulf between the language of the law and that of sociology appears to be far less glaring than otherwise seems to be the case. In other words, whereas there has generally been something about the language of rights that social scientists baulk at – hence Jeremy Bentham's reference to rights as 'nonsense on stilts' and the Marxist talk of them as 'mystifications' and instances of 'commodity fetishism' – there is much less of a problem when the Hohfeldian language is used. Indeed it seems to me to be relatively easy to see how such concepts as capitalism and class and their specification in terms of possession and separation from the means of production may be brought to bear on such questions as to whether or not particular individuals possess 'liberties' to perform certain actions or can enforce their 'claims' on others (and vice versa, of course). This is because, for example, limitations on possession – separation – imply restrictions on 'liberties' and/or 'claims', whilst enhanced 'liberties' and/or 'claims' imply reduced separation or enhanced possession.

What all of this means, then, for the capitalist employment relation within which labour law has its primary effects is that one can see very clearly how labour law is both affected in its content and enforcement by class balances and constitutive of the same balances. Here I will speak only of the constitutive role of law, since this enables one to summarise the possible effects of class balances on the law's content and so enables one to very readily appreciate its indexical character. In sum, when one brings the Marxist and Hohfeldian concepts together one may grasp something of the complexity of the relationship between the law and class relations and explain how labour law provides an index of class balances.

(1) The law may alter the balance with respect to the economic *possession* of the means of production to labour's advantage by granting certain 'liberties' to bargain over the terms of employment and/or by inscribing certain 'claims' within the conditions governing the hiring of labour and therefore the validity of the employment contract. These are generally referred to as 'labour standards' and include rules governing the payment of wages, rest periods and holidays. However, they also include such aspects of collective labour law as those pertaining to the permissibility or otherwise of the closed shop. The inscription of such 'liberties' and/or 'claims'

may or may not be accompanied by the granting to labour of participative 'powers' of one kind or another with respect to the setting of such standards.

(2) The law may alter the balance with respect to political or disciplinary *control* of the means of production to labour's advantage in three ways; first, by granting certain 'liberties' to bargain over the conditions of employment and/or by inscribing either certain 'claims' within the employment contract in the form of those aspects of 'labour standards' that refer to workplace rules; second, by limiting the contract's purview through specifying certain additional 'liberties' which may allow its temporary suspension for bargaining purposes; third, by specifying in either workplace rules and/or the employment contract certain 'claims' that allow for the exercise of 'powers' of one kind or another which allow varying degrees of co-determination as well as the adjudication of disputes by tripartite tribunals or mutually agreed third parties.

(3) The law may alter the balance with respect to *title* to the means of production to labour's advantage by granting certain liberties to bargain over ownership and/or by inscribing various 'claims' within property, company and taxation law in order to achieve such as profit-sharing, employee share-ownership, nationalisation, and/or distribute social benefits of one kind or another. Again, the inscription of such claims may or may not be accompanied by the granting of certain participative 'powers' to labour at the enterprise and/or national levels.

Finally, I would like to bring out the national and transnational context-dependency of the effectiveness of these modes of intervention in the capital/labour relation by comparing two cases. In a Western economy (like that of the United States in the 1950s) composed primarily of medium-sized or first-generation corporate capitals, operating at the heads of commodity chains, within a protected market, and producing goods for which there is strong demand, a traditional labour law system configured in terms of 'liberties' and focused on possessory relations is likely to be adequate to secure the 'attachment' of the pertinent rights to labour. Under such circumstances an employer possesses some autonomy and labour is free to attempt to take advantage of this. However, in a strongly dualistic Pacific-Asian economy (like that of the Philippines in the 1990s), wherein a large number of petty commodity producers and small capitals are organised by a small number of large capitals (many of which are transnationals), operating within an open market at the lowest level of the commodity chain, a traditional labour law system configured in terms of 'liberties' is most unlikely to be adequate to secure the 'attachment' of labour's rights. This is because, although possessory relations may continue to be the most salient of the elements within the property relation to local capitals as such, the economic context and the latter's subordination to transnational capital means that the control relations that are most salient to transnational capital take effective precedence in the governance of the small enterprises and so render moot the effects of a labour law system based on 'liberties'. In sum, under such circumstances the employer possesses very little autonomy and so it is often beside the point that one has the liberty to attempt to force him or her to exercise it to labour's benefit. As in the case of Japanese domestic main contractor/sub-contractor relations, if the exercise of such a liberty interrupts production the corporation at the head of the commodity chain will simply increase its orders to other suppliers or seek new ones.

CONCLUSION

In sum, then, the benefits of working with the set of concepts outlined above are twofold. First, complementing the work of Sassen (1996) and Soysal (1994) it adds what might be termed a geological dimension to the study of globalisation and rights in that the latter is not understood to be simply a matter of investigating transnational 'flows' or whatever but also a matter of investigating the embeddedness or otherwise of any such flows and the problems that this may pose. Second, it allows one to understand that, given the primacy of the transnational, all boundaries are permeable, and all national sets of social relations have transnational as well as domestic conditions of existence and indeed effects. In other words, thinking only of the transnational/national flow and not of its reverse, it allows one to understand how, especially as the forces making for globalisation intensify, changes in transnational conditions of existence as well as direct institutional linkages may affect domestic social relations; that is, through the differences they make to political, economic and discursive relations both as distinct dimensions of sociality and, synthetically, as dimensions of the class structure.

As far as the substantive issue with which the current study is concerned, these concepts enable one to make two further summary points.

(1) That, regardless of considerations of spatial propinquity, trans-
     nationally produced extra-legal discourses may enter national legal
     systems (that is, simply by virtue of 'modelling' or their incorpor-
     ation, however idiosyncratically or partially, into state projects,
     legislation and judicial pronouncements).
(2) That such politically and/or discursively prompted changes in the
     law may or may not affect the balance of class forces within a
     particular nation state, depending on the differences they make to
     the 'liberties', 'powers', 'claims' and 'immunities' of those
     positioned by the class structure.

Stepping back from the immediate concerns of the present study, the
larger significance of this set of concepts is that it enables one to overcome both the governmentalist (Burchell, et al., 1991) and the postmodernist (Laclau and Mouffe 1985) challenges to my kind of Marxisant
sociology, since it enables one to make the following more general points.

(1) That sociality is not to be identified with an aggregate of the
     supposedly totalising bounded entities known as nation states, but
     is instead to be understood as an open, transnational system that
     only in part exists in the form of nation states and then only if
     states are conceived of as loosely bounded and always
     underdetermined, incomplete, and themselves open, territorial
     entities.
(2) That so far from being the occasion of a totalising economic
     reductionism, the rethought categories of 'capitalism' and 'class',
     like those of 'economy', 'polity' and 'ideology' upon which they
     depend (Woodiwiss, 1990b, p. 55, n. 1), are to be understood as
     the means for overcoming such reductionism because of *their*
     intrinsically multidimensional and mutually underdetermining
     character.

In this way, then, some reflection on the nature of substantive social
change has facilitated not simply the resolution of a particular methodological problem – how to understand the determination of the effectivity
of rights regimes – but also the resolution of a set of metatheoretical and
theoretical problems within the Marxist tradition thought by some to be
insuperable.

To conclude, by looking behind, so to speak, individuals, trade unions
and labour law and instead at the social and legal conditions within
which they exist, I hope to show that one can specify what is favourable

or unfavourable about these conditions in relation to the maintenance of the human rights upon which unions and employees depend. And to do so with far more precision than if I were to maintain the traditional focus of representationalist sociology on the actors involved and their conflicts. Methodologically, what all this means for the nature of the analytical framework deemed appropriate for the understanding of the nature and effectiveness of labour and human rights that gives proper regard to their transnational context is the following. First, that national systems of governance must be clearly related to the transnational flows that affect the domestic political, discursive/ideological, economic, and therefore class relations that pertain to employment relations and individual/state relations. Second, that the reciprocal interrelationships between these relations and the relatively autonomous legal relations should be specified. And third, that a judgement may be made as to what all the foregoing tells one about what legal measures, if any, have been effective in 'attaching' rights to labour organisations or individuals and under what conditions. In other words, as in my other studies of labour law systems, I will be seeking to answer variants of three basic questions. Why, on what occasions and under what social-structural circumstances did the law enter industrial relations? How were these interventions legally specified and received and therefore become constitutive of the same social-structural circumstances? What were the consequences of these interventions for the conditions that gave rise to them?

CHAPTER TWO

THE CHALLENGE OF PACIFIC CAPITALISM: FROM PAX AMERICANA TO THE JAPANESE WAY?

To attempt an exhaustive account of the transnational structures and flows pertinent to employment relations in Pacific Asia would be a mammoth task that is not only unnecessary but would also seriously slow the pace of and unbalance the narrative that I wish to present. Instead, I will provide a highly condensed but analytically pointed synoptic reading of some of the principal texts in the field before focusing on the structures and flows most pertinent to labour law. This said, each of the case studies will provide a specification of the more general flows pertinent to employment relations, labour law and human rights in the country concerned.

In his landmark study *Rethinking the Pacific* (1990), Gerry Segal presents a powerful argument against the view that it is or soon will be possible to speak of a Pacific social entity or 'community' in the sense that it is possible to speak of the communities of Western European or North Atlantic states (see also, Dirlik, 1993). He suggests instead that we learn to 'think Pacific' through combining an appreciation of the region's diversity with an acknowledgement of the increasingly global nature of the forces that are shaping it. Whilst I have no particular problem with this conclusion as such, it seems to me that the denial of the existence of a trans-Pacific social entity that it incorporates is more a function of the way in which Segal makes his argument than it is a conclusion that necessarily follows from the data he provides. The definition of 'community' he works with is a very tight one: to wit, an entity that 'shares values, expectations, communication, levels of transaction, predictability of behaviour and capabilities' (Segal, 1990, p. 3). Indeed it is so tight that I would doubt that any individual nation states would qualify as communities so defined, outside of the representations of them to be found in their ceremonial discourses. Certainly, those aggregations of Western European and North Atlantic states against which Segal measures the claims of those who would talk of the Pacific Rim would not qualify. But in case his definition should prove insufficient to silence any such talk, the way in which Segal goes about investigating such claims guarantees just such a result. This is because, not only does he unproblematically take nation states as his units of analysis, and in this way accept their claims to particularity at face value, but he also then goes on to ask, in the manner of an empiricist seeking a generalisation, if these states have anything in common. Not surprisingly, the answer that he gets is 'no'. In sum, then, Segal's conclusion that there is no such thing as the Pacific Rim is predetermined by the representationalist, nation-centred conceptualisations and empiricist assumptions that he shares with traditional International Relations theory.

THE SPECIFICITY OF PACIFIC CAPITALISM

Predictably, things look rather different when the Pacific Rim is considered from a transnationally oriented perspective. To begin with, although of course the interactive effects of the economic, political and ideological transnational processes include the nation states of the Rim, these effects also include the clustering of these states which justifies us in talking about them as a regional entity of some kind. Since at least the beginning of the War in the Pacific, this clustering has become steadily more visible. First, because of Japan's efforts to construct a Greater East Asian Co-prosperity Sphere. And, second, because of the United States defeat of the same effort. The net result was the initiation of a process of decolonisation, which ultimately proved to be irreversible and which eventuated in the political separation of the region from Europe. Since 1945 and under the 'protection' afforded by United States military hegemony, and notwithstanding the latent and actual threats posed by the presence of the two most powerful communist societies (the USSR and China) in the region, the Pacific Rim has gained its own societal core for the first time in history (Chan, S., 1990, ch. 2; So and Chiu, 1995).

In representationalist terms, this core is Japan and its links with the other countries of especially the North American, Asian and Australasian segments of the Rim. Institutionally, it is:

(1) The web of bilateral international political alliances forged

between Japan, the United States, other nation states, and such regional sub-groupings as ASEAN (Segal, 1990).

(2) The economic links forged by the activities of international financial institutions, foreign aid donors, multinationals, and associated with commodity chains and trade in general (Abegglen, 1994; Clark and Chan, 1992; Tokunaga, 1992).

(3) The cultural links represented by Islam, Christianity, Confucianism and Buddhism, as well as the Mandarin, Malay and especially the English languages.

However, in the non-representationalist sociological terms deployed in this text, this core consists of a phenotypically distinctive combination of the general political, economic and discursive/ideological conditions that are universally constitutive of the capitalist mode of production. Thus the distinctive way in which these conditions were secured in Japan as compared to the United States has, contrary to the expectations of the 'convergence theorists' of the 1960s (Kerr et al., 1993; and critically, Goldthorpe, 1964), become steadily more pronounced over time. The significance of this is that, despite apparent Japanese disinterest in becoming a regional economic hegemon (Thurow, 1992, pp. 84, 213–14; but see: Nester, 1990; Steven, 1990; and Bowring, 1992), and despite the United States actual political and military hegemony as well as its continuing importance as a major if relatively shrinking source of investment and markets for Pacific manufactures, it is Japanese-style rather than American-style capitalism that has become archetypal within the region (Lubis, 1985). Thus, although Japan has also become steadily more and more enmeshed in global structures of one kind or another, as symbolised by Tokyo's ascension to the status of a 'world city' (Sassen, 1992), its position as regional archetype, reinforced since the mid-1980s by its overtaking of the United States as the region's leading investor (Chew et al., 1992, p. 115), has already resulted in Pacific capitalism acquiring a distinctive institutional silhouette. The main lineaments of this silhouette are as follows.

(1) A centralised, sometimes authoritarian and variously interventionist state.

(2) An organised enterprise structure wherein state-supported coordination is achieved either through the institutions of a dual economy, whereby a small number of very large companies at the head of domestic producer-driven commodity chains dominate a large number of smaller companies (the South Korean *Chaebol* and the

Japanese *Keiretsu*, for example), or as in the case of 'overseas Chinese' capital, by quasi-familialistic groupings responding to the demands of buyer-driven commodity chains usually headquartered overseas.

(3) A patriarchalist ideological/legal formation, within which, regardless of whether it draws on Confucian, Christian, Islamic or Buddhist forms, the owner's entitlement to the surplus is strongly reinforced by a patriarchalist expectation of loyalty and filial piety on the part of employees and subordinate owners.[1]

That said, it is important to make a couple of qualificatory points. The first is that, as a matter of 'social geology', some societies for historical and social reasons of very different kinds (as in the case of the United States, Australia, New Zealand, China, Hong Kong, Indonesia and the Philippines) and/or geographical ones (as in the case of the Pacific countries of Latin America, but see Petersen, 1992) remain relatively unaffected by this archetype. And the second is that even some that have been strongly affected, such as Korea, Taiwan, Malaysia and Singapore, continue to be marked by inherited social particularities and/or to have experienced attempts either to deny its influence or to differentiate their institutions from the Japanese model for historical, political and/or religious reasons.

Still, despite such obstacles to its diffusion and the difficulties that the 1995 Osaka and 1996 Manila meetings of the Asia Pacific Economic Conference (APEC) confirmed still stand in the way of formal regional economic coordination (Noland, 1990, ch. 5; Shibusawa, 1984, pp. 144–8), the model continues to have a profound influence, as will become apparent in Part II of the present study. This is because the model's attractiveness is reinforced not only by the inherently transnational nature of the forces that have produced and sustained it, but also both by the prestige that has accrued to its Japanese instance as a result of that society's continuing economic pre-eminence, and by the more direct disciplinary consequences of either trading with Japan or playing host to Japanese transnational capital. Moreover, the proliferation of Export Processing Zones (EPZs) in even the most socially and geographically distant parts of the region is a testament to the archetype's attraction, since the regulations which constitute them generally replicate what is from labour's standpoint a very harsh form of Pacific capitalism and so provide capital with a beachhead in what might otherwise appear to be very unpromising circumstances (for accounts of China's EPZs, see Crane, 1990; Sklair, 1996). All this said and despite the oppressive connotations with respect to labour and human rights that are evoked when one considers Pacific capitalism's institutional forms, what I will suggest below is that such connotations are reversible under certain conditions.

AMERICAN POSTMODERNITY, HUMAN RIGHTS AND INCREDULITY ALONG THE PACIFIC RIM

To my mind, there is perhaps something tragically ironic about the faith currently evinced in the dominant liberal variant of the discourse of human rights by some Western NGOs, since several of such rights, most pertinently those relating to labour, appear to be well on the way to becoming one of the principal victims of another transnationally pertinent change; namely that represented by the onset of postmodernity. Although postmodernity as a properly social rather than simply cultural condition is thus far confined to the United States (Woodiwiss, 1992b; 1993), where it represents a possibly terminal instance of ideological self-destruction, its arrival there is nevertheless an occurrence of the most profound transnational significance, especially along the Asian segment of the Pacific Rim. This is because, given the demise of the so-called Socialist Bloc, the regional weakness of social democracy, and notwithstanding the United States government's many actions to the contrary, American Social Modernism has been the principal source of ideological support for the discourse of human rights in the region since 1946.

Social Modernism was the discourse most of whose component elements first crystallised in President Truman's 'Fair Deal' speech of 1948, and which included amongst its key tenets, alongside 'self-reliance', 'opportunity' and 'loyalty', a 'responsible unionism' which both rests upon and is one of the principal social guarantors of a significant sub-set of human rights. These elements were identified by American academics such as Daniel Bell as defining social modernity from the late 1940s onwards. This identification became official, so to speak, when President Kennedy repeated it in the early 1960s. However, its accuracy as a description of the United States hegemonic public discourse ended after Richard Nixon's election in 1968. Thereafter it seems to me to be more accurate to refer to Social (Post)Modernism since, despite the repetition of the promises made in the name of Social Modernism by him and every president prior to George Bush, the state: (1) no longer willingly helped those who could not be 'self-reliant'; (2) no longer felt that it should actively enhance the 'opportunities' available to its citizenry; (3) no longer sought but rather assumed the citizenry's 'loyalty'; and therefore

(4) no longer had any use for a 'responsible unionism' whose most valued role had been to support state paternalism with respect to the poor, distribute opportunities, and ensure the loyalty of its membership (Woodiwiss, 1993, ch. 7).

Not only have trade unions now lost their place in the hegemonic discourse of the United States, but their right even to participate in the construction of public discourse has been challenged by the rise of a Japanese-inspired discourse on labour for Pacific capitalism (see below). Moreover, the latter currently appears to be antipathetic not just to some social and political rights but also to several of the civil rights that have, rightly or wrongly, always been identified with Western capitalism. In the remainder of this chapter I will do two things: first, outline what the arrival of postmodernity has meant in American labour law; and second, outline the consequences for Japanese labour law of what I will refer to somewhat carefully as the 'passing of modernism' rather than the arrival of postmodernity.

POSTMODERNITY AND LABOUR RIGHTS IN THE UNITED STATES

American labour legislation applies to a comparatively narrow segment of the labour force. The basic text, the National Labor Relations Act of 1935, initially excluded all agricultural workers and government employees from its coverage, whilst the Taft-Hartley Act (1947) which reformed it imposed numerous constraints upon unions (e.g. the banning of the pre-entry closed shop, sympathy strikes, communist office-holders, and direct contributions to political parties). Nevertheless, the postwar history of American labour law has most often been interpreted as having been favourable to labour. At least it was so interpreted until the late 1970s when radical labour law scholars, like Katherine Stone (1981), Karl Klare (1981) and James Atleson (1983) began reflecting on the significance of the 1971 case known as *Boys Market*. This was the case that brought the notorious 'labour injunction' back to American industrial relations after an absence of nearly forty years, albeit only in the case of wildcat strikes.

Ironically, what had made this return possible was the earlier and ostensibly pro-union decision in the *Lincoln Mills* case of 1957, and the judiciary's assumption of the right to invoke and indeed define 'the general welfare' (Woodiwiss, 1990b, pp. 253ff.). The decision in *Lincoln Mills* established the doctrine that, where a contract included a no-disruption pledge on the part of the union, the union had a right to expect that, as a *quid pro quo*, all otherwise strikeable grievances should be made subject to third-party arbitration. In this way the Social Modernist discourse pertaining to 'responsible unionism' became embedded at the core of an emerging federal common law of collective bargaining in which the discourses of contract and property played an increasingly determinative role. Thereafter, the Supreme Court's prime concern became the maintenance of the coherence and consistency of this body of law regardless of which substantive interests were winning or losing. In a striking parallel with what happened in Japan, these interests disappeared behind another discourse. But, in an equally striking contrast, the discourse behind which they disappeared was that of arbitration rather than that of conciliation (see below, p. 66).

Thus, the wholly unintended result of the return of the signs 'property' and 'contract' as the means to legally enforce what may initially have been an equalitarian vision of industrial pluralism (Stone, 1981), was to recreate the possibility of a collective labour action becoming the cause of 'irreparable damage' and thereby of a tort that in equity could only be remedied by the issuance of a labour injunction. This was the unseen logic which eventually took the symptomatic form of the *Boys Market* injunction: a profoundly ironic result since, to repeat, in arriving at it the Court was applying a logic which had long been thought, by unions as well as judges, to be pro-union.

What had produced this reversal were two developments: first, the hitherto marginal dimension of property relations which relates to control of the labour process and to which *Boys Market* spoke had become central with the change in the nature of corporate capital and the increased competitiveness of the conditions in which it operated (see above, p. 51); and second, the forgetting of Social Modernism that was eventually to result in the arrival of postmodernity had commenced. The net result was that labour and its legal friends found themselves fighting new battles over control issues, whose successful prosecution required that they take up weapons that they had long ago voluntarily sacrificed the right to carry, namely, various means of slowing or stopping production. In Hohfeldian terms, then, the postwar development of American labour law has seen the manner in which the central jural relations are specified change from an emphasis on wide 'liberties' and vaguely specified duties to one on a disempowering combination of narrow 'powers' (to seek arbitration during the lifetime of a contract), far more sharply defined duties (to desist from any disruptive actions), and some, as it has turned out, ultimately unenforceable 'claims' (to company health and unemployment plans, for example).

In this way, then, American labour made its entry into a literally postmodern and therefore hyper-real world in which things are both not and only what they seem – a world from which the only currently conceivable modes of escape would appear to be nostalgic fantasies such as those which during the 1980s informed the AFL-CIO president Lane Kirkland's repeated calls for a revocation of the National Labor Relations Act and a return to the harsh, bareknuckle reality of American industrial relations before the New Deal. In sum, even without the rightward shift in the balance on the Supreme Court and the National Labor Relations Board which occurred during the 1970s and 1980s, it seems to me that *Boys Market* and all it legally represented has long been irreversible because of the effects of extra-juridical discursive developments which diminished the significance of organised labour, and which even liberal justices would have found it difficult to resist. It therefore seems more than a little ironic, not to say hypocritical, that it should be the United States that is currently taking the lead in calling for the respect for labour rights in Pacific Asia. There are therefore good grounds, unfortunately, for the incredulity/anger directed towards the United States when it adopts the role of the workers' protector, since it is seen to be seeking to impose on other capitals restrictions that it would rather not see on its own.

JAPAN, PATRIARCHALISM AND THE RULE OF LAW

If the United States is surprisingly ill-equipped to act as either a model or an enforcer in the sphere of labour rights, Japan would seem, equally surprisingly, to be far better placed on both counts. I say 'surprisingly' because according to the *Kokutai no Hongi*, the official statement of prewar *Tennosei* (emperor-system) ideology produced by the Ministry of Education in 1937, traditional Japanese patriarchalism allowed no space for a discourse of rights of any kind:

> the relationship between the Emperor and his subjects is, in its righteousness, that of sovereign and subject and, in its sympathies, that of father and child. This relationship is an 'essential' (in the sense of having to do with natural qualities) relationship that is far more fundamental than the rational, obligatory relationships, and herein are the grounds that give birth to the Way of Loyalty. From the point of individualistic personal relationships, the relationship between sovereign and subject in our country

may (perhaps) be looked upon as that between non-personalities. However, this is nothing but an error arising from treating the individual as supreme, from the notion that has individual thoughts for its nucleus and from personal abstract consciousness. Our relationship between sovereign and subject, is by no means a shallow, lateral relationship such as (means) the correlation between ruler and citizen, but is a relationship springing from a basis transcending this correlation, and is that of self-effacement and a return to (the) one, in which this basis is not lost. This is a thing that can never be understood from an individualistic way of thinking. In our country, this great Way has seen a natural development since the founding of the nation, and the most basic thing that has manifested itself as regards the subjects is in short this Way of Loyalty. Herein exists the profound meaning and lofty value of loyalty. Of late years, through the influence of the Occidental individualistic ideology, a way of thinking which has for its basis the individual has become lively. Consequently, this and the true aim of our Way of Loyalty which is 'essentially' different from it are not necessarily (mutually) consistent. That is, those in our country who at the present time expound loyalty and patriotism are apt to lose (sight of) its true significance being influenced by Occidental individualism and rationalism.

We must sweep aside the corruption of the spirit and the clouding of knowledge that arises from setting up one's 'self' and from being taken up with one's 'self' and return to a pure and clear state of mind that belongs intrinsically to us as subjects, and thereby fathom the great principle of loyalty.

Given such an ethical baseline, the fact that Japan now scores 82 per cent on the *Humana Human Rights Index* (1992) is therefore the mark of a considerable achievement, especially since the Index rates countries exclusively on their civil and political records and not on the social and economic ones in relation to which patriarchalist societies such as Japan in particular would claim to have greatly improved over the postwar period.

When Japan's postwar constitution was formulated great efforts were made by the Occupation authorities and their Japanese allies to correct the manifest weaknesses of the prewar constitutional and legal order as a system of rights protection (Oppler, 1976). Individual rights in general were greatly strengthened both by increasing their number and by their less qualified constitutional expression. In addition, individuals acquired rights of redress against the state through new administrative courts. The autonomy of the judiciary was considerably enhanced thanks to the Supreme Court's gaining of the power, if requested by the citizenry, to review government actions and legislation with a view to establishing their constitutionality. The judiciary's position was also strengthened by its gaining of the power to impose the sanctions of the criminal law on its own behalf, although this power remains very underdeveloped as compared to the 'contempt power' available in common law societies (Haley, 1982).

Finally, as if to symbolise the potential significance of both these and the accompanying extra-legal developments, the local *Koseki* (registers), which had been the most important prewar legal texts and very powerful instruments of social control, were restructured on the basis of the nuclear rather than the extended family. By depriving the *ie* (the traditional patriarchal household), both institutionally and ideologically, of its critical role as *the* intermediary institution between the individual and the state, the restructuring of the registers struck at the heart of *Tennosei*. This was an attack continued by the two-stage reform of the Civil Code which occurred in 1947 and 1948, and whose principal concern was the reform of family relationships. As a result of the changes to the code, primogeniture was abolished, wives gained control over their own property, mothers gained equality with fathers with respect to matters concerning children, women gained the same divorce rights as men and in numerous other ways the bases were created for a more egalitarian family structure and, by extension, a more individualised citizenry.

By and large, despite some continuing ambiguity as to the status of the constitutionally given rights, these legal reforms and the social developments that accompanied them have successfully transformed the rights position of the ordinary Japanese citizen (Beer, 1984, ch. 12; in addition, see the cases reported in Itoh and Beer, 1978, ch. 10 and Maki, 1964, pp. 3–155). This said, a closer look at where Japan loses points on the *Humana Index* suggests what has also been confirmed by more detailed research, namely that there are two categories of people whose human rights are not as well protected as they are, for example, in Western Europe. First, isolated and/or poor individuals who come face to face with the state in antagonistic circumstances. They can expect: violence from the police; long periods of detention without either the laying of charges, legal advice or a hearing; little media or pressure group interest in their fate; and little hope of a fair trial since most often these pressures induce them to confess before coming to trial (Foote, 1992; Ramlogan, 1994). I emphasise that all this is likely to happen to isolated and/or poor individuals because, as is well known, suspects who are well integrated with their families, neighbours and workmates and who both confess and apologise will not suffer such abuses and, even if found guilty, may often escape punishment altogether. The second group of rights-losers includes members of minorities (Koreans, Ainu, Okinawans, and Burakumin (untouchables)), as well as the entire female gender. This latter group's rights are more often violated indirectly because of state-condoned discriminatory practices of one kind or another than directly by the actions of the state or the operation of the criminal justice system (Buraku Liberation Research Institute, 1984). Finally, I would like to suggest that a third group has suffered at least a partial derogation of its rights over the postwar period, namely trade union members. However, this loss of freedom has been at least partially offset in terms of increased job security, especially but not only for the relatively privileged group of employees whom unions tend to represent. And this has occurred in a way that I intend to show may yet prove to be highly propitious for both trade unions and human rights throughout Pacific Asia and perhaps beyond.

THE PASSING OF MODERNISM AND THE RECONFIGURATION OF LABOUR RIGHTS IN JAPAN

It is widely known that the Occupation authorities hoped that the promulgation of a system of labour rights would help to democratise Japanese industrial relations by enhancing labour's autonomy and so underpinning the constitutional and legal changes outlined above. My general thesis (Woodiwiss, 1992a) is that, whilst this hope was initially fulfilled, it has since been somewhat disappointed but not without compensation. My more specific thesis is that the prime reason for this disappointment has been the hegemonic accession of *Kigyoushugi*, an ideological formation wherein the virtuous company replaces the virtuous *Tenno* at the core of the Way of Loyalty, and which for similarly patriarchalist reasons continues the prewar hostility towards fully autonomous and assertive trade unions.

In what follows, I will suggest, first, that the statutes upon which the postwar labour law system was based may be read as instances of a fundamental ideological continuity between pre- and postwar Japan; and, second, that the reason why labour law has latterly become at least as much of a hindrance as a help to trade unions is because, given its intrinsic patriarchalism, it has proved to be highly susceptible to *Kigyoushugi*-inspired interpretations on the part of the judiciary – interpretations which have resulted in these continuities becoming in general ever more marked with the passage of time. The result of the latter movement is that it has reduced still further labour law's anyway inherently limited capacity to serve as a means for the enforcement of a certain democracy in the workplace. In sum, then, what I intend to indicate here is the concrete nature of *Kigyoushugi* in the employment sphere.

Although it has seldom been fully acknowledged in the pertinent literature, the same residual but nevertheless significant ambiguity as to what it might signify (that is, democratism or patriarchalism?) character-ised even the amended and partially Americanised Trade Union Law of 1949 as characterised the 'New Constitution'. On the one hand, the passage of the law, like the presence of labour rights in the constitution, undoubtedly granted labour in both the private and public sectors rights and a degree of social recognition which it had never possessed before (only the police, firefighters and prison staff were excluded from this dispensation). On the other hand, it did so on the basis of a bill which, highly suggestively as Sheldon Garon (1987) has pointed out, had first been prepared by the Home Ministry's Social Bureau in 1925.

Also passed into law during the early days of the Occupation were three other labour laws which, although this has been commented upon even less often, similarly owed much to prewar state patriarchalism, the Labor Relations Adjustment Act (LRAA) of 1946, the Public Corpor-ation and National Enterprise Labor Relations Law (PCLL) of 1948, and the Labor Standards Act of 1947. I do not intend to attempt to justify my reading of these texts as patriarchalist here since I have already done this at some length in the text already cited. Suffice it to say that throughout the legislation the fact that labour rights were granted for a purpose rather than for the sake of a principle is explicit (i.e. they were granted in order to enable *trade unions* to fit into a surprisingly pre-systematised framework of industrial relations, rather than to enable *employees* to contribute to the construction of such a system). Instead of saying any-thing further by way of justification, I will proceed more or less immedi-ately to a summary characterisation of the judicial interpretations of the same texts – interpretations which make it clear that, especially after 1972, the majority of Supreme Court justices may be read as having supported my claim as regards the patriarchalism of the basic texts, albeit whilst placing an opposite and positive valuation upon it. I say 'especially after 1972' not so much because during the preceding two years the make-up of the Supreme Court was transformed by the arrival of seven new and very conservative justices, but more because *Kigyoushugi* was hegemonically established by that time and so readily available for enunciation by such justices.

Prompted by a conciliatory methodology for dealing with conflicts over rights that Lawrence Beer has appropriately termed 'harmonising' to distinguish it from the 'balancing' performed by American judges, the Japanese Supreme Court has depended upon *Kigyoushugi*-inspired ideas to weaken trade unions and strengthen hierarchical relations within companies in the following ways: by strongly favouring conciliation over arbitration as well as over adjudication and as a result refusing to define either rights or duties with any precision; by allowing that constitutional freedoms, such as those relating to speech, may be negotiated away in the case of 'contracts that have been freely entered into'; by reasserting the constitutionality of suspect and ILO-challenged restrictions on the right to strike in the public sector; by allowing the legality of joint consultation arrangements that undermine the independence of trade unions, despite the existence of the same unfair labour practice provisions that disallow such arrangements in the United States; by making involuntary overtime as well as transfers to so-called 'related companies' impossible to resist by individual employees; and, finally, by making an important surrogate for strike action illegal – the wearing of slogans critical of management while continuing to work ('ribbon struggles') (Woodiwiss, 1992a, ch. 5).

Because the last of these developments is so suggestive of the particularity of the restrictive side of Japanese labour law, I will end this section by discussing it in a little more detail. When the Tokyo Local Labour Relations Commission first considered the 'ribbon struggle' tactic in the *Hotel Okura Case* (1972), it allowed that when a dispute was in progress the works rules were suspended and so it found nothing wrong with the staff's wearing of ribbons critical of the management. By contrast, when the Tokyo District Court reconsidered the same case on appeal in 1975, it found that 'ribbon struggles were illegal in general'. Quoting only from that part of the judgement in which the court explains why the practice of ribbon struggles is bad for employees as well as employers, the dependence of the court's reasoning on *Kigyoushugi* is very clear: it creates 'a psychological dual structure which on the one hand is obedient and on the other is antagonistic towards superiors and [so] divides the psychological operations of people who are logical beings, paving the way for the formation of split personalities'. On this reasoning, then, ongoing face to face disagreement with one's superior is to be discouraged because it is likely to lead to schizophrenia – of course it does not, but what it does do is violate the patriarchal familialism upon which *Kigyoushugi* rests. In 1982 the Tokyo Labour Commission appealed the case to the Supreme Court on behalf of the union concerned. The Supreme Court upheld both the judgement and the amateur psychological reasoning of the lower court.

To conclude, the entry of *Kigyoushugi* into labour law has transformed the conception of the employment relationship in the private sector that was basic to both the new constitution and the amended Trade Union Law; i.e. the Social Modernist recognition of the different interests of capital and labour that was fundamental to the postwar legislation has been ever more confidently denied as the social and judicial commitment to the limited communitarianism or patriarchalism of the company has grown. In a surprising and fascinating instance of transnationally inspired hybridity, it seems that, alongside *Kigyoushugi*, arguments drawn from the Weimar Republic's social-democratic labour law by lawyers acting for the unions played a significant role in helping the judiciary arrive at this commitment (Kettler and Tackney, 1996). In Hohfeld's terms, then, the period since 1949 has seen a striking reduction in the 'liberties' and 'immunities' of Japanese employees and unions as, similarly to the United States, the control dimension of the property relation has become ever more salient within large companies, and as an anyway very prescriptive legal framework has become more and more proscriptive. This said, and despite therefore a move in the direction of industrial absolutism that is comparable to that which has occurred in the United States, the same period has also seen these reductions compensated for not only by a small increase in 'powers' (to participate in joint consultation fora) but also by very substantial increases in 'claims' to such as company welfare benefits and, most importantly, to an apparently irreversible claim to 'lifetime employment'.

Restricted though the numbers concretely as opposed to nominally benefiting from these 'claims' may be, it is nevertheless important to acknowledge that, thanks to the demand for consistency inherent in legal discourse under conditions of legal autonomy, successful but as yet not fully tested efforts have been made to extend the legal entitlement to 'lifetime employment' beyond the confines of the corporate sector (Schregle, 1993; Sugeno, 1992, pp. 65, 156). Thus, in the absence of a written contract to the contrary (a very common state of affairs in Japan), the courts will generally find an implied promise to provide lifetime employment no matter what the size of the company. Moreover, the wider legal, social-structural and cultural supports that this doctrine possesses have thus far proved robust enough to sustain it through a prolonged recession and the continuing 'hollowing out' of the economy as production has been relocated to other countries including others in Pacific Asia. Of course, many companies have sought either to reduce their exposure to the doctrine's consequences by taking on far fewer 'regular' employees, or to avoid them by offering inducements (not all of them pleasant) to those whom they would like to see take early retirement. However, the very fact that such measures have had to have been adopted suggests the legal strength of the position of young and mid-career regular employees.

In sum, then, these developments in Japanese labour law represent an instance of how the obligations inherent in the Confucian concept of 'benevolence' have been made legally enforceable and so instance a neo-patriarchalism rather than simply a paternalism. In Japan this was the result of the Supreme Court's inclusion and expansion of bargained terms as implied contractual terms. In the light of the favourable cultural environment, there is therefore every reason to think that a similar result could by achieved in other Pacific-Asian societies by legislatively specifying 'powers' to participate in decision-making, 'claims' (to training, security of employment, and/or social programmes, for example), that must be granted if 'liberties' and 'immunities' are to be reduced.

As indicated earlier, if it is to be successful, any attempt to inscribe the discourse of rights within that of patriarchalism has both to be rigorously enforced, preferably by unions as well as by the state, and therefore to involve the maintenance of certain irreducible 'liberties' and 'immunities', as well as labour access to political power. Here again a critical lesson may be learnt from the Japanese case. In my view the most important of these liberties and immunities are those that protect the freedom of ordinary employees to withhold their consent without having to choose 'exit' over 'voice'. In other words, where one has enterprise or 'in-house' unions, as in Japan, it is essential not simply that labour rights are fundamentally employee rather than union rights, but also that, again as in Japan (Woodiwiss, 1992a, pp. 142–4), they are continuously exercisable not only *vis-à-vis* employers but also *vis-à-vis* incumbent unions through employees exercising a 'liberty' to create a second or sustain a 'minority' union. In other words, from labour's standpoint and contrary to Western labour's experience, the possibility of dual unionism should be seen in a positive rather than in a negative light – that is, where the efficacy of the negative labour rights represented by employer 'unfair labour practice' provisions are reduced, as they invariably are where there are enterprise unions, it is important that this be balanced by a strengthening or a broadening of a positive and transferable right to self-organisation on the part of all employees (see also Leader, 1992, ch. 10).

CONSTRUCTING A DISCOURSE ON LABOUR FOR PACIFIC CAPITALISM

In the remaining sections of this chapter, I will, first, specify the role assigned to labour within Pacific capitalism; and second, suggest how labour rights and, by extension, human rights more generally might best be designed if they are to be enforceable in Pacific Asia. As is well known, the critical weakness of all international law, including human rights law, is that its subjects (nation states), in contrast to those of national legal systems, exist in a Hobbesian 'state of nature' (Carty, 1986) wherein there is no sovereign power and therefore little chance of the law being enforced. Thus, for example, because of the play of ideologies within them, nation states are easily able to exempt themselves from the obligations contained within international law (for exemplifications of this point as it relates to human rights, see: Campbell et al., 1986; Cassese, 1990, ch. 3). In the explanations provided in Part II as to how such exemptions have occurred in the Pacific-Asian region, I will assume without elaboration the correctness of those analyses that have pointed to the pertinence of the globally unique absences of both a regional polity and an associated regional human rights convention (Acharya, 1995; Welch, 1990; Woods, 1995). Similarly, I will assume the correctness of the arguments of those who have stressed the historical responsibility of Northern governments and transnational capital for these absences (Feldman, 1990; Muzaffar, 1993b).

What will be novel about the explanation presented here is the argument that what has been at least as damaging as any of these factors in the case of labour rights has been the recent *selective* borrowing from a transnational ideological current of apparently Asian origin, namely the Japanese Employment System (JES). Thus, the overseas effects of this current not only differ from their domestic ones, but also run counter to those of Japan's official support for human rights (Peek, 1992). The net effect of this current's positive reception in Pacific Asia has been two-fold. First, to make manifest the shared but, of course, not uncontested patriarchalism of the region's cultures. And second, to give this patriarchalism a new lease of life by suggesting not only ways in which it may be made congruent with the capitalist economic relations which they also share, but also ways in which it may contribute to making these relations a source of what is claimed to be the general enrichment.

In the immediate aftermath of the Second World War and as instanced by its labour policy in Japan, the United States government regarded trade unions in a very positive light and strongly encouraged their development on the grounds that they represented a bulwark of democracy. The United States stance changed, however, with the onset of the Cold War. The Occupation authorities imposed legislative and public order restrictions on the rapidly growing Japanese labour movement, and the United States supported the repressive policies towards left-wing trade unionism of the colonial governments that still dominated much of Pacific Asia. With the onset of decolonisation, the International Confederation of Free Trade Unions (ICFTU) and its component International Trade Secretariats (ITS) such as the International Metalworkers Federation (IMF) became the chief conduits through which the AFL-CIO, supported by the State Department, sought to exercise influence in the region. This effort became more focused with the formation in 1968 of the Asian-American Free Labour Institute (AAFLI).

In some tension with the social democratically inclined Western European members of the ICFTU and the ITSs, as well as in clear conflict with the largely communist World Federation of Trade Unions (WFTU), AAFLI has consistently advocated a strongly anti-communist and apolitical variety of trade unionism modelled on American 'unionism pure and simple' (Busch, 1983; Neuhaus, 1982; Spooner, 1989). In this way Pacific-Asian conceptions of the proper nature and role of trade unions, which with the exception of the Philippines had otherwise been largely shaped by social-democratic and communist ideas mediated through or in conflict with the mainly European colonial regimes, also became subject to a pronounced American influence. Latterly this influence was supplemented and in part displaced by the simultaneously evolving Japanese ideas (see Williamson, 1994, for a detailed and institutionally focused account of Japan's 'labour diplomacy'). Together, these two discursive flows were constitutive of a new disourse on labour for Pacific capitalism. Since the manner in which the Japanese current became part of this story is not only central to the present study but also provides a striking incidence of what is involved in Braithwaitian social modelling (see above, p. 28, n. 1), I will devote the remainder of this chapter to outlining the central aspects of this otherwise untold story.

As early as the late 1950s, lifetime employment, seniority-related pay and enterprise unionism were recognised by some as the defining features of a distinctively Japanese industrial relations system. However, those like Abegglen (1958), who regarded these features in a positive light were out of step with mainstream opinion both inside and outside Japan. For such opinion regarded them as feudal (that is, patriarchalist) survivals that would disappear as the society continued to modernise. Only in the late 1970s did the positive reading of the significance of these features receive widespread support and admiring talk of the Japanese Employment System (JES) become common (for instances of the growth in support of a 'non-culturalist' version of Abegglen's argument, see Clark, 1979; Cole, 1971; Dore, 1973; Nakayama, 1975; OECD, 1977; Rohlen, 1974). The proceedings of the biennial Asian Regional Conference on Industrial Relations organised by the Japan Institute of Labour (JIL) provide a unique, especially pertinent, and hitherto neglected opportunity to examine the process whereby the discourse summarised as the JES was formulated. What is particularly notable about the formulation emerging from these conferences is the stress placed upon enterprise unionism in what might be termed the 'export version' of the JES, as compared with that placed on lifetime employment in the domestic version and indeed the wider Western literature on Japanese industrial relations. What is equally notable is the significance of non-Japanese scholars in the preparation of the export version, which suggests that their focus on enterprise unions tells us as much if not more about what they considered to be the principal problems faced by their own countries' industrial relations systems as it does about the nature of the Japanese system.

According to Rob Steven (1990, ch. 3), the interests of Japanese companies in the region have developed through three phases, each associated with the particular but by no means exclusive salience of a different problem arising from the dependence of Japanese capital's position in the world system on the low-cost exports initially made possible by the low-wage regime established during the postwar recovery period (see also, Thurow, 1992, pp. 125–6). The first period (1962–72) was marked by a search for low-wage production sites in such labour-intensive industries as textiles and was prompted by the rising domestic wage levels in these industries. The second period (1973–8) was initiated by the substantial cost increases that resulted from the 'oil shocks' of those years. It was characterised by a general search for cost reductions, especially as regards raw materials and on the part of the heavy metallurgical industries. The third period (1979–90) began with the price rises consequent on the rising value of the yen. It was marked by the addition of North American and Western European investments to Pacific ones as Japanese transnationals sought ways to avoid the barrier to their exports created by the high yen.

Returning to the changing agenda of JIL's Asian Regional Conferences on Industrial Relations with this periodisation in mind, what one notes as one follows its development is not only the crystallisation of the discursive dimension of the JES, but also the way in which this process very closely tracked the developing interests of Japanese transnationals in the region. The conferences began in 1965 with a general discussion of the development of the Japanese industrial relations system in the context of American and Western European developments. It included a paper by Bernard Karsch prefiguratively entitled 'The Exportability of Trade Union Movements'. Its subtitle, 'The Japan-United States "Cultural Exchange Program"', and its content indicate, however, that it was written in another world. For what Karsch reports on is a very intense effort on the part of the American government and the AFL-CIO to teach their ways to Japanese trade unionists. This seemed to him to be failing because of the Japanese participants' inability to understand how their American opposite numbers could disavow any class consciousness, could work so hard, and could cooperate so enthusiastically with management!

After this first conference the organisers gave the series the Asian focus that has since been reflected in its title. Appropriately, the 1967 conference provided an overview of the industrial relations systems of the region. More purposefully, the 1969 meeting included sections on 'industrial relations in the public sector', manpower problems and policies in developing economies, and the design, role and management of industrial relations centres or institutes. In 1971, reflecting Japan's growing direct involvement in the region, the conference turned its attention to what its chair termed 'the deeper forces at work which tend to shape industrial relations within a country', namely their 'social and cultural background'. The section headings were 'the development of management', 'the making of industrial workers' and 'social and cultural norms in industrial relations'.

Significantly, the latter section featured two assessments of Japan's role in the future evolution of industrial relations in the region, which are more alike than the subsequent careers of their authors would lead one to expect. One, by Robert Ballon, was entitled '"Organized Labor": a Japanese Technological Transfer?' Written by a long-time, Western enthusiast for the Japanese way, it is a far more uninhibited celebration of the then newly crystallised hegemonic discourse of *Kigyoushugi* than any offered at the time by Japanese industrial relations scholars. In it, several of the most controversial characteristics of the 'new unions' that emerged in the wake of the 1960s government/management onslaught on their more assertive predecessors are recommended for emulation by employees in developing countries. Thus, according to Ballon, a useful union in a developing society should be:

> spontaneously enterprise-wide, and limiting its membership to the 'regular' employees [i.e. those not hired temporarily];
>
> jealous of its autonomy [e.g. excluding 'outsiders' from the bargaining table];
>
> directed by officers who are not professionals, but employees kept on the payroll while exercising their union responsibility;
>
> careful in the representation of their interests not to jeopardise the enterprise. (JIL, 1971, p. 199)

The other paper was by Robert Cox, and was entitled 'Approaches to a Futurology of Industrial Relations on a Global Scale'. In it, although Cox gives voice to his now justly famous insights into the consequences of the arrival of transnationals in developing countries, he not only mis-identifies the Japanese industrial relations system with those of North America and Western Europe on the basis of their shared 'powerful autonomous trade unions' (JIL, 1971, p. 287, but see Cox 1987, p. 73 for a different view), but he also predicts a still closer convergence between these three systems (such are the perils of futurology!).

The year 1973 saw the first of the 'oil shocks'. Interestingly, therefore, the preface to the 1973 conference proceedings, which was written by the president of JIL, opens with a low-key but somewhat exclusionary claim that the participants had a common aim, namely 'to promote mutual understanding and contribute to cooperation in this region'. It then goes on to explain the reasoning behind the choice of that year's theme, 'industrialisation and manpower policy in Asian countries'. This was that 'the expansion of employment opportunities and manpower development' was one of 'the most fundamental problems of Asian Industrialisation'. Unsurprisingly in view of the more developed nature of Japan's labour market structures and of the research thereon, as one peruses the papers one gains an unmistakable sense of Japan's status as a model. This sense is confirmed by two comments made during the conference's concluding session. In the first, a participant from Hong Kong noted, presumably favourably, 'that he sensed a feeling of "Asianness" . . . as exemplified by the use of Japanese language with simultaneous interpretation and the presence of a large Japanese delegation, permitting a greater exposure and exchange of ideas between Asians'. And in the second, the JIL president referred to a recent OECD report, which identified 'lifetime commitment, seniority system, and enterprise unionism as the major factors accounting for the rapid growth of the Japanese economy'. Perhaps the most important event in the region during the year before the 1975 conference was Prime Minister Tanaka's tour of the Asean countries, which was marked by numerous hostile demonstrations. According to Shibusawa (1984, p. 151), 1975 was the year in which Japanese transnational investment in Pacific Asia took off. On cue, the theme of that year's conference was 'foreign investment and labour in Asian countries'. The opening address by JIL President Naka-yama and the 'greetings' offered by the administrative vice-minister of labour, both attest to the anxieties felt by the Japanese side in the light of what the latter referred to as 'increasing criticism of Japanese firms abroad'. Thus the vice-minister continued:

> There is no need to say that management should follow the institutional practices of the host country. However, it often happens that the management of a foreign firm do not fully understand those practices. In view of this situation we look forward to the presentations of researchers and other specialists assembled here today.

Fascinatingly, in view of the prestige that Japanese management prac-tices have since gained throughout the region and the world, it is clear from the conference papers and the often tense discussions between the participants, that the vice-minister's criticism's were rather specifically directed at Japanese transnationals. Perhaps because the first wave of Japanese investors in the region were from the less sophisticated sectors of Japanese industry, certainly because of the still apparent failure of Japan to come to terms with its colonial and aggressive past, and despite the fact that they were most often engaged in joint ventures, these trans-nationals appear to have been blissfully unaware of the sort of reaction that any sort of 'high-handedness' on their part might evoke in the host countries. This said, Professor Taira's (JIL, 1975, p. 157) suggestion that, once the unfortunate impression created by the 'cultural aggression' of the first wave companies subsided, 'the evolution of management struc-tures in these countries in the future may be more in the Japanese direc-tion than the Western' has proved to be prophetic. In the light of the current insistence by most commentators on the cultural diversity of Pacific Asia, and of course because of my own view to the contrary, it is important that I indicate the nature of Professor Taira's reasoning. After fully acknowledging both the religious and cultural diversity of the region and the varying levels of criticism of Japanese companies (then, interestingly, most intense in Singapore, Malaysia and Thailand), he puts his central proposition thus:

> Asian values are not individualistic, egalitarian, or democratic . . . Individuality is usually subsumed, protected, and developed within the crust of the family, while families are informally organized into kin groups. The predominant Asian worldview is hierarchical and social inequality is not bad per se if legitimized by an accepted code of behavior . . . Effective group action is supported by shared feelings of participants under affective leadership (which goes by the name of charisma in the West) rather than under democratic leadership on the basis of a consensus through a rational discussion of issues, methods, and goals . . . Thus a high degree of interdependence [is] obtained within the hierarchy of a group through 'spiritual' communications, which are invisible and cannot be caught by the technical antennae of the Western man.

> The description of the 'Asian man' in the preceding paragraph contains most of the institutional factors and socio-psychological forces that evoke an association with 'familialism', 'groupism', 'paternalism', 'welfare corporatism', and so on that are said to characterize the Japanese employment system.   (JIL, 1975, pp. 157–9).

Professor Taira's somewhat regretful view that, in Pacific Asia at least, history was on the side of what I have been calling Pacific capitalism appears to have done little to calm the anxieties of governmental and corporate opinion in Japan, since the 1977 conference was a continuation of the 1975 one. Indeed so great was this anxiety that in the course of his greetings the vice-minister of labour made JIL's closeness to government far clearer than is usual, when he stated that:

> These problems created by international investment activities are important ones which we can no longer afford to disregard . . .

> In dealing with these problems, in Japan, a committee of representatives from trade unions, firms and government has been set up . . . to examine them. The Japan Institute of Labour with the cooperation of labour and management concerned is collecting information and materials concerning labour problems created by Japanese firms . . . and offer these (sic) information widely within the country.   (JIL, 1977, p. 212)

Despite the underlying anxiety that the 1977 conference shared with its predecessor, the later conference saw little of the handwringing apparent in its predecessor. On the contrary the papers included one by Professor

Ishida which another Japanese discussant referred to as breaking a taboo, in that it spoke positively about the 'exportability of the Japanese employment system' (JIL, 1977, p. 235). Moreover, the comments of many of the Japanese participants to the discussions were noticeably aggressive in their dismissal of any criticisms of Japanese corporate behaviour overseas.

In 1979 Japan ratified the 1966 UN Conventions on civil, political, economic and social rights (the United States only ratified the civil and political convention in 1992 and has yet to ratify the economic and social convention, Wessner, 1996). This was something that it had long resisted, not least because the Conventions included articles relating to strikes by public sector employees, the freedom of unions to join international confederations, the limitation of working hours, payments for public holidays, and the right of women to equal pay that showed Japanese labour law and industrial relations practice in a bad light (for Japan's continuing difficulties in meeting international human rights standards in these and other areas, see Peek, 1992; Buraku Liberation Research Institute, 1984). Perhaps for this reason, the tension of the 1977 conference appears to have been completely absent from that of 1979. Also the theme was the broader and less touchy one of 'social tensions and industrial relations arising in the industrialisation process of Asian countries'. Whatever the reasons for the initial bad reaction to the arrival of Japanese companies in other Pacific-Asian countries, there was clearly no doubt amongst the participants that the Japanese system seemed to have done a very good job at reducing labour-inspired social tensions at home. Moreover, despite some sceptical remarks relating to who benefited from it by a Hong Kong based British participant, Joseph England (JIL, 1979, pp. 320–2), and perhaps as a pat on the back for signing the UN Covenants, the chief of the ILO's Industrial Relations and Labour Administration Department, Johannes Schregle, gave a paper which emphasised what the West could learn from the Asian notion of *Wa* (harmony). He also specifically congratulated Japan on its success in keeping the law – perhaps he should have said 'liberties' – out of industrial relations, and emphasised how much could be learnt from the publications of the Japan Institute of Labour. His concluding remarks included the following: 'Japan's unique position (economic, geographical and cultural) gives her an important role in comparative industrial relations both in highly industrialized countries in the West and in developing countries in Asia' (JIL, 1979, pp. 236–7). Here, and at last, was praise indeed – the imprimatur of a major global institution. All the more welcome, since it came from an organisation that had long been very critical of certain aspects of the Japanese system (see Harari, 1973, for example). JIL President Nakayama's pleasure at this outcome was very evident in his closing address, which contrived both to assert Japan's uniqueness, as well as to claim the status of a model that others might attempt to emulate:

> The Japanese system of conflict resolution consisted of something like joint consultation. Unlike some countries a class conflict consciousness is not present, but both sides make cooperation efforts . . . in their way of seeing and solving problems the Japanese are perhaps peculiar . . . We have to be cautious [however] in equating the Japanese way of thinking with that of all other peoples in Asia.

At the end of 1980, Prime Minister Lee Kwan Yew of Singapore declared that the Japanese model was the one for his country and as a result its population was, in the words of one commentator, 'blitzed with the ideological discourse of team work' (Rodan, 1989, p. 162; see also, Soesastro, 1985). The confidence created by such a practical confirmation of the intellectual gains confirmed by the 1979 conference was manifest in both the title chosen for the 1981 conference, 'Agenda for Industrial Relations in Asian Development', and the choice of one of the sub-themes: 'In Search of Alternative Models for Asian Industrial Relations'. The other sub-themes related to the informal sector and technology transfer, but as the new JIL president, Professor Sumiya, made clear in his opening address, both were connected with, and subordinate to, the 'alternative models' theme. As it happens, the discussion of the informal sector appears to have excited by far the most animated and prolonged discussion. A fact which should come as no surprise since, after all, the sector encompasses the vast majority of the non-Japanese, non-communist, Asian labour force. Indeed, the absence of any discussion of the informal sector at earlier conferences serves to underline the Japan-centredness of their agendas.

Compared to the discussion of the informal sector, that of 'alternative models' seems to have been distinctly lacklustre. It also seems to have been pretty mystical in that it included a paper on the I Ching and industrial relations as well as some very odd ruminations by Ballon on 'the problem of the use of words for realities'. Other papers and discussants were more down to earth and clearly had no time for any notion of Asian particularity. Even when Schregle repeated his thesis about the potential of the 'Asian idea of harmony' he did so in a very much more careful way.

Nevertheless, when the rapporteur for the small group that had discussed the topic further made his summing-up, he identified the key themes of a specifically Asian approach to industrial relations as state intervention, enterprise-centredness, antinomianism and 'the emphasis placed in some Asian countries on duty, rather than on right, and on obedience as opposed to equal footing' (JIL, 1981, p. 364).

Although the 1981 conference may not have quite delivered the further ringing endorsement of the Japanese system as the prototype Asian system that the organisers may have hoped for, the declaration later that year by Prime Minister Mahathir of Malaysia that his country too was adopting a 'Look East' policy (Jomo, 1990, pp. 202–5; see also Soesastro, 1985), and the publication and massive sales in the early 1980s of books such as Ezra Vogel's *Japan as Number One* confirmed the regional influence and the global acceptability of the Japanese system. Thereafter, and thanks also to the difficulties encountered, and changes undergone, by Western capitalisms in the ideological contexts created by the election of such high-profile free-market conservatives as Ronald Reagan and Margaret Thatcher, the Japanese model was 'de-orientalised' and indeed denuded of its benevolent features to become 'flexible specialisation' or 'lean production'. Since that time and despite Japan's recent economic difficulties, it has come to serve as a model for a Pacific capitalism whose influence as well as power has been felt far beyond the Pacific Rim.

Thus, what is borrowed from the Japanese experience is neither the 'liberty' exemplified by the ease with which unions may be formed, nor the 'claims' represented by company welfare programmes and 'lifetime employment' (see Atsushi, 1995, for example). Rather, what are borrowed are such techniques of labour constraint as are represented by:

(1) the careful vetting of all new employees;
(2) the purposive segmentation of internal and external labour markets to produce a variety of employment conditions. (Interestingly, one mode of segmentation that has not been widely taken up in Pacific Asia is the introduction of a plurality of legal statuses within a single workplace, namely regular, temporary and part-time.);
(3) the institutionalisation of continuous job-rotations and involuntary transfers to other plants and companies;
(4) the establishment of quality circles, and seniority-based and bonus payment systems;

(5) the transformation of any existing independent unions into enterprise unions; where independent unions do not already exist often not even an enterprise union will be allowed, although state-sponsored unions may be as in Indonesia and China.

Taken in turn and together, these techniques represent a veritable engine of authoritarian familialism in that they:

(1) distinguish an inside from an outside;
(2) make clear the specialness of those on the inside;
(3) make explicit the special demands made on those who are chosen;
(4) establish mechanisms whereby the chosen ones discipline themselves;
(5) provide the regular workers with a non-disruptive means of protecting themselves.

In sum, then, the techniques of industrial governance made possible by a particular set of class-structural relations in one country have been disaggregated and formalised so that they may be used to affect the balances with respect to possessory, disciplinary and discursive relations in others.

The third wave of Japanese investment in the Pacific Asia region encountered little of the hostility that greeted the first and second waves. On the contrary, the fact that it involved the now famous names of Japan's world-beating electronic sector and the local production of their very popular, relatively high value-added consumer goods seemed only to confirm the high hopes of the 'Look East' ideologues. It must be acknowledged, of course, that these ideologues, and especially their most forthright representatives in Singapore and Malaysia, also drew heavily on their own countries' ideological resources (see Chapters 5 and 6 below) and therefore nothing changed in their labour policies even after they had to tone down their Japanophilia in the mid-1980s for local political reasons. Nevertheless, whether they have since spoken instead, like Senior Minister Lee, of 'Confucian Capitalism' (Rodan, 1989, pp. 172–4), or, like Prime Minister Mahathir, of an Islamicised capitalism (Mauzy and Milne, 1984), the ideological success of the discourse of Pacific capitalism has become very clear.

In these circumstances, then, JIL's Asian regional conferences continued through the 1980s with a very technical, even technocratic, focus on the problems encountered by Japanese transnationals as regards human resource utilisation, the industrial relations side of technology transfers, and managerial strategies. Only in 1992 did the focus shift to the broader issues raised by the ongoing economic development of the region. In that year the conference theme was: 'Present Issues of International Migration: How Can the Sending and Receiving Countries Cooperate?' That is, it related to what is widely seen in Japanese policy-making circles as the grave threat posed by the immigration of unskilled labour from other parts of Asia to one of the principal supports of what by then was generally capitalised as the Japanese Employment System – Japan's supposed 'racial' homogeneity (Hingwan, 1996).

A couple of even more recent events suggest, however, that Japan's critical role in the region's emerging industrial relations regime is perhaps becoming a source of anxiety in Tokyo. The first is the JIL's recent initiation of an international seminar series on comparative labour law. The second seminar in the series was held in March 1993 and took as its theme 'The Effects of Foreign Laws and Legal Policy Concerning the Rights of Labour Unions – The Case of Asian Nations'. Tantalisingly, *The Japan Labour Bulletin* (May 1993, p. 4) reports that 'five foreign participants from Asian countries and some 20 Japanese attendants participated in often heated debates'! The second is the appearance in the same *Bulletin*'s June 1993 edition of an article by the Institute's research director which not only calls into question common conceptions of the JES but also contains the following comment: 'In discussing transfer of Japanese-style employment practices overseas . . . the danger is transferring individual elements . . . only as techniques.' Information networks and, therefore, discursive flows such as that which has just been outlined have, of course, developed greatly in both breadth and intensity over the past decade or so with the proliferation of both Asian research institutes and Japanese private sector institutes which are often financed by securities companies. The net effect of all this may be summarised by repeating the recent and entirely uncritical comment of a Malaysian academic:

> Transference is made easier due to the interest in Japanese HRM [Human Resources Management] practices [which academics transfer] to their students in their own academic institutions. The local news media also play a role in disseminating such information to the general public. The groundwork for creating awareness and understanding of Japanese HRM practices has been started and still continues. This helps to ensure that when Japanese companies transfer manufacturing and service activities offshore, their presence and activities will not prove to be a cultural shock to the local populace.
>
> (Thong, 1991, p. 149; see also, Koike and Inoki, 1990, ch. 4)

CONCLUSION: AUTHORITARIAN FAMILIALISM OR ENFORCEABLE BENEVOLENCE?

Very likely, the discursive flow related to industrial relations is of far less immediate importance to regional politicians and policy-makers than those similarly increasingly Japanese-dominated ones (Morris-Suzuki, 1992) which exist in relation to transportation, communication, technological and financial matters (for a detailed overall description of these, see Tokunaga, 1992). However, the special significance of the existence of the flows that relate to industrial relations is that they represent a particularly potent *political* resource with the potential for long-lasting nationwide impact that can be deployed either by or against such politicians and policy-makers. In other words, alongside and generally to the detriment of such flows as those that revolve around the discourse of human rights, they represent important resources in the making, or challenging, of 'state projects' that are especially pertinent to populations (see above, p. 39).

In sum, then, the most important social consequence thus far of the co-presence of American ideological bankruptcy but continuing military hegemony, footloose transnational corporations and selective borrowings from the Japanese archetype is the addition of a distinctive set of transnational conditions of existence to those anyway pertinent to the state of class relations within the nation states of the Pacific Rim and especially the Pacific-Asian region. The possibility and profitability of the symbiosis between capitalism and patriarchalism represented by Pacific capitalism was first discovered in Japan. Interestingly, Japanese commentators prefer the term 'synergy', presumably because it downplays the differences involved. However, the shock waves created by the occurrence of this symbiosis have already played a part in undermining and transforming extant domestic modes of governance in much of the rest of the world including the advanced capitalist world (for its effect within British industrial relations see Bratton, 1992). The net result is that, whatever form any future systems of social regulation or governance may take, they are unlikely to bear much resemblance to those that emerged in Western Europe in the postwar period.

As already indicated and as I will make clear in Part II, the most important social consequences of the distinctiveness of Pacific capitalism's institutional silhouette and its associated discourses are its effects on class relations within the region. For, as industrial capitalist class relations have come to replace and/or dominate those produced by the

hitherto prevailing combination of agricultural (or plantation) capitalism, simple commodity (or peasant) production and primitive communist
(or tribal) production, the chief consequence of the replication of Pacific
capitalism (by Western European and American companies as well as by
Japanese and local companies, it should be noted) has been an increased
asymmetry in class relations. Thus, for this reason and in some tension
with the common claims as to the relatively egalitarian nature of income
distribution in Japan and the East Asian NICs, wages throughout the
region, including Japan, represent a much lower share of the national
income than in Western Europe and the United States (Thurow, 1992,
pp. 125–6). This is not simply because the human and institutional
embodiments of labour tend to lack political, economic and ideological
power, despite the rights promulgated in the region's post-colonial
constitutions, but also because the Pacific capitalist discourse on labour
and the transnational processes with which it is imbricated have allowed
the formation of a very fully worked out pre-emptive strategy in relation
to any possible future attempts to claim such rights and assert such
powers. That is, and this is the point of articulation between class-
structural and governmental developments, wherever either the highly
conditional nature of transnational capital's sojourn in a particular
nation state, or the special restrictions on labour imposed within Export
Processing Zones (EPZs) are insufficient to constrain labour, *selective*
managerial and/or legal borrowing from the Japanese model provides a
wealth of techniques which can be deployed either alone or, more
effectively, together in order to maintain both labour's tutelage and the
resulting low share of wages in GNP.

All that said, and notwithstanding Japanese labour's own 'citizenship
deficit' (that is, the legal impediments it faces in trying to turn its economic power into a Marshallian 'surrogate' political power; see Woodiwiss, 1992a, p. 157), it should not be forgotten that the domestic version
of the JES represents a much better deal for labour than the export
version, at least for some employees. That is, pursuit of the Pacific
Capitalist model and therefore emulation of Japan's success does not
necessarily have to mean that employees should remain passive and not
seek compensation for their legal as well as their other sacrifices. Moreover, what the Japanese experience also suggests is that, in the absence
of legislation to the contrary but because of the region's shared patriarchalism, any Pacific-Asian unions pursuing such compensation in the
form of 'claims' on their employers' benevolence should find the courts
on their side, provided of course that the rule of law exists. This is

because the syllogism that has come to dominate Japanese labour law should gradually reappear within other Pacific Asian jurisdictions too. This syllogism is as follows: if the loyalty that the employee owes to the company justifies restrictions on employee 'liberties' with respect to industrial action and this leads to economic success, then the companies that benefit from this loyalty must fulfill the expectations of those who have placed their trust in them and provide labour with economic security (n.b. the political restrictions that Japanese labour operates under are in no way a necessary corollary of this syllogism).

In other words, what Japan instances is not simply a very well-known symbiosis of patriarchalism and capitalism, but also a much less widely recognised but potentially equally powerful symbiosis of patriarchalism and the rule of law. Thus, the strategic political proposition that the Japanese experience prompts is that the labour law, and by extension human rights, regime that stands the best chance of being respected is one that is written in such a way that it: (1) mobilises the patriarchalist cultural and social-structural biases, so to speak, of a particular locale in its favour; and (2) is pertinent to the forms of the property relation obtaining amongst the capitals it seeks to regulate. Encouragingly, what the case studies that follow will demonstrate is that, despite their social and legal differences, both of these desiderata are already 'immanent' within the population of the region. This is especially significant because it suggests that there is widespread, latent political support for a labour law system and human rights regime premised on 'enforceable benevolence'. This is a possibility that suggests in turn that there may eventually come a day when transnational corporations are no longer able to play either one Asian-Pacific country off against another or the East against the West, or at least that it is not merely the powerful who will benefit from this divide and rule strategy. In sum, 'enforceable benevolence' may yet become an Asian-produced way in which the Eurocentrism of human rights discourse may be overcome and the human rights project gain the additional ideological and cultural weight made necessary by the waning of American Social Modernism. This, then, is the thesis whose plausibility will now be investigated in Part II.

PART TWO

HUMAN RIGHTS, LABOUR LAW AND PATRIARCHALISM IN PACIFIC ASIA

CHAPTER THREE

THE PHILIPPINES AND MENDICANT PATRIARCHALISM

At first glance the Republic of the Philippines might seem a strange case with which to begin a study of the relations between patriarchalism and labour/human rights in Pacific Asia. It is typically regarded as the odd person out in the region. This is because it was a colony for longer than any other territory in the region, is largely Christian, and has often seemed to value its relations with Spain and the United States more highly than those with the rest of Pacific Asia. Finally, although it was second only to Japan as a developing economy in the early 1960s, it is now far less successful economically than most of its neighbours. However, it nevertheless represents an instance of a society in which the hegemonic public discourse has long been and remains a variety of patriarchalism. Moreover, *de jure* if not, I will argue, *de facto* the Philippines was the first territory to begin the process of decolonisation and therefore has had the longest experience of democracy in the region. Thus, it also represents the longest established instance of that attempted symbiosis between patriarchalism and the rule of law in the sphere of labour law that is the central concern of the present study. However, the main reason why a discussion of the Philippines is important in the present context is that it represents a limiting case in that it enables one to understand that the exchange that I term 'enforceable benevolence' cannot be a costless one for capital if it is to be effective in moderating industrial disruption as well as for the state if it is to be effective in protecting human rights. If these costs are not accepted, and they have not been in the Philippines, the result is likely to be economic disaster and social disruption of a revolutionary kind. In the words of the National Unification

Council's 1992 Report '"unequal justice" [was found] to be one cause of rural people's sense of grievance and dissatisfaction . . . 30 per cent of all rebels it talked to declared they had "direct, personal experience of injustice"'.

The Philippine labour movement is very weak. It is divided along many dimensions, organises less than 10 per cent of the labour force and has little or no effective political representation.[1] Nevertheless, for complex reasons that will be elucidated below, labour has achieved a far stronger position within legal and indeed more general political discourse than its weakness within class relations would suggest was possible. Because of the labour movement's general weakness it has had to depend upon the state for the protection of its liberties and the enforcement of its claims. Although such protection has been legislated for with an almost baroque floridity and detail, the state has been unwilling and/or unable to enforce its own laws.

Analytically, what follows will be structured by posing my three questions. Why has the state legally intervened in industrial relations in the way that it has? How has it intervened? To what extent has any diminishment of labour's civil and political rights, especially its freedom of association, been compensated for by enhanced social and economic rights? Substantively, the aim is twofold. First, to explain how labour obtained the legal gains represented by: (a) the rather extensive protective legislation passed between 1908 and 1936, which included the establishment of a system of compulsory arbitration; (b) the Industrial Peace Act (IPA) of 1953 which replaced arbitration with collective bargaining; (c) the Labor Code of 1974 which restored compulsory arbitration; and (d) the 1987 amendments to the Code which rescinded compulsory arbitration again in an effort to return to the IPA system. And second, to explain why these gains have always been less significant than they might have appeared because they have seldom been effectively enforced. Significantly, the explanation for the gains, their lack of substance and the lack of enforcement may be found in the same social-structural attribute – the persisting mendicancy of Philippine patriarchalism.

THE FORMATION OF A PATRIARCHALIST POLITICS

Like all the other nation states within the region, the Philippines is a product of centuries of transnational and international effects arising from the arrival of settlers, traders, colonisers, missionaries and ideologies of all kinds (McCoy and de Jesus, 1982). As a result, although they still number some 12 million, the indigenous peoples have either been marginalised in all senses and/or have intermarried with the incoming Malays, Chinese, Mexicans, Spaniards and Americans. All of these developments have left their mark on Filipino politics. Thus, although the Spanish and American colonialisms have had a profound effect on the social structure, indigenous and Malay customary terms such as the 'barangay' (originally a kinship group of between thirty and fifty families but now the smallest local government unit) are sometimes invoked to describe these Western effects in the local variant of the apparently universal phenomenon of the 'invention of tradition'.

The Philippines achieved independence from Spain through an American-supported armed uprising which began in August 1896 and ended in August 1898 when Manila fell to the American fleet. In January 1899 the commander of the revolutionary forces, General Aguinaldo, promulgated the largely European derived and liberal-democratic Malolos Constitution. Less than a month later the Philippine–American War began. It ended in November of the same year. Until 1902 and the ending of a 'pacification' campaign that cost between 200,000 and 1,000,000 Filipino lives, the islands were ruled under the war powers of the United States Congress. Between 1902 and 1935 the country was ruled by a colonial government that was very similar in structure to those in the rest of the region. Ultimate power rested with the American Congress which delegated it to a governor, who consulted with an executive body known as the Commission and a legislative Assembly (a purely legislative upper house, the Senate, replaced the Commission in 1916). There was also an independent judiciary. Equally striking, however, were the differences as compared to the British colonies in the region. Reflecting the democratism and rights consciousness characteristic of American political thought, the Assembly as well as the Senate were elective bodies from the beginning, albeit resting on a very restricted franchise. Only male Filipino citizens over the age of 21 with a year's local residency and who either owned property, paid taxes or were literate could vote – 1.41 per cent of the population in 1907. Also, the colonial government had to respect a Bill of Rights administered by the judiciary, and the local population was allowed to have its own resident commissioners in Washington. Moreover, not only were the executive and the judiciary, but significantly not the educational system (Fry, 1977; Hunt, 1978), localised relatively quickly, but also the Assembly became a critical (Constantino, 1969, pp. 40–1), active and, in many American eyes too, a legitimate advocate of the restoration of independence. The Assembly's efforts were rewarded in 1934 with the passage of the Tydings–McDuffie Act, whose provisions were repeated in the Assembly's Independence Act. This provided for a ten-year period under a transitional form of limited self-government to be known as the Commonwealth. The constitution was to be decided by Filipinos, save that it should include a Bill of Rights and should maintain the sovereignty of the United States for the transitional period. A constitution was rapidly created by the Convention set up for the purpose and was ratified by a plebiscite held in May 1935.

The governmental structure so created was modelled on that of the United States. There were, however, five principal divergences from the American model. First, the constitution began with a list of underlying principles – popular sovereignty, the duty to defend the state, the renunciation of war, support for the family, and 'the promotion of social justice'. Second, the president's term of office was limited to six years and a second term was not allowed. Third, the president possessed a particularly unencumbered power to declare martial law 'when the public safety requires it', as well as to issue executive orders, to veto single items or provisions in legislative bills, and to decide whether to release, transfer or withhold legislatively approved funds. Fourth, the legislature was unicameral, literacy but not property ownership remained a requirement for electors, and the possibility of female suffrage was provided for. Fifth, all land and natural resources were both nationalised and only to be exploited by Filipinos or by companies that were at least 60 per cent Philippine owned – mineral rights were only to be leased and only agricultural land could be sold.

In 1940 a set of constitutional amendments was promulgated which reduced the length of the president's term to four years but allowed the possibility of a second term, replaced the unicameral legislature with a bicameral one consisting of a Senate and House of Representatives, and created an Electoral Commission to guard against fraud and corruption. With these exceptions, then, the 1935 Constitution defined the structure of the Filipino state when independence was finally achieved in 1947 – two years later than promised because of the Japanese Occupation of 1941–5. Although the Ordinances appended to the Commonwealth Constitution that assured American sovereignty automatically lapsed on the achievement of independence, it is important to note that the new Philippine Republic did not possess full sovereignty. Two measures in particular account for this: the United States Congress' Bell Act (1946) and the Military Bases Agreement (1947). The first made the continuation of free trade between the two countries and the availability of war damage compensation conditional on the granting of constitutional 'parity' to American individuals and corporations in respect of the exploitation of natural resources and the ownership of land – the necessary constitutional change was supported by a 4:1 majority in a plebiscite. The second granted rent-free use to the United States of 23 bases covering nearly 200,000 hectares for 99 years (this agreement ended in 1994). The military might that the bases represented constituted a powerful implicit sanction should Philippine politics develop in a direction disapproved of by the United States.

As elsewhere in the region, one of the proudest boasts of the colonisers was that they had brought the rule of law and therefore capitalism and prosperity to the Philippines. As Governor W. Cameron Forbes said in the course of his Inaugural Address and with a frankness that would be hard to find amongst the speeches of his British equivalents:

> Capital demands stable government. Capital is not particularly interested in the color or design of the flag, it wants just and equitable laws, sound and uniform currency on the part of the government, just and fair treatment in the courts. The faith of the United States is pledged that all these benefits shall be permanently assured to the Filipinos.
>
> (Quoted in Salgado, 1985, p. 20)

Apart from the continuing effort of the United States to maintain Filipino tutelage, there is very little about the first constitution that would appear to offer any support to the development of a patriarchalist politics, especially given the prominence accorded the Bill of Rights. On closer examination, there turn out to be at least four elements that did offer such support and which were of specifically Filipino provenance. The first was the imposition on the state of duties to support the family and pursue 'social justice'. The second was state ownership of all land and natural resources. The third was the state's capacity to set limits to the size of landholdings and redistribute them as it sees fit subject to the payment of compensation. And the fourth was represented by Article 14, section 6, which reads as follows:

> [T]he State shall afford protection to labor, especially to working women and minors, and shall regulate the relations between landowner and tenant, and between labor and capital in industry and in agriculture. The State may provide for compulsory arbitration.

In other words, the Constitution was in part at least the product of an already established and supposedly patriarchalist politics. I will now briefly outline the nature of this politics before discussing in more detail its culmination/nemesis in President Marcos' 'smiling martial law'.

When one first considers the development of Filipino parties there is little in their platforms to suggest the existence of a patriarchalist mode of politics. However, as Renato Constantino has argued in his highly influential book *The Making of a Filipino* (1969), the American presence was at least a factor in the growth of the debased form of patriarchalism that gradually subverted the rule of law. As explained in 1960 by the subject of Constantino's study, Claro Recto, it began as follows:

> Political patronage, a characteristic of the American party system, was established . . . by Taft [the first American governor-general] himself under a policy of this tenor:
>
>> In the appointment of natives, the fact that the man is a member of the Federal Party is a good recommendation for him for appointment, for the reason that we regard the Federal Party as one of the great elements in bringing about pacification . . .
>
> This frank, forthright statement presents the principal characteristic of the new colonisation policy, which was to establish a government with a semblance of Filipino representation through trusted Filipino agents enjoying the respect of the people because of their social position or intellectual reputation. For in a country with such limited economic opportunities, men of intelligence and ambition had to look up to the government to further their personal advancement. Government appointments carrying handsome emoluments and distinction, were adequate rewards for acquiescence, loyalty and cooperation.
>
> (Quoted in Constantino, 1969, p. 36)

Developing Recto and Constantino's insight, Ruby Paredes (1989, p. 6) has put the point even more explicitly:

> Denied equality with Americans under law, Filipino leaders adopted tactics of guile and manipulation to win from American patrons political concessions they needed to maintain the loyalty of their Filipino clients. Since American colonials were ambitious careerists, they needed Filipino cooperation to give them the aura of administrative success necessary for further advancement.

In this way, then, Filipino politicians gained the resources necessary to develop a populist style of politics (see also, Agpalo, 1972; McCoy, 1994). Whilst this style was largely made possible by the structure of the colonial state, it owed its inspiration to American agrarian populists such as William Jennings Bryan and his successors in the Democratic Party, who, fearing the competition, opposed the colonisation of the Philippines from the beginning and often provided advice to the main political party, the Nacionalistas.

Granted all this, patronage in the socially more significant form of patron–client relations was already a well-established feature of indigenous Filipino social and political relations (Agpalo, 1972; Carroll, 1968; Lande, 1956), especially in the rice and corn growing areas where the dominant form of economic relations was known as the *kasama* (share-cropping) system. Because the share of their crops that farmers (clients) were allowed to retain was seldom sufficient to enable them to meet their needs, they were often in debt and therefore very dependent upon their landlords' (patrons') benevolence. The resulting sense of obligation (*utang na loob*) on the part of the tenants became an important political resource as the franchise was broadened, since one way to repay one's 'debt of honour' was by voting for or as directed by one's landlord. For this reason the political parties developed as loose, fissiparous alliances of regional political fiefdoms with little in the way of ideological differences. Hence the frequency with which party allegiances were and still are switched in pursuit of access to political spoils. And hence also the tendency for political struggles to revolve around efforts to wrong-foot opponents with respect to otherwise shared ideological commitments such as independence before the Second World War and 'social justice' afterwards. This treacherous political terrain finally found its postwar master in 1965 when Ferdinand Marcos was elected to the presidency for the first time. Marcos repeated his victory in 1969.

On David Wurfel's (1988) analysis, although the patronate, which included the Marcos family, retained formal power throughout the first two decades after independence, their capacity to satisfy their increasingly diverse and assertive constituents through the patron–client system became ever more doubtful and the system itself ever more distasteful to the population at large. Additionally, on Willem Wolters' (1984, pp. 185–200) analysis of developments in central Luzon, as the *kasama* system was replaced by leases and wage labour whilst the landowners diversified into the processing and manufacturing sectors of the economy, political relations became disarticulated from economic ones. The political spoils, especially the various permissions, licences and tariffs necessary to set up and run readily profitable enterprises, were within the gift of the national government with which capital could either deal direct or through national party organisations. In sum, politics no longer rested wholly on local patron–client relations but instead on centralised, 'pork-barrel' patronage and, I would add, contradictory ideological appeals.

In response to the citizenry's concern with the graft that had become so apparent in state/capital relations, as well as for his own reasons, which at this stage were primarily political, President Marcos convened a constitutional Convention to propose solutions. A wide-ranging and serious debate ensued both within the Convention and outside in the 'parliament of the streets'. Marcos, however, simultaneously suborned many of the delegates and skilfully heightened the anxieties associated with the increasing structural disjunction between political and economic relations by sponsoring various violent provocations which he blamed on the guerillas of the emerging, quasi-Maoist New Peoples Army (NPA). He also presented himself as a technocrat who sought to change the Constitution merely in order to speed the modernisation of the country. And, finally, he won the clear support of the military. In this way, then, Marcos succeeded in making his 1972 proclamation of martial law seem more like an act of social reform than self-aggrandisement (Marcos, 1974). On the part of many Filipinos as well as of the American government, there was consequently less interest in the thousands of arrests that occurred than in what Marcos meant by a 'New Society'.

In the event, the only thing that was new about Marcos' vision was that he sought to concentrate all power, whether legislative, executive or judicial, and all patronage within his own hands as the single *padrino* or godfather. In an attempt to legitimate this move he damned almost every institution of what he termed the 'old society'. Thus he either suspended their operations (as in the case of the legislature), intimidated their members (as in the case of the judiciary, who were required to lodge their pre-signed resignation letters with the president (Vejerano, 1991)), or required the graft obtained by others to be handed over to himself (as in the case of the civil service). Additionally, and in line with its claimed familialism, substitute but largely sham institutions such as the reinvented *barangays* were established throughout the country. Supposedly, they represented a direct link between the ordinary people of the *barrios*, the victims of the old society, and the presidency. In fact they opened up new lines of patronage in exchange for which their officials were expected to deliver popular endorsement of the regime in successive referenda, by whatever means necessary (Pinches, 1991, p. 174).

The only other things that were new about the regime were an unusual degree of concern for enforcement in some areas and unconcern for it in others, as well as an unusual degree of modesty about either these efforts or their absence. Illustrating the concern with enforcement, during the first five years of the 'New Society' some 70,000 people were imprisoned for their political beliefs and actions at one time or another, many were tortured, and a minimum of between 30 and 50 people per year were 'disappeared' between 1976, when counting began, and 1978. Illustrating the unconcern with enforcement in other areas were the decisions to greatly reduce the number of workplace inspections and not to collect data on poverty. The regime's modesty about all of these 'achievements' was demonstrated by its refusal to let the media publicise them. In all other policy fields Marcos' government was indistinguishable from its predecessors. It continued to violate the land rights of the authentic *barangay* of the Muslim people of Mindanao, and then sought to quell the rebellion it provoked by the use of military force (George, 1980). It pretended to introduce a radical programme of land reform (Wurfel, 1988, pp. 165–76). It sought both to reject neo-colonial status and to take advantage of it in foreign policy (ibid., ch. 7). And finally, it failed economically.

As a result of Marcos' successful monopolisation of most lines of patronage, the mainstream parties quickly atrophied under martial law. The chief opposition to the regime came therefore from 'progressive' Catholics and a rapidly growing and armed Left that arose out of the student movement of the late 1960s. The most important element amongst the Left was the new and quasi-Maoist Communist Party of the Philippines (CPP), which with its armed wing, the NPA, grew in direct proportion to Marcos' efforts to suppress it. This growth continued despite both the lifting of martial law in January 1981 and the development of new channels of patronage such as the Kilusang Kabuhayan at Kaunlaran (The Movement for Livelihood and Progress) and Marcos' self-interested reorganisation of the coconut industry (Wurfel, 1988, pp. 256–61). By 1981 the NPA claimed to organise 40,000 activists, 15,000 of whom were armed, and to be supported by 10 per cent of the population. In 1983, it was said by the army to control, or have influence in, some 20 per cent of the country's villages. The event that probably did most to stem the further growth of the NPA as well as of the Left more generally was the assassination of the most vocal spokesman of the 'moderate' opposition, Benigno Aquino, as he stepped from his plane at Manila Airport on 21 August 1983. It so galvanised the Catholic Church and the forces that Aquino had represented that they: first, organised very seriously to contest the election that Marcos had been forced to call for1986; and second, refused to accept its rigged result. On 23 February,

Defence Minister Juan Ponce-Enrile, General Fidel Ramos and forces loyal to them also declared Mrs Corazon Aquino the victor, and were supported by hundreds of thousands of people who for four days encircled their base alongside Manila's main highway, Epifanio de los Santos Avenue (*Edsa*) – 'people power'. By October of the same year the country had a new constitution, closely modelled on that of 1935 except that the president is allowed only one six-year term and the House of Representatives has to face an election every three years instead of every two years.

The alliances and their component parties that exist today have different names to those of the pre-martial-law period. However, little if anything divides them ideologically, floor-crossing is still frequent, and the twelve successful senators in the 1995 election included the families of former Presidents Macapagal, Magsaysay and Osmena. The unsuccessful senatorial candidates also included a Marcos – Bong Bong – and the successful House candidates included another – Imelda (for detailed evidence of political and economic continuity, see Guttierrez, 1994) – *plus ça change plus c'est la même chose?*

THE MAKING OF A DEPENDENT ECONOMY

Part of the reason why Filipino politics changes so little is because the economy also changes so little – at least as regards the continuing importance of agriculture, its incapacity to meet the needs of a population whose growth is only minimally controlled, and its dependency. The patronage that the continuing dependence on overseas sources of finance helps to make possible remains an efficient or at least effective means of using scarce economic resources to secure political loyalty amongst the needy as well as the greedy. And the pervasive scarcity of domestically produced finance that makes it necessary has endured despite recurrent bouts of optimism as to the imminence of an economic breakthrough, such as that which occurred in the late 1950s when the Philippines was regarded as second only to Japan as a Pacific-Asian economy with good prospects.

Before the Second World War the Philippines was almost entirely an agricultural country. After what can best be described as Japan's four years of 'looting' between 1941 and 1945, the Americans returned, and, reflecting the fact that by the late 1930s the Philippines had been the first or second most important export market for a very long list of American products, forced the change in the constitution represented by the 'parity clause'. The reimposition of free trade with America in the context of the Philippines' severely war-damaged economy and the pegging of the peso to the dollar had disastrous consequences. The huge inflow of imports prevented domestic industry, such as it was, from re-establishing itself and since it was not matched by a similarly large outflow of exports, the result was the near bankruptcy of the country in 1949. In the context of the newly declared Cold War and the commencement of the communist-led Hukbalahap (Huk) Rebellion, the United States grudgingly agreed to waive the constitutional rights of its corporations and citizens and allowed the imposition of import and exchange controls as surrogates for the still-banned tariffs. It is important to note, however, that by 1951 20 per cent of the country's productive wealth was already owned by foreign companies, mainly American, and that these controls had little effect on them. Indeed, they too prospered greatly behind a protective wall that raised the domestic prices of manufactured commodities by up to 300 per cent above world market prices. The creation of a wide range of import-substitution industries produced a marked improvement in economic conditions generally, as was summarised by an average growth rate for the period 1952–68 of 5.7 per cent. It also produced the beginnings of an apparent Filipinisation of the economy in that, by 1961, 88 per cent of new investment was of Filipino (including Filipino-Chinese) origin as compared to 55 per cent of such investment in 1949.

By the early 1960s, the Philippines was the second most industrialised country in Asia outside of Japan. However, as John Power and Gerrado Sicat (1971, p. 18) have pointed out, the 5.7 per cent average growth rate hides a significant deceleration of the rate of manufacturing growth. This was 12.5 per cent for the period 1952–6, but less than 5 per cent throughout the 1960s. Moreover, what the relatively impressive average figure also distracts attention from is the fact that, although this upsurge in manufacturing increased its share of output to 27.07 per cent of GNP by 1970, the sector still only employed 11.8 per cent of the labour force. In that year the majority of the labour force (53.8 per cent) was still employed in agriculture which only accounted for 28.18 per cent of output. In other words, the processes allowing what later proved to be the critical transformation of the employment structure in the Asian NIEs were stalling – the Philippines was not succeeding in mobilising its great comparative advantage, its cheap labour power, by developing the domestically sourced, labour-intensive and export-oriented industries that could best take advantage of it (Ofreneo, 1993, ch. 4).

Again it seems that the country's patriarchalist political system combined with the nature of its relationship with the United States was the root cause of this failure. The Laurel-Langley Agreement of 1954 provided for the accelerated phasing out of free trade by 1974, and the unfixing of the peso/dollar rate, but also for a compensatory immediate extension of American 'parity' to the whole economy. Although many of the companies in the import-substitution industries were American-owned and repatriated two-thirds of their profits back to the United States (Salgardo, 1985, p. 39), it seems that they had reached the view by the late 1950s that it was already time to lift the import and exchange controls. Filipino opinion, however, had become ever more positive as regards the controls and their beneficial economic consequences – hence President Garcia's initiation of the popular 'Filipino first' policy of 1958, which offered government support to the Filipinisation of foreign-dominated industries. External pressure was therefore applied to effect a change in policy: first, through the IMF; and then through the CIA's partisan involvement in the elections of 1959 and 1961. In 1962, the Agency's favoured candidate, President Macapagal, lifted the controls, proudly acknowledging the personal support of President Kennedy.

Although candidate Marcos was highly critical of the damage done to the import-substitution industries in the course of his successful 1965 campaign for the presidency, he did not reverse the de-control policies introduced by his predecessor and thus remained loyal to his original, export-oriented, domestic and American agri-business connections – the opposition of the import-substitution industries was greatly weakened by the fact that many of their owners were from landed families and so had interests in agro-exports too (Carroll, 1968; Doronila, 1992; Rivera, 1994). Thus, thanks to his particularly energetic manipulation of the multitude of trade and industrial regulations (McCoy, 1994, pp. 17–18), the companies owned by Marcos' connections – 'crony capitalism' – benefited disproportionately as EPZ manufacturing was added to the country's export base and the growth rate improved during the 1970s to between 6 and 7 per cent per annum. However, all this came to a dead stop amidst the chaos of the 1980s (Hawes, 1987; Ofreneo, 1993; Salgardo, 1985, ch. 4.; Seagrave, 1988). In the words of one wit, reflecting on the activities of the president's wife, the answer to the question, 'What was the most important growth industry during the 1970s?' was 'Mining' – as in, 'that's mine, that's mine, and that's mine'.

That said, after several false starts under the preceding Magsaysay and Macapagal Administrations, the most serious effort to do something for the rice and corn tenants was that undertaken by the Marcos regime. However, even these efforts only placed at most 11 per cent of rice and corn farmers on the road to owning their own land, and this happened so slowly and so inefficiently that the process embittered as many as it pleased. One result of this failure is that the number of landless labourers increased dramatically, creating an ever larger pool of unemployed and underemployed labour which, whilst it has kept wages low across the economy, cannot be productively employed and therefore has sunk ever deeper into a poverty which means that there is only a very small domestic market in value terms. Also, because of chronic capital flight (Boyce, 1993, ch. 10), and without the savings of prosperous small farmers and well-paid wage earners to draw upon, there was relatively little Filipino capital around to take advantage of the establishment of several large EPZs in 1979. Even by 1989, on average only around 20 per cent of the firms taking advantage of the conditions within the EPZs were wholly Filipino (Orbeta and Sanchez, 1995, Table 30).

The major difference made by the Marcos Administration's many moves to open up the economy and encourage investment was the broadening of the sources from whence foreign direct investment comes. The Americans retain their traditional hold over the agri-business, oil and banking industries. However, new industries like garment and semiconductor manufacturing, which moved to EPZs in countries such as the Philippines, during the 1980s, to get around the quota system which governs the export of the products of such industries to the United States and Europe and once costs increased in Hong Kong and the other NIEs (Ofreneo, 1983), have provided opportunities for European and especially Japanese and Hong Kong companies (Salgardo, 1985, pp. 85–141). Thus although the level of foreign ownership had reached around 40 per cent (Yoshihara, 1985, p. 41) by the early 1980s, the proportion held by American companies declined as their share of annual direct investment declined from 64.6 per cent in 1973 to 45.3 per cent in 1993. Over the same period the share made by Europeans stayed steady at just under 20 per cent, whilst that made by the Japanese rose from 9.7 per cent in 1973 to 20.3 per cent in 1993, and that made by Hong Kong companies rose from 1.3 per cent to 6.7 per cent between the same dates.

Although these investments mean that in most years since 1970 more money has been invested in the Philippines than extracted from them (Orbeta and Sanchez, 1995, Table 8), it is important to note that this level of outside investment is far lower than that enjoyed by other ASEAN states (ibid., Table 9), although a higher proportion of Philippine industry is foreign owned. Nevertheless, foreign investment has transformed the country's export profile so that agricultural exports have declined from 69 per cent of the total in 1975 to 25 per cent in 1990. However, the significance of this changed export profile as a contributor to economic autonomy has been virtually nil because not only has it been made possible by foreign investment, but also until very recently the country has suffered from massive balance of payments deficits, caused by the importation of production goods and raw materials for the import-substitution industries, and the borrowing that financed 'crony capitalism'. As a result, the Philippines became heavily dependent on loans begged from the IMF and other, primarily American and Japanese, governmental and private sources. By 1983 the country was paying out more in debt repayments than it was gaining in new loans. And between 1986 and 1991 on average just over 50 per cent of the government budget was devoted to debt servicing (Boyce, 1993, ch. 11).

The Philippines suffers from shocking levels of underemployment, unemployment and poverty. The Marcos regime did not collect statistics on poverty, but when the Aquino government did so in 1985 it found that 59 per cent of the population lived on or below the poverty line (Mangahas, 1994, p. 129), most of them disqualified from participation in the country's rudimentary social security system by their prior low income, if any, or by their occupational status (Serrano, 1992). However, the clearest summary evidence of the gap between the Philippines' national aspirations and its economic performance is the huge growth in the number of overseas contract workers (OCWs) (Battistella and Paganoni, 1992). Reflecting the country's American-inspired belief in education as *the* means of social mobility, relatively high proportions of young Filipinos at least begin their secondary and tertiary education. However, because of the underdeveloped nature of the labour market there are not nearly enough jobs for those who graduate (for example, employment in the manufacturing sector actually shrank during the 1980s to stand at 9.7 per cent of the labour force in 1990). Hence, they have been forced to seek work overseas. In the 1960s the principal destinations were the United States, American-managed construction projects in South-East Asia, and, for musicians and female 'entertainers', Japan and Hong Kong. In the 1970s, the Middle East became an important destination, as did the world's shipping industry, and Hong Kong and Singapore began to employ a large number of Filipino domestics (Asian and Pacific Development Center, 1989). Most recently, large numbers of skilled workers have started to find employment in Taiwan.

In 1974 the export of labour became official policy with the promulgation of the *Labor Code* and the attendant establishment of the Overseas Employment Development Board (now the Philippines Overseas Employment Administration). The Board was charged with undertaking 'a systematic program for overseas employment of Filipino Workers in excess of domestic needs'. In this way the Marcos government began to send many of its citizens off in search of new colonial masters and mistresses, and opened up a new income stream for itself, private employment agencies and the country as a whole. Thereafter, no Filipino could accept a job abroad except one obtained through the Board or an accredited agency, both of which receive fees from either or both contracting parties. In addition, and with rich irony considering governmental collusion with capital's illegal flight from the country, the Board requires the OCWs to remit part of their earnings (currently between 80 and 50 per cent depending on category of employment) back to the Philippines. In return it now provides some minimal support and welfare services overseas, plus a quasi-judicial grievance procedure, which claims 'original and exclusive jurisdiction', and a disciplinary system. The latter enforces a code that, in a patriarchalist manner, comprises a long list of 'duties' to, in this order, family, fellow contract workers, country, agency and/or employer and host country.

There were 20,553 officially processed OCWs in 1976, 176,511 in 1980, and by 1995 there were probably close to 2 million Filipinos temporarily working abroad or at sea, many of them with university degrees. In addition, some 1.5 million Filipinos are currently living as permanent immigrants abroad. Indeed, it has been estimated that fully three times as many locally trained professional and technical workers are employed abroad as in the Philippines (Orbeta and Sanchez, 1995, p. 13). Wasteful of national resources as this subsidising of the development of other already more developed societies undoubtedly is, the remittances that the OCWs return to the Philippines have become vital to the economy. By the 1990s they accounted for more than 4 per cent of the GNP, fed 25 per cent of the population (Ofreneo, 1992, p. 14), and provided some compensation for capital's 'illegal' flight. If unrecorded remittances are brought into the reckoning they accounted for possibly twice this proportion of the GNP and feed many more people (Floro, 1995, p. 1). Finally, remittances on this scale produced the Philippines' first balance of payments surplus for many years in 1994. No wonder President Ramos has called OCWs the 'new heroes' of the economy.

Whether or not the Ramos Administration can find a way to take advantage of the increased room for manoeuvre that the OCWs' efforts have created for it in its dealings with its international creditors remains to be seen. The Administration's strategy document 'Philippines 2000', which projects an incredibly optimistic vision of NIC status by that year, is informed by some recognition of the structural and political obstacles that have to be overcome if this goal is to be achieved. Specifically, but apparently inspired by an extremely oversimplified conception of 'Japan Inc.', it recognises that the state must attain a degree of autonomy from the contradictory pressures exerted by the fractured bloc of closely held local capital (only 10 per cent of the top 1,000 are public companies) that was restored to dominance after *Edsa*. The aim is to foster the growth of a reformed agriculture and a diversified industrial base, whilst at the same time remaining democratic (Rocamora, 1994, ch. 6). The problem, of course, is precisely that the restored bloc of local capital once again dominates both the legislature and the economy, with the result both that it prospers whether or not the society as a whole stagnates and that there is no legislative pressure on it to change its economically regressive, rent-seeking ways (McCoy, 1994, pp. 10–12). In July 1995, President Ramos introduced a tariff reduction programme intended to improve the economy's degree of integration within the regional and global economy. The programme projects a uniform tariff rate of 5 per cent in 2003. Amongst the publicly acknowledged exceptions were many agricultural chemical imports whose tariff moved to 3 per cent immediately, finished cars whose tariff stayed at 40 per cent, and the promise of non-tariff 'additional incentives' for the petrochemical industry (*Manila Bulletin*, 23 July 1995) – clearly, the great rent-seeking game continues.

THE MAKING OF A MENDICANT PATRIARCHALISM

The term 'mendicant' means 'begging' and it has been used in the Filipino literature, notably by Constantino (1969), to denote the debased form of patriarchalist practice that has become the established mode of exercising power within the society – political leaders before and after independence begged the Americans for favours so that they could in turn respond to those who were begging favours from them. Filipino writers have rightly stressed the role of this mode of discourse in sustaining dependency on the United States. Without in any way gainsaying the analyses that result from this stress, there is a problem with it in that it deflects attention away from the domestic consequences of the presence of such a discourse. Here what I have in mind is that a mendicant patriarchalism is a weak patriarchalism, specifically one that is unable to respect itself and therefore its clients and so follow through on its larger promises. Thus, as Claro Recto eventually came to see with particular lucidity (Constantino, 1969, pt. 4), the *sine qua non* in relation to the achievement of the social justice to which the constitution commits the nation, is a certain nationalism. Not a nationalism in the sense of an aggressive, expansionist or even anti-American creed but in the sense of an ability to see where the national interest lies in any particular set of circumstances and to follow through at the level of policy formulation and enforcement – two things that are very hard to do in the mendicant position, since there is no patronal autonomy. Hence the frequently repeated public and inter-personal responses to those whom politicians and even ordinary people disappoint – 'What can I do?', or the invocation of *pakikisama* (the need to get along with others). Hence the generalised fatalism that allows such a response to be acceptable. Hence too the ironic humour that pervades conversation with friends or a trusted audience. But hence, finally, the cynicism of those who choose not to follow through on their promises even when they can – fate, not they, will be blamed.

Because mendicancy generally does not announce itself in public discourse, its presence can only be known by its effects, as exemplified by the land reform charade referred to above and the startling enforcement failures in relation to labour law that will be discussed below. However, its presence as a sub-text should be borne in mind throughout the account of the development of Filipino public discourse that follows. This is something that I hope will be made easier to do by the fact that, as I shall point out and as was the case with land reform, what is promised in a slogan is often taken away in the exposition of what it means. Moreover, there was at least one famous and particularly pertinent occasion when the largely rhetorical nature of Filipino reform was unwittingly made explicit.

Both reflecting the strong desire for independence and the need to hide its absence, the core theme in Filipino public discourse has always been the nation. For the same reasons, plus because of the great importance of especially the Catholic religion (Bolasco, 1994), the Filipino conception of the nation has always had a utopian character: that is, as the state that Filipinos will finally arrive at after they have redeemed all their sins. In the words of the first president, Emilio Aguinaldo, at the opening of the Malolos Congress in 1898:

At this opening of the temple of the laws, I know how the Filipino people, a people endowed with remarkable good sense, will assemble. Purged of their old faults, forgetting three centuries of humiliation, their hearts open to the noblest traditions and their soul to the joys of freedom, proud of their own virtues, without pity for their own weaknesses . . . they will assemble . . . to bring together the assistance of our thinkers and politicians, of the defenders of our native soil and of our profound psychologists of the Tagalog language, of our inspired artists and of the eminent personages of the bench, to write with their votes the immortal book of the Filipino constitution as the supreme expression of the national will.

(Bananal, 1986, pp. 156–7)

In other words, even at the nation's formative and proudest moment, with the revolution against the Spaniards all but won, there was a doubt – expressed at the same moment that it is denied – as to whether or not Filipinos are good enough to be a nation; there was, in other words, a fear of mendicancy. However, as is also clear from this passage, Filipino nationalism as a discourse if not a practice was from the beginning remarkably free of ethnocentrism. The revolution was led, if not initiated or only fought for, by *ilustrados* (educated ones) who considered themselves to be more Spanish than *indio* (indigenous). However, even the *ilustrados* seem to have been very aware of their *mestizo* character. It is also true that this awareness was often expressed in the language of race in that this mixedness was seen primarily in biological rather than cultural terms. In this way, then, although the Filipinos' view of themselves as a 'brown race' people – Governor-General Taft had referred to his 'little brown brothers' – placed them relatively high up in the global racial hierarchy, domestically it came to stand as a metaphor for their ambiguous feelings about themselves as in some sense a flawed people who were not quite worthy of the redemption represented by the true nationhood achieved by the 'white races'. All this said, it is still striking that Aguinaldo should have seen an important role for the 'profound psychologists of the Tagalog language' in the making of the Republic. And it is equally striking that, having appropriated for themselves the name Filipino, which initially referred only to Spaniards born in the islands, not only did the *ilustrados* freely extend it to all their fellow countrypeople but also the latter quickly claimed it for themselves. In other words, the Philippines has long been a self-consciously hybrid culture. However, it is also important to say that this hybridity is not entirely universalistic or all-inclusive, since it has always privileged those with lighter complexions, marginalised the indigenous, and excluded the Muslims of Mindanao as well as the Chinese in general (Filipinas Foundation, 1976). The latter, for example, were as much the targets of the 1950s 'Filipino first' policy as the Americans.

The man who more than any other confirmed the central themes of what rapidly became a hegemonic and thoroughly Christian public discourse as sin (inferiority), suffering (colonial subjection), independence (heaven) and hybridity (uniqueness) was Manuel Quezon. At various times he was resident commissioner, senate president, and president of the Commonwealth – in sum, he was the single most powerful and influential political figure of the American period and the 'father of his country'. As he said in 1923 when resident commissioner in Washington in an exultant passage which encompasses each of these themes:

> The Philippines of yesterday was consecrated by the sacrifices in lives and treasure of your patriots, martyrs, and soldiers . . .
>
> The Philippines of tomorrow will be the country of plenty, of happiness, and of freedom. It will be a Philippines with her head raised in the midst of the West Pacific, mistress of her own destiny, holding in her hand the torch of freedom and democracy and pointing the way to the teeming millions of Africa and Asia now suffering under alien rule; a Philippines heir to the Orient and the teachings of Christianity . . .
>
> (Bananal, 1986, p. 160)

All these themes, plus the patriarchalist voice in which they were enunciated and their racist framework were given a more elaborate, classic and somewhat more chastened expression in a speech Quezon made in 1938 on the occasion of his birthday:

> National strength can only be built on character . . . The Filipino is not inferior to any man of any race. His physical, intellectual, and moral qualities are as excellent as those of the proudest stock of mankind. But some of these qualities, I am constrained to admit, have been slumbering in recent years . . . There is no substitute for suffering and privation to bring out the finer qualities of man . . . This is in accord with biological laws . . .
>
> We, the Filipinos of today, are soft, easy-going. Our tendency is towards parasitism. We are uninclined to sustained strenuous effort. We lack earnestness. Face-saving is the dominant note in the confused symphony of our existence. Our sense of righteousness is often dulled by the desire of personal gain. Our norm of conduct is generally prompted by expediency rather than by principle . . . Our greatest fear is not to do wrong, but to be caught doing wrong. We are frivolous in our way of life . . . We are inconstant; we lack perseverence . . .
>
> Social decorum is fast becoming prostituted by a mistaken conception

of so-called modernity. A wrong adaptation of foreign customs creates in us, especially amongst the young, a feeling that politeness is commonplace, and that smartness and insolence are the equivalent of good breeding . . . Self-restraint is not an active power in us . . .

Socially we are inefficient. We look upon our government as the fountain source of living, to which we are reluctant to give anything . . . This appraisal of the character of our people today may sound too severe . . . But my responsibility as head of this Nation compels me to face and state facts . . .

To ensure the accomplishment of this task of national spiritual reconstruction, we shall formulate and adopt a social code – a code of ethics and personal conduct – a sort of written Bushido – that can be explained in the schools, preached from the pulpits, and taught in the streets and plazas, and in the remotest corners of our land . . .

We are orientals. Orientals are known for their placidity and passivity . . . I refuse to allow the Filipino to be so regarded . . .

The Filipino people are on the march, toward their destiny, to conquer their place in the sun.   (In Bananal 1986, pp. 160–4)

Since this speech represents a veritiable template for Filipino presidential speeches, I will not cite any further evidence as to the thematic unity of Filipino public discourse. However, before moving on to look at what made this discourse of redemption hegemonic, I wish to draw attention to the positive references to Japan in the speech. These are represented by the patriarchalist critique of 'so-called modernity' and the need for 'a sort of written Bushido' to be taught throughout the nation (cf. the Japanese government's *Kokutai no Hongi* which was published a year earlier). Not only does this instance a conscious cultural hybridity, but it also suggests an assumed level of knowledge of, and respect for, Japanese ways of doing things that, along with the statism of *ilustrado* discourse (Quirino, 1971, p. 277), helps to explain two things. First, why so many of the *ilustrados* (notably Jose Laurel and Recto, the *éminences grises* of the postwar Right and Left respectively) collaborated with the Japanese Occupation forces. And second, why they were so readily forgiven afterwards (for a detailed study of wartime collaboration with the Japanese Occupation, see Steinberg, 1967).

Archetypal though the themes of sin, suffering, heaven and hybridity – the discourse of redemption – rapidly became, their presence does not in itself explain why they could become themes in a hegemonic discourse. Certainly, these themes established the basis upon which national

unity could be constructed but they did not contain any acknowledgement of the socio-economic or class-produced tensions within the population, let alone discursively resolve them. That such a resolution was
necessary early on was a consequence of both the long history of rural
uprisings and a growing fear of trade unions. The text within which this
resolution occurred was the Commonwealth Constitution with its
imposition on the state of a patriarchalist duty to achieve 'social justice'.
Moreover, there is also evidence that some at least of the *ilustrados* even
recognised that this resolution and hence the claim to hegemony was to
be achieved by, to use Ernesto Laclau and Chantal Mouffe's (1985)
vocabulary, transforming previously 'antagonistic' discursive elements
into 'equivalents'. As the then Supreme Court justice and soon to be
president of the Japanese puppet republic, Laurel, said in 1940:

> The promotion of social justice, however, is to be achieved not through a
> mistaken sympathy towards any given group. Social justice is neither
> communism, nor despotism, nor atomism, nor anarchy, but the
> humanization of laws and the equalization of social and economic forces
> by the state so that justice in its rational and objectively secular con-
> ception may at least be approximated. Social justice means the promotion
> of the welfare of all the people, the adoption by the government of
> measures calculated to ensure economic stability of all the component
> elements of society . . . constitutionally, through the adoption of measures
> legally justifiable, or extra-constitutionally, through the exercise of
> powers underlying the existence of all governments on the time honoured
> principle of *salus populi est suprema lex.*
>
> Social justice, therefore, must be founded on the recognition of the
> necessity of interdependence among diverse units of a society and of the
> protection that should be equally and evenly extended to all groups as a
> combined force in our social and economic life, consistent with the funda-
> mental and paramount objective of the state of promoting the health,
> comfort, and quiet of all persons, and of bringing about the greatest good
> to the greatest number.   (In Bananal 1986, p. 38)

A more recent Catholic commentator, Professor Aranata, explained its
meaning rather more pithily and brought out both its patriarchalism and
its Christian character particularly clearly, when he pointed out that the
concept of 'social justice' was derived from that of God the Father. He
further reasoned that since God is Father to all people, all are his
children and as such equal to one another. What this patriarchalism
meant in practice was rather less impressive. Again to quote Laurel, only

this time from 1965 and thus with some of the candour of old age if still without apologies:

> It is our duty to help in the promotion of social justice so that every Filipino may have the opportunity to acquire *through toil* his necessities in food, clothing and shelter, together with reasonable comforts, and a leisure which will permit cultural self-improvement and a participation in the blessings of civilisation. (In Bananal, 1986, pp. 167–8, emphasis added)

Even more candid and equally without apologies was the unknowing and often equally unknowingly repeated admission by one of his successors in the presidency, Ramon Magsaysay, that social justice, Filipino-style, might only be a matter of words: 'I believe that he who has less in life should have more in law' (ibid., p. 199). As will be explained in more detail below, many of the words of the law were to be American in the 1950s both in general public discourse and labour law.

The major difference between Marcos and his predecessors was that he sought to abrogate all power to himself when he declared martial law; Philippine reality having failed to match even the restricted promises made by the new American legal vocabulary. At the level of discourse, there was very little to distinguish Marcos from his predecessors, since he simply articulated a somewhat ethnicised and more authoritarian variant of the established patriarchalist discourse of redemption. What did differentiate his version of the discourse, however, was that he exaggerated the sins of his people, called for greater suffering (that is, by adding the self-flagellation represented by martial law to the woes of the Filipinos), and promised an improved, less American, somewhat ethnicised and more imminent heaven (the New Society). Although the 'Presidential Couple' wrote at length, and often in a decidedly kitsch style on these themes (Imelda Marcos was especially fond of the term 'love', see Tiongson et al., 1986), it is both more economical as well as apposite to quote their advisors and one particularly well-placed observer. The need to stress patriarchalism was emphasised by a committee convened to advise the president on matters of ideology:

> What is recommended therefore is an expansion of the family to a larger group – the country. We should treat the country as our very own family, where the President of the Republic is the father and all the citizens as our brothers. From this new value we develop a strong sense of oneness, loyalty to the country and nationalism. Because all Filipinos are brothers, we will become just and sincere. (Quoted in McCoy, 1994, p. 16)

Breathtakingly naive though this advice was sociologically, the president seems to have acted on it in all its literalness:

> In many ways, the Martial Law years saw the Marcos family establish themselves as supreme patrons. Thus in Tatalon [a Manila squatter community] Christmas gifts would be dispersed through the National Housing Authority or through barangay local officials as presents from the First Couple. Relief Aid and state employment were distributed in a similar fashion. (Pinches, 1991, p. 174)

Finally, the redemptive theme is clearly brought out by a gloss on the president's views provided by his leading spokesman in the early days of martial law, Carlos Romulo, his secretary of foreign affairs and a Pulitzer-Prize-winning writer:

> In developing societies, democracy as Americans know it, and as we have experienced and lived it, cannot successfully operate. We had too much politics, uninhibited politics. Our people had to have something that will help us to develop and develop fast . . . If you have our legislature and our licentious press, you can't develop as fast. To do that you have to impose certain stern measures . . . You have to have surgery if you need it. Sometimes a scalpel is more merciful than to allow cancer to continue festering in a man's body . . . In only four months of martial law, the Philippines has become a 'new country', free of guntoters, political warlords and crime czars, and crooked civil servants and policemen . . . Here tradition is in the family and in the tribe which has always been authoritarian. One man must rule. (Ibid., p. 138)

Edsa signalled the exhaustion of such authoritarian discourse and a return to the democratic glossing of the discourse of redemption. The sins, though, remain the same (graft, indiscipline, casualness), as does the need for continuing penance (the retention of many of the legal constraints on unions is the most pertinent example), and even the heaven is the same, namely 'development' or 'Philippines 2000'. However, the means to be used in the pursuit of the millennium are now democratic, the continuing high level of human rights violations appears to lack presidential sanction, and even state mendicancy is more avoidable thanks to the remittances of the OCWs.

The Marcos years coincided with and indeed stimulated an upsurge of academic and popular interest in Filipino 'native' culture. Some of the resulting work suggested that the islands' indigenised and therefore hybrid form of Christianity, especially the rural *pasyon* (passion play), could be and indeed had been a form and mode of resistance to oppression and not simply an opiate (Ileto, 1979). More often, however, the work on 'native culture' involved the discovery that it had 'migrated' like many of its rural bearers to the cities. An important milestone in the dissemination of this discovery was the text edited by Frank Lynch and Alfonso de Guzman II and entitled *Four Readings in Philippine Values*. First published in 1964, this text has been through many printings and several editions (for a discussion of the literature as a whole, see Hennig, 1983). To give a pertinent example of the literature it spawned, according to one of the very few and as far as I am aware unchallenged studies of workplace relations, the central and critical institution as far as day to day workplace relations is one of the 'migrant' cultural elements, namely the *kumpadre* (or where a female labour force is concerned, *kumadre*) system:

> The *kumpadre* system manifests a functional extended family system, sometimes stronger than ordinary kinship ties, particularly after first degree family relationships . . . [Although it grew out of the god-parent/child relationship] . . . as in parts of Latin America, where the Catholic Church is strong, the *kumpadre* system in the Philippines has taken a particular drift . . . the central point of interest shifted to the relationship between the godparents and the child's parents. They develop a very close relationship with each other, exchanging favors, material and otherwise, which are not normally available to mere friends.
>
> (Ramos, 1978, p. 53;
> for a more recent and confirmative study see Torres, 1988)

As Elias Ramos goes on to point out, ties which engender a similar sense of *utang na loob* (obligation/debt of honour, cp. the Japanese concept of *giri*) can also develop between friends and between inferiors and superiors in workplaces. Thus they provide both a means of gaining employment and of solving grievances once employed that tends to personalise and so supposedly 'soften' hierarchical relations in the workplace. This said, as Michael Pinches (1991) has emphasised, dependency in the workplace is also often just one more source of shame on the part of those who cannot reciprocate and therefore sometimes provokes an antagonistic 'class-conscious' response (see also, Aquino, 1984). Nevertheless, generally it appears to be so effective that employees will far more often request the help of their *kumpadre* than their union representative even when one is present. Ramos notes, however, that this is less likely to be the case where the employer is a foreign-owned and managed company. This said, although some companies (see below) go to some trouble to formalise and build on such relations, it is necessary to add a cautionary note at this point because of the paucity of data on

Filipino workplace relations. This is that, despite the similarities between the *kumpadre* system and the Japanese workplace *oyabun/kobun* or
sempai/kohai systems, one Japanese researcher has reported Japanese
expatriate managers in joint venture but largely locally managed factories as being shocked by the harshness of supervisory relationships
(Tsuda, 1978).[2]

Since 1964 a small industry has grown up around the propagating of
Filipino values. As in the case of the parallel but as far as I know initially
unconnected Japanese *Nihonjinron* literature, for most writers the sheer
existence and presumed historicity of these values is sufficient to
guarantee their legitimacy as well as their appropriateness to all
circumstances of contemporary Filipino life. (For a *Nihonjinron*-style
suggestion that their appropriateness has a biological guarantee in the
'right-sidedness' of the Filipino brain, see Bautista, 1988.) In other
words, although many of the propagators of these values are social
scientists, none of them seems to have noted the imbrication of these
values with particular political and economic circumstances either as
elements in pre-capitalist sets of social relations or as 're-invented'
traditional elements in capitalist settings. Indeed, none of them seems to
be aware that by contributing to the popularity of these ideas they are
precisely engaged in such a process of 'invention'. Thus, not only is the
patriarchalist nature of these values not commented upon, but also,
corroboratively, they seem to have found their most enthusiastic
proponents amongst human resources academics and some of their
corporate clients – an acknowledgement of the Japanese model is
apparent in the work of some of the academics (see, for example, Jocano,
1988, pp. 8–9). A couple of quotations from the prolific anthropologist
and human resources consultant, F. Landa Jocano, will be sufficient to
illustrate both of these points (see also, Gatchalian, 1983). The
patriarchalism is clearly apparent in the set of 'national ideals' that he
has recently distilled from his work:

> Belief in God
> Love of country before self
> Care for the family
> Respect for the individual
> Desire for consensus
> Preference for unity and harmony. (Jocano, 1992, p. 18)

Lest the fourth of these ideals seems a little discordant, it is necessary to
quote the gloss that Jocano (ibid., p. 19) provides, since this makes it

clear that what is being recommended is certainly not 'Western individu-alism' but rather something that strongly echoes the *Nihonjinron* literat-ure (Harootunianin in Miyoshi and Harootunian, 1989, pp. 80–1):

> Respect for the individual is one of the core values . . . It is a fundamental demand in Philippino value system. This is why one of our core values – the *asal* (character) – lays great stress on the importance of *kapwa-tao* (fellow human being), *damdamin* (feelings) and *dangal* (honor, dignity).

The reasons for the attractiveness of such Filipino values to human resources academics and some of their clients is brought out with similar clarity by the note appended by Jocano to this quotation from the work of Marie Aganon (1990, p. 35):

> United Drug was founded by Jose Y. Campos . . . Its founder was said to be the one who initiated the 'Bayanihan' concept of employee–employer relationships . . . He believed that the human asset is 'the greatest asset of a business' and that for the business to thrive, a spirit of brotherhood must prevail . . .
>
> Thus was born the *bayanihan* as a way of life in Unilab. 'Bayanihan' . . . means '*tulong-tulong tayo*' system (we help one another) . . . It is accepted to mean the sharing of one's burden . . . This way of life (*sic*) has been transmitted from generation to generation of workers at the Unilab. (Note: the system has been working effectively for 20 years with only one attempt to organize a union.)   (Cf. Matsushusita, 1984)

Aganon herself, on the contrary but indeed like Jocano (ibid., pp. 141–50) in his conclusions, is concerned to bring out something which reinforces the central thesis of the present study. And this is that when patriarchist values are taken seriously in the industrial relations context they *oblige* the employer to be benevolent. More specifically, Aganon stresses the low labour turnover at Unilab, which as it happens is a Chinese–Filipino company, and comments that its attitude to its employees is not simply paternalistic but also 'approximates lifetime commitment'. Moreover, she describes the reasoning involved in the following terms:

> These values work in this way: *May utang na loob ka sa akin* (you have a debt of honor to pay me = productivity); *may utang na loob din ako sa igo* (I also have a debt of honor to you = profit-sharing); so for smooth interpersonal relations, *nakisama tayo* (let's go along).
>
> (Aganon, 1990, p. 45)

In other words, what may be seen in this reasoning is the classical patri-archalist exchange of benevolence for loyalty. However, thanks to the wider dominance of mendicant patriarchalism, such benevolence in the Philippines remains utterly a matter of discretion and in no way enforceable.

THE INSTITUTIONS OF MENDICANT PATRIARCHALISM AND THE CLASS STRUCTURE

I will now summarise the social-structural significance of the foregoing and thereby structurally explain why Philippine labour law has the character it does by outlining the class-structural balances that have characterised the society as it has developed. The balance of power within the class structure constituted by the imbrication of the sets of social relations condensed within the structures outlined above is at first sight rather hard to discern. However, it becomes rather easier to discern once one realises that, perhaps even more so than in the developed societies and the NICs, the class balances in the Philippines are very variable over time, from workplace to workplace and especially from region to region. In the twentieth century, first the American colonial government and its allies amongst the large landowners, and then the latter with American support monopolised political power. Thus capital has never been legitimately challenged along either the macro (public order) or micro (workplace) dimensions of control relations (Ofreneo, 1980; Wolters, 1984).

However, precisely because of this monopoly of political power, agricultural capital in particular has been almost continuously and illegitimately challenged at both the macro and micro levels by various revolutionary or separatist movements such as the Colorums of the 1920s, the Sakdalistas of the 1930s, the Huks of the 1940s and 1950s, and the NPA and the Muslim Moros of Mindanao from the 1960s to the present (Constantino, 1978, pp. 70–5; Terami-Wada, 1988). To a lesser extent, industrial capital too has been politically challenged by revolutionary movements, most notably by the Kilusang Mayo Uno (KMU) or May 1st Movement from the 1960s to the present. Although the effectiveness of the industrial organisations has been very limited, the rural organisations have from time to time succeeded in controlling large areas and making sometimes rather sustained military challenges to the central state. In the event, however, the army and its American allies have thus far always proved to be equal to these challenges.

Similarly, and largely because of its official political strength, the possessory power of capital, or its capacity to set the terms and conditions of employment, has seldom been challenged where insurgent groups have not succeeded in taking control of the means of production. And this despite the extensive constitutional and statutory protection and empowerment of labour that will be discussed further below. Finally, this supposed protection and empowerment was only possible because the one dimension of class relations along which capital has had to concede ground since 1935 is the discursive one of title, as is indicated by both the hegemony of the sign 'social justice' and the seriousness of the problem of capital flight, much of which was simply the illegal re-export of loans from foreign banks and governments (Boyce, 1993, ch. 10).

The net result, then, is a curious and bifurcated set of class relations. Within the more extensive set, capital's title could have been legally revoked at any time. This has not occurred as yet since labour has not even been able to force the government to extract the legally mandated taxes on capital and high-income earners (70 per cent of taxes are raised indirectly, whilst total tax-take represented only 14.7 per cent of the national income even as late as 1991), let alone replicate its discursive encroachment on capital's power along the control and possessory dimensions of class relations. Instead, thanks to the *kumpadre* and/or the much harsher systems with which it is almost always entwined, reinforced by the growth of EPZs (Ministry of Labor and Employment, 1984), workplace relations in the Philippines continue to take at best a paternalist form even where unions are present. More effective still in its prophylactic effect is the dissolution of directly supervised workplaces thanks to the huge growth in outworking that the creation of the EPZs has stimulated (Pineda-Ofreneo and del Rosario, 1988). According to Amelita King (1984), such informal activities produced between 39 and 42 per cent of GNP between 1980 and 1984. Finally, in the countryside and in the absence of revolutionary or separatist arms, the *kasama*/leasehold system has proved more likely to inhibit challenges to landlords than to stimulate them (Mojares, 1983; Ofreneo, 1990). In all these ways, then, any attempt at the revocation of capital's title is very effectively pre-empted within most sets of social relations. Within the less extensive set, however, such challenges have been successfully mounted, except that revolutionary military power rather than constitutional sanction has been the enabling element.

In sum, capital's retreat with respect to title has meant that its maintenance of control and possession depends upon the absence of challenges by labour along the latter two dimensions. Hence the structurally determined nature of mendicant patriarchalism and, as will become clear below, its labour law. In other words, to answer my 'Why?' question, rather than simply pointing to graft and budgetary niggardliness, the structural causes of the state's failure to deliver on its promises of protection and empowerment are twofold. First, such an abnegation of responsibility is necessary to the survival of capitalism since successful delivery could mean capital's liquidation. Second, such abnegation is possible because the state has access to external funds that allow it to deliver a highly selective form of paternalism. The constitutional commitment to the pursuit of 'social justice', which must have seemed relatively unthreatening when all that was envisaged, in the American populist manner, was land reform in the sense of the transfer of title and the formation of a petite bourgeoisie. However, in the event it has turned out to represent a substantial hostage to fortune in the changed circumstances represented by an even partly industrialised economy. The confinement that 'social justice' imposes is something that only military force can release capital from, should Mendicant Patriarchalism and its selective paternalism ever fail. This is especially the case given that the striking underdevelopment of a 'new middle class' contradictorily positioned by capital means that currently there is no at all plausible escape route from poverty even for those 'lucky' enough to be in the waged sector of the labour force.

As an indicator of the underdevelopment of the middle class, the percentages employed in 'professional and technical' and 'administrative, executive and managerial' occupations actually declined during the Marcos years. This was because of the combined and interrelated consequences of the rise of the OCW phenomenon and the low level of demand for technical and managerial labour from 'crony capital' and EPZ producers – in one EPZ only 1.32 per cent of the labour force were 'managerial workers' (Orbeta and Sanchez, 1995, Table 31). Specifically, the proportions engaged in those occupations most likely to be contradictorily positioned fell from a combined total of 7.5 per cent in 1976 to 6.5 per cent in 1986. Moreover, more than a third of those included in these categories were employers. By 1991 the combined figure had risen again to 7 per cent. Thus the 'new middle class' in the Philippines is tiny, currently around 5 per cent of the labour force if one strips out employers, and insignificant as either an escape route for individuals or a drain on capital. Thanks to the failure of land reform the same may be said of the 'old middle class', since the number of sharecroppers who have become leaseholders or gained title to their land and hence joined the ranks of the petite bourgeoisie has been so very small.

The effectiveness of Mendicant Patriarchalism, the balance of military power between the forces of capital and labour, and the support of the United States for the former, therefore, have long been the Philippine class structure's critical conditions of existence. The one feature that distinguishes the present from the past is the rather sudden and remarkable addition of a very concrete transnational dimension to these conditions of existence. The Philippines, like everywhere else, is necessarily affected by global developments in the political, economic and discursive spheres such as the appearance of computer technology and the ending of the Cold War (see Rocamora, 1994, for the latter's consequences within the CPP and the NPA). However, thanks to the opening of the economy, the country's international indebtedness, and the poverty and vulnerability of its population, the Philippines is also host to a huge number of foreign government agencies and global NGOs, ranging from the IMF, through the various intergovernmental land reform support schemes and Amnesty International, to myriad smaller organisations. In other words, transnationality has become institutionalised within the Philippines. Whether or not this will make a difference to the possibility of the society finally freeing itself from the structural constraints summarised by Mendicant Patriarchalism is of course an open question.[3]

MENDICANT PATRIARCHALIST SOCIETY, THE LAW AND HUMAN RIGHTS

In my view, the critical transudatory interface between any set of social and class relations and labour law is that represented by the general structure of the law and the content of its major bodies of doctrine. This is because, although these doctrines speak to many other sets of social relations, in the sphere of industrial relations specifically contract law speaks to possessory relations, tort law to control relations, property law to relations of title, and public law to the overall relations between the state, capital and labour. In this way legal doctrines may be seen to be both constituted by and constitutive of class relations as well as one of the several ways in which macro structures have an effect at the micro level. Thus, to develop Emile Durkheim's famous insight, the content of the doctrinal structure is both an indicator of the nature of the overall balance of class forces, and an important, relatively autonomous determinant of developments in specific areas of law and therefore of said overall balance.

116

To pass laws that favour the poor and powerless whilst prohibiting them from using the means whereby such laws might be enforced, and having failed to vote or release the funds that would allow their enforcement by the state, transforms the invocation of the law too into a variety of begging or mendicancy. However, before I demonstrate this in some detail by giving an account of the development of Filipino labour law, I will first say something about the development of Filipino private law in general since Magsaysay's dictum concerning the supposed legal wealth of 'those who have less' applies to it too, but with this very significant difference: in effect if not in name, the weaker party actually as opposed to merely rhetorically favoured by the private law is Filipino (including Filipino–Chinese) capital as opposed to foreign or even local Chinese capital. This is because, unlike other weaker parties, Filipino capital has had the means, including especially the legal expertise and political connections, to enforce its rights. The advantages that follow from the possession of local legal knowledge when combined with local and especially family connections is brought out very clearly in Alfred McCoy's (1994, p. 25) study of the rise and fall of the Lopez family. As he says in drawing out the general significance of his study: 'the Philippine state's . . . legal codes governing elections, commerce, and corporations are complex and comprehensive, enveloping the whole universe of politics and business with nominally strict regulations. Through legal education, politicians learn to manipulate these regulations in their quest for rents.' The foundation of Filipino private law is the Spanish Civil Code which was belatedly introduced into the colony in 1889 (for an outline of Philippine law in the Spanish and pre-Spanish periods, see Gamboa, 1955, chs. 7, 8.). Although the institutional and ideological context within which the Code was thenceforth enforced changed dramatically with the changeover from a Spanish to an American colonial government, it nevertheless remained in force throughout the American period (Aquino, 1969). However, its purview shrank and in some aspects its meaning also changed rapidly during this period as it was applied in the light of American-originated or influenced legislation and American common law precedent (ibid., pp. 87–91). As Perfecto Fernandez (1969, p. 51) has said:

> The greater bulk of our rules have been derived immediately from American jurisdictions or enacted under American authority. This is especially evident in branches of the law dealing with our system of government, public administration, international relations, trade and commerce, social welfare, and procedure in our tribunals and other public bodies.

With the passage of time and especially with the arrival of, first, the constitutional commitment to 'social justice' and later independence, there naturally arose a need to reconcile the sometimes discordant consequences of so tangled a hybrid growth by reconstructing the whole edifice from first principles (on the nevertheless continuing importance of *stare decisis*, see Villanueva, 1990). In 1945, Kenneth Kurihara outlined the problem faced by any would-be codifiers:

> The practical difficulties of the Social Justice program were caused not so much by capital or labor opposition as by its own inconsistencies. Hence the contradiction between theory and practice. President Quezon said that 'social justice can only mean social justice to each and every social group', and 'so long as capital is not unmindful of the social purpose and duties of property, so long will our government give it whole-hearted support and protection'. To do every group justice is of course rhetorical, the idea being ipso facto impracticable under the existing economic arrangements ... In an attempt to accord both capital and labor equal protection and just treatment, the government frequently satisfied one party at the expense of the other. To reconcile conflicting economic interests is a ticklish problem, the adequate solution of which would require a program much more drastic than a program of palliative measures.
>
> (Kurihara, 1945, pp. 27–8)

As it turned out, in the law as well as in other spheres, palliative rhetorical elaboration proved more attractive to the country's rulers than drastic action. This elaboration was undertaken by a Code Commission created by President Roxas in 1947 under the chairmanship of a leading legal academic and a Supreme Court justice during the Japanese Occupation, Jorge Bocobo. Within a year the Commission completed work on what the author of the major study of its development, Juan Rivera (1978), calls the 'first brown race civil code' (see also, Agabin, 1991) – an appellation whose apparent acceptability further illustrates the increased ethnocentrism of the Marcos years. According to Bocobo, 57 per cent of the new Code was simply a restatement of the Spanish Code, whilst the remainder was new and comprised borrowings from the common law tradition, other civilian traditions, and, as enjoined by President Roxas, 'the customs, traditions, and idiosyncracies of the Balangayan (Filipino) people'. Also according to Bocobo (ibid., p. 167), the 'outstanding reforms in the new civil code' were the following:

(1) the elevation of moral principles into positive law under certain conditions;

(2) the strengthening of democracy as a way of life;
(3) the introduction of equity jurisprudence as found in the English
     and American legal systems;
(4) the liberalisation of women's rights;
(5) the implementation of social justice;
(6) the elevation of Filipino customs into law;
(7) the exaltation of personality.

Even without going into the details, the aptness of Magsaysay's dictum
seems clear, since this represents a remarkably comprehensive list of
ways in which weaker parties might be rhetorically advantaged. This
impression is strengthened even when one only considers the illustrative
details given by Bocobo himself. The first reform took the form of Article
21 which states that: 'Any person who wilfully causes loss or injury to
another in a manner that is contrary to morals, good customs or public
policy shall compensate the latter for the damage.' The second took the
form of Articles 32 and 358, which make public servants and employees
liable for damages if they interfere in any way with the rights of another
person. The third coloured the whole Code, whilst the fourth improved
the status of married women with respect to their freedom of contract
and, suitably in the light of the bilateral nature of Filipino lineages, the
disposal of conjugal property. The fifth pertains directly to the employment relation and was given form by such articles as the following:

> Article 24: In all contractual, property or other relations, when one of the
> parties is at a disadvantage on account of his moral dependence,
> ignorance, indigence, mental weakness, tender age or other handicap, the
> courts must be vigilant for his protection.
>
> Article 25: Thoughtless extravagance in expenses for pleasure or display
> during a period of acute public want or emergency may be stopped by
> order of the courts at the instance of any government or private charitable
> institution.
>
> Article 1702: In case of doubt, all labor legislation and all labor contracts
> shall be construed in favour of the safety of and decent living for the
> laborer.
>
> Article 1703: No contract that practically amounts to voluntary servi-
> tude, under any guise whatsoever, shall be valid.
>
> Article 1704: The laborer's wages shall be a lien on the goods manu-
> factured or work done.

The sixth reform was given substance by various articles pertaining to
family life, such as those that enhanced the status of women, restored

parental control over the property of children, and required consultation with grandparents on all important family matters. And finally, if somewhat bathetically, the Code sought to 'exhalt the personality' by introducing American tort law to the Philippines in order to make possible various forms of 'independent civil action' (see Articles 26, 33, and 2217).

Without doubt each of these provisions strengthens the positions of weaker parties. However, at the same time, and consonant with the acknowledged aim of 'the consolidation of the family', each of them also increases the patriarchal responsibilities of the state since it is the judiciary that has to be 'vigilant for [their] protection'. This is even the case with respect to the introduction of tort law which Bocobo and his colleagues otherwise felt would introduce a 'spirit of rugged individualism' (ibid., p. 191) into Filipino law since it would allow individuals to seek redress instead of continuing to be dependent upon the vagaries of public prosecutors. However, if the tort provisions are read in the light of Article 21, one has the basis for American-style promissory estoppel or a tort of 'bad faith breach', as well as for other policy-motivated incursions of tort into the otherwise sacrosanct realm of contract. Finally, because in the United States the occasions for such incursions have typically involved commercial or consumer relations, the continuing openness of Filipino law to both American legislative example and common law precedent (Fernandez, 1969, p. 51) has encouraged rather than discouraged this particular mode of increasing the judicial power to interfere in 'private' relations.

Taken together with the constitutional commitment to social justice, what the reforms incorporated into the Civil Code represent, then, are a series of *potentially* rather severe restrictions on domestic, let alone foreign, capital with respect to the relations of possession, control and title that constitute it. Moreover, these are restrictions that exist prior to any exercise by the state of its powers of eminent domain, taxation and police (as in the American concept of 'police power'). This said, and neatly illustrating both the problems created by the inconsistencies pointed out by Kurihara and the continuing discursive primacy of property rights within the law, the Supreme Court opined as follows when it first attempted to reconcile property rights with 'social justice' in 1948:

> the Constitution did not propose to destroy or undermine property right, or to advocate the equal distribution of wealth . . . Evincing much concern for the protection of property, the Constitution distinctly recog-

nises *the preferred position which real estate has occupied in law for ages.*
Property is bound up with every aspect of social life in a democracy as
democracy is conceived in the Constitution. The Constitution realizes
the indispensible role which property, owned in reasonable quantities and
used legitimately, plays in the stimulation to economic effort and growth
of a solid social middle class that is said to be the bulwark of democracy and the
backbone of every progressive and happy country.

(Quoted in Francisco, 1967, p. 105, emphasis added)

What is also striking about this passage, which is clearly a rather creative
piece of transnationally inspired legal reasoning, is the way in which it
claims to find a justification for property in land in what is very clearly
the American Social Modernist discourse on the middle class (Woodiwiss, 1993, ch. 2). In other circumstances the invocation of the possibility of a 'solid middle class' might possibly have served to soften the
legal and discursive antagonism between 'social justice' and 'property',
as indeed it did in the United States. However, in the Philippines the
move failed for at least two reasons. First, ownership of a *hacienda* is in
no way comparable to a mortgage on a piece of a suburban track housing
as either a piece of real estate, a source of motivation or a determinant
of social conduct. And second, a large and relatively open middle class
failed to appear precisely because of the continuing hegemony of landed
capital and its consequences for the structure of the Philippine labour
market.

Given the failure of this effort to neuter the potentially disruptive
effects of 'social justice', the latter concept was free to return to the
centre of legal as well as political discourse on the next major occasion
of crisis within Mendicant Patriarchalism. This it did in a still more
inflated rhetorical form in the 1971 Marcos Constitution. In this text the
existence of the set of constitutional limitations on property rights
connoted by 'social justice' that had long been largely implicit (that is,
only occasionally acknowledged in case law) finally became explicit with
the enunciation of the concept of the 'social function of property' in a
series of amendments to the 'social justice' clause and the various sections of Article 14. According to one constitutional scholar:

> The concept of property invested with social function means that
> property has to be used not only for the personal benefit of the individual
> owner, but also for the purpose of advancing the common interests and
> welfare of society. Thus the individual has no longer the right to abuse in
> the exercise of his right to property, like allowing his land to remain idle
> when there is a need to cultivate it . . . or . . . for housing . . . Thus the

121

> State has the power to regulate the acquisition, ownership, use, enjoyment, and disposition of private property, and equitably diffuse property ownership and profits.   (Santos, 1976, p. 88)

I emphasised the term 'potentially' when talking above about the restrictions on capital's freedom of contract, control and title just outlined because they are instances of private or public law and therefore to have any effect they have to be activated by either citizens or the state. By contrast, under the criminal law the state not only has a duty to act but also has a means so to do in the form of the police force. For the most part, these restrictions have not been activated in the Philippines because of a combination of the impoverishment or understandable cynicism of the pertinent sections of the citizenry, a remarkably comprehensive dereliction of duty on the part of the state, judicial passivity and patriarchalism. Thus, although the tort of 'bad faith breach' has been available, so to speak, since the mid-1950s to protect weaker contracting parties, it has very seldom been used apart from in some cases involving jilted fiancées from wealthy families. Moreover, Filipino consumers still do not enjoy the protections provided by the doctrine of 'strict liability'. Interestingly, one reason sometimes suggested for the latter is that it is particularly difficult in personalistic patriarchalist societies to see non-human entities such as firms or corporations as having any responsibilities.

Pertinent examples of the state's dereliction of duty with respect to its powers to affect control relations in workplaces include violations of the *Minimum Wages Law* and the article in the IPA that specifies certain 'unfair labor practices', since they were originally defined as criminal offences, unlike most of the rest of labour law. However, the attitude of the state as regards its duties under such circumstances was well put by the first chairman of the NLRC:

> legally, unfair labor practice cases cannot be conciliated because they are supposed to be public crimes . . . Anyone found guilty of unfair labor practice is liable to be jailed depending on the gravity of the case . . . But all these years, I do not know of any employer or labor leader who has been jailed for committing an unfair labor practice . . . Violations of the Minimum Wages Law are supposed to be unfair labor practices but I can assure you, on my word of honor, that 95% of all bakeries . . . gasoline stations . . . department stores . . . [and] drug stores in the country are not complying with the Minimum Wages Law . . . The reason why no employer has been jailed for unfair labor practice is because it is not good policy

and not because the government does not have the will to jail the
employer.   (Inciong, 1974, pp. 104–5)

Nevertheless, the following year the insistence on the criminal nature of
unfair labour practices was repeated in the Labor Code. Under such
circumstances, and noting too that criminal offences require a higher
standard of proof ('guilt beyond reasonable doubt') than civil infractions,
the passage of legislation purporting to favour those who 'have less in
life' can only be described as encouraging mendicancy. This is because,
as when one is faced by a beggar, the decision on how or whether to
respond to the plea represented by the legislation remains more or less
completely at the discretion of the potential benefactor no matter how
strong the moral or legal claim to benevolence may be. Finally, although
the limitations on title inherent in the notion of 'social justice' have been
invoked in support of the various land reform efforts, they have not
proved effective in preventing their avoidance. Nor has the Supreme
Court ever countenanced any suggestion that considerations of 'social
justice' might justify any encroachments on the managerial prerogatives
that flow from title and limit the possibilities of encroachment along the
dimensions of control and possession.

Disappointingly, despite the encouragement to judicial activism represented by the strengthening of the Supreme Court's powers of judicial
review in the post-Edsa, 1987 Constitution (Agabin, 1991), the Court
has continued its partiality towards capital. Thus, for example, it has
found the compensation offered to landlords under the land reform law
to be 'unjust', whilst it has refused to be active on labour's behalf, for
example, by preventing that avoidance of the Labor Code that could be
achieved by broadening the definition of 'labor-only contracting' that it
contains.

Unsurprisingly given the social and legal context, the history of
human rights in the Philippines displays a depressing symmetry, since it
begins with literal mendicancy and ends with the arrival of its social-
structurally produced equivalent. A representative newspaper appeal to
the Spanish government in 1889 read as follows:

> The nation that gave all to Spain begs Spain for affection. It does not ask
> any sacrifice on her part; but nothing more than respect or justice; it asks
> only a small share in the exercise of rights recognized and respected by
> Spain . . . it asks only a little consideration for human dignity.
>   (Quoted in Jimenez, 1979)

The begged-for rights were included in the Malolos Constitution, all the American colonial instruments of government after the ending of the state of war, and in the 1935 and all subsequent Constitutions. After 1935 there was a possibility of conflict over how to balance the civil and political rights carried over from the American period, whose language was purposely retained so as to ensure both a settledness of meaning and continuing access to American lines of precedent, with the social and economic ones attendant upon the pursuit of 'social justice'. However, this possibility did not become an issue until Marcos' declaration of martial law. This was because, prior to this declaration, respect for human rights was a victim of the social-structural mendicancy discussed earlier, as well as because the relationship between the two sets of rights was most often seen by politicians as well as jurists as one of means (civil and political) to ends (social and economic).

Even President Marcos maintained that he saw no intrinsic conflict between the two sets of rights and, anticipating many of today's 'Asian values' ideologues, only wished to reverse the means/ends polarity so that social and economic rights became the means, and civil and political rights the ends (Marcos, 1977). More concretely, he also claimed that only the civil and political rights of those engaged in sedition, insurrection and rebellion were suspended *pro tem*. And indeed not only were most of the principal martial law decrees challenged before, and in the event legitimated by, an intimidated Supreme Court, but also the courts continued to hear and rule on numerous human rights cases throughout the martial law period including those pertaining to *Habeas Corpus* (Jimenez, 1979). However, flagrant abuses did occur because suspicion of sedition, for example, was sufficient to lead to detention. Also, there were numerous disappearances, often carried out by paramilitary civilian and vigilante groups (Turner, 1991) perhaps precisely to avoid what the authorities recognised as the real possibility of judicial intervention. And finally, if one reads the juristic commentary of the time, it is clear that the ultimate and widely shared justification for the circumstances that produced them (that is, martial law) was that, in the words of an Appeal Court justice: 'the civil and political liberties of a few persons should never prevail over the right of the masses to truly enjoy the same civil and political liberties through social and economic reform' (Gutierrez, 1979, p. 41; see also, for example, the lectures and discussions reproduced in Quisumbing, 1979 and Quisumbing and Bonifacio, 1977). The problem with such a rationale is not so much that the masses were not in fact significantly helped by the reforms, since that would grant more legitimacy to the rationale than it deserves. Rather it is that it fails to see that there is any problem with the fact that what martial law necessarily entails, as President Marcos frankly and even proudly acknow-ledged, is the denial of the right to determine their own destiny not just to the fortunate few but also to the masses. And this because, in pater-nalistic terms, the masses are not thought to be mature enough to be able to resist the blandishments of a licentious press, a venal legislature or political extremists. They are therefore only entitled to beg for respect.

Although today peace and state power seem to be returning to the countryside and civil and political rights have been formally restored, they have not yet been restored in fact (Plantilla, 1997; Muyot, 1992; Tuazon, 1993; for a defence of the Aquino Administration's record, see Bello, 1992). Legally, the biggest obstacle to their restoration is the maintenance in force of Presidential Decree 1850 (1981) which grants military courts exclusive jurisdiction with respect to claims against the military (Angeles, 1994; Turner, 1991). Moreover, as the desperately slow process of land reform indicates, the promise contained in the constitutional and legal commitments to social and economic transformation remains not only unfulfilled but also, given the lack of both economic means and political will, a social-structural guarantee that, *mutatis mutandis*, it will not be fulfilled.

THE LABOUR LAW OF MENDICANT PATRIARCHALISM

The first labour organisations in the Philippines were the *gremios* that emerged in the 1850s. Because of the Spanish conspiracy laws these were secret mutual aid societies. In 1872 the first recorded strikes occurred, and in 1899 the Malolos Constitution was promulgated which contained as Article 20:

> The right to join any associations for all objects of human life which may not be contrary to public morals.

The American colonial government was initially silent on the topic of trade unions, although it used its *Sedition Law* of 1901 and the Spanish conspiracy law it inherited to suppress a general strike in Manila in 1902 which had been organised by the first Filipino trade union federation, the libertarian socialist Union Obrera Democratica which afterwards renamed itself the Union Obrera Democratica de Filipinas. The latter organisation very quickly included 150 unions and organised a Mayday demonstration in 1903 which called for immediate independence and was attended by some 100,000 people. Again the sedition and conspiracy laws were used against the trade unionists, this time to justify the arrest of the federation's leader, Dr Dominador Gomez. At this point the colonial government switched tactics and with the support of the American Federation of Labour sponsored the setting up of an alternative trade union federation committed to American-style 'unionism pure and simple', the Union del Trabajo de Filipinas (Carroll, 1968; Wurfel, 1959).

Thereafter and although socialist and nationalist unions and federations quickly reappeared, the colonial government seems to have decided on a policy of toleration and there were no further prosecutions of union leaders. In 1908 the Philippine legislature created the Bureau of Labour, which was placed within the Department of Commerce and Police and took on the role of encouraging the development of 'unionism pure and simple', or in local parlance 'rice and fish unionism'. By the 1920s, and limited by the small size of its staff, the Bureau was doing many of the things that, for example, the Hong Kong Labour Department only started doing in the late 1960s, albeit for a far larger percentage of the labour force (see below, p. 175), namely, job placing, facilitating the settlement of labour disputes, pursuing claims for unpaid wages and inspecting workplaces (Villegas, n.d., ch. 1). Also in 1908, an industrial injuries compensation act was passed which, however, merely restated the ungenerous common law tort principles then operant in the United States. In 1912, of its own volition, the Assembly passed an act that made it a criminal offence not to perform the services for which one had been paid and not to pay for those that had been performed. In practice only the first of the offences was acted upon and with such a degree of abuse in the countryside that it had to be repealed in 1927. In 1913, under considerable pressure from the Commission, the Assembly passed an anti-slavery law which resulted in the freeing of large numbers of tribal peoples who had been enslaved by their Malay and *mestizo* fellow-countrypeople. Again under great pressure from the Commission, the Assembly passed laws in 1916 against usury and the truck system, which were intended to ease the problems of share-croppers and rural labourers. In subsequent years, supported by members of both the Commission and the Assembly, efforts were made to introduce the compulsory arbitration of labour disputes, but all of them failed. Apart from some minor measures to ameliorate the plight of some of the already large numbers of Filipinos who were working abroad, especially in Hawaii, the only other pieces of labour legislation of note passed prior to the 1930s were two Commission-sponsored laws: one in 1923 which provided some protection to women and children in the workplace, and another in 1927 which was a proper workmen's compensation act (Calderon, 1968a).

As the Assembly's resistance to much of even the rudimentary protective legislation just outlined suggests, the legal tolerance extended to trade unions by the colonial government did not make their presence any more palatable to Filipino employers than they were to American employers. What is more, the Supreme Court reinforced employer resistance when in the case of *People* v. *Pomar* (1924) it declared the maternity leave provisions of the Working Women and Children Act unconstitutional on the following American-inspired grounds:

> Clearly . . . the law has deprived every person, firm or corporation . . . to enter into (sic) contracts of employment upon such terms as he and the employee may agree . . . Such persons are, therefore, deprived of their liberty to contract. The Constitution of the Philippine Islands guarantees to every citizen his *liberty*, and one of his *liberties* is the *liberty to contract.*
>
> (46 Philippines 440, emphasis in original)

Although there is a dearth of material relating to the history of the colonial labour movement, it seems safe to conclude that it was the occurrence of vigorous employer resistance which explains why the membership of registered unions grew so slowly (that is, from 63,652 in 1920 to 78,781 in 1930), engaged in very few strikes, and remained restricted to the sugar processing, land transportation, mining, stevedoring, coconut and tobacco industries. Thus labour only reappears as an important actor in most accounts of Philippine history in the 1930s when real wages were declining rapidly because of the Great Depression, and in the form of militant, communist or socialist-led urban federations and rural peasant movements whose combined membership has been estimated at around 190,000 (Carroll, 1968; Kurihara, 1945, ch. 6; Wurfel, 1959).

TOWARDS A FILIPINO SYSTEM OF LABOUR LAW:
COMPULSORY ARBITRATION

In response to this upsurge, the colonial government sponsored legislation relating to such issues as employment agencies, wages bonds, emergency medical care in companies with more than thirty employees, the protection of wages and workman's compensation claims in the event of bankruptcy, and rice tenancies (Calderon, 1968a, p. 24). More importantly, in 1935 the Commonwealth Constitution was promulgated with its commitment to the pursuit of 'social justice' and its specific promise of protection to labour. This commitment and promise, in turn, both stimulated the establishment of a system of compulsory arbitration applicable to some tenants as well as to some workers and protected the system against challenges to its constitutionality on the grounds that it violated liberty of contract (Calderon, 1968d). In 1936, Commonwealth Act 103 was passed which set up a Court of Industrial Relations that administered the arbitration system and was modelled on a similar, populist-inspired Kansas statute. The act both fulfilled a long-established patriarchalist aspiration on the part of President Quezon and the Nationalistas, who consciously opted for it over a New Deal inspired system of collective bargaining, and provided them with a weapon to use in their struggle with the Left. Also passed in the same year was Commonwealth Act 213, which allowed the minority of 'rice and fish' unions a role as representatives of labour by granting them the 'power' to appear before the Court. This it did by providing for the registration and therefore, for the first time, the full legal recognition of trade unions, 'except such whose object is to undermine and destroy constituted government or to violate any law or laws of the Philippines'. Thus only those unions which survived a rigorous, pre-registration police investigation – a minority – could expect any protection from the Court against employers who attempted to intimidate their actual or potential members.

A further limitation was that the compulsory arbitration system applied only to employees in firms employing more than thirty people and to tenancy disputes involving more than thirty tenants – again, a minority. Either or both parties could choose to submit their dispute to the Court, but if they did not the secretary of labour could do so without their agreement. A dispute could also be decided by the Court if it involved an appeal against an order, ruling or decision of the Department of Justice which was charged with enforcing the statutes relating to tenancies, principally the Rice Share Tenancy Act. Before commencing its own investigations, the Court was enjoined by the act to attempt the conciliation and/or mediation of the dispute. But once any such attempt had failed it was armed with all the powers of a regular court, including the contempt power. Finally, its decisions were only appealable to the Supreme Court and only on points of law.

According to Cicero Calderon's authoritative analysis of the Court and Supreme Court's joint record, the two Courts oscillated from one pole to the other of their discursive universe. Thus, on the one hand, the Supreme Court in particular consistently sought to enlarge the scope of the right to organise where registered unions were concerned, sometimes as in the *Manila Hotel* case (1941) even against strong government opposition. Also, both Courts consistently ordered the reinstatement of employees dismissed or laid-off without 'just cause'. But, on the other hand, neither Court did much to encourage collective bargaining, perhaps unsurprisingly given their commitment to the arbitration system, nor did they do anything to encourage 'union security', whether through allowing the closed-shop or the 'check-off'. Finally, both Courts used the Eight Hour Labor Law (1933) to deny the payment of overtime rates where prior permission to work overtime had not been obtained from the secretary of labour by the employer and the employees involved (that is, in most cases).

No doubt additionally encouraged by the latitude anyway allowed both by the civil law system and to arbitrators in any system, and apparently unconstrained by the later attempt at ensuring consistency represented by the *Civil Code* of 1948, the Industrial Relations Court made widely divergent decisions even on the same issues. Thus, on some occasions it interpreted the statutory phrase 'a just and fair wage' generously and on others narrowly; on some occasions it accepted the right of unorganised workers or those represented by an unregistered union to avail themselves of its services, but on others it did not; on some occasions it upheld the right to strike if a dispute with an allowable purpose was not pending before the Court, but on others it did not.

In sum, Commonwealth Act 103 required employees and tenants to place a lot of faith in the two Courts as repositories of patriarchal authority, since it turned employees and tenants into supplicants. This it did by requiring them to give up their most effective means of exerting pressure on employers if they either sought or were forced to seek arbitration – namely, the right to strike and the right to be represented by a self-chosen bargaining agent. It should also be said that the numbers of the latter were rapidly decreasing as unions either failed to survive the pre-registration police investigations, were deregistered (391 in 1952), or tried to avoid both fates by refusing to register in the first place (Abbas, 1988, p. 77). In return, employees, and especially tenants, received very little – some encouragement to employees to form approved unions and some protection against 'unjust' dismissal. And what gave the whole bargain its mendicant character was the fact that, because of underfunding, the justice the courts dispensed flowed ever so slowly. By

1948, only 50 per cent of cases were decided within a year, and by 1952 none were.

RETREAT FROM THE FILIPINO WAY: THE ARRIVAL OF COLLECTIVE BARGAINING

It seems most unlikely, however, that the rapid build-up in the backlog of cases was the major reason why a radical transformation of the industrial relations system was affected in 1953. The process that led up to this change was initiated by the critique of compulsory arbitration contained in the American sponsored *Bell Report* of 1950 which also permitted the commencement of the import-substitution policy. What seems to have been far more important in creating the pressure for change was the fact that the transnational circumstances pertaining to industrial relations in the postwar period were very different to what they had been before the war. After the war, state intervention in industrial relations became associated with the defeated fascist regimes, and the collective bargaining systems of the Allied Powers reigned supreme (Australia excepted). They were *the* model of industrial relations for democratic societies. Collective bargaining was supported by both European social democrats and the United States government, and its model status was confirmed by the ILO's adoption of the conventions on freedom of association and collective bargaining in 1948 and 1949 respectively. For this general reason, then, as a sign of respect for their American 'benefactors', the model for the collective bargaining regime introduced by the Philippine government was the American National Labor Relations Act (NLRA) as amended in 1947; that is, the most legalistic and the least favourable to labour of those then available. Indeed it was the NLRA's legalism that made the statute attractive since legalism was equated with regulation within the ruling patriarchalist discourse. In sum, then, given that they introduced the signs 'responsible unionism' and 'loyalty', in the sense of anti-communist, into Philippine public discourse, the 1953 changes represented simply, and quite literally given their source of inspiration, the attempted 'modernisation' of a segment of Philippine patriarchalism. However, as in Japan (see above, p. 65), the imported signs nevertheless quickly gained a strongly patriarchalist inflection, as was portended by the title chosen for the act which contained them, the Industrial Peace Act (IPA).

Evidence of the general ideological exigencies to which the act was a response is provided by two particularly striking differences between the

NLRA and the IPA. First, the absence of a list of excluded occupations from the act's definitions as provided in Section 2 – appropriately in an act proclaimed as 'Labour's Magna Carta'. However, as Vincente Francisco (1967, pp. 359–65) explains, the exclusions specified in the American legislation in respect of domestic, non-profit and agricultural employees, were nevertheless all achieved in the Philippines by early judicial decisions which found these exclusions in the use of the term 'industrial' in the act's title. Strangely, the Courts did not, however, find that this term excluded government employees from the purview of the act. The second difference was the presence in the Philippine legislation of the term 'legitimate labour organization' where the American legislation speaks only of 'labour organizations'. In this way extra emphasis is placed on the fact that the only permitted labour organisations are those that are neither company unions nor led by communists. Thus, in general terms the act represented a rather clear continuation of the state's established labour policy – paternalistically rewarding friends and punishing enemies.

In sum, by simultaneously increasing the value of the benefits offered to 'legitimate labour organizations' by including collective bargaining amongst them, as well as by tightening still further the criteria for assessing legitimacy, the act provided the basis upon which patron–client relations might be further developed between the state and certain trade unions. Moreover, the commencement of the import-substitution programme had commended the search for a *modus vivendi* with industrial labour. By contrast, the Huk rebellion had demonstrated the disloyalty of the agricultural labour force which was not considered to have expiated its guilt until 1963 when its equivalent to the IPA, the Agricultural Land Reform Code in 1963, was passed and share tenancies were replaced by leases.

More direct signs of the act's patriarchalist inflection are apparent in the Declaration of Policy with which the act begins, especially if one compares it with the equivalent sections of the American original. Section 1(a) states that the right to self-organisation that the act enshrines is granted to employees not only, as in the case of the Taft-Hartley Act, for the predefined purpose of collective bargaining, but also for 'the promotion of their moral, social, and economic well-being'. In addition to stressing, again like the American original, the limiting concept of the 'general welfare', the Declaration then goes on to give a far greater degree of prominence to the availability of 'full and adequate governmental facilities for conciliation and mediation'. And finally, the Declaration announces that the act will 'avoid or minimise differences which arise between the parties to collective bargaining by prescribing certain rules to be followed in the negotiation and administration of collective bargaining agreements' (see Sections 13–16).

At first sight, Section 3 of the Declaration appears to be far more collectivist than its American equivalent. It specifies the employee's right to self-organisation, backed up by a list of unfair labour practices on the part of the employer and a state-administered secret ballot for the selection of a 'sole bargaining agent', but without including the additional entitlement not to exercise such a right contained in *Taft Hartley*. However, this latter entitlement eventually appeared in a 1963 case in which American case law was invoked amongst the grounds for the decision (Francisco, 1967, pp. 397, 398). Also included amongst the grounds for this decision was the list of unfair labour practices on labour's part specified in Section 4. Subsequent case law confirmed the prohibition of sympathy strikes (ibid., p. 407) and secondary picketing (ibid., p. 472), but allowed the closed shop under certain circumstances (ibid., p. 399, pp. 428–30). Despite these restrictions, Section 3's inclusion of the phrase 'to engage in concerted activities for the purpose of collective bargaining and other mutual aid or protection' in its elaboration of what was entailed in the right to self-organisation certainly gave to 'legitimate' labour organisations far more freedom to engage in strikes and picketing than was the case under the compulsory arbitration system. The only limitations were again the standard, American-derived ones: to wit, that the union had attempted or was attempting to 'bargain in good faith', that neither activity involved violence, that their object was not 'trivial, unjust or unreasonable' (ibid., pp. 405–83), and finally that they did not involve government employees nor affect an industry 'indispensable to the national interest' (ibid., pp. 705–11).

The last sign of the IPA's patriarchalism that I wish to draw attention to was that represented by the persisting importance of the CIR. The Court retained its arbitration function in the case of disputes concerning 'indispensable industries' and was charged, like the National Labor Relations Board in the United States, with enforcing the act. But it was also charged with enforcing the Eight Hour Law as well as, most significantly, the Minimum Wage Law (1951), whose agricultural equivalent, like that of the IPA, also made its delayed appearance in 1963. As Elias Ramos (1976, p. 209) has argued, what made the Minimum Wage Law so significant was the fact that in the face of very widespread employer violations, and given the over-supply of labour as well as the absence of strong unions, the 'legitimate' unions especially pursued a strategy of seeking to see that the Minimum Wage Law was enforced. This, of course, contributed to making them supplicants to the state, since the government sets the minimum wage and the Court supposedly enforces it. This remains the case even today, since by the mid-1970s the percentage of union members covered by collective bargaining agreements, which might occasionally set pay levels above the minimum, had still only reached 17 per cent (Ramos, 1990, p. 127) and has not risen since.

The union movement grew rapidly under the new dispensation. The membership of registered unions increased from 150,430 in 1953 to 500,000 in 1956 (Abbas, 1988, p. 81). Unsurprisingly, it was concentrated in the large and medium-sized companies of the so-called industrial sector of the economy (that is, in manufacturing, commerce, transportation and services, Ramos, 1990, p. 97). Equally unsurprisingly, it was a bitterly divided movement. The largest sector was composed of the mainstream 'legitimate' organisations which were structured on either an industrial, a general or a mixed basis, whilst the smaller sectors were similarly structured but were also either 'illegitimate' revolutionary or 'legitimate', Catholic-inspired but self-described 'independent' unions that criticised the first sector and the government with varying degrees of ferocity (Dejillas, 1994, ch. 2; Ramos, 1990, ch. 5). More interestingly, the 'legitimate' unions were incredibly fragmented since their federations were typically led by labour lawyers who regarded them as business enterprises and whose best hopes of wealth lay in enlarging the federations led by themselves. Naturally, it was in the interests of other federation leaders or leadership aspirants either to prevent the growth of such federations or to split them. Ramos (1990, pp. 118–19) explains how this was possible in the following terms:

> The reliance of labor federations upon labor lawyers for leadership dates back to the period of compulsory arbitration from 1936 to 1953 when practically all labor disputes were settled in court. The intricacies of handling labor cases in this manner inevitably made labor unions highly dependent on legal counsels. Lawyers, for their part, found this method congenial to their profession and thus built a regular clientele . . .
>
> What happens is that, where the labor federation is relatively small and financially unstable, federation officials are paid from the legal office's payroll. In such cases, it is inevitable that officials of the labor federations be lawyers . . .
>
> The rivalry therefore between nationally prominent labor leaders is a phenomenon that goes much deeper than just personal rivalry . . . Although very few leaders are known to have built their fortunes from the

labour movement, the career patterns of many union leaders indicate the significance of purely economic interests.

Finally, the same economic interests and paternalistic leadership style also contributed to the unions' lack of militancy as reflected in their only slowly decreasing reluctance to use the strike weapon. Between 1953 and 1971, there was a fluctuating but nevertheless rising trend in strike activity, but only from 13 strikes at the beginning of the period, when 9,683 workers were involved, to 157 in 1971, when 62,138 workers in public service and transportation especially were involved (ibid., pp. 150–7). Consistent with what was said earlier about the state's predominance with regard to wage setting and the Department of Labor's resource-starved enforcement effort, the most frequent causes of strikes were employer violations of the unfair labour practice provisions of the IPA and, increasingly, the Minimum Wages Law. However, the enforcement effort on the part of unions was apparently sufficient since the level of violations discovered on both scores in the course of the department's inspections during the ten years before martial law was tiny. On average, the department conducted some 18,000 inspections per year, covering 3.76 per cent of the labour force. For the first half of the period the level of violations discovered was around 20 per cent. And in the second half of the period it was around 14 per cent (ibid., Table 18.11). The level of minimum wage violations was never more than 4 per cent and always less than 1 per cent in relation to 'discharge and discrimination' (ibid., Table 18.12). The fact that the decrease in the level of violations occurred despite a slowing of the rate of economic growth suggests the necessity and effectiveness of unions' exercise of their freedom of action under patriarchalist systems since the second half of the period was a time of increasing strike activity. This will become still clearer when the conditions just described are compared with those that resulted from seven years of martial law.[4]

Freedom of action, however, is precisely what the unions lost with the declaration of martial law in 1972 (Fernandez, 1982; Villegas, 1984, ch. 5). Not only did unions lose the right to strike, but they also lost control of their funds, saw many of their more left-wing leaders imprisoned, and witnessed the return of compulsory arbitration in the form of an interim National Labor Relations Commission, operating under the control of the Department of Labor. As the content of these measures suggests, they were but a prelude to the reimposition of an exclusively paternalistic system, which this time took the rhetorically monumental form of the Labor Code of 1974. This complex statute combined all the existing labour-related laws and presidential decrees concerned with both the industrial and agricultural sectors into a single integrated text. Disappointingly, it also made explicit the apparently irresistible tendency for patriarchalism to degenerate into paternalism even in the realm of discourse, since the elements of the previous laws that had to be excised in order to give coherence to the whole were all those that might engender union autonomy. Thus what unions lost was not just the right to strike and indeed to accumulate strike funds, but also the right to decide on the nature of their potential constituency. How the first of these losses was inflicted textually was both staggering in its simplicity and, because of this, made the paternalistic nature of the whole utterly transparent. The right to strike was not withdrawn but made a matter of the state's discretion. The phrase 'consistent with the national interest' was simply inserted in Article 264 which otherwise announces that 'workers shall have the right to engage in concerted activities . . .' As the supplementary *Letter of Instruction No. 368* explained: 'The Ministry of Labor may include in – or exclude from the above list [of indispensable industries] any industry, firm or company as the national interest, national security, or general welfare may require.'[5] Unions lost their legal freedom to decide on what the basis of their organising strategies should be as a consequence of one of the relatively few new elements in the Code, namely Article 238 which imposed an industrial union structure on would-be 'legitimate' unions. However, in contrast to the strike ban which was strictly enforced by the police and the army, the state did not enforce this article but instead left the 'legitimate' unions to re-organise themselves. This had the consequence that: 'the labor movement was held in check politically. Instead of focusing its attention to significant national issues including the freeze on wages and prices, the labour movement's concern up to about 1980 was diverted to the resolution of organisational problems' (Ramos, 1990, p. 111). In the meantime, the number of 'illegitimate' unions greatly increased, partly because some unions preferred to deregister themselves in an effort to avoid the arrest and/or harassment of their officers, but mainly because the state created a large number of new grounds for deregistration, including prohibiting any unions of supervisory and government employees, as well as (pursuant to Article 238) competing unions in industries where a 'legitimate' union already existed. Some 5,000 unions were deregistered in 1977 on such grounds (Dejillas, 1994, pp. 29–30).

In sum, if they wished to be considered loyal clients, 'legitimate' trade unions were required to give up the strike weapon, collude in the repression of many of their fellow trade unionists, and accept the considerable obstacle to organising represented by the increase from 10 per cent to 50 per cent in the proportion of signatures needed before a certification election could be called. In 1975, at the government's behest and with the Asian–American Free Labor Institute's financial support, the vast majority of 'legitimate' unions formed themselves into the Trade Union Congress of the Philippines (TUCP). In exchange for their loyalty they were offered certain corporatist 'powers' and, most importantly, the Modernisationist promise of 'development' and its hoped for 'trickle down' effects. This was in addition to the continuation of such established 'claims' as the labour standards concerning employment agencies, hours, wages, rest days, bonuses, paid holidays, overtime pay, maternity leave, gender discrimination, the minimum wage, redundancy, and the protection of women, children, domestic servants and homeworkers. The code added a generous definition of permanent employment by declaring that no probationary period should exceed six months and so prevented the creation of a permanent 'temporary' labour force on the Japanese model. It also strengthened the existing protection against 'unjust termination'.

The most important of the new 'powers' was the strong expectation that five TUCP officials would be appointed to the tripartite National Labor Relations Commission (NLRC) which replaced the old Court of Industrial Relations. The NLRC, which still exists, is a quasi-judicial body to whom appeals are addressed by parties dissatisfied with the decisions made by the agency's regional officers or arbitrators once they have decided that neither conciliation nor mediation will bring about a settlement. The Commission's decisions are appealable on matters of law to the Supreme Court. However, first, these 'powers' were rendered insignificant by a dramatic decline in the number of Labor Department inspections and therefore cases for the Commission to hear (see below, p. 140). And second, union representation did not prevent the Commission from using the sheer fact of a strike to deprive a union claim of any merit, regardless of any provocative wiles and procrastinations on the part of employers (Abbas, 1988, pp. 136–43).

Since *Edsa*, the pace of labour law reform has been very slow. In 1989, the Labor Code was amended and significant changes were made to the letter if not the spirit of the law. Nevertheless, most of the changes that have occurred have been to labour's advantage, with one exception. The latter is the significant narrowing of the code's applicability brought about by increasing the size of the retail and service establishments excluded from the code's coverage from five to ten employees and by waiving its applicability for 'two or three years' in the case of any new enterprises established outside of the National Capital Region (basically Metro Manila) and the EPZs. The most important positive changes from labour's point of view made then and later were the following.

- The granting of enhanced autonomy to the NLRC *vis-à-vis* the secretary of labour.
- The restoration of organising rights to supervisory/managerial employees.
- The restoration of very limited organising and bargaining rights to government employees – almost any form of association short of a union is allowed, but even 'negotiation' (an exchange of views) as opposed to strike-backed collective bargaining is only allowed where the issue has not already been decided by legislation, which is not often.
- The granting of full organising rights to private sector security guards and the employees of non-profit organisations for the first time.
- The reduction in the number of signatures needed for the holding of a certification election to 20 per cent of the proposed bargaining unit.
- The reduction in the size of the plurality vote needed to call a strike from two-thirds to a simple majority.
- The encouragement of voluntary rather than compulsory arbitration in relation to grievances arising from disputed terms in collective bargaining agreements.

Significant though these reforms are, they represent neither a sufficient alteration in the balances between labour and capital to end the practice of selective paternalism nor a change to the patriarchalist grounds upon which legitimacy is claimed. Indeed the private sector has been given an even freer rein to exercise selective paternalism in an increased number of new or retail and service establishments. In the retail sector alone, on 1991 figures, 115,097 employees or 42 per cent of the retail labour force in establishments employing more than 5 persons have lost the protection of the law (Department of Labor and Employment, 1992, Table 6.4a). Meanwhile, state paternalism has been maintained with respect to the remainder of the labour force. Despite the fact that the rewritten Declaration of Policy that opens the labour relations book within the code states that its primary purpose is 'to promote and emphasise the primacy of free collective bargaining and negotiations', this purpose is immediately subverted by the way the section ends – 'including voluntary arbitration, mediation and conciliation, as modes of settling labor or industrial disputes'. What this means in practice is that it is both almost equally difficult and equally rare for a 'legitimate' union to make the best (that is, quick) use of its strike weapon as it was during the Marcos years. Unions still have to bargain first, reach a deadlock, and give thirty days notice of a strike (fifteen days in the case of an unfair labour practice). The only difference is that during the notice period the Department of Labor and Employment (DOLE), as it is now called, is mandated to attempt conciliation or mediation or recommend voluntary arbitration instead of referring the case for compulsory arbitration. Moreover, the provisions relating to the right to strike still include the 'national interest' clause. Although unions seem to be more prepared to challenge the government's classificatory powers, recent case law suggests that the Supreme Court has thus far only been prepared to decide against the government in 'national interest' cases where there has been flagrant abuse of these powers. That is, although it was not prepared to accept the claim that the production of telephone directories was vital to the national interest, it had no trouble accepting that the Nestle Corporation's food-processing and a private academic institution's teaching activities were vital. In addition, 'illegitimate' unions and unorganised workers still have no rights to bargain let alone strike and picket, except that the latter may now call upon a legitimate union to act for them.

Finally, turning to the continuation of a patriarchalist justificatory rhetoric, in 1987 the government sponsored a Code of Industrial Harmony which the peak associations of capital and labour signed, and which included what is perhaps the first post-Marcos formal endorsement of the discourse of traditional 'Filipino values' in its reinvented 'sociological' form: 'We accept the preferential use of voluntary modes of dispute settlement including conciliation, mediation and voluntary arbitration, consistent with the Filipino value system of consultation, consensus, cooperation and compromise.' Confirmatively, in the same year a Center for Labor Studies was created within DOLE, which has as one of its principal goals: '[To] study and develop innovative and indigenous approaches towards the promotion of harmonious and productive labor–management relations and the improvement of workers' welfare services.' In sum, then, I have answered my 'How?' question by outlining the development of mendicant patriarchalist discourse within Philippine labour law and showing how it both initially structured the law and latterly was used to justify a policy of selective and niggardly paternalism and so subverted the one serious attempt, the IPA, to free the labour movement from its fatal embrace. What remains to be seen is whether or not the post-*Edsa* reforms will be sufficient to strike a balance between labour's still forgone 'liberties' and its restored 'claims' and 'powers' which is considered fair by all parties. As things stand, particularly as regards the still severe restrictions on labour's use of the strike weapon, the nature of this judgement will be determined in large part by the effectiveness of the state's enforcement effort; that is, by the state's capacity to deliver ordinary social and economic justice (the enforcement of legitimate 'claims', in particular), let alone its more exalted forms. In what follows I will provide my own judgement on the fairness of the current position by answering my 'What?' question.

CONCLUSION: FROM MENDICANT PATRIARCHALISM TO ENFORCEABLE BENEVOLENCE?

The labour movement that emerged in the1980s after Marcos' very determined effort to suppress and restructure it had been terminated was far less fragmented than it had been before martial law. It was also somewhat more autonomously minded ideologically though still bitterly divided. However, it was much less effective than it had been. By 1983, 89 per cent of union members were affiliated to one of three union confederations. By far the largest was the TUCP which claimed 1 million or so industrial members and 2.6 million agricultural members. The second largest was the Catholic-led Federation of Free Workers (FFW) which claimed some 400,000 members. And the smallest was the revolutionary but constitutionalist and therefore 'legitimate' KMU. This last is a 'social movement union' organising non-workers as well as workers and politically as well as economically active. Although it was formed as recently as 1980, it grew very rapidly to claim 270,000 members in 1983 (for detailed histories of each of these organisations and their activities, see Dejillas, 1994; Ramos, 1990; Yu, 1981).

Ideologically, the movement's centre of gravity appears to have shifted somewhat to the left, largely thanks to the success of the KMU's self-described 'genuine unionism' and the TUCP's adoption of a more critical stance towards government in the latter years of the Marcos era and an accompanying shift towards what it describes as a 'social-democratic' rather than business unionist stance. That is, the TUCP both sought the restoration of political democracy and continues to seek the diffusion of participative tripartism throughout the economy through the mobilisation of political influence. Not the least of the reasons for this ideological shift was the demonstrable failure of the TUCP's previous strategy of collaboration, which it nevertheless maintained, albeit 'critically', to the very end of the Marcos regime. This was apparent not so much in its failure to use the strike weapon as in the consequent rise in the number of labour standards violations, the non-implementation of promised wage increases, and, of course, the failure of development to occur.

In what follows I will focus on the rise in labour standards violations since what it demonstrates is that the 'legitimate' unions had in fact sacrificed far more than they realised – they had accepted nothing less than the abrogation of the rule of law. By 1976, the number of inspections carried out had dropped to 11,801, and 65.5 per cent of firms inspected were found to be in violation, 13.5 per cent for failure to pay the minimum wage. After 1979 inspections occurred only on the basis of complaints to the Department of Labor. Two years later only 367 inspections occurred. The declining interest of the state in enforcement was also reflected in both the declining rate at which compulsory arbitration cases were settled and the declining overall caseload of the Commission. After a dramatic increase in its caseload from 19,704 in 1975 to 53,347 in 1976, the number of cases handled by the Commission declined rapidly to stand at 6,427 in 1984.

Since *Edsa,* regular inspections have restarted leading to an increase of nearly 100 per cent in their number, which stood at 12,044 in 1985. In that year 42.7 per cent of establishments inspected were found to be in violation, 13.7 per cent for failure to pay the minimum wage. Finally, in the last year for which figures are available, 1993, 37,485 workplaces were inspected, 60 per cent were found to be in violation, 18 per cent for failure to pay the minimum wage (Department of Labor and Employment, 1993, Table 19.3). The figures that would allow one to calculate what percentage of either the labour force or workplaces was covered by these inspections are no longer published, and it is therefore impossible to compare the present level of enforcement activity with what it was before martial law with any precision. All one can say is that, whilst the labour force has doubled in size since 1973, the number of inspections has risen by only 48 per cent. Since the level of violations has risen astronomically over the same period, it is patently clear that this level of enforcement is wholly inadequate to guarantee to labour even the trivial compensation in the form of 'claims' that is currently on offer for the legal constraints it continues to operate under and the loyalty it continues to display.

Thus, to answer my 'What?' question, there is still a huge amount to be done before the rule of law is fully restored, any enforceable 'claims' compensate for 'liberties' that have already been long forgone, and one may speak with any confidence of either labour or human rights being securely and patriarchalistically 'attached' to their ostensible bearers. It is therefore very difficult to resist the argument that, as in the pre-martial-law period, the quickest and most cost-effective way to correct this imbalance would be by restoring to labour its 'liberty' to deploy the strike weapon freely. Only then, it seems, will there be any real chance that Mendicant Patriarchalism might eventually give way to an 'enforceable benevolence' that would have to be the outcome of bargaining since the state has proved to be incapable of disciplining itself let alone capital.

Encouragingly, despite or because of the state's disappointing efforts, unions have again begun to grow, especially the KMU which now claims more than 700,000 members, including 350,000 under collective bargaining agreements. Finally, symbolic and juridical gains as well as tactical innovations have been made. The major symbolic gain was the Aquino Administration's creation of the Labor Advisory and Consultative Council (LACC) to advise the secretary of labour. All the major federations were invited to join, but the TUCP soon left – apparently miffed by the loss of its status as the sole government confidante on labour matters. The juridical gains are instanced by a developing trend in unjust dismissal cases that clearly favours employees, although its positive consequences for labour have been partially offset by decisions allowing pay in lieu of reinstatement under certain circumstances and staff transfers under almost any circumstances. Finally, the tactical innovation is the KMU's development of the *welga ng bayan* (People's Strike), in which the union mobilises its non-industrial supporters (that is, shopkeepers, housewives, students etc.) as well as its industrial ones to bring activities in a particular town, city or region to a standstill for a day or two in support of demands that have wide community support. Recent examples of such demands have included the halting of the construction of a nuclear power plant and protesting heavy-handed military or police operations. Despite their clear illegality, several of these *welga* have been very successful. All this said, the critical weakness that must be overcome if labour is actually to secure the benefits promised under patriarchalism has still not been corrected – lack of political and therefore budgetary power. Depressingly, despite the TUCP's ideological shift and the KMU's tactical breakthrough, patron–client politics and their promise of quick fixes for some individuals' and indeed some unions' problems, appear to have gained a new lease of life thanks to their identification with the return of democracy.

In the past, diagnoses such as mine which stress the repetitive character of the pathologies afflicting Philippine society have prompted calls for the shock treatment represented by dictatorship or armed insurrection. Today, perhaps one can begin to think in an alternative and transnationally oriented way about how the undoubtedly huge obstacle to national progress represented by local capital, its debased form of patriarchalism and the consequent hopelessness of Filipino politics might be overcome. The hope, therefore, is that as the Philippine economy becomes more and more integrated into the transnational flows that define Pacific capitalism and the global system of governance, whether through ASEAN, APEC or the WTO, rent-seeking for its own sake will become harder and harder to arrange and the cancer of mendicancy forced into remission. For all its 'oddness' in the region, it is striking that despite the best efforts of the United States, its institutional silhouette already corresponds to that which defines Pacific capitalism. What must be hoped therefore is that the set of transnational and international processes and attendant disciplines to which it is now subject will finally ensure that such institutions can now begin to generate the sort of social cohesion, primarily by disciplining capital, that they have in other parts of the region.

CHAPTER FOUR

HONG KONG AND PATRIARCHALIST INDIVIDUALISM

It may also seem strange to include a British colony in a sample of case studies chosen to suggest how human and labour rights might best be protected in societies where patriarchalism is hegemonic. In fact, this is one of the main reasons why Hong Kong was chosen. Non-settler colonies have typically been governed on the basis of the rule of law and a patriarchalism, albeit deeply flawed because of its racism – the infamous 'white man's burden'. Moreover, under normal circumstances and thanks to its largely economic rationale, a preference for arms-length or 'indirect' administration has historically informed British, as opposed to, say, French or Spanish, colonialism. The result was that private governance in Hong Kong has remained patriarchalist with respect to both its justification and its practice. For this reason, despite the long persistence of a virulent anti-Chinese racism and its myriad attendant discriminations (Wesley-Smith, 1994a), public governance in Hong Kong too became more and more fully patriarchalist as it was 'localised'. To begin with, however, this earlier localisation was of a *de facto* rather than a *de jure* kind and involved a very narrow and capital-oriented definition of a 'local'.

Thus the first reason why Hong Kong was chosen was because it represents an instance of a society wherein the mendicancy to which all colonised patriarchalist societies would seem to be prone has been largely overcome thanks to the enforcement of the rule of law. Despite the continued absence of full democracy, what Hong Kong exemplifies today is an example of what, even in the absence of democracy, a labour law/human rights regime can look and operate like in a patriarchalist social formation that corresponds to the Pacific capitalist model, and possesses an independent judiciary, a commitment to enforcement, and relatively little graft. Of course, what cannot be known is whether the level of acceptance by capital that the system presently enjoys would survive the full democratisation of the territory and therefore the possibility of equalising the quid pro quo upon which it rests. Ironically, given China's officially socialist ideology, all the signs are that this is also not a question that is likely to be posed now that Hong Kong is a Special Administrative Region (SAR) of the People's Republic of China (PRC).

The second reason the Colony was chosen was because, or so I will argue, the trajectory taken by the development of its labour law system corresponds with that which my basic thesis suggests should be the case in relatively advanced capitalist-patriarchalist societies as they democratise and where the rule of law obtains. Specifically, a movement from assuming and enforcing the loyalty of the labour force to acknowledging and positively valuing it to the extent that it becomes recognised as providing the basis for legally enforceable 'claims' against capital, or what I have termed 'enforceable benevolence'. Of course, it may be, and often has been, argued that this discursive shift, which began in Hong Kong with the passage of the Employment Ordinance in the wake of the 1967 riots and continued with the development of extensive public housing and educational upgrading programmes in the early 1970s, was simply a belated instance of enlightened self-interest on the part of a worried colonial administration. This may be true, but the significant points are that it was structurally possible as well as successful.

Analytically, what follows will again be structured by posing the three questions. Why has the state legally intervened in industrial relations in these ways? How has it intervened? To what extent has any diminishment of labour's civil and political rights, especially with respect to freedom of association, been compensated for by enhanced social and economic rights? Substantively, the chapter will focus on the slow pace of collective labour law's development prior to the Second World War, the growing importance of individual as compared to collective labour law in the postwar period, and the wider socio-legal significance of the content of the Employment Ordinance.

THE MAKING OF A PATRIARCHALIST STATE

As a colony Hong Kong is rather obviously the product of international and transnational forces. Indeed, as will become clear as the present chapter proceeds, changes within, as well as between, Britain and China in particular have had a profound effect on the territory's development even where there have been no negotiations and no formal enactments (Chan, 1991). This said, the Colony was created as part of the international negotiations that ended the Opium Wars in 1842. Its subsequent expansion to include Kowloon and the New Territories was also marked by the signing of treaties in 1860 and 1898 respectively. Indeed, the Colony disappeared in 1997 because the last of these treaties took the form of a 99 year lease. The contents of these treaties were repeated in the three acts of the British royal prerogative called *Orders in Council* which constituted the territory as a colony. The structure of the colonial state was specified in the *Letters Patent* and the *Royal Instructions*. The first created and defined the powers of the governor/commander-in-chief. It also provided for an Executive Council (Exco) and a Legislative Council (Legco) with which the governor had to consult. Additionally, it allowed the governor to make grants of land and to appoint but not dismiss judges. The *Royal Instructions* specified the modes of appointment to, and procedures to be followed by, the two Councils, as well as the areas of policy that required London's direct assent. Until 1997, these were: divorce law, gifts by the governor to the governor, currency matters, banking associations, differential tariffs, various matters relating to foreign and military policy, proposals to discriminate against non-Europeans and, finally, any measures that have already been rejected by London. The only other limitations on the governor's legislative power were those that might arise from a conflict with either the provisions of an act of parliament that had been specifically extended to Hong Kong or the common law. There was seldom any such conflict, mainly because very few acts were so extended, and there were only a few occasions when the courts found items of legislation to be *ultra vires*.

The final documents of constitutional significance were the *Colonial Regulations*, which were advisories that from time to time were amended in line with domestic British developments, and *Captain Eliot's Proclamation* of 1841. The latter is important in the current context despite its contested legal significance. This is because it includes the statement that: 'the natives of the island of Hong Kong and all natives of China thereto resorting, shall be governed according to the laws and customs of China, every description of torture excepted' (quoted in Miners, 1986. p. 65). Although Lord Palmerston immediately disavowed it, this statement has nevertheless on occasion been invoked by judges, Legco members and elements within the Chinese community as legitimating the possibility of there being different laws for the expatriate and local populations. In the words of Norman Miners: 'It would seem that the proclamation makes a good debating point whenever Chinese rights appear to be infringed.' It therefore provides some sort of constitutional support for the *de facto* localisation that I will now outline.

It was clearly the wide powers and the broad area of discretion granted to the governor which created the possibility of this *de facto* localisation or what Lau Siu-Kai (1987) has termed 'decolonisation without independence'. Chan Wai-Kwan (1991) has explained in detail how the Chinese merchants organised themselves in the latter part of the nineteenth century so as to be able to make their case, whilst Henry Lethbridge (1970) has explained how the senior civil servants (the 'cadets') chose to respond. All I will do here is outline the mechanism which made the resulting localisation possible, and which Ambrose King (1975) has referred to as the 'administrative absorption of politics'. Essentially, this is a matter of describing the structures of the two Councils and their evolution. Appointments to Exco were made by the secretary of state in London but, especially recently, the governor's recommendations were always followed. The permanent members are still all *ex officio* and for most of the Colony's history they included: the commander British forces, the chief secretary, the attorney general, the financial secretary, and as many others as London and the governor from time to time decided. The office-holders are referred to as 'official members' or 'the Officials' and the others as 'unofficial members' or 'the Unofficials'. In 1948 the numbers of Officials and Unofficials were both increased to six. This expansion allowed the beginnings of *de jure* localisation to occur. Exco now includes the director of home affairs (formerly the secretary for Chinese affairs) and one other secretary as official members. This represented a formal recognition of the 'Chinese interest', albeit initially as mediated through an expatriate civil servant. As the system evolved it became customary for these two seats to be filled by Chinese. The number of Unofficials was further increased to eight in 1966, nine in 1978, and ten in 1983. Since 1946 half of these have always been Chinese, and since 1974 the majority were Chinese. Without going into the details, a similar process of localisation occurred within Legco as the size of its membership too was increased. Finally, the proportion of Unofficials to Officials increased, and so, after 1985, did the number of elected members.

Although the two Councils might appear to correspond to the executive and legislative branches of democratic governments, it is important not to draw this conclusion despite the increase in the elected membership of Legco which means, for example, that labour is now represented in the legislature. The two Councils are formally only entitled to be consulted, have little control over the budget, and seldom take up the cases of individuals who have a grievance against a government department. Since 1970 the latter task has, however, been placed in the hands of an Ombudsman-type institution known as UMELCO (the Office of the Unofficial Members of the Executive and Legislative Councils). In fact, not only have Legco members very rarely initiated legislation (this is done by the governor's Secretariat) but for many years they very seldom challenged, amended or even voted on bills (Miners, 1977, lists only sixteen divisions or 'revolts' between 1946 and 1975). Although they too were belatedly transformed into elected bodies, a similar caveat as to their formal powerlessness must also be entered in relation to the institutions of local government – the Regional Council, the Urban Councils and the District Boards.

That said, localisation has never been purely symbolic, even if, equally, it has never been fully representative of the Hong Kong people (for an important instance of local capital forcing the government to change its mind, see Wong, 1988, p. 90). The consultation with the representatives of capital and some professions during the preparation of legislation is real and, moreover, extends beyond the Councils (Davies, 1977; Leung, 1990a, 1990b; Rear, 1971). Most importantly, each government department has one or more Advisory Committees attached to it which provide another means of gauging local opinion. These committees have existed since the nineteenth century but have grown exponentially since 1950 when there were 50. In 1987 there were 436 and their growth seems to have been closely correlated with moments of crisis in relations between the colonial state and sections of the local population (de Barros, 1989). However, the membership of these committees too was until recently uniformly and very heavily weighted in favour of Chinese capital and the professions. Hence the latter two groups' vigorous opposition to the possibility of introducing an elective element into Hong Kong government when it was first suggested in the early postwar period (Tsang, 1988). In 1982, when many committees were restructured, things changed on some but by no means all of them. However, interestingly, the Labour Advisory Board has always consisted of the commissioner for labour as chair and equal numbers of employee and employer representatives.[1]

THE MAKING OF A MICRO ECONOMY

From its foundation until the 1940s, Hong Kong was primarily an entre-pôt serving the needs of those who wished to trade between China and the rest of the world. At first such traders were largely British or other non-Chinese, but they were very quickly joined by Chinese merchants who followed the foreigners down from Guangzhou (Canton) after the ending of the Opium Wars. Both groups were attracted by the opportunities provided by a freedom to trade that was rare in China itself and a legal system that protected their gains from arbitrary sequestration by the authorities (Geiger and Geiger, 1973, pp. 6–7; for the general significance of the rule of law in explaining Hong Kong's development, see Wong, 1992). An entrepôt, especially one so close to one of its markets and so far from others, is very seldom just a dock and a collection of warehouses. As Geiger and Geiger (1973, p. 7) have pointed out, whilst the goods imported from Europe and the United States simply needed to be stored, those from the Chinese hinterland often needed 'combining, sorting, grading [and] semi-processing' as well. In addition, trading implies the need for shipping, insurance, banking, retailing, communications, as well as for ship-repairing and supply services. It was this range of activities, then, that laid the foundations for Hong Kong's rapid post-1945 growth as a manufacturing and, latterly, an international services centre.

However, the transition from entrepôt to 'industrial colony' (Hopkins, 1971) and later to 'regional services hub' was not a smooth or gradual one. The combination of the Japanese Occupation, the Chinese Revolution, and the political ramifications of the Korean War virtually destroyed Hong Kong's traditional entrepôt business. In addition, a flood of refugees, legal and illegal immigrants, and a dramatic increase in the birth-rate (the population grew from 600,000 in 1945 to 2.2. million in 1952) threatened to overwhelm not just the Colony's feeble economy but social order too. However, amongst the new arrivals, especially after the ending of the civil war in China, there were many Shanghainese entrepreneurs (most of whom brought capital – on one estimate US$50 million – and some even brought machinery) and skilled workers (Haggard and Chung, 1984, p. 89; Wong, 1988). With remarkable speed these resources, combined with local finance, the support of the colonial government and access to the British market created an industrial base which soon involved local Cantonese entrepreneurs too. The latter were both traders and manufacturers in their own right, and their deepening

economic participation led to the rapid further localisation and internat-
ionalisation of the economy. Whereas in 1947 manufactures accounted
for only around 10 per cent of Hong Kong's exports, by 1972 they accounted for 80 per cent. At the heart of this industrialisation were the
growth of the cotton textiles and clothing industries and their success as
exporters. By 1960 these two industries provided more than 40 per cent
of the colony's manufacturing employment. Equally fast growing and
export-oriented if smaller were such as the footwear, torch, glovemaking,
and aluminium kitchenware industries. Finally, fastest growing of all was
a plastics industry which produced housewares, toys and flowers (Youngson, 1982, pp. 3–6).

Full employment was attained in 1960 and the publication in the
following year of the first postwar census showed that Hong Kong's GDP
was growing at the exceptionally rapid rate of 10 per cent per annum.
There were successful moves upmarket, sometimes thanks to advice and
support from overseas retailers, and forward along the commodity chains
in existing industries (for example, in the clothing industry, from assembling pre-cut pieces finished in Japan to cutting, finishing and now even
designing and selling whole, high quality garments, Gereffi, 1995, pp.
33–4). There were also lateral moves into the manufacture of synthetic
fibres, consumer electrical goods, watches and electronic components.
The last arrived in 1961, in the form of the American company Fairchild
Semiconductor (Henderson, 1989, pp. 80–101). The result was that the
high, export-driven rate of growth was sustained through the 1960s,
1970s and 1980s if the figures are averaged out to compensate for the
two mid-decade slowdowns (T. Wong, 1994). By the mid-1980s, 90 per
cent of Hong Kong's manufactured output was exported. This output
was also growing at 10 per cent per year and at double the rate of the
growth of world trade.

Thanks in part to its position as a freeport and thus the first Export
Processing Zone (EPZ) in the region, as well as to its highly favourable
tax regime, the Colony's second phase of growth saw a rapid increase in
foreign investment in the textile and electronic industries in particular.
The result was that by the early 1980s it has been estimated that between
8 per cent and 40 per cent of all industrial employees worked for companies with some element of foreign ownership, mainly American and
Japanese (Youngson, 1982, p. 16). This meant that Hong Kong became
even more deeply and comprehensively embedded in transnational
economic flows than before (Sum, 1994, chs. 5, 6; T. Wong, 1994, pp.
546ff.). Both of these developments were confirmed and reinforced by

149

the simultaneous rise of the financial services industry, whose contribution to GDP rose from 6 per cent to 20.6 per cent between 1960 and 1990 (Jao, 1994). In employment terms these developments, plus increasing automation (T. Wong, 1994, p. 566) and a somewhat less than commensurate rise in government provided services and social provision, have led to a fall in manufacturing's share of the working population from 44.6 per cent in 1976 to 35.8 per cent in 1986, 28.2 per cent in 1991 and 18.9 per cent in 1996.

Because most of the growth and indeed the survivors in the manufacturing sector have been in firms operating in the middle and lower reaches of buyer-driven commodity chains originating in the United States, Japan and Western Europe, there has been considerable instability amidst the overall progress (England, 1989, pp. 26–29; for an exemplary study of the specific causes and different consequences of the resulting 're-structuring' in the textile and garment industries, see Chiu and Levin, 1995). This remains the case today despite two recent developments; first, the creation of a market in the export quotas (that is, the permissions to export to the European and American markets introduced in the 1960s) which has helped to smooth out the ups and downs in market conditions for some individual producers; and second, much of the more cyclical lower-end production activity has been shifted, still under Hong Kong or joint Hong Kong–PRC ownership, to the neighbouring Pearl River Delta region of South China (for how much in which industries, see Chiu and Levin, 1995, p. 159). Since 1989, 3 million jobs have been created/shifted in this way. In addition, Hong Kong has regained its entrepôt function but, because of containerisation, few of the unskilled and/or casual jobs that were formerly associated with it. Despite the instability, the continuous inflow of immigrants and refugees (Sit and Wong, 1989), plus an increase in the female labour market participation rate (from 42.8 per cent in 1971 to 51.2 per cent in 1986) and the more recent outflow of jobs, unemployment has remained very low since the 1960s and real wages have risen by an average of 5 per cent per year. There was some alarm in the Colony when the unemployment rate reached 3.5 per cent in 1995 which sounds over-anxious unless one remembers the underdeveloped nature of the welfare system.

The instability, which reflects great differences in seasonal demand, changes in fashions, competition from other low-cost producers, and the ebbs and flows of economic conditions in the Colony's export markets, has had its effect in two main ways. First, in producing recurrent booms, bankruptcies and their associated effects on labour turnover. And second, in contributing to the apparently ever-decreasing size of manufacturing firms as local industries have added their own multiplying and ever-extending domestic and sub-regional tendrils to the transnational commodity chains within which they are located (Henderson, 1989; Sit and Wong, S.-L., 1989). In 1954 the average firm size in manufacturing was 44.6 persons, in 1970 27.8, and in 1984 18.4 (Redding 1990, p. 106). Moreover, in 1981 as many as 5 per cent of the labour force were employed as 'outworkers'. As Frank Leeming saw the system in 1977:

> There is a visible continuum . . . from small workshops, street stalls and family shops . . . through bigger but hardly less domestic workshop or retailing arrangements, through retailers with a wholesaling side or work-shops doing sub-contract work for export manufacturers, to big whole-sale/retail suppliers of factory machinery with sophisticated catalogues and extensive contacts . . . , or to manufacturing businesses which have risen within a generation . . . to clear 'firm' status.
>
> (Quoted in England, 1989, p. 29; see also Sit, 1983; Ng, 1992)

Although this picture of Hong Kong's economy and what it implies about its occupational structure remains accurate, it relates to only one sector today, albeit still a very important one. What has changed the overall picture on both scores is the combination of the arrival of the new and often white-collar industries of the 1980s and the export of manufacturing jobs to southern China.

THE EMERGENCE OF PATRIARCHALIST INDIVIDUALISM

Taken together, the colonial government's racist patriarchalism, its much-trumpeted but always somewhat misleadingly labelled *laissez-faire* policy stance (that is, its stress on individual self-reliance, if not full-blown individualism), and the rise of a patriarchalist 'Chinese manu-facturing economy' are the major structural factors accounting for the increasingly patriarchalist if particular character of Hong Kong's simul-taneously increasingly hegemonic public discourse, especially in the industrial relations arena. The description of the government's policy record as *laissez-faire* is misleading for at least three reasons. First, what governments do not do is often as significant as what they actually do (Bachrach and Baratz, 1970). For this reason and despite its 'Whitehall' cleverness, the description preferred by a former chief secretary, Sir Philip Haddon-Cave, namely 'positive non-intervention', seems a more accurate one for the period prior to the 1960s. Second, after the mid-1960s the

Hong Kong government became increasingly active in the economic, social and welfare spheres (Chow, 1989; Youngson, 1982, ch. 4). Apart from the passage of the 1965 *Employment Ordinance*, the most significant result of this increased activity was the acceleration of the public housing programme that occurred after 1973 and which now provides accommodation for around 50 per cent of the Colony's population (Chiu, 1994). Third, the one thing that the government could never be *laissez-faire* about, especially as a colonial government, was its own security. Moreover, and again because it was a colonial government, it exhibited a relatively high degree of autonomy in relation to 'local' opinion when it came to deciding what policies its security required and so defining and redefining its 'state project'. The result has been that in several policy areas it went against or ahead of such opinion. However, whether by luck or good judgement, it generally managed to find a way of doing what it thought necessary in such a way that it went with rather than against the grain of the local elite's admixture of individualism and patriarchalism and so made it difficult for them to object. As will become apparent below labour law is very much a case in point.

Before I outline this local elite discourse, perhaps I had better explain why I am continuing to use the term patriarchalist to refer to it despite the fact that I am now talking about Hong Kong rather than about a general regional phenomenon and so could be using the term Confucianist. The most important reason is that, following the lead of James McMullen (1987), I do not regard the discourse I am about to outline as specifically Confucianist in the sense that it has been rigorously derived from that body of moral teaching in order to inform the proper governance of a capitalist society in general and the workplace in particular. This is not to say that philosophies of governance having such objects could not be so derived from Confucianism, but only that they have not been. Rather, what one sometimes encounters in Hong Kong, as in Japan (Woodiwiss, 1992a, pp. 148–51), Taiwan and Singapore, is a *post hoc* attempt to rationalise and dignify practices undertaken for decidedly more mundane political and economic, or what I term 'ordinary patriarchalist', reasons by referring to them as Confucian or indeed Chinese. Referring to the ideologically central area of family law, Carol Jones (1994a, pp. 118–19) has concluded that

> the British consolidated hitherto flexible and changing customary practices into rigid and inflexible written law, thereby ensuring that a set of dominant values particular to an undeveloped Hong Kong of the 1840s, and favourable to the interests of a few powerful groups, became en-

shrined as the authentic text of 'Chinese tradition and culture' . . . In courts of law . . . missionaries [amongst others] . . . were called upon by various departments of government to advise on all aspects of things Chinese . . . their view was filtered through their own patriarchal world-view.

Thus it comes as no surprise to read Wong Siu-Lun (1986, p. 310) making the following point when reporting some of his own findings with respect to immigrant Shanghainese entrepreneurs:

> When asked to name a book that they would recommend to a young entrepreneur, they gave diverse answers ranging from the works of Beaver-brook and Edward de Bono. None of them mentioned the Confucian Classics. Not Confucianists in the strict sense, they have blended Western elements with their own tradition with apparent ease.

Moreover, as Wong (ibid., pp. 67–8) states earlier in the same study of the avowedly patriarchalist mill owners, even they constructed their managerial philosophy on a trial and error basis. However, as Gordon Redding (1991), also reflecting on his own findings, has said:

> a secular form of Confucianism pervades and structures the consciousness of the key actors . . . The head of the family business lives out values of paternalism, the disciplined exchange of vertical obligations, and the cultivation of specific horizontal bonds of obligation and friendship, all of which appear as selections from the wider Confucian ethic. State Confucianism, with its theories of government and its practices of aloof and obscure superiority via scholarship, is abandoned or at least put on one side as of only marginal interest. Instead certain key lessons, bound up with the perpetuation of social order via family discipline and family coherence, are selected out and retained . . . The ideology of Chinese chief executives is an elaboration around the theme of control in the face of limited trust.

Finally, Lui Tai-Lok and Thomas Wong (1994) have argued on the basis of data obtained from their study of social mobility that there is nothing specifically familialist, let alone Confucian, about the motivation of Hong Kong entrepreneurs. Rather, entrepreneurial activity is simply one of a number of strategies for economic advancement. However, they too add:

> Our emphasis on the strategising aspect does not deny the relevance of the family as a unit of economic action. In fact, social advancement is still a collective, familial effort for Hong Kong Chinese (see, for example, Salaff, 1981). The family serves as an agent for pooling and allocating

> resources for an individual's mobility. While the abstract ideal of family
> prestige may have faded, the economic well being of the kins is still an
> important practical concern . . .　　　　　　(Lui and Wong, 1994, p. 25)

In stressing this point, I am not for a moment wishing to deny the role of
distinctive discursive/ideological factors in the making of Hong Kong
society and labour law, but only insisting that this factor was an ordinary
patriarchalism arising out of the contemporary circumstances rather
than a set of moral beliefs with an ancient lineage. Moreover, as England
and Rear (1975, chs. 4 and 5; see also Lee, 1993) have shown, the significance of even ordinary patriarchalism for conceptions of the nature of
proper governance of workplaces in Hong Kong was and is highly variable. What, however, I am hoping to undermine by this stress are the
arguments of those on the wider Pacific-Asian stage who might seek to
justify their equally ordinary authoritarianism by claiming that there is a
specific ethical imperative behind it.

Notwithstanding Jones' point about the actual genealogy of 'Chinese
culture', one neat, no doubt too neat, way of summarising the development of Hong Kong's hegemonic discourse over time is to say that,
whereas before 1945 the colonial state provided the stress on individual
self-reliance and the local elite provided the patriarchalism, since then
these roles have gradually been reversed. Lau Siu-Kai and Kuan Hsin-
Chi (1988, p. 19) are correct, of course, when they state that, 'there has
not been an elaborate, systematic theory, explicitly articulated [like
Marxism-Leninism], to buttress the legitimacy of authority in Hong
Kong'. Nor indeed is there a clear privileging of a central summary concept like the *Kigyoushugi* or the collection of concepts summarised as
Social Modernism that I and others have claimed exist in Japan and the
United States respectively. However, this does not mean that an hegemonic discourse does not exist in Hong Kong, in the sense of a widely
accepted and structurally embedded set of ideas defining the commonsense of the society on both sides of the public/private divide. Indeed,
and I am not sure that Lau and Kuan would agree with this since hegemony is not a concept they use, it seems to me that evidence for the
existence of precisely such a discourse is what they unknowingly provide
in their study. I say 'unknowingly provide' because Lau and Kuan present
this discourse as if it was in fact two different discourses, one produced
by the colonial government and the other dispersed through the Chinese
population. This reflects Lau's earlier (1982) characterisation of Hong
Kong as a 'minimally integrated socio-political framework'. There seem

to me to be two reasons for Lau and Kuan's dualism. First, it is a product of the implicit and unintended Orientalism that is a function of them narrativising their account of the 'Hong Kong Ethos' as a process of deviation from what, in their text too, is a largely Western reading of the Confucian canon. And second, it perhaps also represents a wholly understandable reaction to that earlier exclusion of the Chinese population from Hong Kong's historiography that Chan (1991, p. 2) has made so clear. Concerning the government's ideology they summarise their findings by saying:

> the nature of governance in Hong Kong comprises a set of inconsistent elements, viz. authoritarianism, ambiguous legitimacy of authority, limited government, benign and enlightened rule, separate but blurred public spheres, rule of law and quasi-democratic appurtenances. Some of these features are compatible with traditional or modern Chinese governance, while others are additives to Chinese political culture. Together they furnish a peculiar but congenial ambience for the fostering of a particular ethos among the Hong Kong Chinese.   (Lau and Kuan, 1988, p. 33)

Concerning the ideology of the Hong Kong Chinese they summarise their findings by saying:

> The individual, social and economic values of the Hong Kong Chinese represent a mixture of old and new orientations; these orientations maintain an uneasy coexistence.
>
> The freedom enjoyed by the individual in an open socio-economic system provides the condition for individual success and individual expression. Personal freedom is the predominant value in Hong Kong Chinese people's view of the individual. Nevertheless, the value of the individual emphasised by the Hong Kong Chinese seems to be an instrumental one, and a person is valued by his achievements rather than by any Western conception of the intrinsic value of the individual. The Confucian idea of the natural equality of men still lingers on, but it seems not to have much effect on interpersonal relationships. While the Hong Kong Chinese have progressed quite a bit in their decent level of abstract social trust, still, in their action tendencies, mistrust of others is the dominant theme. Hong Kong Chinese have no qualms in restricting the enjoyment of civil rights by others if those rights would engender social disorder . . .
>
> The emphasis placed on social order and social harmony and the loathing of social conflict still persist strongly in the ethos of the Hong Kong Chinese. Many of the traditional virtues centring on the family are still strong, thus simultaneously producing depoliticizing effects and

buttressing the competitive capitalist system and its concomitant economic values.   (Ibid., pp. 67–8)

(For a re-reading of Lau and Kuan's text in the light of more recent data, which stresses the 'utilitarian individualism' of the Hong Kong Chinese, and for the willingness of Hong Kong people to turn to sources of support other than the family, see Wong and Lui (1994).)

Reading these two statements from the perspective provided by my stress on a gradual but long-developing process of localisation, their relationship looks rather different. If one combines the first of these statements with the government's oft-stated commitment to individual self-reliance and the market, it seems to me that one does not have one discourse fostering another but rather the same one being repeated on both sides of the public/private divide as mirror images of one another. This is a result of mutual borrowing and, to use Laclau and Mouffe's (1985) terminology, previously 'antagonistic' discursive elements such as 'state'/'Chinese', 'individual'/'family', and 'Hong Kong'/'working class' having become 'equivalents' and thus, for this reason, components of a hegemonic discourse.

In the current context, perhaps the most pertinent instance of the development of the syncretism that has just been outlined is the fact that the following statement, first, was constructed for survey purposes and, second, attracted a high level of agreement (virtually 70 per cent): 'the rights possessed by a person in society are not in-born. It is because of his good performance that society gives him the rights as rewards' (Lau and Kuan, 1988, p. 51). This does not seem to me to be an instance of 'thinking in the same terms as traditional Chinese' (ibid., p. 51). Rather, the use of the concept of rights to refer to an attribute of an individual which Lau and Kuan's findings tell us their respondents regard as useful for personal advancement, and also the notion of rights as rewards for performance, both either suggest or have their equivalents in Western discourse. Indeed, within the Marxist tradition the last two are viewed as closer to the heart of the actual history of that discourse than the natural law notion of rights as 'in-born'. If one wishes to summarise the developments outlined above, one may speak oxymoronically of the transmutation of 'individualistic patriarchalism' into 'patriarchalist individualism' (the adjective referring to the state side of the discourse and the noun referring to the popular or local side). What such a formulation points to and summarises is a process of reciprocal inscription between two formerly antagonistic discourses.

In sum, and largely displacing any possible class antagonisms, the 'citizenry' have become ideologically more or less what the state has wanted them to be, whilst the state has become ideologically more or less what the citizenry has wanted it to be. This, at any rate, is what it seems to me must have happened for the reversal to have occurred of the ideological polarity of state/popular relations with respect to the prime loci of the insistences on individual self-reliance and patriarchalism. Thus the reversal of the relations between the terms 'individualism' and 'patriarchalism' both registers the tension within the dominant public discourse and suggests how it was resolved – that is, by reversing the loci of its carriers.

SOCIAL INSTITUTIONS, CLASS STRUCTURE AND LABOUR LAW

The imbrication with one another of the social-structural conditions and developments outlined above has, because of its effects on the relations of possession, control and title within which classes subsist, produced a class structure marked by a particularly striking imbalance between the powers of capital and labour. The state which is a condition of capital's hegemony has until recently been a colonial state and hence not without liabilities in terms of its longevity and legitimacy. However, Hong Kong capital has been constituted politically by its virtual monopoly of access to this state, with the result that the securing of public order and the control of the production process on its own terms has never been seriously in doubt despite the occasional serious strike or riot.

Hong Kong capital has also been constituted by the externally organised and managed global commodity chains upon which it depends for both its inputs and the sale of its output. In addition it has had to acknowledge the obligations acquired as a result of Britain's ratification of many ILO Conventions as well as the International Covenant on Civil and Political Rights. Notwithstanding any of this, it has also been constituted economically by its very seldom challenged possession of the means of production. In other words, the result has been that, in the context of an evolving patriarchalist discourse and thanks largely to its access to a plentiful supply of labour either through immigration or relocation to China, its possessory power to specify the conditions under which production will take place whether in the Colony as a whole or within particular workplaces has also never been in doubt. And this despite the occasional presence of trade unions, the ministrations of the Labour Department created out of the Department of Chinese Affairs in

1947, and most recently the occasional interest of the Labour Tribunal established in 1973. Finally, capital's title too has never been under threat at either the macro or micro levels, despite the fact that in the case of local land property is held on a leasehold basis under somewhat uncertain political conditions. This lack of threat is largely the result of the transfer of much of the Colony's wealth overseas and China's forbearance. The latter's stance has gradually become more positive as the PRC government has increased its own stake in Hong Kong (Wong, S.-L., 1994, pp. 224–5).

In sum, although or, perhaps, because Hong Kong is deeply embedded in, and dependent upon, transnational flows of one kind or another, the SAR's class structure has been constituted in such a way that it was only recently that labour became capable of at all qualifying capital's power along any structural dimension, and then only with the state's contingent and differently motivated support. This, then, it seems to me, is the structural context which explains why Hong Kong has the particular and patriarchalist labour law system that it does. It is also the structural context within which the particular factors stressed by other scholars – 'refugee mentality', over-politicised unions, patriarchalist values, prosperity, Chinese foreign policy (see Turner et al. 1981 for the most elaborate discussion) – may be seen to have had their effects in inhibiting labour action and solidarity. In addition it is important to note that capital has not weakened itself by having to extend many of its rights or perquisites to a so-called middle class.

Much has been made of the political significance of the growth of middle-class positionings in Hong Kong as well as in other parts of the region (see, however, the critical comments of Leung, 1994, p. 63). For example, the rise of a middle class is commonly supposed to lead to the liberalisation and democratisation of patriarchalist societies. In fact, in the Hong Kong case liberalisation, if not democratisation, preceded rather than followed from the emergence of a substantial middle class. In the present context, therefore, the growth of the middle class in Hong Kong is of interest largely because of what it can tell us about the state of class relations more generally rather than about political relations specifically. Here again the reality is less exciting than theory suggests it could have been. Specifically, it is less exciting than is suggested by my own view that the rise of the middle class represents not just an elaboration of capital's control mechanisms but also a qualification of its power at the point of production (see above, p. 43). The main points here are that the growth of the middle class has neither been that dramatic, nor turned out to be as critical a symptom of the state of class relations as it sometimes is in other societies. Using the unfortunately only recently redefined official occupational classification schema and data from the 1991 Census, those most likely to be contradictorily positioned ('Managers and Administrators', 'Professionals' and 'Associate Professionals') presently account for less than 20 per cent of the labour force once employers and the self-employed are stripped out. Using a combination of survey data and the two principal classificatory schema available to sociologists, one arrives at a figure for the size of what might be termed the 'core' middle class in 1990 of either 31.7 or 20 per cent (T. Wong, 1994, p. 37). Whichever classificatory schema is used, this suggests that the size of the group contradictorily positioned on either side of the boundary between capital and labour is still small in comparative terms. For Britain, where the size of this group is also relatively low compared to the United States (Wright, 1985), the equivalent figures in terms of the sociological categories were 36.3 or 27.3 per cent (Marshall et al., 1988, pp. 22–4).

It is also clear that most of this increase is related to changes in the functions of Hong Kong plants and offices as well as in the employer mix. Thus the increase is a far less reliable indicator of pressure on profitability than it is or has been in some other societies. The proportion of contradictorily positioned employees in manufacturing did rise dramatically between 1986 and 1991, but most of this seems to have been a result of, and indeed has been more than compensated for by, the relocation of low-end production to China and a corresponding increase in the administrative labour performed in Hong Kong (for an indication of how this has nevertheless contributed to the increase in inequality, see Chiu and Levin, 1995, pp. 161–3). It would be difficult to think of a more dramatic example of the necessity these days of thinking of class relations within a theoretical framework that takes account of transnational effects.

In 1986, 52 per cent of 'Professional, Administrative and Managerial' employees were to be found in service industries as compared to 34.3 per cent in manufacturing. However, the symptomatic significance of the contradictorily positioned in service industries is far less than in manufacturing, since such industries are far more dependent upon the knowledge of a few key personnel and upon marketing than on labour or indeed fixed capital as a source of value-added (T. Wong, 1994, p. 554). In addition, the overall growth in the number and significance of contradictory positionings is also the result of a large increase in what I regard as non-class-positioned, civil service jobs (Woodiwiss, 1990a, p. 184, n. 4).

Thus, if the profit margins of manufacturing companies nevertheless appear to be rather narrow (T. Wong, 1994, p. 554), this would seem more likely to reflect the tightness of global market conditions, or indeed a preference for 'declaring' profits in the PRC or elsewhere, than the state of class relations at the point of production in Hong Kong.

The result of the basic asymmetry in class relations, the relatively small size of the capital drain ascribable to the maintenance of a middle class, and therefore of the asymmetrical effect of the legal interventions that I am about to describe too, has been that the overall profitability of Hong Kong companies has increased year by year. Also, the ratio of profits to wages as percentages of the GDP has increased to capital's benefit. Moreover, income inequality as measured in terms of the changing Gini Coefficient has steadily increased from .43 in the latter half of the 1970s to .46 and rising in the 1980s (Turner et al., 1991, pp. 14–18, but see Chau, 1994 for an attempt to discount the significance of these increases in inequality on an 'all boats must rise' basis). This means that Hong Kong is a significantly more unequal society than the United Kingdom, for example, since the comparable Gini numbers there were 24.3 and 32.4 respectively (Crafts, 1997). In addition, despite the widespread popular belief that Hong Kong is a highly mobile society (Wong, S.-L., 1994, p. 226), the chances of a person from a manual working-class background as compared to someone from a professional background gaining a professional job (intergenerational mobility) are very small (Tsang, 1994). Indeed, they are three times worse than in Britain (Marshall et al., 1988, p. 272; Wong, 1992, p. 54)! In other words, in spite of the pressure on profits initiated by the rising organic composition of capital consequent upon the increasing proportion of fixed capital to labour power, what Marx termed the 'counteracting influences' have operated effectively. This is not surprising since to list them is to call to mind many of the transnational conditions of existence that constitute the Colony's specific set of class relations: increasing the intensity of labour; the cheapening of elements of fixed capital; ready access to supplies of un- or underemployed labour; the ability to import and export capital freely; an increase in 'cheap' capital raised on the stock market; and finally, one that Marx did not mention, low corporate taxation.

LEGAL DOCTRINE AND THE POWER OF CAPITAL

In this section I will begin by outlining some of the particularities of Hong Kong legal discourse with respect to contract, tort and property in order to confirm what was said above about the nature of the class balances in the society. I will then illustrate the transmutation of individualist patriarchalism into patriarchalist individualism by looking at the development of the Colony's labour law and its consequences for unions and employees.

As has been indicated several times already, the shared appreciation of the rule of law by all sections of the Colony's population has been a critical condition of possibility with respect to the emergence of Hong Kong's syncretic public discourse.[2] For the present day this is, again unknowingly, confirmed by Lau and Kuan's findings. After listing what they refer to as 'many inconsistencies', which they seem not to be aware would be replicated in Western countries too (for such similarities, see Hsu, 1992, ch. 6.), they conclude that there is majority (that is, typically 60 per cent) approval of the legal system on most counts, but minority worries about unjust laws or regulations, and their 'foreignness': 'the reception of the common law system . . . has proceeded largely on an instrumental, utilitarian and egocentric basis, whereas the philosophical and ethical foundation on which the legal system operates still contains traces of traditional Confucian and familistic considerations' (Lau and Kuan, 1988, p. 143; see also Hsu, 1992). Both the fact of this approval and its basis are confirmed by the litigiousness of the local population – as measured in terms of cases per 1000, Hong Kong 'citizens', even in 1969, were nearly twice as likely to bring a civil case as Britons and nearly five times as likely as the Japanese (Lau and Kuan, 1988, p. 142). What makes this a particularly significant outcome in terms of the present argument concerning the syncretism of Hong Kong public discourse is that this high approval rating has been achieved despite the fact that there is very little explicit evidence for the presence of specifically Confucian or even ordinary patriarchalist elements in either the basic structure of the common and statutory law as it applies in Hong Kong or, in contrast to Japan, in judicial reasoning.

As 'clarified' by the Application of English Law Ordinance (1966), the sources of Hong Kong's law are legislation, the common law, equity, and local customary law (Wesley-Smith, 1993, 1994b). Initially and naturally enough, all of Hong Kong's legislation was of British origin and included the statutes then in force in Britain unless they were, as it states in the Supreme Court Ordinance of 1844, 'inapplicable to the local circumstances of the colony or of its inhabitants'. Once the Colony obtained its own legislature in 1843, and despite the clear sovereignty of the 'Queen in Parliament', its government was free to make its own laws save those that were applied to Hong Kong by either an Order in Council (as exemplified by those included in a schedule attached to the Supreme Court Ordinance), express provision in a British statute, or passage of a local ordinance. The common law and equity continued to be fundamentally English law, since they are officially regarded as found and not made by judges and so as unchanging. In any event, the final arbiter as to their nature was the House of Lords or the Judicial Committee of the Privy Council, and English precedents have generally been presumed 'applicable' in Hong Kong (Wesley-Smith, 1994b, pp. 106–10).

The exceptions have largely been where local customary law is considered to apply, which is chiefly to some areas of family law, such as those that formerly allowed concubinage, and some aspects of land law in the New Territories (Haydon, 1962; but see again Jones, 1994b on the 'invented' nature of this customary law). The fact that, on the one hand, Hong Kong makes its own laws and, on the other, that English justices have to be mindful of English legislation which may have no equivalent or application in Hong Kong (a possibility that Legco insisted on in its 1971 amendment to the 1966 Application Ordinance) might have been expected to have caused problems in identifying the law. These, however, have either not occurred or when they have the English precedent has been followed anyway regardless of the absence of local legislative support (Wesley-Smith, 1994b, pp. 111–12). As Wesley-Smith has wryly commented: 'In the last resort, it might be concluded, law is not really what the legislature lays down, or what the courts say it is, but is to be found in the practice of lawyers. On that test, the Application of English Law Ordinance seems to have been a success' (p. 128). This said, there are still many points at which Hong Kong law differs from English law because statutes in effect in England either have not been applied or have no equivalent in the SAR (an exceptionally clear and skilful account of how the two sources are blended in judicial labour law reasoning may be found in Williams 1990).

The significance of these differences to industrial relations issues, although many of them do not directly relate to them, is negative so far as labour is concerned. This is because the differences I have in mind, relating as they do to the basic doctrinal infrastructure to which judges refer when they are having difficulties, all tend to be to the advantage of stronger rather than weaker parties. Although it is not directly pertinent to the issue of the balance of advantage as between parties, I will begin my brief account of these differences by referring to one that relates to capital alone. This is because it both suggests where the law's sympathies have tended to lie and instances the long-established localisation of the law. In nineteenth-century, pre-revolutionary Chinese law, the liabilities of the parties involved in partnerships were proportionate to their actual investment. Thus Chinese businessmen found the English law of partnership very onerous since it imposed full liability for all debts on all partners irrespective of the size of their investment. In 1911 the Chinese Partnerships Ordinance was passed which made liability proportionate to a registered interest. After 1945 trading as a limited liability company gradually came to be seen as more advantageous with the result that the 1911 Ordinance disappeared from the statute book, but not until the 1970s (Li, 1985, pp. 4–5).

More pertinent to the issue of the balances between stronger and weaker parties are some particularities of Hong Kong contract and tort law. The points that relate to contract both illustrate the continuing importance of relatively untrammelled 'freedom of contract' in Hong Kong. The first of these particularities is not a difference between Hong Kong and English law but rather a consequence of the fact that the Colony follows English rather than other lines of common law precedent. Put simply, the weaker party to a contract in Hong Kong does not have the benefit of the broader doctrine of 'promissory estoppel' that he she or it would have if they had access to American courts. That is, a judge will not look for anything beyond a surrogate for the 'consideration', the equivalent of a down payment, that makes a contract binding if such consideration has not actually been provided – specifically, he or she will not look at the structure of the relationship between the parties. Thus, in the United States but not in England or Hong Kong, a tradesman who is let down by a corporate client with whom he thought he had a contract but who had not yet bought any raw materials or turned down other work would still have grounds for an action *because of* his weaker bargaining position. The second particularity I want to mention is a difference between Hong Kong and English law. It relates to 'exemption clauses'. These allow a contracting party to limit or exclude some of its liability for breach of contract, but in Britain as elsewhere in the West weaker parties such as consumers have since the mid-1970s been provided with statutory protection where such clauses have been thought to involve an unfair sloughing-off of responsibility. Such protection only arrived in Hong Kong in 1990.

In the area of tort, which relates to instances of non-contract-related injuries and damages, and where again Western legislatures have acted to protect weaker parties by either broadening the scope of so-called 'strict (that is, unavoidable) liability' or expanding governmental res-ponsibility, the Hong Kong government has again not acted. A perusal of the judicial reasoning deployed in the employment-related cases refer-red to in the list of differences between Hong Kong and English tort law so usefully provided by Robyn Martin (1987, p. 233) makes it very clear that, again, these differences are all to the benefit of capital. It is clearly thought by both Legco and the Bench that where at all possible employ-ers should not be encumbered by such responsibilities whether directly or indirectly (that is, by having to face either court actions or increased taxes to pay for enhanced consumer protection, improved health and safety measures, or health care). Thus, for example, Hong Kong employ-ers are not liable if their employees are injured by defective machinery, stabbed in a public toilet on their way back to work from a lunch break, attacked by a fellow worker whilst waiting to be allowed to leave the workplace, or unable to establish that the mosquito that gave them malaria bit them on board the employer's ship rather than ashore. A detailed discussion of the pertinent legislation and its failure to stem the rising tide of industrial accidents may be found in Williams (1990, ch. 9).

The critical consequence of the minimal protection offered to weaker parties in relationships known to the law is, of course, that the rights of private property owners – the fulcrum of any capitalist legal system – are still relatively unconstrained as compared to other jurisdictions. This means that individual capitals have remained relatively unencumbered in their relations with each other, with their employees, with the general public, and with the overseas owners of intellectual property.

That said, it should nevertheless be pointed out that property in land in Hong Kong is not as securely held as elsewhere since, because the crown itself was merely the leaseholder of a large part of the territory, private entities too could only hold property in land on this basis. Thus, most property is held, sometimes renewably, on 75 year leases, with some also held on 99 and 999 year leases (Shum, 1994). Although it does not pertain in any direct sense to capital's freedom to deploy its property in the means of production as it sees fit and so has little direct relevance to employment relations, this fact is perhaps pertinent to the assessment of the general level of security of title in the SAR and so to both the overall character of class relations and in particular to the relations between the state and capital. Here what I have in mind are two consequences. First, that capital flight is made more likely. Additionally, as Wong (1988, p. 110) has suggested, 'immigrant' Chinese capital might be particularly affected by the absence of entirely secure title because of the importance to some Chinese of the possibility of purchasing landed property in gaining their commitment to a new regional identity or *jiguan*. And second, that capital is structurally even more dependent on the good opinion of the state than is commonly the case. Thus, if the latter may grant favours, as exemplified by utility price rises (see, for example, the discussion of the 1966 Star Ferry Riots in Lethbridge, 1984), planning permissions, and export quotas, it may also refuse them. Since, unlike that in the Philippines, the government has not been mendicant, its good opinion has been a valuable asset and therefore a source of discipline on capital. These, then, are perhaps some of the chief structural reasons why local capital should sometimes have been prepared to defer to the government against its own better judgement, as well as why much of its wealth has been invested overseas (De Mont, 1989; Ng, 1989; Wong, 1992). Most importantly, it also explains why the government has been able to play, gradually and belatedly, a more explicitly patriarchalist role. The sale of leases provides close to a third of its revenue and has allowed it to increase social provision and, in so doing, take on some of the expenses previously borne on a voluntary but discretionary basis by individual capitals (see below, p. 179) without increasing taxes. This is a system that China seemed to be committed to maintaining when it resumed sovereignty.

What has also allowed the government to take on a more patriarchal role is the fact that, as a matter of public law, despite the greater dangers of legislation being declared *ultra vires* in a colony whose powers are delegated to it, the judicial presumption in favour of the legality of legislation was carried over from Britain where, in the absence of a written constitution, a clear separation of powers and especially a Bill of Rights, parliament is supreme (Wesley-Smith, 1994b). Because of ambiguities in their drafting, it is hard to say whether or not the passage of the Bill of Rights Ordinance in 1991, now incorporated into the Letters Patent, and the arrival of the Basic Law of the Hong Kong Special Administrative Region may in time begin to undermine this presumption. A pointer, perhaps, is the fact that there is no place for the right to own private property in any of these documents.

HUMAN RIGHTS IN HONG KONG

As Peter Wesley-Smith (1989, p. 30) has recently reiterated, under the common law everything is permitted unless it has been forbidden by legislation whether in the form of statutes or judicial decisions. However, there is now a huge amount of such legislation, plus much subsidiary regulation. As in my view is also the case as regards the UK, it would therefore seem particularly important that the liberties of the citizenry should be clearly spelt out, especially given the supremacy of the legislature. Until the passage of the Bill of Rights, Hong Kong was singularly lacking in any such specification. The Letters Patent say nothing pertinent save for establishing judicial security of tenure and invoking the rule of law. Many of the sources of civil liberties in England – Magna Charta, the 1688 Bill of Rights and the Act of Settlement of 1700 – were not included in the original schedule of laws applicable in the Colony. The only relevant statutes included were the Slave Trade and Habeas Corpus Acts.

More recently, the British government failed to apply the European Convention on Human Rights to Hong Kong although it was applied to other colonies. Similarly the international Conventions relating to discrimination against women, torture and the treatment of refugees have not yet been applied. The UN's International Covenant on Civil and Political Rights was applied (unannounced and with seven reservations) to the Colony as an automatic consequence of Britain's ratification in 1976. Not only did the people of Hong Kong not know of this until the Sino-British Joint Declaration of 1984, but also, because Britain did not ratify the Optional Protocol of the ICCPR, the 'citizens' of Hong Kong were denied access to the UN's Human Rights Committee (Britons have access to the European Court of Human Rights). Also unannounced and therefore not discussed within the Colony (either before or after its submission) was the report on implementation that the British government submitted to the Committee in 1978. After much delay a second report to the Committee was submitted in 1988, and largely as a result of briefings by well-informed local lobbyists, the Committee produced a very critical report which found problems in many areas. These are summarised by Nihal Jayawickarama (1989) and discussed in detail in Wacks (1992). Most pertinent in the present context are two of the problems that the Committee highlighted. One concerned the limitations on freedom of assembly caused by the Public Order Ordinance, which, because it requires pre-notification, gives the commissioner of police very wide discretionary powers. The other concerned the limitations on freedom of association caused by the intrusive powers of the Societies' Registrar with respect to trade union federations. The latter generally fail to qualify for the exemption allowed to trade unions as such because of their political goals and activities and/or their cross-sectoral membership (see below, p. 173).

Because of the weakness of their international and domestic statutory protections, the people of Hong Kong have therefore had to depend upon their self-activity, the statutory response to such activity, the self-restraint of government, and those protections that, somewhat precariously, have entered the SAR's versions of the common law and equity – the last two in particular have often disappointed them.

LABOUR LAW AND THE TRANSMUTATION OF INDIVIDUALISTIC PATRIARCHALISM INTO PATRIARCHALIST INDIVIDUALISM

Neither the English Combination Acts of 1799 and 1800, which declared the incipient unions of the time to be criminal conspiracies, nor the Acts of 1824 and 1825 which partially repealed them and removed combination as such, if not such incidents as picketing, from the purview of the common law were included in the schedule of statutes considered to be applicable to Hong Kong conditions in 1843. No local legislation directly relating to trade unions was introduced in Hong Kong until the Illegal Strikes and Lockouts Ordinance of 1927. This means that, strictly speaking, the law that governed collective labour actions for the first 100 years of the Colony's existence was the common law of England as it stood in 1843 without its statutory clarifications. Contra England and Rear (1975, p. 121), this could have been to the benefit of the trade unions as they gradually emerged in the Colony. For it seems that this law, which owed much to that body of legislation that has become known as the Tudor Industrial Code, is very ambivalent as to whether or not combinations were *ipso facto* criminal conspiracies or even guilty of restraint of trade (Abrahams, 1968; Mason, 1925). Of course, this ambivalence was dramatically reduced and to the unions' detriment when the English courts 'discovered' the possibility of the tort of 'irreparable damage' on the part of trade unions in trade disputes in the *Taff Vale* case of 1901. In Hong Kong, however, all of this was moot since the government chose to deal with Chinese labour organisations (there were none involving 'Europeans' until the postwar period) on the basis of a combination of the following elements: first, the Societies Ordinance, which related to triads, guilds and secret societies; second, assumptions drawn from English common law developments despite their dependence upon statutes that had no force in Hong Kong; and third, locally promulgated public order legislation.

The most important of these sources was the Societies Ordinance.

This was first passed in 1845 and then amended in 1887, 1911 and 1920. As England and Rear (1975, pp. 121–33) have demonstrated in their comprehensive study of the history and structure of the Colony's labour law, despite some exclusions (pp. 123–4) these ordinances were used systematically to ban Chinese labour organisations until the 1920s with scant regard as to whether or not there was any justification for treating them as either triad or triad-influenced organisations – a usage that illustrates the racism of the government's discourse in the industrial relations arena. A comment made by a speaker at a meeting of the General Chamber of Commerce at the time of a 'coolie' strike in 1895 brings out the vulgar patriarchalism of the wider 'European' discourse: 'With regard to dealing with the strike, the Chinese, no doubt, are children. But parents don't discuss with children; they simply say that this or that is to be done, and they insist on it being done' (quoted by Chan, M.-K., 1990, p. 159). Nevertheless, unions continued to form, grow, involve themselves in China's chaotic politics, and strike. All this activity culminated in the seamen's strike of 1922, which involved 120,000 men at its peak, and in the even bigger action of 1925. The latter lasted for sixteen months, thanks to the support given to labour by the Canton government and that given to capital by the Hong Kong government. In England and Rear's (1975, pp. 128–9) words:

> By 1926 trade unionism in Hong Kong had adopted its characteristic form: a multiplicity of associations in the crafts and traditional industries of the Colony, each heavily influenced by guild traditions of exclusiveness combined with mutual aid for members; and in addition a group of large unions organized on an industrial basis – notably amongst seamen, dockers, tramway workers, and printers – motivated by political ideals of nationalism and anti-imperialism.

In April 1927 the Kuomintang leader, Chiang Kai-shek, turned on his erstwhile communist allies and adopted a far more conservative policy with respect to trade unionism. In the same month the Hong Kong government turned on the Colony's trade unions, proscribed one of the major labour federations, declared the seamen's union unlawful, and simultaneously both severely constrained union political action and afforded trade unions their first statutory recognition. The text which achieved this unlikely combination of effects was the Illegal Strikes and Lockouts Ordinance of 1927. The passage of this ordinance neatly illustrates both the way in which British statutory law was in fact received into the Colony despite the absence of formal reception and the ease with which transnational effects may occur. Because it was based on the Trade Disputes and Trade Union Act passed in the aftermath of the British General Strike of 1926, it brought to Hong Kong the legislation it amended and so, for the first time, all the immunities that were the legislative response to *Taff Vale*. It did so thanks to its use of the words of the 'golden formula' first enunciated in the Trade Disputes Act of 1902. Thus only those strikes and lockouts were declared illegal that had 'objects other than or in addition to the furtherance of a trade dispute'. Since it seems to have been received without judicial protest, the arrival of the 'golden formula' appears to confirm that, in theory at least, the Hong Kong judiciary had already incorporated large chunks of 'un-applied' English legislation into the Colony's law. The Colony's version of the 1927 Act was even more oppressive than the British original with respect to union political action in that it prohibited not just sympathy strikes and the taking of economic action for political purposes, but also incitement to, and financial support for, any such actions. However, its passage also meant that for the first time trade unions were formally if still implicitly recognised as not conspiracies *ipso facto*, and also that, as England and Rear (1975, p. 129) put it: 'No offence was committed by those who merely ceased work or refused to work or to accept work in the course of an illegal strike.'

SHRINKING IMMUNITIES AND COLLECTIVE CONSTRAINTS

Unsurprisingly, for some years after these momentous events the trade unions either turned in on themselves, content to pursue mutual aid activities where they could, or simply disappeared. After a brief revival in their fortunes in the late 1930s, and episodic expressions of support for the development of 'responsible unions' from the Colonial Office (Roberts, 1964), the disruptions caused by the Second World War and the civil war in China meant that the colonial government did not turn its attention to trade unions again until 1948. In that year the Trade Unions and Trade Disputes Ordinance was passed. In contrast to British domestic law, the ordinance recognised and offered its immunities only to registered trade unions and not simply to 'any two or more persons' engaged in a trade dispute. In this sense, when compared to the 1927 ordinance, it took away from labour as such and even from trade union officials the immunities against actions in tort that it simultaneously granted to unions. Thus, reflecting what would appear to be an extra-ordinary degree of distrust in relation to Chinese individuals, not only did ordinary employees and union officials who participated in industrial action remain subject, like their British counterparts, to the threat of dismissal, the withholding of pay and suit for breach of contract, but also, unlike their British counterparts, they also remained subject to the threat of suits in tort – it is as if the Colonial government simply could not bring itself to grant any rights directly to any Chinese person. A point confirmed for me by the fact that unregistered combinations fell and continue to fall within the stigmatising racist as well as paternalistic ambit of the Societies Ordinance.

Another contrast with the position in Britain is that the requirements for registration were and continue to be rather onerous. That is, the powers of the Registrar of Trade Unions have become ever more intrusive as the pertinent Ordinances have been amended. Today, the Registry possesses apparently unlimited inquisitorial powers in connection with its need to be satisfied as to the credentials of a union's officers and the 'lawfulness' of its objectives. In the latter case, the test it applies allows the Registry wide discretion, since it is required to assure itself as to the economic (as opposed to criminal or political) character of a union's 'principal objectives'. Moreover, not only do a list of officers and a copy of the union's rules have to be submitted on registration, but also any changes on either score have to be notified to the Registry. They then have to be scrutinised to ensure that no provision of the Ordinance has been contravened. Additionally, the Registry must give its assent to any amalgamations and it supervises the secret ballots that it requires with respect to union elections, amalgamations, membership of federations, the establishment of electoral funds and several other matters. The only restraint on the Registry's exercise of its powers is that represented by the provision which allows refusals of registration to be appealed to the Supreme Court – in other words, there is no protection as regards any vexatious use of the Registry's regulatory powers short of refusal to register. As Kevin Williams (1990, p. 101) has said: 'It is apparent that trade unions are not seen by the law as private organizations, but rather as quasi-public bodies whose objects should be oriented towards economic goals and whose internal processes require careful scrutiny.' As rewritten and reorganised in 1961 for the amended and retitled Trade Union Registration Ordinance, the 'immunities' that are so critical to these paternalistically supervised entities are and remain the following:

> The purposes of any registered trade union shall not, by reason merely that they are in restraint of trade, be deemed to be unlawful so as to render

any member of such registered trade union liable to criminal prosecution for conspiracy or otherwise.

The purposes of any registered trade union shall not, by reason merely that they are in restraint of trade, be unlawful so as to render void or voidable any agreement or trust.

No suit or other legal proceeding shall be maintained in any civil court against a registered trade union in respect of any act done in contemplation or furtherance of a trade dispute to which a member of such trade union is a party on the ground only that such act induces some other person to break a contract of employment or that it is an interference with the trade, business or employment of some other person or with the right of some other person to dispose of his capital or of his labour as he wills.

An action against a registered trade union, whether of workmen or employers, in respect of any tortious act alleged to have been committed in contemplation or furtherance of a trade dispute by or on behalf of such trade union shall not be entertained by any court.

The value of even these limited immunities was, however, greatly reduced by later additions to the Ordinance. In 1961 a very restrictive proviso was added to the section dealing with the picketing that the Ordinance originally allowed in a much less encumbered form. When read in conjunction with equally restrictive provisions with respect to demonstrations contained within the Public Order Ordinance, England and Rear (1975, p. 343) were able to deduce nine separate grounds upon which permission to picket could be refused.

The year after the passage of the Trade Unions and Trade Disputes Ordinance, the unions claimed to have approximately 100,000 members spread through 180 unions, most of whom were, and still are, organised into two historically bitterly competitive federations: the bigger of the two is the (communist) Federation of Trade Unions (FTU), which consists largely of unions organising the British-owned utilities and transport undertakings; and the other is the (nationalist) Trade Union Council (TUC), which consists largely of craft unions. In the 1970s many independent unions and several other federations emerged which catered largely for the new white-collar industries (see Leung and Chiu, 1991). In 1961, the Societies Ordinance was amended to exclude trade unions. Also the Illegal Strikes and Lockouts Ordinance was first revoked and then restored because of a dramatic increase in strikes in the late 1940s, many of which were successful. This upsurge in militancy has never been equalled since. The year 1950 began, however, with a re-sounding defeat for the FTU-affiliated Tramway Workers Union, which seems to have inspired both the government and capital to take vigorous counter-measures against the union movement in general by, respect-ively, rounding up and deporting suspected communists, and refusing to negotiate. The unions thereafter largely turned their backs on industrial action and returned to their mutual aid activities.

The result of the combination of employer intransigence, union dis-interest and high levels of unemployment (unofficially estimated at 25 per cent in 1950), was that the explosive postwar growth in Hong Kong's manufacturing sector took place with minimal union participation. In 1976 when union density reached its overall high point of 25.2 per cent, only 11 per cent of workers in manufacturing industry were organised. Indeed, manufacturing labour has remained the least organised sector of the Hong Kong labour force. In the other major employment sectors, including the much newer and largely white-collar occupations, the density of union membership is sometimes far higher. In 1986, when the overall organisation rate had fallen to 15.7 per cent, only 6 per cent of those in manufacturing were organised. However, 11 per cent of employ-ees in the financial services sector and 50 per cent in the public service were organised. Continued union success in these sectors saw the overall organisation rate climb to 21 per cent by the mid-1990s. The net result of this still low and now declining level of organisation as well as its uneven spread is not only that, despite a flurry of protests in the Civil Service at the end of the 1980s, industrial actions of all kinds have become increasingly rare, but also that collective bargaining is exceed-ingly rare. Collective bargaining currently covers less than 4 per cent of the labour force, mainly amongst those employed by the SAR's largest and originally British-owned companies.

In order to understand why unions have failed to prosper in Hong Kong's manufacturing sector and therefore not had a more substantial voice in the localisation process despite the opportunities granted them by what has been known since 1971 as the Trade Unions Ordinance, one has to take account of two sets of factors. First, there are the unpropi-tious circumstances outlined in the first part of this chapter and rep-resented by the transnational, international and domestic political, economic, discursive/ideological and class structures in which they and their potential membership have existed. And second, there are the more directly workplace-related and, as it turned out, generally equally unpropitious circumstances represented by the developing and specifically legal structures in which they and their potential constituency have had to function.

It is the latter set of structures that I will now outline. In so doing I will draw attention to the irony of the fact that along this dimension most of the developments that I will refer to have been positive for unions and individual employees, but at some cost in terms of their autonomy and therefore the unions' chances of becoming what European social democrats like to refer to as 'social partners'. The irony arises because these developments have had their effects within a framework structured by an overarching patriarchalist discourse whose existence is most clearly seen in its net effect – the emergence of an embryonic form of 'enforceable benevolence'. Internationally, there have been several positive developments. First, the establishment of a *modus vivendi* between Britain and China and the agreement to return the Colony to China reduced Government House's level of paranoia with respect to unions and the working population more generally and so allowed a more cooperative relationship to develop. Second, as a result and also in response to accusations of 'sweated labour' from trading partners that were particularly intense in the 1960s, transnational developments have also been positive. Thus the British government ratified many of the most important ILO Conventions on Hong Kong's behalf during the 1970s and 1980s. By 1994, forty-nine out of a possible seventy had been ratified, including the critical ones relating to freedom of association (Convention No. 87) and the rights to organise and bargain collectively (Convention No. 98). It remains the Hong Kong government's policy, as stated by the governor in 1976, that the Colony should have a 'level of legislation . . . broadly equivalent to the best in our neighbouring countries, excluding Japan'. However, the ILO has condoned but not accepted some deviations from the Conventions. An important deviation is that represented by the limitations on the freedom of association and the stigmatisation that are a consequence of trade union federations having to register with the anti-triad Societies Registrar (a police official with broad discretion to refuse registration and wide powers of entry and search). Moreover, even today there are also serious gaps in ratification and implementation with respect to the following areas: male hours which are not regulated (which in turn means that overtime may be compulsory and extra payment can be avoided), paid holidays, collective bargaining, equal pay for work of equal value, minimum wages and pensions (Hong Kong Labour Department, 1994).

What the rapprochement with China meant domestically was that the Colony's government felt able to continue the containing rather than the repressive side of its response to the very serious riot of 1966 and the strikes and riots of 1967 (England and Rear, 1975, pp. 17–23). With respect to collective labour law, the Registrar of Trade Unions' powers were further enhanced in 1971 so as to allow greater control over the internal affairs of unions and the distinguishing of unprotected political strikes from protected economic ones. The basic legislation was also retitled as the Trade Unions Ordinance. However, as if to compensate for the tightening of the main legislation, the Illegal Strikes and Lockouts Ordinance was repealed in 1975 and a new Labour Relations Ordinance passed. The most important provisions of the latter were, first, the encouragement it offered to the Labour Department's already existing but hitherto legally unsupported conciliators to take a more active role. And second, the granting to the governor of the power to order an extendible 'cooling-off' period of thirty days in cases where there is deemed to be a strong public interest.

None of this, however, did much for either union or collective employee rights more generally. Indeed, it seems that formally the right to strike has been restricted to contractual issues. This appears to have occurred as an accidental consequence of a failed effort at clarification attempted in the course of the redrafting made necessary by the creation of two ordinances out of what was formerly one. What is protected is described as a trade dispute whereas unprotected political action is described as a conflict of interest. This, then, could result in strikes undertaken in pursuit of non-contract-related economic interests lacking protection (Carver, 1989, pp. 385–7). To make matters worse, the establishment in 1973 of a Labour Tribunal to hear claims with respect to rights established under the terms of the Employment Ordinance (see below) appears to pre-empt resort to strike action arising from some contractual disputes. And finally, regardless of how little protection they may formally offer, the immunities still apply to unions alone. Individual employees, as well as union representatives or officials, and whether acting on their own or collectively, have no protection whatsoever in the face of claims for damages in respect of any possibly tortious action they may engage in, and no immunity in the face of injunctions to cease such actions (England and Rear, 1975, pp. 340–7; Williams, 1990, p. 226, n. 10). What makes this state of affairs particularly constraining is the fact that the areas of the economy in which strikes are most likely to occur – manufacturing, catering, construction – are where unions and *therefore* legal protections are also at their weakest. This said, none of these theoretical suppositions have yet been tested in the courts, either because employers have not sought to rely on them when faced with strikes, or unions have not raised them, or because they have been 'conciliated away' (Carver, 1994, p. 341). This 'soft cop/hard cop' strategy would seem to have been successful in that it goes a long way to explaining why, as the number of strikes declined, the number of cases conciliated or otherwise handled by the Labour Department rose rapidly and has since remained stable (for the pertinent figures and additional commentary, see England, 1989, pp. 217, 224).

EMPLOYMENT LAW AND THE ESTABLISHMENT OF SOME INDIVIDUAL CLAIMS

I wish to turn now to individual labour law where the changes that followed the disturbances of 1967 were even more dramatic and had the same exclusionary effect with respect to trade unions. This was because the state increasingly took up the role of labour's protector – access to the valuable protections afforded to individuals by the Labour Tribunal is normally on referral from the Labour Department, which will first attempt conciliation. Here, then, is where the state's assumption of the patriarchal role became both explicit and very hard to resist on labour's part. The first step in this direction had already been taken in 1961 when the applicability of the very rudimentary protections afforded by the Employers and Servants Ordinance (1902) was extended to cover all employees earning US$700 per month or less. In 1968 this Ordinance was replaced by the Employment Ordinance, whose coverage extended to all manual workers and to all non-manual workers earning US$8,500 or less.

Today, the Ordinance applies to almost all employees equally. However, illustrating the continuing sensitivity of government to employer pressure, awards under it only take account of pay up to US$15,000. Reflecting also the continuing sensitivity to both patriarchalist structures where they are presumed still to exist and/or capital's needs, the largest category of employees entirely or in part excluded from the coverage of the Ordinance are a group of 'contingent' workers of varying and uncertain size. Amongst the sometimes overlapping categories of such workers are the following: unpaid family members who live in the same place as the employer; those with no claim to a 'continuous contract', namely either part-time workers who work less than three days per week, outworkers, or some 'ambulatory', temporary and casual workers; and finally, those who have contracts for service rather than of service. Rather surprisingly, but because of the declining importance of the other categories and its own increased importance within the manufacturing labour force, the last category is today by far the largest and most significant economically. In 1991, there were roughly 100,000 self-employed clerical, service, skilled, semi-skilled and unskilled workers. There were also roughly 39,000 of the same categories of workers who were classified as employers (1991 Census, Table 3.7). Taken together, these two groups accounted for around 5 per cent of the labour force and appear to have taken up the statistical place if not exactly the same economic role as that formerly played by the now much reduced category of 'outworkers'.

Unfortunately, no studies have focused directly upon these casual entrepreneurs. Clearly, many of them are petty proprietors, hawkers, craftspeople, lorry drivers, plant-owners, and service providers of one kind or another. However, the numbers are such that one suspects that all that many of them possess is their own labour power, and that perhaps they are simply the formerly important categories of contingent labour retitled so as to avoid completely any possibility of falling within the ambit of the Employment Ordinance. This is a suspicion prompted by two sources. The first is Chu Yin-Wah's (1992, pp. 434–6) subtle account of how use of the traditional categories of contingent labour facilitates avoidance of the Ordinance (women outworkers can easily be made to work longer hours than is allowed, for example). And the second is the record of legislative and case law developments since the initial passage of the Ordinance. The latter shows that some elements and aspects of contingent labour have been brought within the ambit of the Ordinance. Thus, the courts decided in the early 1970s that some casual workers, and in 1987 that some outworkers too, were to be regarded as employees within the meaning of the legislation (Williams, 1990, pp. 35–7). In addition, a 1977 amendment to the Ordinance made main contractors in the building industry responsible for paying at least part of any wages owed by insolvent sub-contractors (ibid., pp. 88–9). However, a Labour Tribunal ruling in 1983 made it clear that this liability could be avoided where the sub-contractors' 'employees' were themselves sub-contractors. All this said, the import of this segment of the contingent labour force pales into insignificance once one recalls the transnational context. That is, both the economic role performed and the legal-avoidance function fulfilled by Hong Kong's contingent labour are now also performed by more than 100,000 Filipina domestic servants, some

17,000 other immigrant workers, and over 3 million joint-venture employees in Shenzhen and other parts of southern China.

When first passed, the Ordinance covered just three areas: the duration and termination of contracts, wages and the regulation of employment agencies. Now it covers many other areas: maternity leave, rest days, holiday pay, sickness benefits, severance payments, redundancy pay, long service pay, bonuses, the pay of some sub-contractors' employees and protection against anti-union discrimination. Detailed accounts of the Ordinance may be found in England (1989), Williams (1990) and Shum (1989). The last is particularly useful in relation to how the Ordinance has fared in the courts and the Labour Tribunal (see also, Ribeiro, 1985). In general terms the most significant aspects of the Ordinance are the following. First, it has created a large number of what it itself refers to as 'rights' or 'claims' that are legally enforceable, in many instances with the help of government agencies, and which cannot be bargained away. Second, it has been generally well received by employees (Turner et al., 1991, p. 88), employers, and trade unions (Lee, 1988). This said, employees report a much higher number of grievances than is referred to the Labour Department and thence on to the Labour Tribunal. Most of the excess, so to speak, are either not pressed or are simply rejected by employers. Commenting on this survey finding of theirs, Turner et al. (1991, p. 76) state, 'private sector labour relations at the workplace level remain employer-dominated'. However, as Levin (1990) has shown, the phrase 'sweated labour' is no longer an accurate description of the conditions faced by the majority of the labour force. Nevertheless, in 1994 the median working week was still a high 48 hours (23 per cent of the labour force worked more than 50 hours per week and 12 per cent for more than 60 hours per week).

As noted earlier there are, however, signs that a novel category of contingent labour, 'casual entrepreneurs', has emerged to help employers avoid their new obligations. Moreover, the absence of an American-style doctrine of promissory estoppel means that this group are almost as dependent upon the good will of the larger concerns they contract with as when they were simply temporary labourers. In sum, too much insecurity and too much rather than too little work remain the Hong Kong worker's main problems. Third, the rights and claims that the Ordinance grants and allows are nearly all premised on the existence of a 'continuous contract' (for the exceptions, see Williams, 1990, p. 220, n. 14); that is, they are only available to employees who have worked for four weeks, at least three days per week and for at least six hours on those days. As England and Rear (1981, p. 207) put it: 'The objective is to confer benefits only on employees who have some claim, by virtue of their *loyalty*' (emphasis added). In other words, it is patriarchalist.

The preface to the Labour Department's *Code of Labour Relations Practice* states that the government's intervention in industrial relations is made necessary by 'the absence of a strong trade union movement' (that is, by the incapacity of employees to take care of themselves). However, whilst the department has been very active in trying to make the Ordinance work, little has been done by the government to facilitate the activity of trade unions:

(1) no legislation has been passed to preserve unions from the tort of intimidation in a trade dispute – threatening one party to intimidate another – 'discovered' by the English courts in the 1964 case of *Rookes v. Barnard,* and in relation to which British unions gained legislative relief within a year;

(2) the protection the Employment Ordinance offers against anti-union discrimination has turned out to be rather weak (Registrar of Trade Unions, 1994, pp. 7–11);

(3) the Ordinance does not include protection against unfair dismissal and therefore neither supports direct challenges to other employer disciplinary methods, nor contemplates the threat to the patriarch's 'face' inherent in the possibility of the reinstatement of the wronged employee;

(4) the passage of the Ordinance was not accompanied by any strengthening of the rights of either unorganised employees or unregistered trade unions (for the demise of a Labour Department attempt to develop a category of 'temporary unions' thanks to protests from both employers and unions, see England, 1989, p. 146).

Unions, however, have benefited a little in terms of escaping many of the restrictions imposed upon British unions in the 1980s, perhaps most significantly in respect of sympathy strikes. They also benefited politically from gaining a couple of 'functional constituency' seats in Legco and the legal dispensations necessary for them to be able to raise money to compete in these and other elections in the run-up to 1997 (Williams, 1990, p. 98).

That said, nothing in the whole legislative package introduced over the past twenty-five years or so has done anything to strengthen the autonomy of individuals or groups that are not represented by a trade union and so to enable them to set and pursue their own workplace agendas. The undoubted benefits bestowed by the Employment Ordinance have been exactly that, 'bestowed'. Because of the absence of democracy as well as of individual and collective rights in the workplace and therefore the 'secondary industrial citizenship' of which T. H. Marshall spoke, they could be withdrawn at almost any moment and there is very little that could be done about it. In all these ways, then, the assumption of the naturalness of the inequality between the state and the 'citizens' of Hong Kong is maintained, as is the discretionary paternalistic rather than patriarchalist element.

The passage of the Employment Ordinance, then, was the moment when the state assumed the responsibilities of the patriarch and the concept of 'enforceable benevolence' arrived in Hong Kong, at least *pro tem*. This may appear to have been an entirely fortuitous occurrence, since the Ordinance's overall design owes so much to English statutory inspiration and employment law precedent. However, differences that appear to be small adjustments to 'local circumstances' when considered individually add up to a system that is quite distinctive when they are considered together. It was also, at the very least, a fortunate occurrence for Hong Kong capital since, despite the many claims made for, and indeed on, its benevolence (England and Rear, 1981, chs. 4, 5), local capital was finding it increasingly difficult, and indeed pointless, to live up to its patriarchalist values.

As Wong (1988, p. 136; see also, pp. 71ff.) comments in his study of the Shanghainese cotton spinning mill owners:

> Since more work opportunities are available, higher staff turnover is inevitable, which reduces the possibility of a sense of dependence and gratitude in the workforce. As the value of loyal and long service fades among the employees, it is becoming more difficult for owners to maintain a patriarchal stance.

Perhaps this is why the Employment Ordinance has the content that it does? Certainly, a comparison between the obligations that the Ordinance imposes on all employers and those accepted on a discretionary basis towards *cheung-kung* (permanent) as opposed to *cheung-saan-kung* (temporary) employees by the Shanghainese Hong Kong Cotton Spinners Association (Wong, 1988, pp. 70–1) reveals a remarkable degree of overlap. Perhaps, then, this is also why Hong Kong's employers have gradually come to accept the changes in the way that England (1989, p. 15) and Scott (1989, p. 123) outline, as well as why the reversal of ideological roles was possible? The content of the obligations that the Employment Ordinance imposes are consistent with the avowed patriarchalism of the employers, and their universal application means that there is neither competitive advantage nor disadvantage as a result of continuing this avowal. Moreover, to emphasise the point, pensions were never part of the local patriarchalist package. Hence, or so it seems to me, the sustained and vigorous protests on the part of small and medium-sized businesses against any suggestions that they should make any contributions on behalf of employees to virtually any sort of pension scheme.

CONCLUSION: AN EMBRYONIC FORM OF ENFORCEABLE BENEVOLENCE?

Having answered my 'How?' question by outlining the development of a patriarchalist discourse within Hong Kong labour law, I will now turn to my 'What?' question and so begin the conclusion to the present chapter. In order to assess the legal and more general social significance of the difference that the presence of the Employment Ordinance has made, I will conclude with a comparison between Hong Kong labour's current statutorily defined status and what it would otherwise have been under the common law. The fundamental hostility of the common law to employee combination is of course both made explicit and in part neutralised by the statutorily defined 'immunities'. However, the fact that labour's rights depend upon statutory provisions means that they are only as secure against incursions on behalf of capital and the state as those provisions, and only as unambiguous in their significance as the wording used to specify them. Because the legal privileging of capital rests upon not simply the law of property, but also on property's articulation with contract, tort, public law and indeed equity, the possible occasions and locations of such incursions and therefore of the re-emergence of the common law's hostility to employee combination are extremely varied and unpredictable – vide the sudden appearance of the possibility of a tort of intimidation in a trade dispute (see also, Elias and Ewing, 1982; and Carty, 1988).

As indicated above, contract and tort law in Hong Kong have remained particularly favourable towards capital. Thus they also remain a potent source of possible incursions into labour's rights. In other words, labour's rights are unusually dependent upon the strength of the statutory protections that the state can provide and is prepared to enforce. For a combination of reasons having to do with its colonial character, its position as landlord, the mobility of local capital, and notwithstanding its localisation, the Hong Kong government has enjoyed a relatively high degree of autonomy *vis-à-vis* capital, at least when it has felt that its own security was at stake. Thus the post-war history of labour law has seen the passage of a number of statutes that have quite effectively protected organised labour's basic freedoms and improved the terms and enforceability of individual employees' contracts of employment. However, all the collective legislation protects are *organised* labour's basic freedoms and not those of labour as such (this is a weakness of all the UN and ILO texts too, save the Universal Declaration). In other words, unorganised or, better perhaps, unregistered labour, which is currently 85 per cent of the labour force, risks encountering the still largely untrammelled hostility of the common law every time it engages in collective action. And because the sense of justice that informs Equity is constricted by the structure of established rights and duties – 'Equity follows the law' – it too, and specifically its injunctive power, may potentially be turned against such unprotected labour at any moment. The return of the labour injunction in the United States during the 1970s and its appearance in Britain in the 1980s are evidence for this possibility. The fact that unorganised labour in Hong Kong has not encountered this hostility so far does not mean that it is impossible in the future. All it would take is an increased level of employee grievance, perhaps as a consequence of an economic downturn, and a change of employer and/or government policy.

A similar caveat must be entered with respect to the security of individual employee rights. Although they cannot be negotiated away, but because they are generally enforced either through conciliation or through a Labour Tribunal hearing, their currently healthy state (the Tribunal currently finds for employees in three out of four cases, Williams, 1990, p. 23) is also dependent upon circumstances that could change. For all kinds of reasons the conciliators' conception of a fair outcome could alter. And because the Tribunal's decisions do not make precedents, there is not as much clarity about the nature of particular rights and duties as there would need to be if the consequences of a change in the basis for conciliation were to be legally resisted.

Hong Kong's embryonic version of 'enforceable benevolence' rests, then, upon rather insubstantial foundations. It therefore summarises many of the factors that have pre-empted any significant moves towards the democratisation of Hong Kong workplaces. Nevertheless it also possibly instances an oblique and small move in that direction. Thus it already delivers a far greater range and higher level of protection than did the preceding variant of British voluntarism. What is more, it appears to have stimulated an improvement in the status of many employees with the result that, whereas in 1976 only 60 per cent of the labour force were *cheung-kung,* in 1985 87 per cent had this status (Turner et al., 1991, p. 26). In sum, it represents in embryo a form of industrial governance that successfully mobilises what have otherwise been antipathetic local cultural and social-structural particularities on labour's behalf – by contrast, the voluntarist system simply allowed them a free rein that was most often to labour's detriment. It is also more appropriate than the voluntarist system as a mode of disciplining capital given the nature of the class relations obtaining in an economy of small and medium-sized firms operating in the lower and middle reaches of global commodity chains. State enforcement means that at least capital's possessory power is somewhat qualified under conditions where capital could otherwise argue that it needs unilateral power over all the terms of employment, as well as that over the hours and intensity of work which it anyway has. This said, the quid pro quo on the labour side is that it has been asked to accept not only a conciliatory regulatory regime that blurs its possessory rights rather than defines them, but also an almost total absence of any qualifications whatsoever with respect to capital's powers of control and title.

Thus the net result of the coexistence of capitalism, patriarchalism and the rule of law in Hong Kong is a labour law system that, despite the absence of any formal borrowing from the Japanese system, may nevertheless be described as an embryonic form of 'enforceable benevolence'. 'Immunities' rather than 'liberties' have been exchanged for enforceable, albeit lesser, industrial 'claims', supplemented by some significant though still insufficient improvements in social provision with respect to education, housing and welfare. In short, some of the gains along the possessory dimension and in the social sphere made possible in other jurisdictions by the exercise of the right to freedom of association have been received as a reward for accepting some limitations on the occasions when it might be expressed and so are no longer available as means to challenge capital along the dimensions of control or title.

This said, Hong Kong labour currently possesses one 'liberty', at least in the common law sense of something that has not yet been forbidden, which could be important in ensuring that this exchange need not become oppressive – the largely unknown right to reject an incumbent and perhaps 'sweetheart' union by joining another. As has been argued in

Chapter 2, this 'liberty' is critical where, as in Japan, there are enterprise unions and they are the main supports of 'enforceable benevolence'. It is less critical where the main supports are state institutions, except that, especially in the absence of political democracy, having a choice between unions representing different ideologies and strategies provides a way of expressing an opinion on the legitimacy or otherwise of an industrial relations system. However, this is a 'liberty' that could also be easily lost and without the need for legislative or even judicial action. Unions themselves could draw up 'no poaching' agreements such as the British Trades Union Congress' 'Bridlington Rules'. And, again, because of a change in political circumstances, for example, the Registrar of Trade Unions could easily use his or her discretion and fail to be convinced of 'the lawfulness' of the 'principal objectives' of a new or transformed union, especially given that 'lawfulness' essentially means non-political.

Abstractly, it is easy to see how the extant range and level of protection could be better entrenched and therefore made more secure even if not extended and increased. That is, the quid pro quo on the capital side for the continuation of the limitations on the liberties that can allow disruption of capital's control could be added to. Specifically, in the British mode, the 'liberties' and 'immunities' currently enjoyed by trade unions could be extended to all parties engaged in a trade dispute. However, especially in the light of the return to China with its civilian rather than common law system, perhaps it would be best to recast the whole system on the basis of a set of positive 'liberties'. First amongst such 'liberties', this time in the American mode, should be a right to self-organisation whose activation is at the discretion of the individual employee. The closed shop is thereby prohibited, and therefore where, as in the United States, provisions establishing 'sole bargaining agents' also exist, the result can be individual isolation and employee fragmentation. But where, as in Japan, the existence of such a right is not accompanied by such provisions, space is also created for the continuous exercise of collective autonomy without having to go through the time-consuming and expensive process of seeking a decertification election.

The advisability, if not the chances, of pursuing these goals has been increased by the return to Chinese sovereignty, 1997 and the continuing deferral of democracy: the advisability by the possible effects of any alliance between Hong Kong trade unions and the statised unions of the PRC; but not the chances because of the ambiguity of both the Hong Kong Bill of Rights and the Basic Law as to who or what, individuals or organisations, will be the beneficiaries of the right to freedom of association (on the general ambiguity of these two texts, see Ghai, 1993; MacNeil, 1991). However, should such a change ever be achieved, there is no legal reason, especially given the absence of constitutional protection for private property, why they should not lead to the broadening of the scope of 'enforceable benevolence' to include items that no paternalistic administration would willingly allow. However, the same absence of a central principle or *Grundnorm*, to use Kelsen's term, whether it be private property or material equality, means that, as in Japan under the Meiji Constitution (Woodiwiss, 1992a, pp. 51–8), there is nothing at the core of legal discourse that could support resistance to a more hostile form of state paternalism.

In other words, despite the recent efforts to bring the legal corpus into line with the Bill of Rights by, for example, reducing the number of associations that have to register with the Societies Registrar and radically restricting the circumstances under which press freedom may be curtailed, the disposition of the authorities in the PRC is likely to become by far the most significant of the many transnational, international and domestic conditions of labour law's existence which could change in such a way as to weaken Hong Kong capital's local hegemony. Any change in any of them would initiate a restructuring process with predictable consequences in terms of the loci and transfer of strains at the level of the relations of possession, control and title within which classes subsist, but with ultimately unpredictable ones for the 'attachment' of labour and human rights to their intended bearers.

CHAPTER FIVE

MALAYSIA AND AUTHORITARIAN PATRIARCHALISM

Malaysian society exhibits many of the social prerequisites deemed necessary if human rights are to be respected: well-established democratic institutions; success in economic development; a well-trained judiciary and legal profession; and an openness to judicial precedents created in well-established liberal-democratic jurisdictions. However, as it turns out, none of these prerequisites, whether considered singly or together, has prevented what would appear to have been a continuous derogation of human and labour rights in the post-independence period. Indeed, several of these ostensibly positive social characteristics have in fact contributed to the process of derogation (cf. Rubin, 1990). Given the Hong Kong experience, this derogation would not seem to be explainable by simply referring to Malaysia's increasing integration into the circuits of Pacific capitalism. Rather, it appears to have been the result of the manner in which this integration was achieved, which in turn was a product of the social exigencies and political possibilities created by the society's 'racial' or 'communal' diversity. At independence, 49.8 per cent of the population were Malay, 37.2 per cent Chinese and 11.2 per cent Indian. However, what the Malaysian case demonstrates very clearly is that neither successful economic development, the presence of liberal-democratic institutions nor their combination are sufficient to guarantee enhanced respect for human rights. Rather, what seems to be critical is the nature of the discourse of rule that animates these institutions and therefore the nature of this discourse's conditions of existence.

In line with the preceding chapters what follows is analytically structured by my basic 'Why?', 'How?' and 'What?' questions. Substantively,

I will be mainly concerned to explain why labour has been so supine in the face of the myriad restrictions that have been imposed upon its freedoms of association and action, as well as why it has been so minimally compensated for accepting these restrictions. More specifically, I will be concerned to do two things. First, to bring out the significance of the 'racial' diversity of Malaysia's population as part of the explanation for this passivity and parsimony. And second, relatedly, to explain why every significant political and economic move on the part of the postwar colonial, Malayan and Malaysian governments has thus far been accompanied by the imposition of further restrictions on the labour movement.

THE CONSTRUCTION OF A CAPITALIST PATRIARCHALIST STATE

The territory that is now called Malaysia has long been ruled in a patriarchalist manner. What the arrival of British 'protection' meant was the partial rather than the complete displacement of a pre-existing feudal patriarchalist state and set of social relations by capitalist ones. Thus, the rulers of most of the states that existed before Britain offered its 'protection' retained their formal positions afterwards. The exceptions were: Malacca and Penang, which along with Singapore were initially ceded to the British East India Company, and in 1867 became parts of the Colony of the Straits Settlements; North Borneo, which was ceded to the British North Borneo Company in 1881; and Sarawak, which was ceded to the 'White Rajahs' of the Brookes family in 1842. The first wave of 'offers' of protectorate status began when the state of Perak accepted one in 1874 because of, to give the British reasons for making the 'offer', the 'anarchy' that threatened British investments in tin mining, imported Chinese labour, and the infrastructural and commercial developments of the Straits Settlements (Hooker, 1988). Similar offers were accepted by Selangor in 1875, Negri Sembilan in 1877 and Pahang in 1887. What protectorate status meant was that the sultans lost actual sovereignty although they retained their formal positions as heads of states. Substantive power was transferred to British Residents and their staffs whose advice had to be 'asked and acted upon on all questions other than those touching on the Muslim religion and custom'. The Residents also controlled the raising and spending of all revenues and the general administration, and also quickly introduced the Torrens System of land registration and with it English land law (Hooker, 1988). In 1895, the four states were combined to form the Federated Malay

States. A Resident General was appointed who attempted to co-ordinate the activities of the state Residents. In 1910, the second wave of protection 'offers' began when the states of Kelantan and Trengganu, which had previously been under the suzerainty of the Kingdom of Siam, accepted those made to them. Johor accepted in 1914 and Kedah (and Perlis) in 1923. Collectively, this second group of protectorates became known as the Unfederated Malay States.

Perhaps the most baleful long-term consequence of the Japanese Occupation was the deepening of intercommunal suspicions that resulted from the favour shown to the Malay and Indian populations as contrasted to the harsh treatment suffered by the Chinese (Tregonning, 1964, ch. 13). After the ending of the Occupation, the British combined all the Malay states together with Penang and Malacca to form the Malayan Union which became a formal colony of the crown. They also reactivated the labour legislation that, as in Hong Kong, had been hurriedly introduced in 1940. Both moves failed to have their intended ideological effects in the sense of contributing to the relegitimising of colonial rule. Because of strong Malay opposition to what appeared to be the total loss of sovereignty on the part of the sultanate, changes had to be made to the pertinent Orders in Council and Royal Instructions to restore the sultans to their former constitutional positions. The Chinese-dominated labour movement, which had been involved in the waging of a guerilla war against the Japanese for four years and was also inspired by the aspirations of its comrades in the Motherland, used its new freedoms to demand the instant granting of independence. When the union leadership went underground in 1948, the government responded by declaring the beginning of the Emergency that lasted for twelve years, and by discouraging the formation of all but the most moderately led unions.

In 1948, the territory was renamed the Federation of Malaya. Federal level equivalents to the existing state Executive and Legislative Councils were created and given a high degree of control over national affairs. However, since in contrast to Hong Kong the colonial government anticipated the eventual granting of independence, an election was held in 1955 for fifty-two seats in the legislature on the basis of a universal adult franchise. In 1957, the Federation gained its independence (*Merdeka*), and two years later further curbs were imposed on the by now predominantly Indian trade union movement. In 1963, despite strong opposition from the Philippines and Indonesia, who also had territorial claims to the island of Borneo, Sarawak and North Borneo (renamed Sabah) as well as Singapore joined the Federation which was renamed

Malaysia. Once again, these developments were accompanied by the imposition of restrictions on labour's exercise of its rights. These were consolidated by the passage of the Industrial Relations Act (1967).

A new constitution was promulgated to allow for all these territorial acquisitions. This provided for: (1) a position of head of state, the *Yang di Pertuan Agong* (king), to be filled on a revolving basis for five-year terms by the various sultans; (2) an upper house (the *Dewan Negara*) with 26 elected members (2 from each state), and 43 who were appointed by the head of state on the advice of the Cabinet; (3) a wholly elected lower house (the *Dewan Ra'ayat*) of 180 members; and (4) a judiciary whose senior personnel but no others possessed full independence in that, subject to the usual provisos with respect to such as their mental health and good behaviour, they were entitled to retain their positions with no diminution of salary until age 65. Ideologically, the most significant feature of the constitution is Article 153 and its declaration that the Malay population and the native peoples of Sabah and Sarawak hold a 'special position' as the indigenous people of the nation. Thus, they are entitled to the protection of the king who is therefore empowered to ensure that a quota of public service jobs, educational scholarships and licences to engage in certain trades and businesses is reserved for them. Singapore was expelled from Malaysia in 1965 because of simmering 'racial' tensions and especially Malay fears of Chinese dominance. They had been inflamed by the Singaporean prime minister's barely concealed aspirations to federal leadership, and intensified by the stresses induced by the continuing 'confrontation' with Indonesia.

It was, however, the politics that developed after 1946 which gave Malayan/Malaysian patriarchalism its substantive and harsher, as opposed to formal, side. The parties that make up the Alliance which has been the basis of the governing coalition since the first federal elections in 1955, all emerged or solidified in the course of the double crisis represented by the Malayan Union controversy and the declaration of the anti-communist Emergency in 1948 (Andaya and Andaya, 1982; Means, 1970, chs. 8–11). The United Malay National Organisation (UMNO) which has always led the Alliance also led the fight against the constitution of the Malayan Union. The Malayan Chinese Association (MCA) emerged as a non-communist advocate of Chinese interests in the aftermath of the Malayan Union crisis and gradually turned itself into a political party. The Malayan Indian Congress (MIC) emerged a couple of years later in 1951 as a non-communist and Malaya-focused rather than India-focused advocate of Indian interests.

In the course of the successive municipal election campaigns which began in 1951 and thus prepared the way for the first federal elections, these three communalist parties discovered that they were a winning combination and far stronger than any left-wing or non-communal groupings. Led by the UMNO leader Tunku Abdul Rahman, they agreed to continue the existing distribution of spheres of dominance. UMNO claimed Malay predominance in the political, cultural and landholding spheres. The MCA claimed Chinese pre-eminence in the economic and professional spheres. And the MIC sought to ensure that something was left for the Indian population. In sum, each of the parties presented itself, and indeed acted in government, as the protector of a specific section of the population. This arrangement and the enhanced patriarchalist practice it brought with it also brought a significant measure of stability to the new state and improved security to its diverse populations. However, these measures also froze this diversity and its attendant restrictions by institutionalising them and therefore failed to address the sources of the mutual resentments that the restrictions continued to generate (Jesudason, 1995).

Gradually, opposition parties emerged amongst the Chinese and Malay populations that were able to give form to these resentments, namely the Democratic Action Party (DAP) and the Partai Islam (PAS) respectively (Hua, 1983; Lim, 1986; Means, 1991, ch. 1; Vorys, 1975). The DAP grew out of the Singaporean People's Action Party (PAP) but changed its name when Singapore was expelled from Malaysia in 1965. It advocated egalitarian policies and made coded criticisms of the 'special position' of the Malays. PAS was from the beginning strongest in the northern states and, on behalf of the poor peasantry, has consistently advocated the further institutionalisation of Islamic religious and therefore ideological dominance and the strengthening of the Malay's 'special position'. The tensions which the emergence of these parties exacerbated came to a head in the aftermath of the 1969 election. Although the ruling Alliance won 66 of the 104 Peninsular Malaysia seats, its share of the vote had declined by 10 per cent to 48.4 per cent. Much of this decline was the result of Chinese voters switching their support from the MCA to the DAP. The MCA declared that it would withdraw from the Alliance and the DAP celebrated in the streets of Kuala Lumpur. In the course of this celebration racial insults were exchanged by some Chinese and Malays. The next day, 13 May, a counter demonstration by Malays turned into two days of very serious rioting which saw the destruction of much property and at least 178 deaths, mainly Chinese. A new emergency was declared, the election due in Eastern Malaysia was deferred, and once again labour's rights were further restricted. Although the prime minister and his Cabinet remained in office, effective control was passed to a National Operations Council (NOC) which consisted of the heads of the police, armed forces, the domestic and foreign civil services, and one representative from each of the Alliance parties. The NOC created a Department of National Unity and a National Consultative Council, and charged them with finding ways of removing the causes of the inter-communal tensions.

The first thing the Council did was to produce a statement of what it took to be the nation's fundamental beliefs and principles and to formalise it as the national ideology, the *Rukunegara* (Rule of Law). This statement combined patriarchalist elements that were largely Malay and therefore Islamic in inspiration with modernistic American ones that promised positive discrimination to the Malays and economic progress to all. The intention was both to indicate the government's determination to alleviate the poverty of the Malay majority and to appease the minority populations. The patriarchalist elements in the *Rukunegara* were therefore modernistically entrenched by strengthening the constitutional 'special position' of the Malays and prohibiting the challenge or even questioning of any of its incidents. And the modernistic economic elements were given substance by the patriarchalist New Economic Policy (NEP) that was introduced shortly after parliamentary government was fully restored in February 1971. The Second Malaysia Plan was drawn up under the direction of the former head of the NOC, Tunku Abdul Razak, who had replaced Tun Abdul Rahman as the leader of UMNO and therefore prime minister in 1970. It contained this statement of the aims of the NEP:

> The Plan incorporates a two-pronged New Economic Policy for Development. The first prong is to reduce and eventually eradicate poverty, by raising income levels and increasing economic opportunities for all Malaysians, irrespective of race. The second prong aims at accelerating the process of restructuring Malaysian society to correct economic imbalance, so as to reduce and eventually eliminate the identification of race with economic function. This process involves the modernisation of rural lives, a rapid and balanced growth of urban activities and the creation of a Malay commercial and industrial community . . .
>
> (Quoted in Means, 1991, p. 24)

The unity stressed by these economic and ideological developments was repeated politically as the Alliance sought new member parties. It managed to bring PAS into the fold and was also successful in gaining new support in Eastern Malaysia. Reflecting the success of its ideological and economic initiatives, the enlarged Alliance, renamed the Barisan Nasional (National Front), improved its share of the vote by some 16 per cent in the 1974 election and increased its number of seats greatly.

Although the resentments that had exploded so violently in 1969 did not disappear, they were confined to the political margins in that they informed the rise of both a militant and socialistic student movement and radical Muslim organisations (Means, 1991, chs. 2, 3). The major political problem during the late 1970s was the leadership crisis created by Tun Razak's sudden death in 1976. He was succeeded by the deputy prime minister, Onn Hussain, but the latter did not have a strong base of support within the party. Nevertheless, Onn remained in office for five years before resigning on health grounds in 1981. By focusing on the implementation of the NEP, Onn brought a measure of stability to the country and achieved a good result for the Barisan Nasional in the 1978 elections. Onn was succeeded by his deputy prime minister, Mahathir Mohamed. Mahathir had had a very chequered career in UMNO. He had been a very young MP but lost his seat to a PAS candidate in 1969 after only one term. Thereafter he became a sometimes too outspoken champion of the Malay cause and was expelled from UMNO. In 1970, he published a book entitled *The Malay Dilemma*, which was banned because of its inflammatory nature. Rescued from the political wilderness by Prime Minister Onn, he gained a series of rapid promotions, not least because of his effectiveness in dealing with the student disturbances as minister of education.

Prime Minister Mahathir brought a highly modernistic, technocratic and ideologically sophisticated energy to the task of implementing the NEP (Chung, 1987; Mauzy and Milne, 1986; Means, 1991, chs. 4, 5). Thus, he concerned himself with improving the efficiency of the civil service in its performance of the important role in economic development that the state had acquired under the NEP, and he sought to dramatise the seriousness of Malaysia's aspirations as an industrialising country by creating a domestic automobile industry from scratch. Most significantly in the present context, he glossed all of this as inspired by 'Looking East' to Japan rather than remaining tied to a deference to things British. In sum, his nationalism took the form of an assertive, Asian-oriented transnationalism as he sought to speed up Malaysia's development by aggressively seeking Japanese and Korean investment and lecturing capital and labour on the benefits to be gained from copying some elements of the Japanese Way. In this he was highly successful.

However, the concentration of power in the office of the prime minister that the NEP entailed, and which Mahathir's style of leadership made particularly apparent, created political strains (Means, 1991, chs. 6–8). The rulers felt that respect for their privileges and prerogatives was being sacrificed in the pursuit of modernisation, and the rural Malays felt that the benefits of the NEP were too slow in reaching their *kampongs* (villages). Thus, when economic growth faltered in 1984, and although the whole programme had as its rationale the realisation of the Malay's 'special position', it became possible, against tradition, to mount a challenge to even so successful a prime minister as Mahathir. The challenger was the aristocratic Tunku Razaleigh, a longtime and most often losing rival of the prime minister. Razaleigh's challenge culminated in him competing with Mahathir for the post of UMNO president in 1987. Mahathir won the contest, just and somewhat questionably. However, Razaleigh's supporters did not accept defeat gracefully. Instead, they challenged the results in the courts and sought to reinforce their case by painting a picture of a government mired in corrupt, Japanese-style 'money politics' (Gomez, 1991). Once the DAP joined in the fray and therefore, in the prime minister's eyes, created the possibility of a repeat of the 1969 riots, the government invoked its emergency powers and had 106 people arrested, most of whom were non-UMNO critics of the government (see below, p. 206). In 1988, and in an atmosphere soured by many prime-ministerial attacks on the judiciary, the Supreme Court delivered its decision on the Razaleigh camp's challenge: there may or may not have been irregularities in the voting but the evidence revealed a prior and more important problem, some thirty UMNO branches had not been registered under the Societies Act and so the whole party had to be deemed an illegal organisation. In sum, both sides lost. Dr Mahathir refused all calls for his resignation, reconstituted his party as UMNO Baru (New UMNO), sought public declarations of loyalty from all of those who wished to be members of the new party, and turned on the judiciary (see below, p. 206). Defeated in their attempts to regain possession of the UMNO name and its properties, Tunku Razaleigh and his supporters eventually formed their own new party. Harking back to the Malayan Union crisis, they sought to remind the public of their claims to be the rightful heir to the UMNO tradition by calling this party Semangat '46 (Spirit of 1946). In 1989, Semangat '46 managed to lure PAS away from the Barisan Nasional. However, because PAS is an even more vocal advocate of the Malay/Islamic cause than UMNO, this move simultaneously made it difficult for the DAP to join the new alliance and so has meant that the Barisan Nasional continues to be faced by a divided opposition. In the 1995 elections, UMNO confirmed the restoration of its political dominance by polling an unprecedented 64 per cent of the vote and gaining 161 out of 191 seats.

THE MODERNISATION OF A TRANSNATIONAL ECONOMY

Economic relations in the territory that is now Malaysia have long had significant transnational and international dimensions (Bowie, 1991, ch. 2; Jomo, 1990, ch. 1; Tregonning, 1964, ch. 9). These became especially marked as the capitalist mode of production spread through the territory with the arrival of Chinese and British capital to finance the production of such primary products as pepper, tin and latex rubber. The administrations of the British Protectorates rapidly introduced capitalist forms of land ownership in place of the pre-existing feudal and communal forms. This was primarily in order to safeguard their own investments. They also facilitated the establishment of capitalist social relations by allowing the mass importation of landless labourers from China and India. However, these changes also had a profound effect on rural Malay economic relations which, with the arrival of private property in land, gradually bifurcated into a large petty-commodity-producing tenant sector and a small but large-scale and aristocratically-owned capitalist sector. Both of these sectors, however, remained subordinated to the British-owned plantations by virtue of the latter's privileged access to both the best land and more plentiful capital.

Thanks to favourable world market conditions, especially with respect to rubber, which was in great demand because of the growth of the automobile industry in Europe and the United States, the British companies involved in the export of such primary products prospered impressively. The benefits that accrued to the local population were much less impressive. It is true that Peninsula Malaya, in particular, gained a relatively sophisticated infrastructure of roads, railways, ports and utilities to facilitate the export of the primary products, but virtually all of this was financed by locally raised taxes on such as opium, alcohol and tobacco (Jomo, 1990, p. 5). Because of the religious prohibitions to which the Malays were subject, these imposts bore down particularly heavily on the Chinese and Indian populations. Also, because the Malayan territories, like all others in the empire, were valued for the markets they provided for the export of British manufacturers as well as for the primary exports, the prewar period saw little in the way of industrial development.

Serious efforts to create an industrial base began only after *Merdeka* with the creation of some import-substitution industries (Bowie, 1991, ch. 3; Jomo, 1990, chs. 5, 6; Jomo and Edwards, 1993). However, these industries were very few in number when compared to those that had been established a decade earlier in the Philippines. This, however, proved to be a blessing in disguise since, when Malaysia adopted the newly fashionable export-oriented growth strategy in the late 1960s, it encountered very few of the political-economic obstacles represented by the prior existence of the 'rent-seeking' Filipino bourgeoisie (Jomo and Edwards, 1993, p. 21). Instead, through its own huge holding companies – Pernas and latterly Permodalan Nasional (PNB) – the state was free to create and especially to buy its own wholly or partly-owned financial, import-substitution and export-oriented companies (Kok, 1994, pp. 87– 91). What is more, by very rapidly creating EPZs featuring all the familiar inducements to capital in terms of tax breaks and the diminution of labour rights, Malaysia quickly became a major centre for the mass production of electronic components for Japanese and Western multi-nationals (Ariff, 1991). In these ways, then, the state directly and indirectly provided jobs for many of those, mainly Malay women, who could no longer support themselves in the agricultural sector. Thus, in contrast to the Philippines, rural poverty was alleviated if not eradicated without the need for a thoroughgoing programme of land reform. The political benefit of this, of course, was that any such programme would inevitably have aroused the ire of the largely Malay landlords and so divided the Malay population even more than was anyway the case. In the event, the high growth rates that have been the result of the success of such policies have fuelled the rapid growth in the demand for clerical, service and professional labour which has provided new jobs, opportunities and increased social status for Malay males in particular.

Another economic advantage that Malaysia has enjoyed relative to the Philippines was the post-independence discovery, effective development and production of new primary products such as palm oil, tropical hardwoods and oil and gas. The income so generated has helped to finance not just Malaysia's search for greater economic diversity and hence security and autonomy, but also the NEP and therefore the state's efforts both to raise the status of the Malay population and to prevent inter-communal tensions from getting out of hand (Bowie, 1991, chs. 4, 5;

Jomo, 1990, chs. 7, 9). The pre-eminent symbol of the search for a more secure economic future was the coming on stream in 1985 of the Mitsubishi-supported 'Malaysian Car' project (Jayasankaran, 1993, ch. 10), which had been the centrepiece of the Heavy Industries Policy announced by Dr Mahathir in 1980 (Bowie, 1991, ch. 5).

In 1991, the NEP was replaced by the New Development Policy (NDP) which seeks to implement the aspiration for developed country status that is central to the government's *Vision 2020* programme (Kok, 1994, chs. 4–8). The continuing improvement of Malay living standards is still a major policy goal. However, instead of providing *the* criterion against which the success or failure of policy should be judged, it is now seen as an expected outcome of the creation of a capital-intensive, technologically more self-sufficient and therefore transnationally more resilient economy.

In sum, then, Malaysia represents an instance of a transnationally and internationally dependent economy successfully moving itself up the global commodity chains within which it is embedded. In less than four decades, it has transformed itself from a producer of raw materials, albeit high value ones, into not only a processor of these and also other high value raw materials, but also a component and original equipment manufacturing base for many leading transnational corporations and their suppliers. Interestingly, this transformation has been both helped and hindered by the political exigencies created by the 'racial' diversity of its population. The 1969 riots provided the final stimulus necessary for the finding of the political will necessary to undertake the radical change of strategy represented by the NEP. Conversely, the Industrial Coordination Act (1974), which required incoming companies to meet the NEP's 'racial' restructuring criterion, caused a temporary drying up of the flow of foreign direct investment as multinationals attempted to work out the significance of so doing for their bottom lines. However, apart from this internally generated hiccup and the externally caused one brought about by the global economic problems of the mid-1980s, the Malaysian economy's growth rate rose from an average of 5.8 per cent in the 1960s to 7.8 per cent in the 1970s and over 8 per cent in the first half of the 1990s. As a result of the important role of manufacturing in producing this growth, the share of the labour force employed in agriculture declined from 58.5 per cent in 1957 to 31.3 per cent in 1988. Concomitantly, over the same period the proportion of the labour force employed in manufacturing rose from 6.4 to 16.6 per cent, and that in hotel, retail and wholesale services from 9.2 to 17.6 per cent.

THE FORMATION OF AN AUTHORITARIAN
PATRIARCHALIST DISCOURSE

According to an early and in the present context remarkably prescient study by one of Malaysia's foremost champions of human rights, Muzaffar Chandra (1979), a patriarchalist discourse that stressed both the ruler's role as protector and the subjects' obligation to display not just loyalty but 'absolute loyalty' has long been part of the social formations that have from time to time constituted themselves within the territory that is now Malaysia. Thus, like Japanese Confucianism and in contrast to the Chinese original (Morishima, 1982), the indigenous Malay version of patriarchalism has consistently emphasised loyalty at the expense of benevolence, even when proving one's loyalty required the transgression of other ethical imperatives. For this reason the possibility of there ever being a basis upon which rebellion against the ruler might be justified was not only extremely unlikely but also laughable – 'the flea wants to fight the eagle!' However, the arrival of Islam in the thirteenth century qualified this prohibition somewhat. Although Islam is undoubtedly a patriarchalist religion – in the words of the Koran, the sultan is 'the shadow of God upon earth' – there are circumstances under which rebellion might be allowable since, again in the words of the Koran, 'there is no obedience in sin, only in virtue' (ibid., pp. 29–31). This said, there appear to have been no recorded occasions on which the patriarchal authority of the sultans was in fact challenged.

This, then, was the patriarchalism whose hegemony the British sought to take advantage of when they allowed the sultans to retain their formal, customary and religious powers. This, however, was also an hegemony that, consciously or unconsciously, they neither felt able to rely upon fully nor wished to undermine too much. Hence their preference for importing Chinese and Indian labour for their tin mines and rubber plantations respectively; that is, labour that neither expected the 'protection' of the sultans and mullahs, nor felt loyalty towards them. The advisedness of this policy became apparent when, against the expectations generated by the racist stereotyping practised by the British, sections of the Malay peasantry shrugged off their supposed 'passivity' and revolted against the colonial administration both before and during the anti-communist 'Emergency' (Nonini, 1992). It was also apparent during the earlier protests against the misguided attempt to dispossess the sultans of even their formal privileges as part of the preparations for independence represented by the Malayan Union plan.

This said, the localisation of the disposition over substantive power commenced far earlier and was more comprehensive than in Hong Kong. Thus, as again Muzaffar (1979, p. 63) emphasises, a powerful group of Malay 'administrocrats' had emerged by the 1940s as a result of many lesser aristocrats taking up posts within the colonial administration. This group formed the nucleus of the UMNO leadership and by their actions during the Malaya Union affair successfully laid claim to the role of, to use Muzaffar's terms, 'substantive protectors' of the Malays as distinguished from the Sultans' role as 'symbolic protectors'. Thus a discourse of loyalty became constitutive of the social formations of post-independence Malaya and Malaysia. However, reflecting the social realities of the time, as well as a tacit agreement between the leaderships of the Malay and Chinese populations in particular, the benevolence implied by this loyalty had little relevance to the industrial and commercial life of the society. That is, in the name of what was termed 'consociationalism' and because of Chinese dominance within the non-agricultural sectors of the economy, the economic policy pursued by the early UMNO governments was one of *laissez-faire*. However, patriarchalism explains much about the nature of internal UMNO politics as well as national politics (ibid., pp. 86ff.). That is, it goes a long way towards explaining why Tunku Abdul Rahman had to be replaced in the aftermath of the 1969 riots – he had failed to protect the Malays. By the same token and self-evidently, it also explains why the protection and enhancement of the Malays' 'special position' was so prominent a feature of the NEP. Finally, it also explains why fission can so easily lead to not just faction but also schism within UMNO politics, as in the Razaleigh Affair of 1986. Because of the rigours imposed by the demand for 'absolute loyalty', there can only be one ultimate leader. Therefore, the point at which defeated aspirants for the leadership have to split from the party, and their retainers therefore have to choose whom to follow, comes more quickly and more often in Malay parties than in parties with more collegial and conditional conceptions of leadership. Hence the significance of the huge number of public pledges of loyalty that signalled the denouement of the Razaleigh Affair (Muzaffar, 1989, pp. 70–7).

An especially insightful aspect of Muzaffar's (1979, pp. 95ff.) analysis is the way in which he dissolves the apparent contradiction between the patriarchalist framework within which the NEP was located and the explicitly modernisationist language in which it was couched. That is, what he points out is that, precisely by criticising traditional Malay culture as an obstacle to 'modernisation' in terms, I would add, that were very close to those found in the racist colonial discourse, such architects of the NEP as Mahathir actually emphasised both the Malays' need for protection (n.b. not benevolence) as well as UMNO's expectations as to their 'absolute loyalty'. Thus the Mahathir governments of the 1980s were especially robust in their dismissal of protests on the part of students, academics and public sector workers – all were deemed outrageously ungrateful for the opportunities that had been provided by the state. As Muzaffar summarises his argument, UMNO's conception of development is that it is something done *for* the people rather than the result of their labours and therefore their right. And for the same reasons, the party tends to conceive of state funds as its patrimony to be disposed of as it wishes so long as the condition of the Malays is improved in some way. This, of course, can have the effect of sometimes making it very difficult to distinguish between personal and community gain.

The intensity of the ideological crisis to which the NEP was both a response and a contributor was registered in the attempts to formulate an official state ideology that accompanied it. As one of the leading participants in this ideological work put it: 'The sad days of May 1969 came like a seizure attacking the heart of the nation – Kuala Lumpur. For this minor stroke, we should be grateful to God, for in his wisdom and mercy a warning signal was registered in the hearts of all men' (Ghazali, 1985, p. 68). This ideology was formulated by a communally representative National Consultative Council specially set up for the purpose and was eventually dubbed the *Rukunegara*. It was presented as a reaffirmation of the basic principles of the constitution and featured a Statement of Beliefs and a Statement of Principles which provided a 'lifting hand for the downtrodden and a direction finder for the lost' (ibid., p. 70). The statements of beliefs and principles read as follows:

> Our nation Malaysia . . . [is] dedicated –
> - to achieving greater unity of all her people
> - to maintaining a democratic way of life;
> - to creating a just society in which the wealth of the nation shall be equitably shared;
> - to ensuring a liberal approach to her rich and diverse cultural traditions;
> - to building a progressive society which shall be oriented to modern society and technology.
>
> We, her peoples, pledge our united efforts to attain these ends guided by these principles –
> - Belief in God,

- Loyalty to King and Country,
- Upholding the Constitution,
- Rule of Law,
- Good Behaviour and Morality.   (Quoted in ibid., 1985, p. 69)

Although the melding of patriarchalist and modernisationist themes is readily apparent in these Statements, the overall patriarchalism was made most explicit in some of the authoritative commentary on the social role that the statements were expected to play:

> The *Rukunegara* will mould a predictable pattern of behavious capable of rationalisation and will expose for corrective measures deviationism and schimistic (sic) tendencies . . . The *Rukunegara* inhibits the individuals from indulging in subjectivism or solipsism and at the same time will prevent the society from being . . . [defiled by] turning to fascism or communism.
> (Ibid., p. 70)

In the event, despite some attempts to embed the content of the Statements within the routines of the society, especially through the state's cultural policy, they proved incapable of containing 'subjectivism', in the form of factionalism, even within the UMNO leadership itself. Thus the Razaleigh Affair can be read as, in part at least, a battle over which leader could best be trusted to put *Rukunegara* into effect. However, it must also be said that more mundane considerations of access to patronage and therefore to means of securing loyalty as well as a powerful reassertion of traditional Malay patriarchalism with its stress on 'absolute loyalty' appear to have played a more important role in securing Mahathir's eventual triumph than the dexterous deployment of *Rukunegara*. The prime minister's apparently very catchy campaign song was called *Lagu Setia* (The Loyalty Song):

> 'Loyalty'
> For our beloved nation
> A devoted outpouring of loyal service;
> For our much lauded Sultans
> Allegiance is undivided:
> To our leaders and to the people
> Service is rendered in obedient loyalty.
> Working together, striving together
> In faithful service to all,
> Ready to sacrifice anything, everything
> To maintain and secure the people's trust;
> We vow our absolute allegiance

> To our faith, people, and nation.
> 'Loyalty'
> (Quoted and subjected to a detailed analysis in Kessler, 1992, pp. 150ff.)

Moreover, even within the sphere of cultural policy the communal ecumenicalism of the *Rukunegara* has failed to displace or even to check the burgeoning 'Malay culture industry' in its multifaceted invention and celebration of Malay tradition (Kahn, 1992; Kessler, 1992). However, the modernistic images that accompanied the television version of *Lagu Setia*, the modernistic inspiration behind *Vision 2020*, and the recent efforts to assert the applicability of the rule of law to the sultanate (Kok, 1994, pp. 25–6), all suggest that what is being attempted ideologically is something other than a simple invention of tradition. Specifically, they suggest that a strenuous effort is underway to identify the 'substantive protectors' rather than the 'symbolic protectors' as the true protectors of Malay tradition and the rightful recipients of the Malay people's loyalty. Thus, the attempt to give an ideological form to the 'consociationalism' that *Rukunegara* represented is currently off the agenda. No doubt it will remain so until this identification of the Malay community with their new protectors has been securely established. Under such circumstances, the construction of a discourse of consociationalism that is more truely hybrid than the culturally hierarchical *Rukunegara* should not be too difficult to achieve. After all, as the discussions of Hong Kong and Singapore in the present text attest, patriarchalism is typically hegemonic amongst Chinese populations too. Indeed, since his sweeping victory in the 1995 elections this seems to have been appreciated by Dr Mahathir. He has recently made several speeches in which he has sought to specify a sense of citizenship that departs from traditional consociationalism, *Bangsa Malaysia*. This he defines in the following way: '[It] means people who are able to identify themselves with the country, speak Bahasa Malaysia [the Malay language], and accept the Constitution' (*South China Morning Post*, 12 September 1995). However, what is conspicuously absent from this attempt to reconfigure the nature of Malaysian citizenship is any specification of citizenship rights in the Marshallian sense of social entitlements. Jobs, educational opportunities and some help with housing are virtually all any section of the population has ever been promised or provided with. Moreover, despite the fact that a National Social Welfare Policy was belatedly introduced in 1990 which committed the government to the creation of a 'caring society', this seems unlikely to make much difference. As the document that launched the policy declared, the intention is: 'to create a society that upholds the spirit of self-reliance, equal opportunities and the practice of a caring society' (quoted in Mohamed, 1994, p. 70). As this statement, which contains strong echoes of American Social Modernism, suggests, caring is regarded largely as a matter of charity and therefore when performed by the state available only to the most 'deserving' of the poor. The list of groups entitled to benefit from the extremely rudimentary Social Assistance Programme with its stress on workhouse-style 'rehabilitation centres' adds transvestites to the familiar categories but, of course, excludes the unemployed and those who might be termed the 'plain poor'. All this said, if the present skills 'bottleneck' is to be overcome, let alone the massive restructuring envisaged in *Vision 2020* achieved, an equally massive increase in non-discriminatory training and retraining opportunities is and will be required (Kok, 1994, pp. 136ff.; Rajah, 1995, p. 89). Also, some form of income support, again non-discriminatory, will necessarily be part and parcel of any such programme if it is to provide such opportunities of the quality and on the scale required.

In the meantime and in the absence of any more substantive citizenship rights, the loyalty of the minority populations hangs on the rather slender thread represented by the prosperity currently enjoyed and the enhancement promised by *Vision 2020*. The effectivity of this thread is both reinforced and undermined by the limitations on civil rights that apply to the minority communities in particular. These limitations reinforce the attractiveness of the modernistic promises because, of course, they make it very difficult even to argue for anything more. However, they also undermine the allure of these promises in so far as they force the Chinese community in particular both to forge economic links with other *Nanyang* (South Seas or Overseas Chinese) communities as well as with China itself, and, I would suggest, to see their interests lying more in the broader, American-sponsored APEC conception of a Pacific economic community than the narrower 'Asian' conception currently favoured by the UMNO leadership.

PATRIARCHALIST INSTITUTIONS AND THE CLASS STRUCTURE

The results of the NEP and its political and ideological supplements have been impressive in narrowly 'racial' terms. They have also been unsurprising with respect to the distribution of wealth and incomes within the

population as a whole, and disappointing as regards changes in the occupational structure. Malays increased their share of the nation's wealth
from 2.4 per cent in 1970 to 20.3 per cent in 1990, and there are reasons
for thinking that it may have in fact increased still further were one able
to take account of ethnically unidentified holdings (Jomo, 1990, p. 160).
Further, they increased their share of technical and professional jobs,
with the result that it now matches their demographic position, and also
very significantly increased their proportions of administrative, managerial
and sales jobs (ibid., pp. 164–5). It is true that the proportion of the
population living in poverty has been strikingly reduced, from 37 per
cent in 1973 to 17.1 per cent in 1990. However, the state has done little
to redistribute land so as to enhance the independence of the poorer
Malay farmers and so enable them to escape from their present dependence on the government subventions that make them vulnerable to
political pressures (Jomo, 1990, p. 164; Rogers, 1989, p. 783). Although
employment in the secondary and tertiary sectors has increased greatly,
the proportion of the whole labour force employed in middle-class occupations only increased by just over 4 per cent after 1970 to stand at 14.1
per cent by 1985. Corroboratively, inequalities of income and wealth
have increased significantly since *Merdeka* (Jomo, 1990, pp. 89–95).

In sum, by virtue of its Pacific-Asian location and because of the
exigencies of development in the region, a social formation that was very
distant from the core of Pacific capitalism in geographical and social
terms has been transformed at the level of class relations in a distinctive
but apparently inexorable manner. Phenotypically, its class relations have
come to correspond more and more closely with the Japanese archetype:
its state has become more interventionist and authoritarian; its capital
structure has become more organised thanks to the growth of large,
state-owned or created holding companies and enterprises such as
Pernas, which controlled ninety-six companies in 1988 (Horii, 1991, pp.
294–6); and its ideological and legal formations have become more
explicitly patriarchalist, if recently slightly more inclusive communally.

In other words and to answer my 'Why?' question, the class balances
with respect to possession, control and title that, as elsewhere, were so
negative for labour during the colonial period have remained equally
negative and unchallenged by labour because of, rather than despite,
industrialisation and the consequent equalisation of the balances between the 'races'. The stress given to industrialisation as a vehicle for
creating employment opportunities for Malays, combined with the post-
emergency inhibition on the part of the Chinese population in relation

to participating in trade unions, has meant that the unions are still regarded as sectional organisations (albeit now representing the Malays and Indians instead of the Chinese and Indians). Moreover, since the unions owe the very existence of their Malay membership to the political party that the membership identifies with and votes for, it has proved very difficult for the unions to resist the ever-tightening restrictions on their activities since these have always been justified as part of the necessary prerequisites for industrialisation. Additionally, not only was full employment only achieved in the 1990s, but also agricultural employment remains a real and still viable alternative source of employment for those, especially Malays, who are dissatisfied with industrial work and conditions.

THE LAW, AUTHORITARIAN PATRIARCHALISM AND HUMAN RIGHTS

Because of the absence of British royal legal charters from the 'constitutional' arrangements of the Protectorates, there was no formal 'reception' of English law prior to the passage of the Civil Law Act of 1956. However, the Residents, the Brookes Rajahs in Sarawak and the North Borneo Company nevertheless allowed their judges to introduce the common law as circumstances demanded. Sometimes the Residents copied Indian, Straits or English statutes, and often the judges invoked English precedents simply because they knew no other way of thinking. The result was that, although all the principal bodies of English law were in fact received, the law was very unevenly developed and enforced across the states (Hooker, 1988, p. 392). Most interestingly, and despite the degree of uniformity belatedly brought about by the Civil Law Act, this means that in present-day Malaysia Muslim law (especially in Kelantan) and 'native' *adat* law (especially in Sarawak) have been and sometimes remain important sources of law in some states (Hooker, 1972).

However, apart from some elements of 'frozen' *adat* law that offer protection to native land titles in some areas (Hooker, 1972, p. 65), the structure of the civil law has been and remains as highly favourable to capital as the class balances outlined above suggest they should be. Thus, the rights in title of private property owners received constitutional protection in 1957, albeit in a somewhat qualified form that specifically allowed for deprivation 'in accordance with law' and compulsory acquisition with 'adequate compensation'. Similarly, contract law continues to favour stronger parties as regards possessory relations in general, although since *Merdeka* it has shown some solicitousness for the interests of weaker parties by softening the standards to be applied in finding 'consideration'. However, this softening does not yet add up to 'promissory estoppel'. Finally, tort law continues to exclude 'strict liability' in relation to the sale of goods, even in Penang and Mallaca where, because of the form that the Straits Settlements' reception statute took (see below, p. 231), consumers should strictly already have the benefits of the British Sale of Goods Act (1979).

The constitution offers protection to life, liberty, private property, and the rights of speech, expression, association and religion. It also provides that no person should be held in slavery or punished on the basis of retroactive legislation, and declares that all are equal before the law. However, these rights are significantly qualified as a consequence of three other attributes of the constitution (Tan et al., 1991, chs. 11–20). The first is the embedding in the constitution through Article 149 of the wide-ranging emergency powers introduced by the colonial government to deal with the communist insurgency and later made permanent by the passage of the Internal Security Act (1960). The latter allows renewable 'preventive detention' of up to sixty days if ordered by a police officer, and of up to two years if ordered by the minister of home affairs. Also supported by the same Article are a rigorous system of press licensing which appears to be unappealable and a Police Act, which requires all public meetings of more than five people to apply for a licence and allows the possibility of police controlled delays in the allowing of any appeals to the courts.

The breadth of the power to order preventive detention and the 'subjective' nature of the criteria that allow this breadth are both readily apparent if one examines the wording of Article 149 which validates any legislation seeking to give force to it with the following words:

> [If it is necessary because of] action taken or *threatened* by a substantial body of persons, whether inside or *outside* the country
>
> (a) to cause or to cause a substantial number of citizens to *fear* organised violence against persons or property;
>
> (b) to excite *disaffection* against the president or government;
>
> (c) to promote feelings of *ill-will* and hostility between different races or classes of the population likely to cause violence;
>
> (d) to procure the alteration, otherwise than by lawful means, of anything by law established; or
>
> (e) which is *prejudicial* to the security of Malaysia. (emphasis added)

Significantly, the state's 'rights' in this area are far better protected than those whose suspension they may permit. That is, they are superior to all the citizenry's rights save for fragments of *habeas corpus* – specifically, the right to be quickly informed of the grounds for one's detention, and to consultation with legal counsel. The only formal protection provided against the abuse of this truely draconian power is that represented by the existence of an Advisory Board to the minister of home affairs. However, this Board now possesses neither the independence nor the power to make decisions that bind the minister that its colonial predecessor possessed. Moreover, its procedures appear to run counter to those commonly understood to be required by the principle of 'natural justice' in that detainees are not allowed to know the nature of the evidence against them (Kehma-S, 1989, p. 46). Finally, when juridical moves were eventually made to reduce the subjectivity of the criteria which allow preventive detention and move in the direction of a 'clear and present danger' standard, they were overruled by legislative action.

The second unhelpful constitutional attribute is the general rider appended to the rights of speech, expression, assembly and association by Article 14(2)(a), which allows parliament to impose, even on its own members and especially on labour and members of educational institutions, 'such restrictions as it deems necessary or expedient' for purposes of national security, public order, morality, and in cases of contempt of court, defamation, and incitement to offence (Tan et al., 1991, pp. 645, 672). There is also a complicating factor represented by the 'special position' of the Malay population, which is that it allows for some derogation of the right to equality before the law where the interests of the Malays and other sections of the population clash. The 'special position' clause also provides legitimation for the 1970 amendments to the colonial Sedition Act, which restricted speech and expression by outlawing any questioning in any media and in any location (including parliament) of the 'special position' or such incidents of it as the sovereignty, powers or prerogatives of the sultanate, the position of *Bahasa Malaysia* as the national language, and the citizenship laws. Finally, as if all these restrictions were not sufficient, there is also an Official Secrets Act which was first passed in 1972 and has been amended several times since with the result that there are very stringent limits on the free speech of civil servants as it relates to governmental and administrative matters. Offences under this Act carry mandatory jail sentences of between one and fourteen years.

The restrictions on human rights that this set of texts represents have often been actualised. Not only is most of the media either government or UMNO-owned and as a result seldom critical of the status quo, but many of the relatively few independent publications that do exist have been shut down on one or more occasions either temporarily or permanently. Referring to the ISA alone, 3,000 people were detained under it for varying periods between 1960 and 1980, but by the end of 1986 there were only 40 detainees. The most spectacular recent occasion on which the fearful nature of the extent of these restrictions on the exercise of otherwise constitutional rights became apparent was the police sweep in 1987 known as 'Operation Lallang'. In the course of this sweep, and despite the fact that it basically arose out of the intra-UMNO Razaleigh Affair, most of the 106 people arrested were opposition leaders, trade unionists, and NGO activists such as Muzaffar Chandra.

The Supreme Court refused to intervene. However, in the following year the lord president of the Court, Tun Salleh Abbas, publically criticised the government for not respecting judicial independence (Lee, 1995, ch. 3). The government subsequently charged him and two of his fellow justices who had supported him with 'misbehaviour', and appointed a tribunal to decide on the issue. The tribunal's decision went against the justices and they were removed from their positions. Ironically, the lord president's criticisms were confirmed by the passage in the same year of the Constitutional Amendment Act, which diminished the dignity of the Court by depriving it of the 'vesting' power to constitute itself which it had hitherto shared with the executive and the legislature. All this said, by 1989 there were only 70 ISA detainees, and by 1994 only 6 communists remained in detention. However, in the latter year and in a move which perhaps signifies the opening of a new chapter in the history of the UMNO state's difficulties in reconciling the discourse of loyalty with a changing social reality, 11 leaders of a 'fundamentalist' Islamic sect, Al Arqam, were detained under the ISA, whilst 150 of their followers were arrested under the Societies Act.

Thus far I have been content to talk as if the limitations on civil rights that have just been outlined affect all citizens equally. However, I will end this section by indicating that they are particularly restrictive in their consequences for the minority communities. Since the vast majority of the Indian population are property-less labourers, the limitations on the rights of labour whose nature and development I will outline in the following section should be read as particularly detrimental to them. Thus, at this juncture I will only say something about the effects of these restrictions on the Chinese population. This is because, as the largest minority community and the major holders of capital, it is their property and cultural rights that have most often been infringed. Thus, they have been confronted with the absence of government-supported Chinese or English language secondary and tertiary education, reduced opportunities to pursue higher education, the forced transfer of shares in Chinese-owned companies to Malays at below market prices, exclusions from certain areas of activity such as landholding and running taxi companies, and pro-Malay government favouritism in the awarding of contracts (Minority Rights Group, 1992).

LABOUR LAW AND AUTHORITARIAN PATRIARCHALISM

The history of labour organisation in what is now Malaysian territory begins with the arrival of Chinese contract labour in Penang which was then part of the Straits Settlements Colony. As the Chinese established themselves in commercial and handicraft occupations, and as they spread across Peninsula Malaya, attracted especially by the opening of the Perak tin mines in 1850, they also established guilds modelled on those then in existence in China (Gamba, 1962, ch.1). Little is known about the internal workings and history of these guilds. From mid-century onwards the Chinese typically arrived on the Peninsula as contract labourers and therefore with non-negotiable terms of employment. However, on the basis of what we know as a result of Trocki's (1990) pathbreaking work on the Singaporean guilds, it seems safe to assume that, whether they were employer-dominated combinations of employers and employees (*Tong ka*) or employee-only associations (*Sai Ka*), the Malayan guilds too performed some regulatory functions when there were disputes over not just the prices of manufactured items but also the terms and conditions of work, and as well provided some benefits for indigent or deceased members.

Because of their secret character and indeed the complexity of social and political relations amongst the Chinese settler population, it was often difficult for both the Malays and their British 'protectors' to distinguish between the guilds and the triad societies such as the Hung Hoay. The latter is thought to have been a branch of the mainland Tien Ti Hui (Heaven and Earth League), an organisation that originated as a society committed to the overthrow of the Manchu Dynasty. Fear of the triads led to the replication of the earlier Hong Kong Societies Ordinance throughout the Protectorates in 1895. More or less simultaneously, a Protector of the Chinese and an Indian Immigration Agent were appointed for the Straits Settlements and the Federated Malay States.

On the recommendation of these officials, the import of indentured labour from India was prohibited in 1910 and from China in 1914. A Labour Department with special responsibility for Indian and, should need arise, Malay labour was established in 1910 (Jomo and Todd, 1994, pp. 4–6). In 1935, this department also gained responsibility for Chinese labour (Roberts, 1964, ch. 8). Apart from compiling statistics and overseeing some very rudimentary labour standards, the Labour Department sometimes intervened in disputes as a mediator.

Gradually, the regulations defining what sorts of societies could apply for registration were loosened so as to allow the legal existence of the trade-union type mutual aid societies. Between 1928 and 1941, ninety such societies were registered in Peninsula Malaya (Gamba, 1962, p. 4). The longest established and most effective of these was the Selangor Engineering Mechanics Association, which came into existence in 1875 and maintained links with the similarly named societies in Canton and Hong Kong. The most aggressive was the coalminers society in Batu Arang which engaged in a series of violent but successful confrontations with the mine-owners in 1935, 1937 and 1938 (Gamba, 1962, p. 7; Roberts, 1964, p. 25). By this time, as in Hong Kong and Singapore, Malayan Chinese labour politics was very much affected by mainland Chinese politics, its rivalries and the growing strength of the Communist Party. This was eventually to lead to some seventy unions joining the General Labour Union (GLU) sponsored by the Malayan Communist Party (MCP) and involving themselves in both the anti-Japanese and anti-British revolutionary guerilla movements of the 1940s and 1950s.

During these formative years unionism or near-unionism was largely restricted to the Chinese population (Jomo and Todd, 1994, ch. 3). The Malays remained confined within the traditional agricultural sector and its rigorously patriarchalist system of social and economic relations. And the Indian labourers, who had begun arriving as convict and indentured labour in the latter part of the nineteenth century, were largely confined to the British-owned rubber and tea estates and did not begin to form even mutual aid societies until the late 1930s (Gamba, 1962, pp. 11–12). In the meantime, belatedly, but thanks to the same shift in colonial labour policy that was outlined in the earlier discussion of developments in Hong Kong, a basis was created for the eventual acknowledgement of a legitimate role for trade unions by the intoduction in 1940 and 1941 of three Ordinances: the Industrial Courts Ordinance, the Trade Union Act, and the Trade Disputes Ordinance. After the restoration of British colonial rule and in line with Britain's ratification of most of the central

ILO Conventions on behalf of its colonies (Roberts, 1964, ch. 9), London sent a former trade union official, John Brazier, to Malaya to convince both the local administration and the trade unions of the merits of this legislative package and to advise on its implementation (for an account of his activities, see Gamba, 1962, ch. 4).

Given their British origins, the founding texts of Malaysia's labour law grounded labour's rights in the familiar 'immunities'. As in Hong Kong, but much more controversially, this legislative package made registration a prerequisite for the enjoyment of any rights and continued most of the restrictions of the British Trade Disputes and Trade Unions Act (1927) upon which it was based – the prohibition of sympathy and political strikes, the outlawing of the closed shop in the public service, and the imposition of stringent restrictions on picketing and political fund-raising (Gamba, 1957, chs. 7 and 8). What made the package a far greater source of controversy in Malaya and Singapore than in Hong Kong was the existence of a much better organised and militant labour movement in the form of the resurgent, communist-led General Labour Union which engaged in a campaign of strikes and organising drives that has not been equalled before or since (Gamba, 1962, ch. 7; Jomo and Todd, 1994, ch. 4; Stenson, 1970, ch. 6). Additionally, the situation was complicated by the 'racial' dimension given to labour disputes by the fact that the majority of trade unionists were then Chinese whilst both the symbols and enforcers of law and order were Malay. Responding largely to developments in Singapore, in 1948 the GLU leadership decided to go underground and throw in its lot with the insurrectionary forces.

During the first few years of the Emergency the colonial government pursued a policy of deregistering communist-controlled unions and very cautiously encouraging the formation of 'responsible' unions (Gamba, 1962, ch. 10). The number of legitimate trade unionists declined by 78 per cent between 1948 and 1950. There were virtually no strikes. And with the decamping of the Chinese, Indian unionists and leaders quickly became pre-eminent. In 1950, the MCP revived its trade union activities and this forced the government to adopt a more supportive stance as regards the growth of a responsible union movement (Gamba, 1962, ch. 11; Jomo and Todd, 1994, ch. 5). Union membership began to increase again and the government's Labour Advisor brokered the formation of a new federation, the Malayan Trade Union Council (MTUC), whose existence gave the trade union movement a legitimate national presence again. Also the government allowed the public service unions to form their own federation and thus confirmed that in its view there was nothing intrinsically bad about trade unionism. Although some effective organisations emerged, notably the Indian Plantation Workers' Union (PWU), the movement never regained its former vitality, nor much of its support amongst the Chinese population who preferred to place their faith in communally oriented political organisations. Nevertheless, the total number of trade unionists did gradually increase until 1965 when it reached a peak of 325,000. Thereafter, it began a gradual decline that has continued down to the present. However, with the coming of the NEP and its Malay-oriented industrialisation, there has been a gradual rise in the number of Malay trade unionists.

The first post-*Merdeka* piece of labour legislation was the Trade Union Ordinance of 1959. Despite the ending of the Emergency, the amendments to the pre-existing colonial statute that the Ordinance contained required all unions to re-register on the basis of even more demanding registration criteria. The term 'trade union' was defined in very narrow economic and occupational terms, thus outlawing general unions. Also, the Registrar of Trade Unions was given very wide investigatory and decision-making powers in all matters concerned with registration, and some offences under the Ordinance continued to be subject to criminal penalties. Nevertheless the unions prospered and in response to this, as well as to the new Emergency created by the 'Confrontation' with Indonesia between 1963 and 1966, labour's freedoms were further restricted by still more amendments to the Trade Unions Ordinance in 1965 and the passage of the Industrial Relations Act of 1967 (Jomo and Todd, 1994, ch. 6). The 1965 amendments substituted appeals to the Minister of Labour for appeals to the courts in the case of refusals of registration and other complaints against the Registrar, and prohibited inter-union competition in the same trades, occupations and industries. The 1967 Act imposed a set procedure in relation to the granting of employer recognition to unions. This procedure involved a requirement that a majority of the labour force concerned should indicate their desire for a union and, having declared recognition to be a non-strikeable issue, made the enforcement of valid recognition claims a matter for the Director General of Industrial Relations. The Act also consolidated several earlier *ad hoc* measures which had banned industrial action on the part of government employees and imposed compulsory arbitration across a wide range of essential services. However, collective agreements were made legally binding provided they had been submitted to the tripartite Industrial Court set up under the Act.

Subsequently, in the wake of the 'May 13th Incident', a series of 'emergency' regulations were promulgated which resulted in issues such as transfers, job changes, promotions, hirings, and most causes of dismissal becoming non-negotiable and therefore non-strikeable. Additionally, these regulations provided for the availability of government conciliation services and binding arbitration by the Industrial Court, where either the parties concerned jointly, or the Minister of Labour unilaterally, requests it. The latter possibility has made legal strikes a great rarity and even caused the courts to be uncertain as to whether or not the right to strike still exists in Malaysia (Ayadurai, 1985, pp. 88–91). Moreover, although the tripartite nature of the Court means that its establishment meant that labour gained some 'powers' in return for its lost 'liberties' and 'immunities', these were minimal. This is because the union movement has no formal say whatosoever in deciding who its representatives should be since they are chosen by the government. In making its awards the Court is enjoined to act with equity and on the merits of the case, always having regard, however, to the public interest. When these regulations were formally incorporated into the Industrial Relations Ordinance on the reconvening of parliament in 1971, they were accompanied by a further set of amendments. This required that companies designated 'Pioneer Industries' as part of the NEP should not conclude collective agreements that improved upon the minimum conditions of employment set out in the Employment Ordinance that had been passed simultaneously.

The latter ordinance provides for the protection of wages (including those of sub-contracted employees), the limitation of the working week to 48 hours and the payment of overtime rates, the taking of rest periods, rest days, paid sick leave and holidays, the payment of specified minimum termination and redundancy benefits, and finally the holding of a 'due inquiry' in the case of dismissals for misconduct (Ayadurai, 1985, pt. B). All of these rights are enforced by a 'quasi-judicial' Labour Court, whose decisions are appealable to the Director General of Labour and thence to the High Court. Finally, there is also legislation petaining to health and safety, and industrial injuries.

At the same time, two sets of amendments were also made to the Trade Union Ordinance. The first set allowed the Registrar of Trade Unions (now the director general of the Department of Trade Unions) to refuse registration to a union if he or she considered that an appropriate union already existed. In this way the emergence of alternative and possibly more militant unions was preempted even where what might be called 'the licensed unions' had made no attempt to organise the employees concerned. The second set of amendments withdrew the right of unions to create political funds and prohibited union officials from holding positions in political parties. In 1975, reflecting what appeared to be the increasingly corporatist nature of the industrial relations that emerged in the wake of the 1971 legislation, and as was most clearly demonstrated by the increasingly frequent resort to binding arbitration as a way of resolving disputes, the Malaysian Trade Union Congress (MTUC) and the Malayan Council of Employers Associations (MCEO) signed a *Code of Conduct for Industrial Harmony* which hymned the arbitration system and sought to extend it. In this document the parties agreed that:

> only with an abundance of goodwill combined with constant consultation and communication . . . we can hope to contain the destructive expression of industrial conflict and encourage a more equitable and efficient system for the benefit of those involved and the community at large.

The lack of harmony between the parties as to what the actual significance of the Code might be was made very clear later the same year at an ILO-sponsored conference in Manila. The representatives of the MTUC stated that they saw it as the forerunner of a Swedish-style 'basic agreement', but the then director general of Industrial Relations candidly stated that the government aimed:

> to increase employment opportunities through the application of a neo-classical economic theory which posits increased employment opportunities in response to the decrease in labour costs . . . (and) to create an investment climate competitive enough for Malaysia to attract more investments.
> (Rajah, 1975, p. 151; see also, Jomo and Todd, 1994, ch. 7)

These measures do seem to have had at least some of the effects desired by the government (Jomo and Todd, 1994, ch. 8). In the early 1980s, unions still organised a mere 10 per cent of the labour force in small and fragmented organisations. The number of strikes fell from an average of sixty-five per year in the 1960s to an average of twenty-seven in the years 1979–81. Presumably, these two factors, plus the fact that the electronics industry remained unorganised, did indeed contribute to Malaysia's growing attractiveness to overseas investors. One of the 1978 strikes was, however, a long drawn out and internationally very visible affair involving the state airline, MAS, and the detention of several union leaders under the ISA. The coincidence of this strike with the difficult global economic conditions of the late 1970s and the early 1980s, led the new government of Dr Mahathir to attempt another turn of the neo-classical screw on labour, only this time its positive gloss had an orientalist rather than European corporatist tint to it in the form of the 'Look East Policy' and the slogan of 'Malaysia Inc.'(Machado, 1987). In 1980, yet another set of amendments to the industrial relations legislation was introduced which further increased the state's controls over unions and their activities. However, far more significant was the ongoing promotion of a new, Japanese-style 'work ethic' and 'in-house' or enterprise unions (the latter received explicit legislative sanction in 1989). Thanks to the reinforcement of the labour discipline by the increased unemployment levels of the early 1980s, and the encouragement of legal and illegal immigration from poorer neighbouring countries (Jomo, 1990, p. 219), Malaysia was in a very good position to benefit from the revival of the global investment that occurred in the mid-1980s.

All that said, the state and capital have not entirely had things their own way since 1981. When the unions have found the resources to appeal to them, the courts have on occasion thwarted both capital and the state. During the 1980s these occasions became fewer and fewer as judicial autonomy was undermined. The result is that judicial autonomy, in the field of labour law at least, is now more or less restricted to that allowed by the common law principles of equity. Thus, for example, as recently as 1990 the High Court in Penang upheld an injunction freezing the organising efforts of an in-house union that had been recognised by both the company involved and the director general of the Department of Trade Unions (DGTU). The Penang court recognised the fact that the plaintiff, a pre-existing national union, had been denied the chance to win employee support in violation of the principles of equity and so was entitled to the protection afforded by an injunction (*Kesatuan Sekerja Pembuatan Barangan Galian Bukan Logam* v. *Director General of Trade Unions and Others*, 1990 3 MLJ, pp. 231–9).

However, equity is a very labile concept and given also the increased serviceability of English precedent in the area of labour injunctions, it does not seem unreasonable to fear that even the rules of equity may soon cease to protect labour. More specifically, it does not seem unreasonable to fear that the assumption as to the formal equality of the parties to the employment relation which still underpins English law will eventually be replaced by a Japanese-inspired patriarchalist assumption as to their intrinsic inequality that is unqualified by any notion of enforceable benevolence. In words drawn from the Ministry of Human Resources' National Labour Policy of 1991:

> Unions and management *must* regard each other as partners in economic progress . . . The parties *must* also adopt a proactive approach to industrial

relations which requires close rapport and consensus-building . . . There is a need for management to encourage worker participation through consultation such that workers are treated as members of the organisational family . . . Trade unions *should* promote positive work and productivity attitudes among the workforce . . . (emphasis added)

By 1988, the percentage of all trade unions that were of the in-house type stood at 54.5 per cent, whilst their percentage in manufacturing stood at 38.2 per cent. In sum, in the words of two recent commentators:

> There are increasing signs that the current Malaysian government dislikes the adversarial role adopted by trade unions, especially in the government sector, and would rather such organizations devoted their energies to social and cultural activities. Women workers in the government sector have already been organized along these lines by the formation of PUSPANITA, an association of female employees in the government sector. Since 1983, such organizations have been formed in most ministries . . .   (Arudsothy and Littler, 1993, p. 129)

The Ministry of Labour claims that PUSPANITA is intended to 'foster good-will and harmony among female employees and wives of employees of the civil service irrespective of rank, including the families'. It may well be that organisations such as PUSPANITA are intended to be alternatives to unions, which appear to be increasingly regarded by government as an unacceptable 'cultural import' (Arudsothy and Littler, 1993, pp. 122–3). In sum, then, I have answered my 'How?' question by outlining the loyalty-centredness of Malaysian patriarchalism and showing how it articulates with the way in which the tensions associated with the society's 'racial' composition have been institutionalised. In the conclusion that follows I will answer my 'What?' question by arguing that, because of the factors outlined above in answering my first two questions, Malaysia is still a long way from possessing a human rights regime that represents an instance of 'enforceable benevolence'.

CONCLUSION: PATRIARCHALISM AND THE TEMPTATIONS TO AUTHORITARIANISM

To conclude, the features of the Malaysian social formation that would seem to virtually guarantee respect for human rights have failed to secure such an outcome. Malaysia remains a democracy, but because of the demographic preponderance of the Malays, their constitutionally sanctioned 'special position', and the communal nature of political organisation, Malaysia has effectively been a one-party state since *Merdeka*. In the absence of the judicial supremacy as regards constitutional matters which had been advocated by the outgoing colonial administration (Means, 1970, pp. 186–8), and in the absence since the early 1970s of government self-restraint as regards taking advantage of the Malay's 'special position' (cf. Muzaffar, 1990, p. 124), the rule of law has become more a matter of proper procedure than of allowing the autonomy that comes from following the principle of consistency, more a matter of restricting rights in the proper manner than allowing rights to have their effects. In addition, the adoption by both the Bar and the Bench of the self-denying ordinance represented by the English 'black letter' method of law-finding has prevented the former from making, and the latter from accepting, American-style common law arguments that rest upon such factors as the 'intent' of legislative authors and/or issues of substantive justice. Finally, because of the turn of events in Britain, those who have sought to counter the negative consequences of all the above for labour were no longer able to draw upon supportive English precedents. Indeed, the anti-labour nature of those events, legal as well as political, seemed only to offer cosmopolitan confirmation of the correctness of the derogation of labour's rights that was intensified after Malaysia began to 'Look East'.

The net result of these failures has been a repetition of the Japanese experience as regards the shrinkage of labour's freedoms, but, despite the presence of some enforced labour standards, without any of the compensations represented by either the housing provided in Hong Kong or the 'lifetime employment' enjoyed by much of Japan's labour force – that is, with little in the way of traditional benevolence let alone 'enforceable benevolence'. In sum, then, a consideration of the Malaysian case provides striking confirmation of the difficulties created by 'racial' diversity, given the current strength of transnational and national capitalist forces, for efforts to secure the 'attachment' of labour and human rights to their intended bearers. If the consequences of the realisation of the successive 'state projects' that have resulted in Malaysia's integration into the circuits of Pacific capitalism have been so negative for its labour and human rights record, at first sight it might appear that tragically the Philippines may still represent the future for Pacific-Asian labour and that there is little hope for any deep entrenchment of respect for human rights in any of the Pacific Asian nations. Contrary to received opinion, it seems to me that the Singaporean experience suggests otherwise.

CHAPTER SIX

SINGAPORE AND THE POSSIBILITY OF ENFORCEABLE BENEVOLENCE

Issues associated with 'race' have played a much smaller direct role in defining the nature of Singaporean society than they have in Malaysia. This is because a clear majority of the population is Chinese, 76 per cent in 1987. The remainder of the population comprises Malays, who made up 15 per cent of the population in the same year, Indians, who made up 6 per cent, and 'Others', who made up 3 per cent. The Sumatran words from which the name Singapore is derived mean 'Lion Island'. The coat of arms of the present republic features what heraldic experts term a 'lion rampant'. What I want to argue in this chapter is, first, the unsurprising thesis, given that it represents an instance *par excellence* of Pacific capitalism, that Singapore is an island of rampant patriarchalism. And second, the perhaps more novel thesis for a socialist sociologist at least, that this could carry a positive significance. That is, I wish to bring out the luxurious as well as the unchecked nature of the rampancy of Singapore's patriarchalism and so demonstrate that states may achieve very high levels of social and economic justice despite their openness to transnational forces. Indeed what the Singaporean experience suggests is that, where the flexibility and self-disciplining of the population are the keys to economic survival, such levels of social and economic justice are necessary if nation states are to thrive under conditions where transnational forces are dominant. In sum, I wish to argue that for all the undoubted civil oppressiveness of the current structure of Singaporean society, the republic is structurally closer to representing a model of what a human rights regime premised upon 'enforceable benevolence' might look like than any other society in the region, including Japan.

That said, structural proximity does not necessarily imply actual proximity since the practical configuration of social relations sometimes means that massive social mobilisations are required to achieve even very minor structural changes. A case in point would be the very serious riots that finally galvanised the Hong Kong government into introducing a small measure of equity to the individual contract of employment and the use made of the Colony's wealth. Whether actions on anything like this scale would be necessary for Singapore to achieve its potential as a paradigm case of 'enforceable benevolence' is almost entirely up to the party that has ruled the republic for the past thirty-five years, the People's Action Party (PAP).

In what follows, I will seek to give plausibility to my somewhat counter-intuitive thesis concerning Singapore's potential model status by focusing on the more than normally critical part played by a highly restrictive system of labour law in the emergence of its corporatist political economy. Thus, first, I will explain why labour law has played so important a role. And second, I will specify the very small structural changes to the legal system and its discourse that would be necessary to initiate a more libertarian and pluralist reconstitution of these relations.

FROM A COLONIAL TO AN ACTIVE PATRIARCHALIST STATE

The history of the contemporary Singaporean state begins in 1819 when Stamford Raffles, acting on behalf of the East India Company, signed an agreement with the local ruler, the Temenggong of Johore, which allowed the Company to establish a trading 'factory' on the island. Until 1867 when it became a Crown Colony, Singapore and its rapidly growing international but largely immigrant Chinese population were governed in a generally light but sometimes harsh manner by, successively, local agents of the Company, the Company's Straits Settlements presidency located in Penang, and finally the Company's Bengal presidency located in Calcutta (Chew and Lee, 1991; Lee, 1989; Turnbull, 1989, chs. 1, 2). The rule of law arrrived in Singapore in 1826 with the granting to the Company of a Royal Charter of Justice, which replaced the previous system of informal justice administered by the *kapitans* (leaders) of the various communities. The result was that by and large the formal courts dealt with the 'European' community and the other communities instituted their own systems for resolving disputes and dispensing justice. In short, the early Singapore state consisted of a skeletal and under-resourced executive answerable to a distant and uninterested Company

217

bureaucracy, supplemented by a judicial system with a very restricted writ, as well as by occasional and highly transitory legislative institutions (for accounts of the political development and gradual integration of the Chinese community during the nineteenth century, see Yen, 1995; Yong, 1991).

The state of the Crown Colony of the Straits Settlements, which was created in 1867, and whose principal components were Penang and Malacca in addition to Singapore, was characterised by the same relationship to London, possessed the same structure, and operated in the same way as that of Hong Kong – to wit, a governor, an Executive Council (Exco), an independent judiciary whose decisions were appealable to the Judicial Committee of the Privy Council in London, a Legislative Council (Legco) composed of Official and appointed Unofficial members, and a proliferating set of advisory committees. For this reason, it is not necessary to repeat the more detailed account of this structure given in Chapter 4.

After the highly repressive interregnum represented by the Japanese Occupation of 1942–5, the Colony of the Straits Settlements was broken up. Penang and Malacca became part of the Malayan Union whilst Singapore became a separate entity in 1946. Reflecting the British government's assumption that even Singapore would eventually have to be granted its independence, either on its own or as part of a federal Malayan state of some kind, *de jure* localisation commenced within the Singaporean state structure far earlier than in Hong Kong. In 1948, the localisation of the civil service began and an elective element was introduced within Legco. The latter consisted of nine Officials and thirteen Unofficials (seven appointed and six elected). Thus, party politics too came far earlier to Singapore than to Hong Kong, albeit on the basis of a franchise that restricted the right to vote to English-speaking, Straits-born or naturalised British subjects and which therefore excluded 50 per cent of the population (Chew and Lee, 1991; Turnbull, 1989, chs. 7, 8). The election was boycotted by the communist Malayan Democratic Union because it saw such a move as an obstacle to the realisation of its vision of a united Malaya. Three of the Unofficial seats were won by the moderate Progressive Party, an essentially middle-class party committed to a gradual movement in the direction of independence as part of a united Malaya, and the other three by similarly moderate independents.

As in the Malaya Federation, the twelve-year, anti-communist Emergency began the same year. This greatly reduced the civil liberties of all left-wing political and trade union organisations and not simply those of the communists. As a result, the mildly social-democratic Singapore Labour Party became the political standard bearer of the labour interest until it disintegrated because of factional rivalries in 1952. The number of elected Unofficials was increased to nine in 1951 and they were allowed to nominate two of their number to serve on Exco. The Progressives won six seats in the election of that year. In 1953, a much more radical reform of the state structure was proposed and accepted. The core institutions became: an executive Council of Ministers with nine members (three appointed and six recommended by the leader of the strongest party) and responsibility for everything except foreign affairs, internal security and defence; and a Legislative Assembly comprising twenty-five elected members, four nominated Unofficials, and three ex-officio ministers.

With the prospect of so much more to play for and with far better prospects of success thanks to the simultaneous quadrupling of the size of the electorate, the majority of the communist and non-communist Left returned to the constitutional political fray. Unexpectedly, the left were victorious. The Labour Front, led by David Marshall and backed by the moderate Singapore Trade Union Congress, won ten seats. The PAP, backed by the more militant communist unions and led by Lee Kwan Yew amongst others, won three. So unexpected was the result that at first there was chaos as the new government of Chief Minister Marshall sought both to overcome the resistance of the British to his demands for greater autonomy, and to counter the attempts of the left within the PAP and the unions to outflank him. After he failed to gain more autonomy for Singapore in his negotiations with the British, Marshall resigned. His place was taken by another Labour Front member, Lim Yew Hock. In 1957, Lim acted strongly against the extreme left, arrested thirty-five communist leaders, including five members of the PAP executive, and inadvertently greatly strengthened the hand of the non-communist, but not then anti-communist, Lee Kuan Yew. In the meantime, the size of the electorate and the preponderance of the Chinese within it had been further increased by a further liberalisation of citizenship requirements so that naturalisation was automatically given to all those with at least ten years residence who were prepared to swear loyalty to the Singaporean state as it was then constituted.

In 1958, the nature of the political terrain changed once again as a result of further changes to the state structure. The number of seats in the Legislative Assembly was increased to fifty-one, all of which were subject to electoral competition. But this time the nature of the relationship with London had changed also. Singapore had become self-governing in all areas save for foreign affairs, defence and internal security. The first two areas remained the prerogative of the British government, whilst the latter became the prerogative of an Internal Security Council which included representatives of Britain and the Malay Federation as well as of Singapore. The PAP won a landslide victory in the 1959 election, winning forty-three seats. However, it immediately acted to reassure capital by adding further restrictions to those already contained within the inherited colonial labour laws – left-wing unions were deregistered, political and sympathy strikes were banned, and a system of more or less compulsory arbitration was introduced. Not surprisingly, as the party's moderate leadership attempted to focus upon its long-cherished and economically driven goal of union with the rest of Malaya, it was once again challenged by its left-wing which feared the loss of local political autonomy that would result. In 1962, this left-wing bolted to form the Barisan Sosialis (BS). In the meantime the leadership had taken steps to ensure that no such challenge ever occurred again by transforming the party from a mass to a cadre organisation wherein the cadres were chosen by the leadership and were the only members with a vote. The task was made easier by the fact that most of its mass membership had anyway already shifted its allegiance to the BS. Although the PAP leadership won a large majority for its plans to become part of an enlarged Malayan federation, it once again had to resort to mass arrests of its own and other left-wingers before it felt secure. Singapore thus became briefly fully independent in September 1963, and soon after a part of the new state of Malaysia. In the election of that year the PAP won thirty-seven seats against the BS's thirteen.

In its disappointment at gaining so small a number of seats despite gaining close to the PAP's percentage of the vote, the BS turned to direct action, initiated a series of strikes, and saw its affiliate, the Singapore Association of Trade Unions, deregistered and its leadership arrested. For reasons outlined in Chapter 5, Singapore's sojourn as part of Malaysia did not last long and the city state was ejected against its will in August 1965 (for the Singapore government's own reasons for discomfort in the new state, see Turnbull, 1989, pp. 282–5). Aside from creating a non-executive president to fill the role of head of state, renaming the assembly as the parliament, and the very recent severing of the juridical link with the Privy Council in London, the state structure of today remains the same as in 1959.

This said, there have been significant changes as regards the relation-ship between the state and civil society and within what might be termed the infrastructure of the state. First, in 1965, what was termed a 'sym-biosis' occurred between the PAP government and the STUC (thereafter the National Trade Union Congress or NTUC). The latter was given a say in the PAP's decision-making as well as financial and administrative support from the government (Stenson, 1970 p. 249). In return, the NTUC agreed to accept a new set of legal restrictions on its freedom of action, including the granting of legal protection to the exercise of the managerial prerogative. What 'symbiosis' also means is that the NTUC's secretary-general is appointed or approved by the government and is given a cabinet seat. In return, the PAP nominates a number of NTUC officials as parliamentary candidates (currently, there are eight NTUC MPs).

The second change in state/society relations was that the party quickly established a set of new or transformed para-statal institutions (Hill and Lian, 1995, ch. 7). The most important of these were the Community Centres, Citizens' Consultative Committees, Residents' Committees, and the various state-sponsored 'communal' organisations. The community centres, which had initially been created by the colonial government in the early 1950s were given a formal status in 1964 and their adminis-tration was taken over by the People's Association, whose chairman is the prime minister and whose staff are all PAP members. The Citizens' Consultative Committees were created in 1965 and their members are all nominated by the government. The Residents' Committees on the public housing estates were created in 1978 and their members are all co-opted by the state's Housing Development Board (Quah and Quah, 1989). And finally, the various 'communal' organisations elect their own officials but are dependent upon government financial support (Hill and Lian, 1995, pp. 107ff.).

The changes to the state's infrastructure consisted of a steady increase in the number of parliamentary seats, and two changes in the represen-tational system. In 1981, the first of the changes created a special cate-gory of up to six non-constituency MPs who are not members of any political party and whose role, although they cannot vote on money and supply bills, constitutional amendments or confidence motions, is to introduce a non-political 'oppositional' presence into parliament. In 1988, the second of the representational changes grouped some of the constituencies into threes and required that at least one of the PAP candidates should be from a minority 'racial' background. Again, the purpose was to broaden the representativeness of a parliament dominated by a single party. Unsurprisingly, given that all this took place during a period of almost uninterrupted economic success and that the PAP controlled all the principal lines of patronage, the party held every single elected seat in parliament between 1965 and 1981.

Perhaps the most important single result of all these political developments was that prime minister Lee appears to have come to regard himself as the unchallengeable patriarch of his people (Chua, 1995, p. 36). Worse, with the introduction of IQ and altruism tests for PAP candidates, as well as the adoption of an even more rigorous selection procedure in relation to candidates for the elected presidency, it seems that the party came both to consider itself to have a monopoly of political intelligence and to imagine that it might be able to project aspects of his patriarchal virtue and consequent authority into the future. Thus, the principal role of the new elected presidency is to ensure that the nation's reserves (that is, the patrimony that Lee and his colleagues consider that they have bequeathed the nation) are not squandered for political purposes. In making this move, the PAP was responding to what it explicitly regarded as the signs of ingratitude or filial impiety represented by the steady decline in the level of the PAP's electoral support since the early 1980s. Although the party lost very few seats during the 1980s and 1990s, its share of the vote fell from 75 per cent in 1980 to 60 per cent in 1991. Since many of the 'lost' voters were from the lower income groups, in the PAP's view this created the possibility that some future opposition party might be able to gain their support by squandering the nation's reserves on welfare expenditure. In the words of the present prime minister, Goh Chok Tong: 'The PAP has *given* a lot but people want even more. When we are not able to fulfill this, a portion of the people say they will not support us' (*Straits Times*, 15 August 1995, emphasis added).

THE MAKING OF A TRANSNATIONAL ECONOMY

Like Hong Kong, Singapore only exists because of transnational economic forces. It too was created in the nineteenth century as an entrepôt linking Europe and especially Britain with Southeast Asia and beyond. It too was central to the opium trade (Trocki, 1990). It too gained its first experience of manufacturing by semi-processing the primary products of its hinterland, specifically rubber and tin. And finally, it too initially gained experience of the service industries through those associated with shipping and trade. One major difference from Hong Kong, however, was that Singapore's entrepôt activities were not interrupted by the Chinese Revolution. Another major difference was that Singapore was a much more important British military base than Hong Kong. Together, these factors meant that despite all the political strife Singapore's economy continued to grow steadily throughout the1950s and into the early 1960s. Singapore's moments of economic truth came in 1965 when it was expelled from Malaysia, and in 1967 when the British suddenly announced the closing of their bases. The first ruled out the possibility of pursuing the then still fashionable import-substitution industrialisation strategy and forced an export-led one. The second intensified the need to export still more – British military expenditures had hitherto accounted for 12.7 per cent of the GDP and the employment of 20 per cent of the labour force.

Lacking both domestic capital or equivalents to the Shanghainese industrialists who transformed the Hong Kong economy, the turn to foreign capital and the development of state-owned institutions and enterprises was unavoidable (Lim, 1988; Krause et al., 1987). The already existing Statutory Boards in the areas of port activities, housing and utilities were expanded and complemented by the creation of numerous spin-off enterprises – in 1984 government companies employed 8.5 per cent of the labour force in manufacturing (Krause et al., 1987, pp. 117–18). The measures that the government took in disciplining labour and generally making Singapore attractive to foreign capital worked. Foreign-owned manufacturing companies, especially in the electronics and the oil-processing industries rapidly established themselves, as did many banking and financial service corporations. Meanwhile, the government successfully promoted the tourist industry, and its housebuilding programme created a large construction industry. Full employment was reached in 1979, by which time the country had enjoyed fourteen years of average growth rates of around 10 per cent. Since that date the economy has continued to grow at around 8 per cent per year except during the recessionary years of 1985 and 1986. In line with this growth, foreign ownership has also increased: specifically, from 9.3 per cent of GDP in 1966 to 26 per cent in 1985. Foreign-owned companies are especially important in manufacturing where they employed 41.6 per cent of the labour force by 1985.

The industry mix remains more or less the same today, although there has been a concerted effort to move towards less labour-intensive industries since the early 1980s. There were three main reasons for this effort.

First, the desire to move up the global commodity chains and away from the levels where competition from countries like the Philippines and more recently China was intensifying. Second, the desire to increase the skill level of the labour force. And third, a fear of the possible social consequences of an ever-increasing dependence on immigrant labour, especially in the form of Bangladeshi construction workers and Filipina and Indonesian domestics. Since 1980 more than 10 per cent of the labour force have been workers from overseas.

The attempt to move up the commodity chains has been hampered by the fact that it will only happen if the Republic's transnational employers wish to do the same thing. Hence the government's continuing efforts to make the labour force attractive to such companies, most recently by shifting most of it into 'flexible' wage and salary systems. Also, because of the small size of the domestic capital base, promotion up the chain is not something that many Singaporean companies are capable of contributing to on their own. This said, with government support several of the larger local construction companies have recently embarked on large-scale projects in other parts of the region including China, which they manage from Singapore (Kwok, 1995). However, efforts to achieve the second two goals have met with more success through the rapid growth of the Singapore, Johor (Malaysia), Riau Islands (Indonesia) Growth Triangle, wherein Singapore is the administrative/research hub.

FROM *LAISSEZ-FAIRE* TO ACTIVE PATRIARCHALISM

As with Hong Kong, it is somewhat misleading to refer to the dominant mode of state discourse in colonial Singapore with the term *laissez-faire*. Whilst Singapore's colonial government may have been every bit as ideologically taciturn as its East-Asian equivalent, occasionally hymning 'self-reliance', 'free trade', 'the rule of law', and British 'racial' superiority, its actions similarly spoke volumes as to its preference for unfettered capitalism. Thus, on Carl Trocki's (1990) analysis, the major reason for the passage of the Singaporean Societies Ordinance was not so much the desire to control criminal Triad gangs as to suppress the collectivist form of economic organisation that the *kongsis* (societies) represented. Moreover, although the non-Europeans were for most of the nineteenth century largely left to administer themselves and were the recipients of very little in the way of paternalist legislation, the British undoubtedly saw themselves as racially superior social patriarchs. In the words of one late-nineteenth-century governor, Sir Frederick Weld:

> I think that capacity for governing is a characteristic of our race, and it is wonderful to see in a country like the Straits, a handful of Englishmen and Europeans, a large and rich Chinese community, tens of thousands of Chinese of the lowest coolie class, Arab and Parsee merchants, Malays of all ranks, and a sprinkling of all nationalities, living together in wonderful peace and contentment. It always seems to me that the common Chinese feeling is that we – an eccentric race – were created to govern and look after them, as a groom looks after a horse, whilst they were created to get rich and enjoy the good things of the earth. Be my theory true or no, the fact remains that the general purity and high tone of our service is a main secret of our remarkable influence.   (Quoted in Lee, 1989, p. 6)

The net result of the 'benign neglect', as it would now be termed, that this stance inspired was that the system of social provision Singaporeans inherited on the arrival of self-government was woefully inadequate (Lee, 1989). All the basic services existed – education, income support, a surrogate pension scheme (the compulsory savings represented by the Central Provident Fund – CPF – established in 1955), and some public healthcare. However, all failed to come close to meeting the level of need. The education system provided only free elementary education and not in the language most parents would have preferred – English. The public hospitals were too few and the CPF too new to have improved things. Finally, even the British-style, universal Public Assistance benefits were insufficient to keep their recipients above the poverty line. Thus, in 1954, 25 per cent of all households with children were found to be living in poverty.

The PAP had its origins in a student discussion group formed in London in 1949 and in the trade union contacts that Lee Kuan Yew made through his labour law practice in the early 1950s (Turnbull, 1989, pp. 245ff.). Formed in 1954, the party won the election of 1959 on a vague platform of independence and socialism. However, the 'pragmatism' of the moderate section of the leadership, and which was soon to become the party's central ideological leitmotif, was immediately apparent in the new government's economic policy statements. These looked forward to a common market with the Federation of Malaya, a mixed economy and an influx of foreign capital, whilst declaring that 'a PAP government was a government on the worker's side'. Thus the first move towards what may be termed an 'active' patriarchalism was made when a 'fair share' in the country's future wealth was promised in exchange for the disciplines imposed by the trade union and industrial relations laws of 1960. Despite initial resistance, this exchange was apparently accepted by the majority of the labour force, especially because of the government's very active public solicitude for the workers' welfare. Much of this activity was carried out by the government-created and financed Statutory Boards in the areas of economic development, housing and utilities. These rapidly set about providing Singapore with a new industrial infrastructure, dependable utilities and good quality public housing (for a detailed discussion of the ideological significance of the housing policy, see Chua, 1995, ch. 6). In addition, the government dramatically increased spending on education from $600,000 in 1960 to $10 million in 1963. In so doing it both made English available to all through its policy of bilingualism (Hill and Lian, 1995, ch. 3) and demonstrated its commitment to 'multiracialism'. Contradictorily, the latter did not sanction what Lee Kuan Yew termed, in a most unfortunate phrase, the hybridity of a 'calypso society' (Turnbull, 1989, p. 302).

Finally, the PAP developed the CPF as the backbone of its alternative to a welfare state. Thus the CPF now not only provides an alternative to a state pension scheme, but also provides resources for the purchase of property, and the payment of medical bills, and may sometimes be used to support elderly parents. The support that the PAP won in this way and the general appeal of its 'pragmatic' ideology were both reinforced by the trauma of the expulsion from Malaysia which made 'survival' the shared concern of government and people. Both this concern and its beneficial ideological effects – the beginnings of the forging of a specifically *national* identity (Chua, 1995, pp. 14ff.) – were still further reinforced when the nation's largest employer, the British government, peremptorily decided to close its bases in 1967. In this atmosphere the next move in the direction of full-blown patriarchalism was made relatively easily. That is, further limitations were placed on the ordinary citizenry's ability either to follow any path other than that decided on by the government or to ensure that the latter followed through on any promises it had made.

Interestingly, but unsurprisingly in the light of the similarities between the PAP's 'pragmatism' and the political conclusions drawn by the American sociologist, Daniel Bell, from his 'end of ideology' thesis, the language used to justify the necessity of these restrictions was that of the only available, or at all progressive, alternative to socialism and communism, American Social Modernism. Thus, when the party addressed the trade unions it spoke in specifically Modernisationist terms of the technologically determined nature of social progress, and *therefore* of the need for a 'responsible', post-solidaristic, and problem-solving trade union movement (see for example, Chan and ul Haq, 1987; NTUC, 1970). In this case the rewards for agreeing to modernisation, that is, for accepting further curbs on trade union freedoms and increased employer possessory powers through a relaxing of labour standards as regards some contractual terms (hours, holidays, overtime and bonus payments, and white-collar fringe benefits), employees were provided with improved standards as regards other contractual terms (sick leave, redundancy pay and increased employer contributions to the CPF). In sum, labour was once again required to give up some of its means of enhancing its autonomy in favour of future, loyalty-dependent benefits. This move was confirmed in 1971 by the diminishing of the significance of collective bargaining represented and effected by the establishment of a tripartite wage-setting institution, the National Wages Council.

Additional compensation for agreeing to restrictions on popular autonomy was provided in the form of continuing improvements in social provision. Systems of English-centred, bilingual secondary and tertiary education were developed in the 1970s almost as quickly as elementary education had been in the 1960s. The compensatory rather than autonomy-enhancing role ascribed to education was confirmed by the merging of the often troublesome Chinese-medium Nanyang University with the very institution whose colonialist traditions it had been established to counter on behalf of the Chinese population, namely Singapore University. Less ambiguous compensation was provided by the rapid progress of the housing programme. By 1974, 42 per cent of the population lived in government-built housing, by 1980, 70 per cent, and by 1987, 84 per cent, the vast majority as owner-occupiers (Hill and Lian, 1995, ch. 5).

However, the overall patriarchalism of the PAP's state project was confirmed by the increasingly explicit declaration that some people were superior to others. Instances of this elitist sub-text may be found in all major policy areas. A rigorous system of streaming or tracking was introduced in the schools and the growth in the number of higher education places was strictly controlled so that a credentialised elite might be created (Tham, 1989). Higher quality housing was made available to those who could afford to pay more (Chua, 1995). Eugenically inspired attempts were made to encourage young people to marry others of a similar level of educational attainment through the setting-up of separate, government-run matchmaking agencies for the holders of '0' levels, 'A' levels, and degrees, as well as through encouraging graduate women to have more children (Hill and Lian, 1995, pp. 151–5). Ministerial virtue was rewarded by raising their salaries to levels equivalent to those of the best paid chief executives in the private sector (Kwok, 1995, pp. 300–3). And, finally, the psychological and material costs of failure were increased by shifting the administration of welfare services to charitable organisations and tightening still further the eligibility criteria for Public Assistance. The latter are now so strict that even many of the 'deserving poor', let alone the unemployed, are refused benefit in all but the most desperate of conditions (Lim, 1989). The summary term with which the existence of this sub-text was officially acknowledged was the same one that was used to summarise the government's anti-discrimination policy, namely 'meritocracy'.

Finally, the link between patriarchalism and elitism became explicit with the turn to Confucianism (Chua, 1995, pp. 28ff., ch. 7). Again, and in this case particularly ironically, it seems the most important source of inspiration was American. Thus the Confucianism that the government for a time urged upon the population was not so much that of Japan, let alone China, but that to be found in a set of texts written by American social scientists such as Herman Kahn and Ezra Vogel, who had developed a Confucianist twist to Modernisation theory (Chua, 1995, pp. 150–3; Hill and Lian, 1995, p. 202). The turn began in a low-key way with the 'Speak Mandarin' campaign which commenced in 1978. In the words of Prime Minister Lee, the campaign was justified on the basis that: 'The greatest value in the teaching and learning of Chinese is in the transmission of the norms of social or moral behaviour. This means principally Confucianist beliefs and ideas, of man, society and the state' (quoted in ibid., p. 197). In the *Report on Moral Education* to which the prime minister was responding with these words, the object of the exercise was stated as the production of 'good, useful and *loyal* citizens' (quoted in ibid., p. 198; emphasis added). Thus in 1984 a wide-ranging but Confucian-centred Religious Knowledge course became a compulsory part of the school curriculum. However, other religions seem to have benefited more from such measures than has Confucianism. In 1986, many newly assertive Muslim Malays joined in noisy protests against a visit by the president of Israel. And in 1987, sixteen similarly newly assertive young Christian activists were arrested under the Internal Security Act for allegedly being part of a communist conspiracy (Rodan, 1992, pp. 9–14). In 1992, the course disappeared from the curriculum (Hill and Lian, 1995, p. 208).

Despite the fact that what I am terming its 'active patriarchalism' was already hegemonic (Chua, 1995, ch. 3), and the confirmation of the Gramscian insight that ideology is most effective when it is identified with the apparent spontaneity of 'commonsense' represented by the ideological meltdown that occurred in the Soviet Union, the PAP has continued its search for an explicit ideology. Moreover, it continued to be drawn to the societal managerialism of the American orientalist Modernisationists. Thus the next text to attract the party leadership's attention was George Lodge and Ezra Vogel's *Ideology and National Competitiveness* of 1987 (Rodan, 1993). And the outcome was the 1991 *White Paper on Shared Values* (see also Quah, 1990). The chosen values were the following:

(1) Nation before community and society above self.
(2) Family as the basic unit of society.
(3) Regard and community support for the individual.
(4) Consensus instead of contention.
(5) Racial and religious harmony.

Clearly patriarchalist if no longer uniquely Confucianist (cf. the statements of Filipino and Malaysian values discussed above), these ideas are currently referred to in Singapore as 'communitarianism'.[1] Finally, confirmation of the increased importance of the need for loyalty implied by the pre-eminence accorded the first of these values within the state ideology is provided by the nature of the government's response to its declining support amongst the lower income groups – increased benevolence in the form of increased housing subsidies of one kind or another, especially to those in constituencies that have remained loyal to the PAP (Chua and Tan, 1995, pp. 18ff.).

THE INSTITUTIONS OF ACTIVE PATRIARCHALISM AND THE CLASS STRUCTURE

I will now summarise the social-structural significance of the foregoing and thereby outline the class-structural balances that have characterised the society as it has developed and so provide a structural answer to my 'Why?' question. Before the Pacific War, both the general political, economic and ideological balances and their specifically class-structural dimensions were clearly massively in capital's favour. By contrast, after the war and thanks to both the severely disrupted economy and the confidence gained by some sections of the labour movement in the course of their guerilla war against the Japanese, the political balance, and therefore the control balance too, shifted markedly in labour's direction. Although the PAP frustrated the revolutionary efforts of the communists, it nevertheless moved to solidify this shift, but to its own advantage rather than to that of labour in general. Thus social and industrial order was identified with the interests of the PAP rather than with those of labour as such. Likewise, the PAP reserved to itself the power to decide where the balance should be struck between labour and capital as regards the relations of possession and title.

In the event, perhaps because after the British closed their bases the PAP had no other choice but to set up in business on its own account and to woo transnational capital, the party decided to strike balances along the possessory, control and proprietary dimensions of industrial property at points which were uniformly, if to varying degrees, more favourable to capital than to labour. Thus, because the Singaporean state had appropriated to itself virtually all power to define the nature of class balances, under conditions where its most important potential clients demanded that the rule of law should be in place, the same state had no alternative but to specify and enforce its definition of where the balances were to be struck through labour law. This is underlined by the fact that, as in Malaysia, each bout of restrictive legislation occurred at a moment of crisis – that is, when the PAP was first elected, when Britain announced the closure of its bases, and when the country was struck by an unexpectedly sharp recession in 1985. In the absence of such legislation and its effective enforcement, industrial capital would very likely have been expropriated, as indeed happened with respect to landed property (see below).

Finally, although the quantum of expensive, contradictorily positioned or middle-class labour increased rapidly from roughly 12.5 per cent of the labour force in 1977 to roughly 24 per cent in 1990, as in Hong Kong, this does not represent a serious drain on domestic capital resources since much of it is employed either by foreign companies or by the increasing number of Singaporean companies who administer overseas production facilities.[2] What the growth of a substantial and transnationally employed middle class does mean, however, is that whilst absolute poverty has been virtually eradicated, inequality has begun to increase recently. The Gini Coefficient with respect to personal income inequality fell between 1966 and 1975, remained constant until 1981, and began to increase in 1982 when it stood at .47 (Lim, 1988, ch. 14). According to Chua Beng-Huat (1995) the continuing increase in inequality is confirmed by the increasingly obvious lifestyle differences between the middle class and the rest, despite the largely state-controlled media's refusal to draw attention to them.

ACTIVE PATRIARCHALISM, THE LAW, AND HUMAN RIGHTS

As far as the concerns of the present text are concerned, there were no directly significant differences between the law of colonial Singapore and that of Hong Kong (Bartholomew, 1989; Hooker, 1978; 1988). Thus, virtually all of what was said above (see pp. 160–65) about pre-1959 Hong Kong law holds for Singapore too, including the point about the displacement of much of English family law by an invented variant of Chinese law, which in the Singapore case, systematically confused concubinage with polygamy, for example (Leong, 1985). However, there was one important difference which was and indeed remains at least indirectly significant. This is the difference represented by Section 5 (i) of the Civil Law Act (1878), which both provides for the continuing reception of English 'commercial law' and remains in force. This clause solves the 'reception problem' in respect of English legislation passed after the territory passed into British hands, that introduces so great a degree of abstract if not necessarily practical uncertainty into Hong Kong law. It does this by making explicit for a certain category of legislation what has been strenuously denied in Hong Kong, namely the continuing reception of English statutes. The problem, however, is that the phrase 'commercial law' does not have a clear referent in English law, since the line between trade-related matters and others is sometimes hard to draw and the former are the concern of many branches of the common law rather than of a clearly demarcated commercial code as in the civilian tradition (Bartholomew, 1989; Hickling, 1992, ch. 6; Rutter, 1989; Woon, 1989).

In sum, then, capital's rights of title were and remain weakened by the fact that, because the territory was ceded, first, to a proxy for the British government (the East India Company), and then to that government itself, all the land in the colony was initially owned by the state. And the state preferred to sell rather restrictive leases instead of freeholds, albeit more often of 999 years duration than was the case in Hong Kong (Ricquier, 1985, p. 16). However, this weakness with respect to title was compensated for, so to speak, by a high degree of freedom of contract and little in the way of tortious liability. Prior to 1959, in the words of one author, Singapore contract law and by extension tort law also instanced a 'slavish adherence to English law' (Phang, 1990, p. 84).

Since self-government and especially since independence, the development of Singapore law has diverged quite sharply from that of Hong Kong, as the courts and indeed the legislature have looked to countries other than Britain for inspiration. Formally, these changes have all been to the detriment of capital. The weakness of capital's rights of title became especially marked on account of the government's considered refusal to include the protection of private property amongst the rights protected by the constitution. The reason for this was the fear that any such protection would encumber the state's right of 'eminent domain' as developed in the Land Acquisition Act (1966) and so interfere with its planned housing programme (Ricquier, 1985). The consequence has been that the proportion of state-owned land has greatly increased since independence, thanks to the activities of the various statutory boards, especially the Housing Development Board. Whereas in 1949 the proportion of crown land stood at 31 per cent, much of it used for military purposes, by 1975 the proportion of state land had risen to 65 per cent (Ricquier, 1985, p. 17). Apart from private landlords in general who have had their property compulsorily purchased, the principal victims of this assertion of state power have been foreign-owned companies which under the terms of the Residential Property Act (1973) not only can no longer own property in Singapore but also have had to divest themselves of any property they owned before the passage of the Act (Soe, 1992, pp. 228–9). In addition, within the sphere of contract/possession, Andrew Phang (1990, pp. 105–15) has detected signs of definite moves in the direction of promissory estoppel, an increased role for 'public interest' considerations with respect to restraint of trade cases, and a loosening of the definition of 'mistake'. Finally, in the area of tort/control, in this case because of the continuing reception of English law in the sphere of commercial law, strict liability arrived relatively early in Singapore with the British Sale of Goods Act (1979) (Sihombing et al., 1991, chs. 4 and 7).

In sum, then, the structure of the basic legal doctrines that judges have resort to when they encounter difficulties in civil law cases has changed significantly to the advantage of either the state or weaker parties in their dealings with capital or, if they are small enterprises, in their dealings with larger enterprises. Theoretically, this could have meant that when ambiguities were discovered in such areas as employment and industrial relations law, the judiciary had the doctrinal resources to settle such issues to the benefit of labour. There are two major reasons why this did not in fact turn out to be the case. The first is that individual and group rights in general have not been allowed to provide the basis for actions – legal or social – that would have colonised the discursive space left by the retreat of capital on behalf of other interests. Instead, the vacant space has been occupied by the state which has been free to decide whom or what interests it will favour. Thus citizens have been favoured as tenants and sometimes as consumers, but not always as employees and very seldom as trade unionists. The second is that, relatedly and as will be explained below, the development of labour law has not been left to the courts but has been kept firmly under the detailed control of the legislature and the party.

As in Malaysia, what has allowed the state this privilege over the citizenry is the very qualified status of the civil rights contained in the constitution. The constitution offers protection to life and liberty, the rights of speech, expression, association and religion. It also provides that no person should be held in slavery or punished on the basis of retroactive legislation, and declares that all are equal before the law. The qualified status of these rights is a consequence of two factors. First, the existence of structural limitations on the independence of the judiciary – especially regrettable given that trial by jury was abolished in most cases in 1960 and completely in 1969. And second, the existence of a problem with and illiberal elements within the constitution.

Lower court judges are appointed by the president on the recommendation of the chief justice for fixed and revokable periods. The normal route to a Supreme Court justiceship is now through serving time as a judicial commissioner (an assistant justice), also for fixed and revokable periods. Finally, Supreme Court justices are appointed by the president on the recommendation of the prime minister and chief justice and with tenure until retirement. Thus, as elsewhere amongst former British colonies, only Supreme Court justices enjoy the conditions that would normally be considered as necessary to ensure their full independence. What is more, the conditions under which prospective justices have to carry out their duties are such as to offer more than normal encouragement for the practice of self-censorship in their deliberations. Indeed, one seasoned observer of the Singapore legal system has commented that both bench and bar are noticeably reticent when it comes to engaging in judicial review and raising constitutional issues (Hickling, 1992, p. 36).

Strangely, possibly the biggest problem with the constitution is its apparent weakness as a basis for judicial supremacy with respect to constitutional matters! Although such supremacy is formally declared in the constitution, at least one scholar (Tan, 1991) has raised doubts about the robustness of this supremacy. This is because after Singapore's expulsion from Malaysia, the constitution was promulgated by a body, the Singaporean parliament, that did not have such a power. Thus, despite declaring itself to be otherwise, the constitution might simply be an ordinary piece of legislation and as such not a privileged text that would necessarily prevail *vis-à-vis* other pieces of legislation.

The first illiberal element in the constitution is, as in Malaysia, Article 149. In the Singaporean case the Internal Security Act (ISA) that the Article supports allows for renewable terms of 'preventive detention' of up to thirty days if ordered by a police officer, and of up to two years if ordered by the president. Although no one has been subject to preventive detention for the past five years, some of the periods of detention in the past have been very long. For example, a former MP, Chia Thye Poh, was released in 1989 after a twenty-three year period of detention. Thus both Article 149 and the ISA may therefore be safely assumed to be highly inhibitive in relation to some varieties of political dissent, especially if such dissent falls within the government's very elastic definition of 'communistic', as the New Left did in the 1960s and 1970s and the Christian activists mentioned earlier did in 1987 (Asia Watch, 1989; Kehma-S, 1989; United States Congress, 1992).

The state's 'rights' in this area are, if anything, even better protected than they are in Malaysia. First, they are superior to all the citizenry's rights save for fragments of *habeas corpus* – specifically, the right to be quickly informed of the grounds for one's detention, and to initiate but not necessarily to secure a consultation with legal counsel. Second, possibly just in case the constitution should turn out to be the superior law, no judicial review of preventive detention orders has been allowed since 1989. The role of the British Privy Council as the final court of appeal was also greatly reduced after 1989, most likely because of the critical comments it made concerning the treatment meted out to a prominent opposition politician, J. B. Jeyaretnam, when it restored him to the Singapore Bar (US Congress, 1992). Since the inauguration of the first elected president in 1992, the judiciary has been displaced by the president and a consultative Advisory Committee as the ultimate protector of human rights! Finally, the role of the British Privy Council as a final court of appeal was finally abolished in 1989.

The second illiberal constitutional element, as in Malaysia, is the general rider appended to the rights of speech, expression, assembly and association by Article 14(2)(a). This allows parliament to impose, even on its own members and specifically on the representatives of labour and members of educational institutions, 'such restrictions as it considers necessary or expedient' for such purposes as the maintenance of national security, public order and morality, or in cases of contempt of court, defamation, and incitement to offence (Tan et al., 1991, pp. 645, 672).

When less draconian measures are called for, which they seldom are in respect of speech (the state either owns or controls most of the media, including the tombstones of private individuals, Hickling, 1992, ch. 7), or assembly (licences are needed for political meetings of more than five persons and they are infrequently granted), the government has at its disposal the Criminal Law (Temporary Provisions) Act. Whilst this Act is ostensibly directed at Triads and gangsters it can also be used to detain anyone 'on suspicion' of criminal activity – in 1989, 1,000 people were in prison because of such suspicion (Jeyaratnam, 1989, p. 37). And finally, as the Lees, father and son, have successfully demonstrated several times recently in dealings with foreign newspapers, there is always the threat of punitive damages arising from suits in libel and defamation if a political 'thin skin' rather than state security is at stake.

THE LABOUR LAW OF ACTIVE PATRIARCHALISM

As Charles Gamba (1957; 1962) pointed out many years ago, for most of its history the majority of wage-labourers in Malaya and especially in Singapore have not been Malays. Thus, the history of labour law in Singapore begins with various paternalistic attempts, the first initiated by Stamford Raffles himself in 1823, to regulate and ameliorate the terms under which immigrant labour either arrived in or left the island. Most of these were ineffective until the Chinese Immigration Ordinance was introduced in 1877. This set up a Department of Labour which soon became known as the Chinese Protectorate or the *Pi Ki Ling* after the first Protector of the Chinese, W. A. Pickering. The shift from paternalistic concern to paternalistic regulation commenced at this moment, since the chief objective of the *Pi Ki Ling* was the registration and regulation of the Chinese secret societies. The occurrence of this shift was confirmed a few years later when in 1889 the government of the Colony of the Straits Settlements introduced an Associations Ordinance to regulate the Chinese Guilds, which by that time were largely employer groupings, and in 1909 a Societies Ordinance was enacted which provided for the registration, regulation and recognition of a wider variety of associations. However, it was not to be until 1920 that the first employee associations, in the form of Chinese Mutual Help Associations, were recognised and the *Pi Ki Ling* took on the role of an industrial relations mediator. In this way, stimulated also by developments in China and the Federated Malay States, the seeds were planted that eventually led to the formation of the Nanyang (South Seas) General Labour Union in 1925 and the occurrence of several strikes in the three years that followed, including some that involved Indian as well as Chinese workers (Stenson, 1970, pp. 8–10). The Great Depression put an end to these early efforts and it was to be another eight years before any organ-ised industrial actions re-occurred, this time stimulated by the Japanese invasion of China (ibid., pp. 14ff.). By 1941, it was estimated that there were some fifty-one registered trade unions and twenty or more unregistered ones in Singapore (ibid., p. 35). In other words, as in Hong Kong and Malaya, but with somewhat more local official encourage-ment, trade unions gained the status of tolerated institutions in line with the emergence of a more supportive stance on the part of the Colonial Office.

The latter eventually led to the enactment in 1940 and 1941 of the familiar trio of British colonial labour laws: a Trade Unions Ordinance, an Industrial Courts Ordinance No. 4 and a Trade Disputes Ordinance. However, the Japanese Occupation rendered their existence academic until they were resurrected in 1946. Thus, the founding texts of Singa-pore's labour law grounded labour's rights in 'immunities' which relate only to the pursuit of approved economic objectives and apply only to trade unions and their officers. As in Malaya and for the same reasons the content of this legislation was resisted far more strongly than in Hong Kong. Moreover, the Singapore government's official Trade Union advisor, S. P. Garrett, was even more sympathetic to the union's cause than Brazier in Kuala Lumpur, and he colluded in their efforts to avoid registration (Stenson, 1970, pp. 135ff.). However, Singapore's Chinese employers were also quick to organise themselves and to insist both that no liberalisation of industrial relations law took place and that regis-tration was enforced. By early 1947 they had achieved both goals and the level as well as the success of industrial disruption declined steeply thereafter (ibid., p. 204).

In its frustration with this sudden reverse, the Singapore Federation of Trade Unions (SFTU), as the local section of the Pan-Malayan GLU now called itself, tried to lead the workers to revolution. It failed, but took up the armed struggle itself, and left a rump trade union movement to deal with a situation made even more difficult by the addition of emergency regulations to the restrictions anyway contained in the resur-rected labour legislation. Thus when trade unionism revived at the end of the 1940s, its most dependable body of support was amongst govern-ment employees. The latter gave a distinctly moderate cast to the Singapore Trade Union Congress (STUC) that they took the lead in forming in 1950. However, once the Malayan Communist Party dis-tanced itself from the strategy of armed struggle and turned its attention back to industrial organising, Singaporean trade unionism rapidly regained a militant wing outside of the STUC. By 1956, there were 157,216 trade unionists on the island, concentrated in the longshoring, transportation and manufacturing industries, as well as the public ser-vice. This was more than there had been even in the heady days of 1945/6, and again most of them accepted communist leadership. This leadership was the 'tiger' that the PAP rode to power in 1959 when it defeated Marshall's STUC-supported Labour Front government.

After the 1959 election, the government made three significant legal moves, which made it clear that it was not going to allow labour to take advantage of the discursive space both its victory and the structure of the law allowed. That is, it set out on a path that led to the eventual creation of a state-corporatist – the term tripartite is officially preferred – political economy (Anantaraman, 1990; see also, Deyo, 1981). This structure pre-empted any possibility of either encroachment by labour on capital's prerogatives, or, it should be emphasised, the establishment of a divisive, Japanese-style private corporatism. First, it amended the Trade Unions Ordinance to reduce interunion competition by increasing the powers of the registrar. Second, it amended the Trade Disputes Ordinance to prohibit sympathy and 'political' strikes. And third, it passed an Indus-trial Relations Act (1960) which replaced the Industrial Courts Ordi-nance and, following the Australian model, made arbitration a routine part of the system for settling disputes and arriving at collective agree-ments.

The latter Act provides that if, after attempting and failing to negoti-ate a collective agreement, and after attempts by the Ministry of Labour to conciliate, there is still no agreement, the parties concerned may submit the dispute to the Arbitration Court for a decision. Such a dec-ision is not formally appealable to the Supreme Court (but see below, p. 242). If the parties do not refer the dispute to the Arbitration Court, it may/will nevertheless be so referred by the prime minister or, 'in special circumstances', the president. In sum, a legal strike is virtually impossible without government connivance. However, because it was initially, and remains, a tripartite body, the formation of the Court also represented the first grant of 'powers' to trade unions in exchange for the 'liberties' and 'immunities' that they had had to forgo. The Court's membership consists of a president appointed on the same terms as a Supreme Court justice and employer and employee representatives who are chosen by the prime minister from panels nominated by the employer and employee organisations. Nobody who has been convicted of an offence under either the Trade Disputes Act or the Industrial Relations Act within the preceding three years may be a member of either panel. Finally, when making an award, the arbitrators are enjoined by the Act to take into account 'the interests of the community as a whole and in particular the condition of the economy of Singapore'. The Arbitration Court also certifies the legality of all collective bargaining agreements and administers them during their lifetime.

The further limits imposed on labour as part of its payment for admission into the state family constituted by the 'symbiosis' of 1965 were again threefold. The Trade Unions Ordinance was further amended to allow the Minister of Labour to freeze union bank accounts in 1963, and require secret ballots before strikes. The Criminal Law (Temporary Provisions) Act was amended in 1967 to prohibit strikes and lockouts in the water, gas and electricity industries. The Industrial Relations Act was amended to define promotions, transfers, hiring, firing and redundancy as aspects of the managerial prerogative and hence non-negotiable, save in the case of dismissal without 'just cause or excuse'. In the latter case, the employee concerned may make representations to the Minister of Labour through his or her trade union. The minister will then decide whether or not to reinstate the aggrieved employee after hearing the views of the employer. No damages but only reinstatement are possible. In exchange for these restrictions, labour received on this occasion a consolidation and expansion of its existing minimalist 'claims' on employers through the passage of the Employment Act (1968). This Act specifies minimum employment conditions, which for most workers are also the best allowable, in respect of contracts, wages (including the liability of principal contractors for sub-contractors), rest days, hours, holidays, servants, women, children and which provided for the availability of employment exchanges and the maintenance of an inspectorate. However, many of these claims were explicitly made conditional on regular attendance and loyal performance of one's duties (Anantaraman, 1990, p. 124). On the other hand, it should also be said that, as a consequence of its colonial origins, the Act like virtually all of Singaporean labour law is backed by criminal as well as civil sanctions on employers.

In 1969, the NTUC held a critical seminar entitled 'The Modernization of the Labour Movement'. In the course of this seminar delegates
heard a succession of ministers, industrial relations experts and NTUC
officials justifying the necessity of the earlier restrictions and giving them
a positive gloss. In some tension with its newly acquired American Social
Modernist vocabulary, this was done by comparing the NTUC's situation and response with those of the West German, Swedish and Israeli
trade union movements. The seminar concluded by mapping out a
strategy for the future which featured: 'strengthening our multiracial
state and the labour movement . . . until we . . . become co-owners of our
new, dynamic society'. There were also calls for the setting up of Joint
Productivity Councils, Joint Health and Safety Councils and Works
Councils (NTUC, 1970).

Since 1969, some of this programme has been put into effect. The
state has been strengthened by the continuing loyalty of the NTUC,
which accepted still more restrictions on labour's freedom of action
when it either accepted or initiated the following changes. First, a
National Wages Council was set up in 1973 to agree guidelines for wage
increases. As with entitlement to 'claims' under the Employment Act,
any increases recommended by the Council are conditional on satisfactory and loyal performance as decided by management (that is, they
are unavailable to employees with less than twelve months satisfactory
service). Second, since 1975, employees have been required to choose
between either an annual wage increase or an annual bonus and cannot
have both, as well as to accept that no annual bonus can have a value of
more than three months' salary. Third, unofficial actions were prohibited
in 1977. Fourth, in 1981, the Trade Disputes Act was extended to any
concerted action 'which would result in any limitation or restriction on,
or delay in, the performance of any duties connected with their employment'. This means that such actions too require a secret ballot before
they may be legally undertaken. Fifth, the Employment Act was changed
in 1984 and 1988 to allow companies much greater 'flexibility' in the
deployment and redeployment of labour by allowing the rostering of rest
days, the lengthening of the working day and the restructuring of wage
systems in the direction of profit (and loss)-sharing schemes (Tan, 1995,
ch. 10). Sixth, the NTUC responded positively to the government's
admiration for Japan's enterprise unions and their contributions to
productivity and the fostering of company loyalty by endeavouring to
restructure its affiliates on this basis (Blum and Patarapanich, 1987). In
this they did, however, encounter some stout resistance and as a result

the policy has not been rigorously pursued since 1987 when the proportion of 'house' unions reached 28 per cent of the total as compared to 13 per cent in 1979 (Leggett, 1988). Seventh, the NTUC delivered a substantial two-year cut in wages and employer CPF contributions during the recession of 1985/6. And, finally, the NTUC has gradually become a highly effective conciliator of first resort for its member unions.

The net result has been that there have been only three strikes since 1977 and Singapore's labour force has been consistently rated as 'the world's best' in recent years by the Washington-based organisation, Business Environment Risk Intelligence. Significantly, this organisation gives 30 per cent of its 'marks' on the basis of the legal framework (Tan, 1995, p. 45). This said, the number of disputes requiring at least conciliation has risen consistently, the number of claims made by non-unionised individuals has also risen greatly, and the number of disputes going to arbitration has fluctuated greatly in line with the changing economic conditions (Ministry of Labour, 1993). In other words, the causes of disputes and claims remain but they are dealt with by means other than industrial action.

In return for all this, the trade unions were allowed to purchase land in 1973, and, in 1977, to own and operate co-operative businesses in their own right (a resort, a country club, an insurance company, a radio station, a large taxi company, Singapores's largest chain of supermarkets, and joint ventures with its opposite numbers in China and Indonesia, for example). Employees have enjoyed full-employment conditions for many years, regular full-time jobs and plenty of opportunities for switching them (Tan, 1995, chs. 3 and 4). Also, even non-unionised employees received the protection of a graft-free and effective labour standards inspectorate. Cases that cannot be conciliated are decided by a Labour Commissioner, whose decisions may be appealed to the district courts. However, the inspectors have uncovered a much higher level of labour standards violations where immigrant workers are concerned. Significantly, they are not allowed to form or join trade unions. Such workers are currently some 13 per cent of the labour force. And finally, labour in general received the benefits represented by the government's housing, medical and educational programmes, as well as, most recently, an employer-financed training and retraining system. In sum, then, I have answered my 'How?' question by outlining the development of active patriarchalist discourse within Singaporean labour law and showing how it has contributed to the transformation of industrial and social relations in the Republic. In the conclusion that follows I will provide an assessment of the degree to which Singapore has witnessed the realisation of a system of 'enforceable benevolence' and so answer my 'What?' question.

CONCLUSION: SO NEAR TO ENFORCEABLE BENEVOLENCE (BUT HOW FAR AWAY?)

Despite the great value of the benefits provided by the Singaporean state, they clearly have not led to the strengthening of the trade unions. Although the absolute size of trade union membership has increased, the proportion of the labour force that unions organise has fallen from 35 per cent in 1957 to 16.2 per cent in 1989. Moreover, the existence of even a substantial body of cooperative enterprises does not have the same social or sociological significance as the co-ownership of otherwise capitalist companies. Also, nothing more has been heard of the Works Councils or even the Joint Health and Safety Councils promised in 1969. Finally, although the recent increases in state benevolence may have been in part the consequence of NTUC pressure within its symbiotic relationship with the PAP, it has neither been able to claim the credit for these improvements nor would it have been able to force the government to introduce them since it lacks the legal means to do so autonomously.

Thus, whilst the value of the benevolence granted by the state is undeniable and is currently delivered, there are equally strong grounds upon which to question its ultimate enforceability. Some of the material benefits are citizenship rights and not just the result of forced savings (see, for example, the criteria for eligibility for HDB housing, which 80 per cent of the population now live in, Wong and Yeh, 1985, pp. 238ff.). However, many of the 'claims' under the Employment Act, whilst legally enforceable, are contingent on the good opinion of management. Also, the 'powers' that the NTUC currently enjoys are contingent upon the good opinion of the PAP leadership. Most importantly, apart from the use of the vote, the means to enforce the continued and fair delivery of benefits, the maintenance of 'powers', and the enforcement of 'claims' as part of the routines of the everyday life of a participative democracy are not possessed as of right by the citizenry. Thus, all the state's benevolence and therefore the 'attachment' of labour and human rights to their supposed bearers remain discretionary and hence instance a paternalism, albeit a highly generous one. This will remain the case until the legal system attains a degree more autonomy and both labour and the citizenry enjoy a degree more freedom of association than they do currently – that is, the freedom to form alternative unions if they are dissatisfied with the incumbent ones and their 'symbiotic' relations with government, as well as to form NGOs of whatever kind they wish, including those committed to monitoring the state's human rights performance.

Remarkably, since no great social programmes need to be ideologically justified or established, the only legislative changes that would be required to bring about a dramatic enhancement of state legitimacy would be the following: the strengthening of the independence of the lower judiciary; the abolition of the judicial commissioners; the confirmation of the currently unused precedent created as long ago as 1978 which allows appeals to the Supreme Court from the Arbitration Court (Anantaraman, 1990, p. 146); and, finally, the clarification of the status of the constitution. Given Singapore's legal history, these changes would be sufficient *to make it possible* for the judiciary to respond to a more pluralistically defined conception of the 'public interest' than that presently articulated by the government. This in turn would then make it possible for labour, if it possessed public support, to take broader advantage of the discursive space that is legally available and pursue again the ideal of co-ownership.

Finally, all that would be additionally required to commence the pluralising of the 'public interest' would be changes in the stances of the Trade Union and Societies Registrars. In the former case, the registrar would simply have to be instructed to cease regarding second unions as necessarily 'against the interests of the workforce'. And in the latter case, he or she would simply have to be instructed to stop seeing sedition in anything and everything the present political leadership dislikes or disagrees with. Although the registrars' adoption of their highly restrictive stances was the PAP's first anti-union move, the restoration of a more liberal stance should be seen as confirmation of the relative equity and resilience of the structures that were created thereafter, rather than as harbingers of their collapse. Moreover, new streams of democratic and creative energy would then become available to the body politic and indeed the economy, and in such a way as to leave intact but reinvigorated most if not quite all of the present political and economic arrangements – even the ISA could stay in place since its application would be in the hands of a more independent judiciary constitutionally charged with balancing the rights of individuals and the prerogatives of the state and responding to a more pluralistic conception of the public interest. This said, everything would depend upon the PAP's willingness to sacrifice a measure of its political security in the national interest. Thus, it would not only have to accept the possibility of the loss of a few more seats now and then, but it would also have to drop its dependence upon a racialised conception of the population and welcome cultural hybridity, as well as be prepared to put as much effort into convincing capital of the benefits of a more genuinely communitarian society as it has hitherto put into convincing labour of the benefits of a pseudo-communitarianism. None of this should be too difficult, given the PAP's claimed monopoly of political probity and talent.

It would be, then, as simple as this for Singapore to displace Japan as an achieved instance of, and not just a pointer towards, 'enforceable benevolence' as a new paradigm for labour/human rights – a hybrid paradigm that combines elements of the socialist, patriarchalist and liberal traditions together in a way that is appropriate to the global economic conditions faced by, as well as to the aspirations of, its population. It would, therefore, also be as simple as this to reverse the valence of the term Pacific capitalism and its authoritarian connotations. The benefits provided in Singapore and enforced *vis-à-vis* transnational as well as local capital already far exceed those available in Japan and many social democracies in their range, universality and quality (one has only to compare the Republic's housing provision with that of Japan and Britain today). Similarly, the mode and structures of economic coordination are already far more inclusive than in either society, if not exactly democratic because of the maintenance of the cadre form of organisation within the party and the NTUC. All that is required is a little more liberty.

CONCLUSION

The question guiding this study has been: 'Is there a fundamental incompatibility between patriarchalism and human rights?' My answer is 'No' and for two main reasons. First, in the absence of the kinship relations that previously legitimated patriarchalist discourses of rule, the latter have to be imbricated with those of liberal democracy and the rule of law as well as their associated institutions and procedures, if they are to be considered as legitimate bases for the exercise of 'joint right' by their now subject populations. Second, thanks to Wesley Hohfeld and indeed the bifurcated nature of human rights discourse, there is a way of enunciating rights that validates heteronomous values and institutions over those that validate autonomy, namely by stressing enforceable 'claims' and 'powers' over 'liberties' and 'immunities' in their writing and modes of institutionalisation. Moreover, my most general conclusion is that it is possible sociologically to descry an apparently emergent if still seriously flawed neo-patriarchalist human rights regime in Pacific Asia that is specified in just these terms.

In what follows I will make no attempt to summarise the evidence for this conclusion contained in the case studies presented above. Nor will I repeat the analytical specifics that explain the presence, absence or degree of enforcement afforded labour and human rights in the different territories I have discussed. Rather, within the theoretical context outlined in Part I, what I wish to do here is to specify what the case studies can tell us about the more general social-structural conditions that either favour or militate against the establishment and maintenance of respect for labour and human rights in societies which claim to be patriarchalist and represent instances of Pacific capitalism. I wish, then, to return to the same level of abstraction as in Part I, only speaking substantively rather than theoretically. In so doing I intend to specify the larger sets of structural relations which are immanent within the populations with which I have been concerned and which either favour or undermine respect for human rights as an attribute of systems of governance. In the broadest terms, these sets relate to the specific forms taken by the always hybrid patriarchalist discourses of the region and the transnationally affected balances of class forces obtaining within the particular territories.

In elucidating the particular effects of these sets of relations, I will not systematically compare and contrast my case studies in an effort to isolate either a set of variables or one or other independent variable whose presence or absence determines the degree to which human rights can be or are respected in patriarchalist Pacific-Asian societies. Working with a realist metatheory and substantively committed to the primacy of transnational social relations, I do not consider my case studies to refer to self-sufficient entities within which social relations are spontaneously and independently constituted. Rather, following Louis Althusser, I assume that there are certain universal properties of social relations, which are commonly referred to these days as the political, economic and discursive dimensions of sociality, and which subsist at the domestic, international and transnational levels. The form and content of the social relations and institutions that provide these properties with their materiality may vary almost infinitely. However, in the cases discussed above, these social relations and institutions exhibit sufficient genotypical similarities with respect to possessory, control and proprietary relations to permit sociologists to refer to them as constituting what Althusser following Spinoza termed 'singular' instances of capitalism. Thus, what determines their capacity to either generate respect for human rights or undermine them is not the presence or absence of these generic relations and institutions – they are always present. Nor is it the degree to which they correspond in their particularity to some supposedly ideal national form such as that projected by American Social Modernism: to wit, a form comprising a liberal democratic state, a market economy, an 'open' class structure and an individualistic value system.

In particular, contra Howard and Donnelly, the degree to which human rights are or could be respected in Pacific Asia does not appear to depend upon the degree to which the patriarchalism whose presence is the most obvious deviation from the modernist ideal has been displaced

by individualism. Indeed, the society that is structurally closest to constituting an alternative human rights regime, Singapore, is the one in
which the new patriarchalism I am interested in is the most fully developed. Moreover, since the components of the Social Modernist ideal
are exclusively domestic in their referents, to use this ideal as a guide
necessarily leads one to neglect the international and transnational
levels of analysis. For good and ill the latter are the levels that have been
important but by no means fully determining of the degree to which
human rights are respected in Pacific Asia. Whilst the UN's Covenants
and the ILO's Conventions have been positive factors, the actions of
colonial governments, transnational companies and global superpowers,
as well as the interpellations affected by American Social Modernism
and the 'export version' of the JES, have been much more ambiguous.
The Philippines provides a particularly striking example of how the
significance for the respect for human rights of a domestic social formation that in its formal aspects corresponded very closely to the Social
Modernist ideal was negated by the consequences of its location in the
international system as a political and/or economic colony of the United
States. In short, it seems to me that there is no set of independent social
variables, let alone any single variable such as an individualistic value
system, that may be usefully thought of as necessarily increasing or decreasing the likelihood of respect for human rights. Instead, one should
approach the question of what set, or better sets, of social relations might
best engender a mode of governance that respected human rights by
focusing on the interactive effects produced by the causal mechanisms
that form the multidimensional social integument within which such
rights subsist. This, at least, is the conclusion that I will be concerned to
justify in what follows as I make a case for my claim that, save for the area
of gender relations, there is nothing about patriarchalism, or indeed
matriarchalism, that is intrinsically any more antipathetic to respect for
the human rights compendium as a whole than liberalism or social
democracy. Indeed, save for its positive validation of supposedly 'natural'
hierarchies, it is very similar to the latter in its stress on 'claims' over
'liberties'. What matters more, then, is the form patriarchalism takes and
the nature of the other social-structural conditions with which it must
necessarily co-exist.

CAPITALISM, LIBERAL INSTITUTIONS, COLONIALISM AND HUMAN RIGHTS

Capitalism as a form of domestic, international and transnational economic organisation *is* intrinsically subversive of respect for human rights. As both a set of structural relationships and a source of motivational structures, capitalism requires that individuals are treated differently depending on how they are positioned within the capital/labour relation. As Anatole France made so clear when he spoke of the unequal effects of the prohibition of sleeping under the bridges of Paris, this positioning determines what substantive positive and negative freedoms individuals have as well as the significance that these freedoms can have for them. By contrast, as both a condition of its own existence and the source of social and legal discipline, the discourse of human rights requires that individuals are treated in the same way regardless of how they are positioned within any set of social relations. This said, the class relations which are constitutive of capitalism are not exhaustive of the dimensions of sociality upon which they depend for their existence. Thus, there is always more to the political, discursive and even economic dimensions of sociality than those relations that separate labour from capital and divide their embodiments from one another. To provide only the most pertinent and obvious exemplifications of this point: the politics of nation states are also about securing domestic and international tranquillity; their public discourse is also about producing a sense of nationality and citizenship; and their economics is about the numerous ways in which human beings relate to nature and therefore to one another apart from through the exclusionary private possession of property in the means of production. It is, therefore, this excess that creates the possibility that capitalism's otherwise inherent subversiveness as regards respect for human rights might be countered in some regards, in some localities and on some occasions: such respect may be structurally required for the sake of, for example, securing domestic and/or international peace, a loyal population or a plurally usable environment.

Of course, none of these requirements are necessarily inimical to the reproduction of capitalism. However, the social conditions under which they arise may make them so: sections of the population may be rioting in the streets, joining revolutionary political parties and squatting on tracts of private property, because a capitalist economy has failed to provide them with enough to eat. All this said, there are other ways of responding to such events than by accepting the discipline inherent in the discourse of human rights – by military repression, for example. Thus, there is nothing that ensures that sociality's capital-transcending relations will automatically lead to the enhancement of respect for human rights. Indeed, where riot, armed struggle and squatting are all that capital's victims have at their disposal, there is every likelihood that repression will ensue – but why?

In my view, thinking about this question takes one to the heart of the sociologically illuminable dimension of the tension between capitalism and human rights. As has been suggested in numerous studies of the development of the welfare state in the West, historically capitalism has become politically and legally more vulnerable as it has become more complex in its internal operations and more demanding of its social context. That is, as the tasks of assembling, managing and supervising capital and labour power as well as realising the commodities that are produced when these elements are combined have increased in their complexity, capital has become ever more dependent upon the mental labour, loyalty and purchasing power of the embodiments of the proletariat and the contradictorily positioned middle class. In this way, then, labour's 'gift' (aka 'surplus value') has had to be recognised as it has become constitutive of the relations of production and not simply a means of production to be exploited. Put another way, labour's active cooperation and not just its simple availability has become a *sine qua non* for the production and realisation of capital. Repression through the use of superior force may ensure the availability of labour but it is not an effective means of gaining labour's willing cooperation. Thus, it would seem that a critical potential source of civilising discipline with respect to capital is its increasing dependence on labour as its operations and the demands on its social context become ever more complex.

In Western Europe and Britain's ex-settler colonies too, what might be termed capitalism's limited self-civilising potential was realised to a significant degree through the 'liberties', 'powers' and enforceable 'claims' instantiated by the labour law and social welfare systems, albeit in many different ways, thanks to the co-presence alongside a capitalist economy of more or less liberal-democratic political, ideological and legal formations. In different nation states one or other of these formations was often more important than the others, as indeed were the changes brought about by wars, but in all of them the net result was the emergence of a substantial segment of the population positioned by the working class and constituted by some form or other of socialist ideology and with some access to political power. The latter was used by socialist political parties and trade union movements to transform the earlier patriarchalist realisations of capitalism's self-civilising potential (the British Factory Acts, for example) into citizenship rights. In the United States too, capitalism existed alongside a full panoply of liberalistic institutions. However, for reasons that have long fascinated historians and social scientists, not only did the discourse of governance largely exclude patriarchalist elements but that which constituted the American working class was not socialist. Thus very few enforceable social 'claims' were established and it was therefore those who were contradictorily positioned (the middle class) who benefited more than the proletariat from the civilising of capital (Mann, 1993; Stephens, 1979; Woodiwiss, 1993).

However, as the history of prewar Japan demonstrates, there is nothing automatic about the realisation of capitalism's self-civilising potential. In Japan, liberal institutions were not an effective part of capitalism's social context and partially as a consequence of this the working class was neither constituted by socialist discourse nor had access to political power. Thus, despite the fact that complex forms of capital were present in prewar Japan, the need for labour's active cooperation was met by mobilising patriarchalist political and ideological forces that constituted the working-class population as loyal servants to the benefit of capital and the embodiments of patriarchal power. Thanks to Japan's defeat in the Second World War, hybrid liberal/patriarchalist formations became constitutive of Japanese society and its classes with the result that a fortunate and quite large minority of the population positioned by the working class became the beneficiaries of a limited form of 'enforceable benevolence' (Woodiwiss, 1992a).

If the histories of my four case studies are considered against the historical and social-structural background that has just been sketched, it becomes possible to do two things. First, to specify the nature of the causal mechanisms at work in the formation of their labour and human rights records. Second, to suggest that there may be forms of 'enforceable benevolence' that are improvements on the Japanese model. In each of my case studies one liberal formation at least was co-present with cap-italism from the beginning of their modern histories, namely an imported, individualistically based legal system. Thus, thanks to their international and transnational conditions of existence (that is, colonialism), there were in each of the territories at least formal limits to the state's power vis-à-vis individuals, especially property holders, and capital's power vis-à-vis individual labourers. In law the state had to respect individual property rights and the privity of contractual relations. Additionally, the holders of property rights had to respect labourers' rights in contract and tort, minimal though they were. There was also an independent judiciary that was required to decide the disputes that were brought before it on a consistent basis and as determined by an evolving body of doctrine whose content was determined by case law and statutory developments in England or the United States. That is, to varying degrees colonial legal systems were in receipt of laws produced within jurisdictions where the civilising of capital was far more advanced than locally, even though they were simultaneously destructive of indigenous laws and social relations. Finally, the presence of the rule of law also meant that there also existed modes of enforcing the rights so imported; that is, by bringing cases to court, seeking injunctions, obtaining damages and meting out fines or prison sentences. Of course, there were marked asymmetries in access to these means of enforcement and in the distribution of rights as between capital and labour in the colonies. This was because of both the continuing inequalities in the metropolitan countries, and the much slower pace at which improvements in labour's rights as compared to developments in capital's property and contractual rights were received by the colonies. There were also great differences in the levels of enforcement that the rights of capital and labour attracted or were able to avail themselves of, thanks to racism and sexism as well as economic inequalities and differences. Nevertheless, an individualistic variant of the rule of law did become a constitutive part of the disciplinary structures of the colonial social formations discussed here, which is a significant difference from the Japanese case.

Notwithstanding the racist patriarchalism that informed colonial governance, what makes this a difference of particular significance is the fact that in these colonies imported capitalism and *its* imported rule of law therefore existed in some tension with the indigenous patriarchalist political and ideological structures. In Japan, this tension was far less because the rule of law as promulgated in the initial nineteenth-century Civil and Commercial Codes continued the privilege traditionally accorded to certain patriarchalist elements (Woodiwiss, 1992, pp. 51–58). However, in the colonies of interest here, as both capital and the state were localised, respect for, or at least acceptance of, the possibility that individual or indeed labour rights might come into conflict with patriarchally defined obligations also became constitutive of the colonies concerned as they moved towards independence, or in Hong Kong's case towards restoration to China. That is, until recently there was little of the demand for 'oneness' that was such a distinctive part of Japan's hege-monic, prewar public discourse. In sum, an individualistic and atomistic conception of rights became embedded in these colonies precisely be-cause they had been colonies rather than independent states like Japan; that is, because such a conception was necessary to secure the colonists' property rights against the threat abstractly if seldom practically posed by the indigenous patriarchalist powers. Thus, in a structural sense if no other, capitalism was a rather less ambiguous ally of rights discourse in the colonies than it was in the metropolitan countries in advance of the emergence of the social-structural support potentially provided by more developed forms of capitalism.

For these reasons, then, despite the long absence of democracy which with the partial exception of the Philippines, was also a product of the international and transnational conditions of existence within which the colonies concerned subsisted, the issue as to whether or not rights are respected has long been an issue within them in a way in which it was not in prewar Japan. Indeed, anger at the hypocrisy of the colonial pow-ers as they spoke of rights amongst peoples whose rights they were at the same moment neglecting or violating did much to fuel demands for independence, as well as to provide a language with which they might be expressed. Thus rights became part, and indeed a privileged part, of the constitutions of all of the territories discussed here when they became independent, or in Hong Kong's case, as it was belatedly prepared for reversion to Chinese sovereignty. That is, rights occupy an important role in such texts not just because their presence is expected as part of the price of admission to the 'modern' or 'civilised' capitalist world, but also because their presence represents a claim to self-respect as well as sometimes to moral superiority *vis-à-vis* their former colonial masters.

That said, once freedom from colonial tutelege was achieved, the domestic, international and transnational social support for rights dis-course provided, albeit very often in the breach, by the colonial state and its capitalist clients, disappeared. Thereafter, a new balance had to be struck between the content of rights discourse and the obligations now more assertively projected in the patriarchalist discourses proclaimed by the new states and emergent national capitals as they formulated their 'state projects'. Moreover, this was done amidst the developing set of international and transnational social relations whose consequences included not just the ever-increasing prominence of the discourse of human rights but the emergence of a Pacific capitalism whose constitu-tive discursive flows featured not only American Social Modernism but also, more importantly, Japanese *Kigyoshugi*. Given that only two of my case studies, Hong Kong and the Philippines, have ratified the UN Covenants and that there is no regional enforcement mechanism (Welch, 1990), the latter development has proved to be a much more significant transnational condition of existence than the former. This, then, is the point in my argument when the differences between my case studies become analytically important, since knowledge of them is necessary if one is to be able to specify the particularity of the causal mechanisms and 'modelling' processes operating in each case.

To put the point in more specific terms, formally there are striking similarities with respect to the structures of the four different labour law systems discussed above. Because of the strength of the patriarchalist institutions that labour faced, the 'immunities' and 'liberties' granted by the colonial authorities were not empowering in Hong Kong and Malaysia. Because of the relative weakness of the same institutions, there is evidence that such rights initially provided labour with some leverage in Singapore and the Philippines. However, even in the Singaporean case where labour did become a force that had to be reckoned with, these rights were insufficient to prevent the establishment of paternalisms, albeit of dramatically different kinds, in both societies. As a result, in all four societies trade union 'liberties' or 'immunities' and therefore labour's capacity to contest capital along the dimension of control relations in particular have been greatly restricted in the name of the employer's hierarchical entitlement. The result is that a legal strike and most of its incidents (picketing and demonstrating, for example) are virtually impossible unless they are either explicitly or implicitly sanctioned by the state. In sum, what each of these case studies would seem to represent is an instance of the social rejection of an alien legal form.

The cogency of this diagnosis is reinforced by the fact that in all four states trade unions or labour more generally have been compensated for this loss of autonomy through:

(1) the provision of 'powers' to represent their members or themselves either before arbitral/conciliatory bodies of one kind or another or within governmental apparatuses;
(2) the establishment of entitlements or 'claims' represented by sets of labour standards whose similarity is a powerful testament to the occurrence of transnational social-modelling.

Thus, and I would suggest to a significant degree because such measures may be more easily embedded within patriarchalist institutions, labour's losses with respect to control relations have been somewhat but unevenly compensated for by gains with respect to possessory relations that can be regarded as required by the need to show benevolence in exercising powers that have their source in a 'joint right'. Moreover, in so far as these gains are enforced by the states concerned, especially where the latter hold title in the means of production, and given Pacific-Asian labour's low level of organisation as well as its vulnerable position with respect to most global commodity chains, they potentially represent a more effective mode of routinely protecting labour's rights than resort to the traditional tactics of industrial conflict. Interestingly, apart from enterprise unionism and despite the presence of many Japanese production facilities throughout the region, and outside of South Korea and Taiwan, the larger features of the JES have been less of a direct influence than one might have imagined. This said, the indirect influence of the Japanese model has been immense thanks to the ideal of 'organised labour' that it projects and the wide take-up of many of its more technical managerial and governmentalist features (see above, p. 78). In sum, the major importance of the Japanese model has been as the catalyst that encouraged the belief in the possibility of a variety of forms of Pacific capitalism constructed out of indigenous resources and involving borrowings from many other models. Thus, as I have shown, the establishment of arbitral and conciliatory alternatives to industrial conflict long predated the occurrence, or at least global awareness of, the 'Japanese Miracle' and drew on British, European, Australian and even, in the case of the Philippines, American models. However, what the Japanese model did when the countries I have been concerned with did eventually 'Look East' was to confirm the claimed cultural appropriateness of these non-juridical alternatives and lend them some of its immense prestige.

The equally striking differences between the four systems relate, first, to the degree to which these compensatory moves have been realised in practice or enforced, and second, to their extent. Because of, in my view, the special significance of labour rights within human rights regimes (that is, because trade unions where they have not been statised remain by far the most important NGOs in most societies), both the formal similarities and substantive differences between the two sets of rights mirror one another very closely indeed. Thus, in each of my case studies restrictions on individual liberties are partially compensated for by promises of social and economic benefits that are both very unevenly fulfilled and very unevenly distributed as between the sexes and ethnic or 'racial' groups (it would require a separate, parallel text to detail and explain this uneven distribution). In sum, then, the most important task for sociologists is to explain the variation in the substantive significance of formally very similar rights regimes by reference to the operation of causal mechanisms that are immanent within the pertinent populations and transnational flows.

THE PHILIPPINES, MENDICANT PATRIARCHALISM AND THE ABSENCE OF HUMAN RIGHTS

The Philippines faced its moment of truth with respect to its ability to sustain and improve upon the mode of governance/human rights regime bequeathed by its colonisers when it ostensibly became fully independent in 1947. That it failed this test was a result of a highly complex concatenation of causal forces, which I will now attempt to set out. First, even today, industrial capital, especially in its more complex forms and as opposed to agricultural capital, has far less of a presence within the Philippine social formation than within my other three case studies. As a result, and as is confirmed by the remarkably small size of the population employed as wage labourers and the miniscule proportion of the labour force that is contradictorily positioned as the middle class, the potentially civilising force represented by capital's need for an actively cooperative labour force is also far less significant than in the other three societies. Second, the independent state's continuing political and economic dependence upon the United States and its consequent mendicancy not only accounted for the primitiveness of its capitalism, but also meant that the state could continue to reward its favoured servants and clients irrespective of their obedience to its formal, legally specified requirements. That is, by distributing as it saw fit the largesse in the form of development aid and export/manufacturing opportunities that the United States made available, the Philippine state was able to suspend selectively the rule of its own law. A particularly clear example of this suspension relates to the many large landlords who have systematically violated the letter and the spirit of the land reform laws but nevertheless have continued to be allowed to fill their shares of export quotas because of their connections with the state and/or powerful American transnational companies.

For these two reasons, there was and is little in the way of structural support for a disciplinary regime favourable to the maintenance of respect for human rights. Instead, a fatal and self-reproducing difference was created between the basis upon which, on the one hand political/ideological, and, on the other, economic calculations were made. Political success required the promising of more and more rights to the mass of the population, whilst economic success required the more and more egregious violation of the same rights. And the latter in turn required the promising of still more rights to redress the new as well as the continuing wrongs. Despite the operation of a powerful, domestically produced patriarchalist logic, qualified somewhat by Social Modernist elements, which generated successive attempts to establish effective labour and human rights regimes, no such regime, no such disciplinary matrix, stabilised in either the industrial or any other context. Armed insurrections, Marcos' 'smiling martial law', and the suspension of virtually all efforts at the enforcement of any rights whatsoever were thus the virtually inevitable results of the underlying structural disjunction caused by the interactive effects of Philippine society's domestic social structure and its international conditions of existence.

To be more specific, at a critical juncture in the sad history of Philippine rights regimes, a patriarchalistically inflected but nevertheless remarkably faithful copy of the American Social Modernist labour rights system was installed in the form of the Industrial Peace Act (1953). At first, the regime appeared to stand some chance of success in that labour at least was reasonably happy and both the Act and the statutory 'claims' that existed alongside it were effectively enforced by the Department of Labour and the courts. However, the 'liberties' that were critical to its apparent success were also its Achilles heel in that they were both expensive to capital and threatened to create a social and political force capable of closing the gap between political/ideological claims and industrial and social practice. That is, they promised to reintegrate the social structure, harmonise the bases upon which calculations of whatever kind were made, and so suture the structural disjunction upon which so much power and wealth depended.

It was structurally possible for martial law to put an end to this possibility for two reasons. First, given the small size of the industrial proletariat compared to that in the United States, the Industrial Peace Act granted industrial labour rights that, like those granted by the legal system as a whole, were wholly out of line with the overall balance of class forces. Second, in a nice demonstration of the inexhaustibility of the various dimensions of sociality in their class-structural effects, the withdrawal of the rhetorical benevolence represented by the IPA was possible because its continuation would have disrupted the political and economic balances as such. The oligarchs who had gained from the structural disjunction that allowed the rhetorical benevolence were collectively powerful enough to prevent the disjunction's repair. However, they were not individually powerful enough to prevent Marcos from adding their property rights to the ever-lengthening list of rights that his government violated. Worryingly, no settled mode of governance respectful of labour and human rights has emerged since the oligarchs regained their property from Marcos. Although it represents an indigenously generated discursive resource, patriarchalism has fallen into disrepute because of its martial law associations, whilst the once again oligarchical state not only refuses to even consider enforcing the 'social democracy' advocated by the core of the labour movement, but also the executive and legislative branches have yet to regain control over a homicidal police apparatus. The set of transnational and in particular international relations within which Philippine social relations subsist have in the past undermined the 'attachment' of human rights. Today, however, the changed character of this set of relations may yet contribute to suturing the fatal disjunction that has caused the Philippines to be such an underdeveloped, unsuccessful and dangerous instance of Pacific capitalism.

HONG KONG, PATRIARCHALIST INDIVIDUALISM AND HUMAN RIGHTS ANXIETY

By contrast, Hong Kong currently demonstrates that even a non-democratic and still colonial but successful and transnationally open Pacific-capitalist society can exhibit a high level of security with respect to the 'attachment' of human rights. Of course, if the Philippines faced its moment of truth in 1947, Hong Kong has yet to face its equivalent. Because Hong Kong was until very recently a colony, nothing more need be said about the causal mechanism that has produced its mode of governance than that it comprises the articulation of a liberal but non-democratic state with a capitalist economy under conditions defined by its status as a British colony and its position as a freeport in an increasingly globalised world economy. This has meant that, after consultation with its major capitalist clients, the state has been able to choose which elements of British legal and rights discourse it wished to receive into the Colony. Hence, the human and labour rights currently enforced in Hong Kong are both no more and only slightly less than those that Britain was committed to respect under its international treaty obligations. In the case of labour rights specifically, their coverage and content is configured so that, with a remarkable degree of precision, the state now meets the patriarchal obligations formerly acknowledged by what were once the most important sections of local capital. Thus, to meet the needs of local and transnational capital, the 'liberties' and 'immunities' enjoyed by organised and unorganised labour have been gradually restricted. However, to a degree this has been compensated for by an increase in individual contractual and wider but individualistically oriented social 'claims' that are currently effectively enforced for fear of the social disorder that might result if they were not. Thus, a minimal set of the behaviours and needs that the discourse of human rights specifies as requiring protection has been protected by transferring the responsibility for carrying out this task from companies and trade unions to the state and its agencies.

In sum, then, the disciplinary matrix, or mode of governance, whereby rights are, to use MacNeil's (1995) essential concept, 'attached' to individuals and labour organisations in Hong Kong consists of a set of state-enforced texts, and state-instructed institutions and agencies. Currently, this mode of governance is effective because there is no significant difference between how it distributes rights and duties and how they might be spontaneously distributed, as suggested by their distribution within the civil law, given the balance of class forces in Hong Kong, and its international and transnational conditions of existence. Perhaps the most important of the latter conditions is the fact that as the Colony has been transformed from a manufacturing centre to a regional hub for high value-added services, the contracts that such employers routinely offer their staff are never worse and more often better than those required under the Employment Ordinance.

In the conclusion to my discussion of Hong Kong, I referred to the SAR's labour rights quid pro quo as an embryonic form of 'enforceable benevolence'. This was not simply because of the still underdeveloped nature of enforceable social and economic claims, but also given the centrality of inspection, conciliation and mediation to the disciplinary matrix that 'attaches' these rights to individuals and unions, no change in the law would be necessary if the state decided to redistribute them to capital's further benefit. All that would be required would be a changed set of instructions to the Department of Labour. Legislatively, nothing would have changed but the disciplinary outcome would have been transformed. Thus, in the absence of democracy and full freedom of association for labour as such and not simply trade unions, and despite their status as legally enforceable obligations, labour's 'claims' remain revokable or 'detachable' at the will of the state and therefore ultimately discretionary and so merely paternalistic. This, then, is why one has to be concerned for the future of human rights in Hong Kong as its international, if not its transnational, conditions of existence are transformed.

The critical structural questions posed by a comparison of the Hong Kong and Philippines experiences are twofold.

(1) Is it ever possible for human rights regimes to be more beneficial to the weak than their environing social-structural balances allow?
(2) If it is possible, what is the particular configuration of balances that might allow it?

In what follows, I will not only outline the causal mechanisms operating within Malaysia and Singapore as regards the 'attachment'of rights, but also argue that a comparison of them with each other and with the Philippines and Hong Kong enables one to answer both of these questions in a conditionally optimistic way.

MALAYSIA, AUTHORITARIAN PATRIARCHALISM AND THE DEROGATION OF HUMAN RIGHTS

The decolonisation of Malaysia has been far more complete than that of the Philippines. Malaysia is not therefore a social formation that remains fractured by neo-colonial mendicancy. It is instead a society that is structured by the presence of a relatively complex form of capitalism, albeit much of it foreign-owned, and liberal forms of governance. However, notwithstanding these favourable conditions, the critical factor determining the fate of labour and human rights in Malaysia since its separation from Britain and its entry into the circuits that have been constitutive of Pacific capitalism has thus far been the replacement of the undoubtedly racist but reserved patriarchalism of the colonial state by the increasingly assertive and authoritarian patriarchalism of the UMNO state. In addition, this replacement occurred within a social-structural context whose dynamics are powerfully overdetermined by domestic 'racial' divisions and the exigencies that arise from the Malay's constitutional 'special position'.

UMNO's patriarchalism stresses the loyalty owed to superiors rather than the benevolence that should be shown to inferiors. Thus, the leadership provided by UMNO has always been regarded as the greatest benefit that could be be granted to the masses of all 'races'. Consequently, whenever this leadership decided that for the good of the nation or for the sake of economic progress it would use its constitutional powers to violate labour and human rights, it has felt under no obligation to offer any apology let alone compensation to those whose 'liberties' and/or 'immunities' it has violated or diminished. On the contrary, not only is social provision far less developed than in Hong Kong, but also the UMNO state appears to have expected the grateful thanks of its victims as well as of the citizenry at large. Moreover, the disciplinary matrix upon which the degree to which the 'attachment' of rights depends has been weakened still further by the removal of the power to order preventive detention from the purview of the courts, the undermining of judicial independence, and the dramatic weakening of the trade unions. There must therefore be great uncertainty as to the degree to which the 'liberties' and 'immunities' that labour and individuals formally retain, as well as the minor 'claims' they have been allowed, are still 'attached' to them – currently, they too seem to be detachable at the will of the state. In sum, then, primarily because of the particular content of Malaysian patriarchalism, the nation's mode of governance is at best paternalist and in any event far less beneficial to labour and individuals than might be expected if one looked solely at the economic dimension or even at the overall balance of class forces as indicated by the distribution of rights and duties within the civil law.

All that has changed since *Merdeka* is that the basis upon which loyalty is demanded has changed. That is, this basis has been 'modernised' or Americanised as the 'substantive protectors' within UMNO have displaced the 'symbolic protectors', the rulers, as those to whom loyalty is owed. This is, however, a development that perhaps suggests a structurally generated possibility of enhanced respect for human and labour rights in the future. Tradition has been replaced by economic prosperity as the basis upon which loyalty is demanded. An indivisible and therefore incalculable basis has been replaced by a numerical and therefore calculable and redistributable one. The net result is that anything that has been given up since the NEP has a price in the form of an expected economic reward, which if it is not forthcoming may in time engender far stronger claims for compensations at the level of rights, especially in the form of contractual and social 'claims', than those currently heard during what continue to be good economic times. Finally, because, thanks to the openness of the Malaysian economy, the most likely source of any future economic disruption will be international or transnational in origin, it may be far easier for the UMNO leadership to respond positively to such claims than it might presently appear – the discourse of rights may therefore yet regain its earlier identification with national dignity.

SINGAPORE, ACTIVE PATRIARCHALISM AND THE POSSIBILITY OF 'ENFORCEABLE BENEVOLENCE'

For reasons that have just been outlined, Malaysia currently instances the negative consequences for the 'attachment' of human rights that can follow from openness to the flows that have been constitutive of Pacific capitalism. Like Hong Kong, Singapore curently instances the positive effects of such openness. In comparison with the Philippines, Singapore shares the same advantages as Malaysia. However, in contrast to Malaysia, from the beginning of its existence as an independent nation, the basis upon which the PAP state has claimed the loyalty of *its* citizenry has been of an economistic kind. Because of its socialist origins and the absence of any effective opposition from capital, the PAP's initial discourse of rule sought to earn the people's loyalty by showing benevolence. However, because the PAP was also engaged in a life or death struggle with a communist movement that was, to begin with, far stronger than itself, its political practice stressed the enforcement of loyalty. Thus, the party simultaneously developed an elaborate system of social provision and demanded an increasingly high price in terms of loyalty from the recipients of its benevolence. That is, the party considered that, since it was the provider of so impressive an array of benefits, it was neither necessary nor appropriate that any other institutions, notably trade unions, should continue to possess 'liberties' and 'immunities' that were no longer required and so were therefore only likely to be used for disruptive purposes. In this way, then, an exchange of 'liberties' and 'immunities' for 'claims' and 'powers' took place that is presently unparalleled in Pacific Asia.

There is a problem, however, with the proposition that this exchange has resulted in the installation of a new mode of governance that, as it stands, is as deserving of global approbation as the liberal and social-democratic regimes that have traditionally enjoyed such acceptance. This problem has its origin in the fact that, over time, loyalty has become much less something that the PAP considers it has to earn than something it considers it is owed. Thus, according to its reading of the needs of the transnational companies that are the Republic's strategically most important employers, it can decide or threaten to withdraw benefits at will from those whom it considers to be disloyal. In sum, the party has become ever more paternalistic in practice if not in rhetoric as it has attempted to re-invent Singapore as, first, an American-style 'modern' society and latterly as an 'orientalized' one. The result is that the benevolence the party now dispenses has become increasingly discretionary, at least in theory if not yet often in practice, and so no longer a matter of right. Structurally, this is because there are no social forces outside of the PAP/NTUC nexus that are legally entitled to enforce 'claims'. Consequently, there has to be some doubt as to how securely 'attached' to the citizenry are their undeniably extensive array of compensatory social rights as well as their remaining 'liberties' and 'immunities'. Moreover, as in Malaysia, the disciplinary matrix upon which the degree of adhesion of the 'liberties' and 'immunities' in particular depends has been weakened still further by the removal of the power to order preventive detention from the purview of the courts, and the undermining of judicial independence.

Thus, what is in theory a novel and, in my view, supportable rights regime that was, as the distribution of rights and duties within the civil law indicates, initially made possible by class balances that were exceptionally favourable to labour, has been flawed from the beginning. In contrast to Malaysia, this was not a consequence of Singapore's ideological particularity but rather simply of the way in which the political force, the PAP, that made use of the autonomy felt compelled to act in the struggle against communism. That is, the source of the fatal flaw in Singapore's claims to represent a new type of human rights regime was a political decision. Since the circumstances that compelled this decision no longer exist, it simply requires an act of political will to remove both it and therefore the basis to any objections to such claims.

CONCLUSION

To conclude, it seems to me, then, that with the help of sociological analysis it is possible to see that there is at least one more conceivable, if so far nowhere fully realised, human rights regime in addition to those projected by the liberal and social-democratic discourses. In other words, contrary to received opinion and despite the repressive use recently made of various imported or invented neo-orientalisms, there is nothing about either patriarchalism as a discourse or Pacific capitalism as a set of institutions that is intrinsically antipathetic to the maintenance of respect for human rights.

In Pacific Asia, as elsewhere, labour is today performed under condi-tions created by an increasingly globalised world economy. Within this economy control relations modelled on Japanese designs have given a new meaning to the phrase 'organised labour' and have gained primacy. The corporations that embody these forces, whether they are European, American or Japanese, can possess anything they like, but they cannot necessarily own it. *Pace* the Philippines' experience, because of the actual or potential pre-eminence with respect to title that patriarchalism can legitimate, only the state and the international organisations it can thereby empower possess the means to design and enforce (juridically or otherwise) a quid pro quo in the industrial arena wherein possessory gains are extracted to compensate the population for their losses with respect to control. However, because of the legislatively driven and so instrumentalist manner in which the law has been deployed in Hong Kong and Singapore, the mode of governance that I have termed 'enforceable benevolence' has yet to receive the support of the juridical syllogism that operates in Japan. However, there are good reasons for thinking both that such support could be forthcoming and that a state-centred human rights regime is more appropriate than one that either leaves enforcement to individuals and trade unions, or off-loads it onto Japanese-style private-corporatist institutions. An unconscious acknow-ledgement of the latter's fading allure may perhaps be present in the Singaporean government's apparent loss of interest in even the 'export version' of the JES – perhaps it too has heard of the increasing number of companies taken over by enterprise unions since the beginning of the present recession? How pleasantly ironic it would be if Japan's minority unions should prove to be the most lasting legacy of the JES.

What, finally, the preceding analysis suggests politically is that, whereas human rights in the so-called 'individualist West' have been pursued primarily as 'liberties' of one kind or another (British labour law's stress on 'immunities' has obviously been a highly suggestive excep-tion to this rule for the present author), they might be more effectively pursued in the patriarchalist East as primarily 'claims' of one kind or another. Because of my conviction that the consistency and therefore also the effectiveness of the law depend upon its articulation with a coherent and, in a Gramscian sense, hegemonic and therefore socially embedded ideological discourse, my point is that any strategy for en-hancing respect for human rights in Pacific Asia that depends upon the advocacy of individualism and liberty is unlikely to be successful for at least two reasons. First, individualism and liberty are subordinate if not entirely alien values within the cultures of the region, even amongst the contradictorily positioned middle classes (Jones, 1995; Robison and Goodman, 1995). And second, insisting on privileging them risks exciting the chauvinistic critiques which still resonate so effectively with the anti-colonialist legacy, as was all too apparent during the 1993 United Nations Human Rights Conference in Vienna. Better by far, or so it seems to me, for regional human rights activists and their supporters to go with, rather than against, the regional ethical and social-structural grain and follow up on the anti-authoritarian possibilities opened up by Neo-Confucianism and the more libertarian currents within Buddhism and Islam. What would give content to such a strategy would be the aim of eventually breaking the links between inequality and patriarchalism. Thus, for example, Confucianism's secular humanism and Buddhism's non-essentialist conception of the self both suggest the possibility of a non-metaphysical individualism which could be developed to make virtually all forms of discrimination unacceptable, including sexism. Of course, if such a breakage could be achieved, it would mean the end of patriarchalism but by its own hand, so to speak. No culture *must* survive for ever.

This, then, is what could be achieved or initiated through the inscription of a state-enforced, claims-based variant of the discourse of human rights within the rites that inform social relations or govern 'proper conduct' in the region. However, this is also what could almost as easily be pre-empted given the temptations to dependency, on TNCs if not foreign governments, and therefore to mendicancy on the part of greedy or failing patriarchs. Chillingly, for this reason if no others, the Philippines' experience remains a possible future for Pacific Asia if the powerful cannot be made to abide by their own values in bad times as well as good, and if therefore a difference emerges between the bases of economic and political calculation. Immanent in the population though it may be, 'enforceable benevolence' remains after all simply a sociologically constructed hope and as yet nothing else. This said, pursuit of a strategy inspired by this hope suggests that there may yet be, for example, a way out of the current stalemate on the 'social clause' at the World Trade Organisation – a claims-based variant could be included alongside the liberties-based one currently favoured by the West and countries allowed to choose the variant that best fits their social-structural circumstances. Thus there may also eventually come a day when employment relations might become globally justiciable like property and contractual relations and when multinational and transnational corporations are no longer able to play 'Southern' and 'Northern' labour off against one another. Such a momentous development could only occur, if not only the countries of the West acknowledged the pertinence of the patriarchalist dimensions of their own pasts, but also if the 'Rest' finally found the confidence to learn from themselves as well as from the West. Under such circumstances we would indeed be witnesses to the commencement of a 'voyage in'.

NOTES

Introduction: the 'clash of civilisations' and the problem of human rights

1. Introducing a recent essay on the background to human rights protection in Hong Kong, Peter Wesley-Smith (1993, pp. 18–19) has provided one of the clearest, most comprehensive and most concise accounts of the nature of the claims made with respect to the rule of law that I have encountered.

   1. '[It is] a formal and rational system . . . its precepts are self-consistent and generalised, made by persons with acknowledged lawmaking competence in accordance with a regular, open procedure.'
   2. 'Law is the antithesis of arbitrary power. It does not depend on whim or caprice but on fixed rules existing prior to conduct which is subject to their standards: it is prospective in operation not retrospective.'
   3. 'The law applies equally to all persons [whatever their personal or social attributes]'
   4. 'judges are independent of political and personal pressure'
   5. 'law is capable of guiding a person's behaviour'
   6. 'Law is advantageous to the individual: it stabilises social relationships, providing a settled framework for social intercourse . . .'
   '[In sum] [t]he legal system which exemplifies and proclaims the Rule of Law as an ideal is characterised by its neutrality, rationality, formality, impartiality, and impersonality.'

Chapter One: Transnational sociality, sociological theory and human rights

1. When the term 'model' is used in the present text I will be invoking the work of John Braithwaite (1994) who has recently attempted to resuscitate the diffusionist tradition by developing a concept of modelling that can be used as a component in otherwise structuralist explanations of social change:

   When the fashion model parades, we say she is modelling, and when the observer copies her, we say she is modelling the model, and we call the whole pattern of fashion diffusion of which this is a part, modelling. This is a good usage because the fact of the process is that the woman who goes to fashion parades herself becomes a model for others. Modelling is therefore defined as action(s) that constitute a process of displaying, symbolically interpreting and copying conceptions of action (and this process itself). A model is a conception of action that is put on display during such a process of modelling. A model is that which is displayed, symbolically interpreted and copied . . . Knowing the structural facts about the past and present will make for poor prediction unless we also discover the models that key actors have constructed of a future toward which they wish to move. (1994, p. 450)

2. One definition of a commodity chain is 'a network of labour and production processes whose end result is a finished commodity'. According to Gereffi (1992, pp. 93–4):

One must follow two steps in building such a chain. First, to delineate the anatomy of the chain, one typically starts with the final production operation for a manufactured good and moves sequentially backward until one reaches the raw material inputs [and forward until one reaches the retailing moment]. The second step . . . involves identifying four properties for each operation or node in the chain: (1) the commodity flows to and from the node, and those operations that occur immediately prior to and after it; (2) the relations of production (i.e. forms of the labour force) within the node; (3) the dominant organization of production including technology and the scale of the production unit; and (4) the geographic loci of the operation in question.

More recently, Gereffi (1995, pp. 14–15) has distinguished between two major types of commodity chains:

two distinct types of governance structures for Global Commodity Chains (GCCs) have emerged (over) the past two decades, which for the sake of simplicity can be called 'producer-driven' and 'buyer-driven' commodity chains.

Producer-driven commodity chains refer to those industries in which TNCs or other large integrated industrial enterprises play the central role in controlling the production system (including its backward and forward linkages). This is most characteristic of capital technology-intensive industries like automobiles, computers, aircraft, and heavy machinery. The geographical spread of these industries is transnational, but the number of countries in the commodity chain and their levels of development are varied. International subcontracting of components is common, especially for the most labor-intensive production processes, as are strategic alliances between international rivals. What distinguishes 'producer-driven' systems is the control exercised by the administrative headquarters of TNC manufacturers.

Buyer-driven commodity chains refer to those industries in which large retailers, branded marketers, and trading companies play the pivotal role in setting up decentralized production networks in a variety of exporting countries, typically located in the Third World. This pattern of trade-led industrialization has become common in labor-intensive, consumer goods industries such as garments, footwear, toys, housewares, consumer electronics, and a variety of hand-crafted items (e.g., furniture, ornaments). Production is generally carried out by locally owned Third World factories that make finished goods (rather than components or parts) for foreign buyers. The specifications are supplied by the branded companies or large retailers that design and order the goods.

One of the main characteristics of the branded firms that fit the buyer-driven model, such as athletic footwear companies like Nike, Reebok, and L. A. Gear, and branded apparel companies like The Limited, The Gap, and Liz Claiborne, is that they usually do not own any production facilities. These companies are marketers that design, but do not make, the branded products they order. They rely on complex tiered networks of overseas production contractors to perform most of their specialized tasks. Branded marketers farm out part or all of their product development activities, manufacturing, packaging, shipping, and even accounts receivable to different agents around the world.

The crucial job of the core company in buyer-driven commodity chains is to manage these production and trade networks and to make sure all the pieces of the business come together as an integrated whole.

Finally, for a comparison between the organisation of Japanese-headed as opposed to American-headed chains, see Dobson, 1993.

3. I say 'particular and non-exhaustive' because, although I consider the class structure to be one of the most important products of the imbrication of the various structural dimensions with one another, I do not consider it to be the only one. Thus these dimensions remain available, so to speak, to produce other structural forms, answering to different imperatives as in the case of gender and 'racial' relations, for example.

4. I owe this tripartite 'sociological' conception of the property relation to the work of Kelvin Jones (1982, pp. 76ff.). I have defined the critical terms elsewhere (Woodiwiss, 1990a, pp. 130–1) in the following way:

> As I read Jones, by 'possession' he means the narrowly economic ability to determine the use or operation, as such, of the production process. By 'control', he means the ability or power to determine the actual deployment of means of production in the production process. Finally, what he means by 'title' refers to the significatory basis upon which claims to any surplus may be made, and so it is not restricted to:
>> the formal legal right to a claim upon a company or an estate but depends upon the sorts of calculations which govern the circulation of legal titles . . . title involves the sort of calculations and conditions that govern the more general provision of finance, the socialisation of debt, the exchange of guarantees and the constitutional position of shareholders.   (Jones, 1982, pp. 77–8)

In addition, and critically, Jones also points out that whereas within small and medium size enterprises the possessory relation is critical, within large corporate enterprises the control relation is critical. Thus, as I have explained elsewhere (Woodiwiss, 1990b, p. 272), where labour law systems do not include provisions relating to co-determination and/or title-sharing (e.g. the Swedish Wage Earner Funds), which means in most of the world outside of Western Europe, their pertinence is largely confined to a set of relations (possessory) that are of decreasing significance as loci of power within contemporary economies. Consequently, one may argue that the legal position of trade unions has been weakened throughout much of the world as much by the increasing irrelevance of extant labour law as by restrictive 'reforms'.

5. For this reason as well as because it may make it easier for a non-legal audience to appreciate the significance of Hohfeld's ideas, I have also altered

his terminology in a couple of instances. That is, where I have used 'liberty' he used 'right ' or 'claim', and where I have used 'claim' he used 'privilege'.

Chapter Two: The challenge of Pacific capitalism: from Pax Americana to the Japanese Way?

1. For Japan, see Woodiwiss, 1992a, chs. 3, 4; for Pacific Asia more generally, see Berger and Borer, 1997; Chan, 1990, ch. 3; Clegg and Redding, 1986, 1990, pt. 1; Deyo, 1987, 1989, chs. 5, 6; Haggard, 1990; Jones, 1997; Scalapino et al., 1985; Whitely, 1992; and, finally, for the especially negative consequences for women in Pacific Asia see: Chann, 1984; Cheng and Hsiung, 1992; Salaff, 1992.

Chapter Three: The Philippines and mendicant patriarchalism

1. Statistics relating to trade union membership in the Philippines are notoriously unreliable. As against the official figure of 25 per cent for the overall organisation rate, Elias Ramos (1990, p. 96) states that on a generous interpretation of the highly suspect data no more than 10 per cent of the whole labour force and no more than 20 per cent of wage and salary earners are organised.
2. For a thorough account of the harsh conditions faced by unorganised employees in the typically non-factory fishing, garment, transport, construction, and retail industries, see the special issue of the *Philippine Labor Review*, 1987. Further confirmation of the variety in the character of such relationships may be found in the larger selection of case studies reported by Aganon (1990) – unfortunately, no one as yet has attempted to estimate the frequency distribution of enterprises between the five different types she identifies.
3. To answer it would require an investigation into the precise nature and location of these interventions and an assessment of their significance at the level of the rules of formation of the discursive formation that makes mendicant patriarchalism possible. Fortunately, such an investigation is beyond the scope of the present study.
4. Although this is very obviously the case under mendicant patriarchalism, this is not a problem confined to mendicant systems alone, as the continuing high level of violations in Japan suggests.
5. The list of indispensable or 'vital' industries was anyway a long one, including the transportation, communications, utilities, banking and fuel industries, as well as the food and export processing industries.

Chapter Four: Hong Kong and patriarchalist individualism

1. For a discussion of the entirely unbalanced sources of advice depended upon in relation to industrial relations matters prior to 1980, see England and Rear, 1975, pp. 8–13.
2. Thus far I have used the term 'the rule of law' in an unqualified way to refer to Hong Kong. There is, however, one weakness in the system that should now be mentioned. Judges in the Supreme and District Courts cannot be dismissed except for reasons of incapacity and misbehaviour as decided by a

committee of judges and approved by the Privy Council in London. Magistrates, however, do not enjoy such protection of their independence, although, interestingly, there were moves to correct this weakness in the run-up to 1997. This perhaps suggests that, in addition to the colonial government's insistence on the use of English in the courts, there may be other grounds for the doubts as to the system's fairness since the magistrates are the judicial personnel that ordinary members of the public are most likely to come in touch with.

Chapter Six: Singapore and the possibility of enforceable benevolence

1. This usage of the term is close to that of Howard and Donnelly (1986). However, it should be distinguished from that associated with Amitai Etzioni (1995), that found in the more general philosophical literature (Mulhall and Swift, 1992), and (contra Hill and Lian, 1995) 'civic republicanism' as found in the wider North American and Australian literature (Wilentz, 1984; Braithwaite and Petitt, 1990). Respect for individual rights remains critical to all of these positions in a way that it does not in the usage that has become influential in Singapore.
2. Official statistics do not allow one to strip out employers and the self-employed from the 'Professional and Technical' and 'Administrative and Managerial' categories that account for the largest number of 'new middle class' positionings.

REFERENCES

Abbas, Datu F. (1988) 'Philippine Labor Policy and its Impact on Trade Union-ism', unpublished Ph.D. Thesis, College of Social Sciences and Philosophy, University of the Philippines, Quezan City.

Abegglen, J. (1958) *The Japanese Factory*, The Free Press, Glencoe.

(1994) *Sea Change: Pacific Asia as the New World Industrial Center*, The Free Press, Glencoe.

Abegglen, J. and Stalk, G. (1985) *Kaisha: The Japanese Corporation*, Basic Books, New York.

Abercrombie, N., Hill, S. and Turner, B. S. (eds.) (1980) *The Dominant Ideology Thesis*, Allen and Unwin, London.

(1990) *Dominant Ideologies*, Unwin Hyman, London.

Abrahams, G. (1968) *Trade Unions and the Law*, Cassell, London.

Abueva, J. and De Guzman, R. (eds.) (1969) *Foundations and Dynamics of Fili-pino Government and Politics*, Bookmark, Manila.

Acharya, A. (1995) 'Human Rights and Regional Order: ASEAN and Human Rights Management in Post-Cold War Southeast Asia', in Tang (1995).

Agabin, P. (1991) 'The Philosophy of the Civil Code', *Philippine Law Journal*, vol. 66, pp. 1–23.

Aganon, M. (1990) 'A Typology of Labor Relations in the Philippines', unpub-lished doctoral dissertation, College of Social Science and Philosophy, University of the Philippines, Quezon City.

Ago, S. (1995) 'The Social Clause as Understood in Asia', mimeo, Faculty of Law, Kyushu University.

Agpalo, R. (1972) *The Political Elite and the People: A Study of Politics in Occidental Mindoro*, Center of Public Administration, University of the Philippines.

Ali, M. R. (1969) 'Legislative and Public Policy Developments in Malaysia's Industrial Relations', *Journal of Developing Areas*, vol. 3, pp. 355–72.

Ames, R. (1988) 'Rites as Rights: The Confucian Alternative', in Rouner (1988).

Amsden, A. (1989) *Asia's Next Giant: South Korea and Late Industrialization*, Oxford University Press, New York.

Anantaraman, V. (1990) *Singapore's Industrial Relations System*, McGraw-Hill, Singapore.

Andaya, B. W. and Andaya, L. Y. (1982) *A History of Malaysia*, Macmillan, London.

Anderson, B. (1991) *Imagined Communities: Reflections on the Origins and Spread of Nationalism*, Verso, London.

Angeles, L. (1994) *The Quest for Justice: Obstacles to the Redress of Human Rights Violations in the Philippines*, Center for Integration and Development Studies, University of the Philippines, Quezon City.

Angoncillo, T. and Guerrero, M. (1970) *A History of the Filipino People*, 3rd ed., Garcia Publishing, Quezon City.

An-Na'im, A. A. (1990) *Toward an Islamic Reformation: Civil Liberties, Human Rights and International Law*, Syracuse University Press, Syracuse.

Appelbaum, R. and Henderson, J. (1992) *States and Development in the Asian Pacific Rim*, Sage, New York.

Aquino, C. (1984) 'A Study of Class Consciousness: the Case of Workers in a Coconut Factory', unpublished Ph.D. thesis, College of Social Sciences and Philosophy, University of the Philippines, Quezon City.

Aquino, C. and her Cabinet (1992) *The Aquino Administration: Record and Legacy*, University of the Philippines Press, Quezon City.

Aquino, R. (1969) 'Legal Landmarks of American Colonial Rule', in Abueva and De Guzman (1969).

Ariff, M. (1991) *The Malaysian Economy: Pacific Connections*, Oxford University Press, Singapore.

Armour, A. (1985) *Asia and Japan: The Search for Modernity and Identity*, Athlone Press, London.

Arudsothy, P. and Littler, C. (1993) 'State Regulation and Union Fragmentation in Malaysia' in Frenkel (1993).

Asia Watch (1989) *Silencing All Critics: Human Rights Violations in Singapore*, Asia Watch, New York.

Asian and Pacific Development Center (1989) *The Trade in Domestic Helpers: Causes, Mechanisms and Consequences*, Asian and Pacific Development Center, Manila.

Atleson, J. (1983) *Values and Assumptions in American Labor Law*, University of Massachusetts Press, Amhurst.

Atsushi, H. (1995) 'Overseas Japanese Plants under Global Strategies: TV Transplants in Asia' in Frenkel and Harrod (1995).

Ayadurai, D. (1985) *The Employer, the Employee and the Law in Malaysia*, Butterworths, Singapore.

Bachrach, P. and Baratz, M. (1970) *Power and Poverty: Theory and Practice*, Oxford University Press, New York.

Bacungan, F. (1990) *Labor and Social Legislation*, Flavdeem Law Publishing, Quezon City.

(1993) 'The Influences of Foreign Law on Contemporary Union Right Policies in the Philippines', mimeo, Japan Institute of Labour, Tokyo.

Bakar, M. A. (1981) 'Islamic Revivalism and the Political Process', *Asian Survey*, vol. 21, no. 10, pp. 1040–59.

Bananal, E. (1986) *The Presidents of the Philippines*, National Book Store, Manila.

Bartholomew, G. W. (1989) 'The Singapore Legal System', in Sandhu and Wheatley (1989).

Barton, C. (ed.) (1992) *Politics and Society in Hong Kong: Towards 1997*, Joint Centre for Asia-Pacific Studies, Toronto.

Bataille, G. (1988) *The Accursed Share: An Essay on General Economy*, Zone Books, New York.

Battistella, G. (ed.) (1993) *Human Rights of Migrant Workers: An Agenda for NGOs*, Scalabrini Migration Center, Quezon City.

Battistella, G. and Paganoni, A. (eds.) (1992) *Philippine Labor Migration: Impact and Policy*, Scalabrini Migration Center, Quezon City.

Bautista, V. (1988) 'The Socio-Psychological Make-up of the Filipino', in Miranda-Feliciano (1988).

Beer, L. W. (1984) *Freedom of Expression in Japan*, Kodasha International, Tokyo.

(1979) *Constitutionalism in Asia: Asian Views of the American Influence*, University of California Press, Berkeley.

(1992) *Constitutional Systems in Late Twentieth Century Asia*, University of Washington Press, Seattle.

Beetham, D. (ed.) (1995) *Politics and Human Rights*, Blackwell, Oxford.

Begin, J. (1995) 'Singapore's Industrial Relations System: Is it Congruent with its Second Phase of Industrializaton?', in Frenkel and Harrod (1995).

Bell, D. (1973) *The Coming of Post-Industrial Society*, Basic Books, New York.

Bello, S. (1992) 'Justice and Human Rights' in Aquino et al. (1992).

Benton, T. (1993) *Natural Relations: Ecology, Animal Rights and Social Justice*, Verso, London.

Berger, M. and Borer, D. (eds.) (1997) *The Rise of East Asia: Critical Visions of the Pacific Century*, Routledge, New York.

Berger, P. and Hsiao, M.(eds.) *In Search of an East Asian Development Model*, Transaction Books, New Brunswick.

Berlin, I. (1969) *Four Essays on Liberty*, Oxford University Press, Oxford.

Bhabha, H. (1994) *The Location of Culture*, Routledge, London.

Bloodworth, D. (1986) *The Tiger and the Trojan Horse*, Times Books International, Singapore.

Blum, A. and Patarapanich, S. (1987) 'Productivity and the Path to House

Unionism: Structural Change in the Singapore Labour Movement', *British Journal of Industrial Relations*, vol. 25, no. 3, pp. 389–400.

Bolasco, M. (1994) *Points of Departure: Essays on Christianity, Power and Social Change*, St. Scholasticas College, Manila.

Bowie, A. (1991) *Crossing the Industrial Divide: State, Society, and the Politics of Economic Transformation in Malaysia*, Columbia University Press, New York.

Bowring, P. (1992) 'APEC May Already be Outdated', *Japan Times*, 17 September, p. 21.

Boyce, J. (1993) *The Political Economy of Growth and Impoverishment in the Marcos Era*, Ateneo de Manila University Press, Quezon City.

Boyle, K. (1995) 'Stock-taking on Human Rights: The World Conference on Human Rights, Vienna 1993', in Beetham (1995).

Boyne, R. (1990) 'Culture and the World System' in Featherstone (1990).

Braithwaite, J. (1994) 'A Sociology of Modelling and the Politics of Empowerment', *British Journal of Sociology*, vol. 45, no. 3, pp. 445–79.

Braithwaite, J. and Petitt, P. (1990) *Not Just Deserts: A Republican Theory of Criminal Justice*, Clarendon Press, Oxford.

Bratton, J. (1992) *Japanization at Work*, Macmillan, London.

Breman, J. (1989) *Taming the Coolie Beast: Plantation Society and the Colonial Order in Southeast Asia*, Oxford University Press, Delhi.

Bresnan, J. (ed.) (1986) *Crisis in the Philippines: An Analysis of the Marcos Era and Beyond*, Princeton University Press, Princeton.

Broad, R. (1979) *Unequal Alliance: the World Bank, the International Monetary Fund, and the Philippines*, Ateneo de Manila University Press, Quezon City.

Buang, H. S. (1989) *Malaysia's Torrens System*, Dewan Bahasa dan Puotaka, Kuala Lumpur.

Buchanan, I. (1972) *Singapore in Southeast Asia*, Bell and Sons, London.

Buraku Liberation Research Institute (1984) *White Paper on Human Rights in Japan: From the Point of View of the Discriminated*, Buraku Liberation Research Institute, Osaka.

Burchell, G., Gordon, C. and Miller, P. (eds.) (1991) *The Foucault Effect: Studies in Governmentality*, Harvester, London.

Busch, G. (1983) *The Politics of International Trade Unionism*, Macmillan, London.

Butterworths (1985) *Handbook of Singapore Employment Law*, Butterworths, Singapore.

Buzan, B. (1983) *People, States and Fear*, Harvester, Brighton.

Byre, A. (1988) *Human Rights at the Workplace*, Policy Studies Institute/British Institute of Human Rights, London.

Byrnes, A. and Chan, J. (eds.) (1993) *Public Law and Human Rights*, Butterworths, Hong Kong.

Calderon, C. (1968a) 'Labor Policy and Labor Law: Beginnings and Development', *Silliman Law Journal*, vol. 1, no. 1, pp. 9–37.

(1968b) 'Constitutional Basis of Philippine Labor Laws', *Silliman Law Journal*, vol.1, no. 2, pp. 67–79.

(1968c) 'The Adoption of Compulsory Arbitration', *Silliman Law Journal*, vol. 1, no. 2, pp. 130–45.

(1968d) 'The Court of Industrial Relations', *Silliman Law Journal*, vol. 1, no. 4, pp. 214–20.

(1968e) 'Judicial Concepts and Attitudes under Compulsory Arbitration', *Silliman Law Journal*, vol. 1, no. 4, pp. 221–54.

Calleo, D. (1982) *The Imperious Economy*, Harvard University Press, Cambridge, Mass.

(1987) *Beyond American Hegemony: The Future of the Western Alliance*, Wheatsheaf, Brighton.

Campbell, T. (1983) *The Left and Rights: A Conceptual Analysis of the Idea of Socialist Rights*, Routledge, London.

Campbell, T., Goldberg, D., McClean, S. and Mullen, T. (eds.) (1986) *Human Rights: From Rhetoric to Reality*, Basil Blackwell, Oxford.

Cardoso, F. and Falleto, E. (1979) *Dependency and Development in Latin America*, University of California Press, Berkeley.

Carino, T. (ed.) (1989) *Transnationals and Special Economic Zones: The Experience of China and Selected Asean Countries*, De La Salle University Press.

Carrier, J. (1992) 'Occidentalism: The World Turned Upside-down', *American Ethnologist*, vol. 19, no. 2, pp. 196–212.

Carroll, J. (1968) 'Philippine Labour Unions', *Philippine Studies*, vol. 9, no. 2, pp. 20–40.

Carty, A. (1986) *The Decay of International Law*, Manchester University Press, Manchester.

Carty, H. (1988) 'Intentional Violation of Economic Interests: the Limits of Common Law Liability', *Law Quarterly Review*, vol. 104, p. 250.

Carver, A. (1989) 'Employment and Trade Union Law', in Wacks (1989).

(1994) *Hong Kong Business Law*, 2nd edn, Longmans, Hong Kong.

Casey, T. (ed.) (1979) *Contemporary Labour Relations in the Asian Pacific Region*, Libra Press, Hong Kong.

Cassese, A. (1990) *Human Rights in a Changing World*, Temple University Press, Philadelphia.

Chalmers, W. E. (1967) *Crucial Issues in Industrial Relations in Singapore*, Donald Moore Press, Singapore.

Chan, H.-C. (1989) 'The PAP and the Structuring of the Political System', in Sandhu and Wheatley (1989).

Chan, H.-C. and ul Haq, O. (eds.) (1987) *S. Rajaratnam: The Prophetic and the Political*, St. Martin's Press, New York.

Chan, J. (1995) 'The Asian Challenge to Universal Human Rights: A Philosophical Appraisal', in Tang (1995).

Chan, J. and Ghai, Y. (eds.) (1993) *The Hong Kong Bill of Rights: A Comparative Approach*, Butterworths Asia, Hong Kong.

Chan, M.-K. (1990) 'Labour vs. Crown: Aspects of Society State Interactions in the Hong Kong Labour Movement Before World War II', in Sinn (1990).

Chan, M.-K., and Young, J. D. (eds.) (1994) *Precarious Balance: Hong Kong Between China and Britain, 1842–1992*, Hong Kong University Press, Hong Kong.

Chan, S. (1990) *East Asian Dynamism*, Westview Press, Boulder.

Chan, W.-K. (1991) *The Making of Hong Kong Society*, Clarendon Press, Oxford.

Chann, L. H. (1984) 'Women Workers in Malaysia: TNCs and Social Conditions', in Norlund et al. (1984).

Chau, L.-C. (1994) 'Economic Growth and Income Distribution in Hong Kong', in Leung and Wong (1994).

Chen, A. and Ng., S.-H. (1987) *The Workers Compensation System in Hong Kong*, Centre of Asian Studies, Hong Kong.

Chen, E., Louisburg, R., Ng, S. K. and Stewart, S. (eds.) (1992) *Labour-Management Relations in the Asia Pacific Region*, Centre for Asian Studies, Hong Kong University.

Cheng, L. and Hsiung, P. (1992) 'Women, Export-Oriented Growth, and the State: the Case of Taiwan', in Appelbaum and Henderson (1992).

Cheng, Tong Yung (1982) *The Economy of Hong Kong*, Far East Publications, Hong Kong.

Chew, E. and Lee, E. (eds.) (1991) *A History of Singapore*, Oxford University Press, Singapore.

Chew, S., Chew, R. and Chan, F. (1992) 'Technology Transfer from Japan to Asean: Trends and Prospects', in Tokunaga (1992).

Child-Hill, R. (1989) 'Comparing Transnational Production Systems: The Automobile Industry in the USA and Japan', *International Journal of Urban and Regional Research*, vol. 13, no. 3, pp. 462–80.

Chiu, R. (1994) 'Housing Intervention in Hong Kong: From Laissez Faire to Privatisation' in Leung and Wong (1994).

Chiu, S. and Levin, D. (1995) 'The World Economy, State, and Sectors in Industrial Change: Labor Relations in Hong Kong's Textile and Garment-Making Industries', in Frenkel and Harrod (1995).

Chow, N. W .S. (1989) 'A Review of Social Policies in Hong Kong', in Kwan (1989).

Christie, K. (1995) 'Regime Security and Human Rights in Southeast Asia', in Beetham (1995).

Chu, Y.-W. (1992) 'Informal Work in Hong Kong', *International Journal of Urban and Regional Research*, vol. 16, no. 3, pp. 420–41.

Chua, B.-H. (1995) *Communitarian Ideology and Democracy in Singapore*, Routledge, London.

Chua, B.-H. and Tan, J.-E. (1995) 'Singapore: A New Socially Stratified

Culture', mimeo, Department of Sociology, National University of Singapore.

Chung, I. Y. (1991) *The Asian Pacific Community in the Year 2000: Challenges and Prospects*, Sejong Institute, Seoul.

Chung, K.-Y. (1987) *The Mahathir Administration: Leadership and Change in a Multicultural Society*, Pelanduk Publications, Petaling Jaya.

Clammer, J. (1985) *Singapore: Ideology, Society, Culture*, Chapman, Singapore.

Clark, C. and Chan, S. (1992) *The Evolving Pacific Basis in the Global Political Economy*, Lynne Rienner Publishers, Boulder.

Clark, R. (1979) *The Japanese Company*, Yale University Press, New Haven.

Clegg, S. and Redding, S. (eds.) (1986) *The Enterprise and Management in East Asia*, Centre for Asian Studies, University of Hong Kong.

(1990) *Capitalism in Contrasting Cultures*, De Gruyter, Berlin.

Clutterbuck, R. (1985) *Conflict and Violence in Malaysia and Singapore*, Graham Brash, Singapore.

Coh, C.-T. (1994) *Malaysia: Beyond Communal Politics*, Pelanduk Publications, Petaling Jaya.

Cohen, R. (1991) *Contested Domains: Debates in International Labour Studies*, Zed Books, London.

Cojuanco, E. (1990) 'The Nature of Industrial Relations in the Coconut Industry' in Teodosio et al. (1990).

Cole, R. (1971) *Japanese Blue Collar: The Changing Tradition*, University of California Press, Berkeley.

Commission for a New Asia (1994) *Towards a New Asia*, The Commission, Kuala Lumpur.

Compa, L. and Diamond, S. (eds.) (1996) *Human Rights, Labor Rights, and International Trade*, University of Pennsylvania Press, Philadelphia.

Constantino, R. (1969) *The Making of a Filipino*, Malaya Books Inc., Quezon City.

(1978) *Neo-Colonial Identity and Counter Consciousness: Essays on Cultural Decolonisation*, Merlin, London.

Cox, R. W. (1987) *Production, Power and World Order*, Columbia University Press, New York.

Crafts, N. (1997) *Britain's Relative Economic Decline, 1870–1995*, Social Market Foundation, London.

Crane, G. T. (1990) *The Political Economy of China's Special Economic Zones*, M. E. Sharpe, Armonk.

Da Cuhna, D. (ed.) (1994) *Debating Singapore: Reflective Essays*, Institute of Southeast Asian Studies, Singapore.

Davies, S. (1977) 'One Brand of Politics Rekindled', *Hong Kong Law Journal*, vol. 7.

Davis, M. C. (ed.) (1995) *Human Rights and Chinese Values*, Oxford University Press, New York.

De Barros, J. (1989) 'An Exploration of the Roles and Functions of Quasi-Governmental Advisory Bodies in the Public Administration of Hong Kong', Ph.D. Thesis, Department of Politics, Brunel University.

de Bary, W. (1988) 'Neo-Confucianism and Human Rights', in Rouner (1988).

De Mont, J. (1989) *Hong Kong Money: How Chinese Families and Fortunes are Changing Canada*, Key Porter Books, Toronto.

Deery, S. and Mitchell, R. (eds.) (1993) *Labour Law and Industrial Relations in Asia: Eight Country Studies*, Longman Cheshire, Melborne.

Dejillas, L. (1994) *Trade Union Behavior in the Philippines: 1946–1990*, Ateneo de Manila University Press, Quezon City.

Deyo, F. (1981) *Dependent Development and Industrial Order: An Asian Case Study*, Praeger, New York.

(1987) *The Political Economy of the New Asian Industrialization*, Cornell University Press, Ithaca.

(1989) *Beneath the Miracle: Labor Subordination in the New Asian Industrialism*, University of California Press, Berkeley.

Diamond, W. H. and Diamond, D. B. (1984) *Tax Free Trade Zones of the World*, 3 vols., Bender, New York.

Dicken, P. (1991) 'The Changing Geography of Japanese Direct Investment in Manufacturing Industry' in Morris (1991).

Dirlik, A. (ed.) (1993) *What is in a Rim?: Critical Perspectives on the Pacific Region Idea*, Westview Press, Boulder.

Dobson, W. (1993) *Japan in East Asia: Trading and Investment Strategies*, Institute of Southeast Asian Studies, Singapore.

Donnelly, J. (1985) *The Concept of Human Rights*, Croom Helm, London.

Dore, R. (1973) *British Factory, Japanese Factory*, Allen and Unwin, London.

Dorman, P. (1992) 'The Social Tariff Approach to International Disparities in Environmental and Worker Right Standards: History, Theory and Some Initial Evidence', in Lehman and Moore (1992).

Doronila, A. (1992) *The State, Economic Transformation and Political Change in the Philippines*, Oxford University Press, Singapore.

Drysdale, J. (1984) *Singapore: The Struggle for Success*, Singapore.

Dryzek, J. (1990) *Discursive Democracy: Politics, Policy, and Political Science*, Cambridge University Press.

Du, G.-J. and Song, G. (1995) 'Relating Human Rights to Chinese Culture: The Four Paths of the Confucian Analects and the Four Principles of a New Theory of Benevolence', in Davis (1995).

Durkheim, E. (1984 [1896]) *The Division of Labour in Society*, Macmillan, London.

Edelman, B. (1980) 'The Legalisation of the Working Class', *Economy and Society*, vol. 9, no. 1, p. 50.

Elias, P. and Ewing, K. (1982) 'Economic Torts and Labour Law: Old Principles and New Liabilities', *Cambridge Law Journal*, vol. 41, p. 321.

Elwell, C. (1995) *Human Rights, Labour Standards and the New World Trade*

Organization, International Centre for Human Rights and Democratic Development, Montreal.

England, J. (1989) *Industrial Relations and Law in Hong Kong*, 2nd edn, Oxford University Press, Hong Kong.

England, J. and Rear, J. (1975) *Chinese Labour Under British Rule*, Oxford University Press, Hong Kong, 2nd edn 1981.

Escoda, I. T. (1994) *Hong Kong Postscript: More Letters from Hong Kong from an Expatriate Philippina*, Mediamark, Hong Kong.

Etzioni, A. (ed.) (1995) *New Communitarian Thinking: Persons, Virtues, Institutions, and Communities*, University Press of Virginia.

Evans, P. (1979) *Dependent Development: The Alliance of Multinational, State and Local Capital in Brazil*, Princeton University Press, Princeton.

(1995) *Embedded Autonomy: States and Industrial Transformation*, Princeton University Press, Princeton.

Ewing, K. (1994) *Britain and the ILO*, 2nd edn, The Institute for Employment Rights, London.

Fabros, W. (1988) *The Church and its Social Involvement in the Philippines: 1930–1972*, Ateneo de Manila University Press, Quezon City.

Fan, Y.-T. (1989) *The UMNO Drama: Power Struggles in Malaysia*, Egret Books, Kuala Lumpur.

Featherstone, M. (1991) *Consumer Culture and Postmodernism*, Sage, London.

Featherstone, M.(ed.) (1990) *Global Culture: Nationalism, Globalization and Modernity*, Sage, London.

Feldman, S. (1990) 'Human Rights and the New Industrial Working Class in Bangladesh' in Welch and Leary (1990).

Fernandez, P. (1969) 'The Structure and Sources of Philippine Law', in Abueva and De Guzman (1969).

(1982) 'The Regimentation of Labor in an Open Economy', *Philippine Journal of Industrial Relations*, vol. 4, nos. 1/2, pp. 7–17.

Fernando, W. (1975) 'Labour Laws in Malaysia' in ILO (1975a).

Ferrer, S., Hernandez, A., Jacinto, V., Padilla, A. and Quevado, R. (1980) 'The Supreme Court Record on Human Rights under Martial Law', *Philippine Law Journal*, vol. 55, pp. 247–97.

Ferry, L. (1990) *Political Philosophy: Rights – The New Quarrel Between the Ancients and Moderns*, University of Chicago Press, Chicago.

Filipinas Foundation (1976) *Philippine Majority–Minority Relations and Ethnic Attitudes*, Filipinas Foundation, Manila.

Fitting, G. (1982) 'EPZs in Taiwan and the Peoples Republic of China', *Asian Survey*, vol. 22, no. 8, pp. 732–44.

Florida, R. and Kenney, M. (1991) 'Japanese Direct Investment in the United States: The Case of Automotive Transplants' in Morris (1991).

Floro, F. R. (1995) *Philippines in the Regional Division of Labour*, International Institute for Labour Studies, ILO, Geneva.

Fong, C. (1992) 'Foreign Direct Investment in Malaysia: Technology Transfer and Linkages by Japan and Asian NIEs', in Tokunaga (1992).

Foote, D. H. (1992) 'The Benevolent Paternalism of Japanese Criminal Justice', *California Law Review*, vol. 80, pp. 317–90.

Foucault, M. (1974) *The Archaeology of Knowledge*, Tavistock, London.

(1979) *The History of Sexuality*, vol. I. Penguin, Harmondsworth.

(1991) 'On Governmentality' in Burchell et al. (1991).

Francisco, V. (1967) *Labor Laws in the Philippines*, 4th edn, East Publishing, Manila.

Frank, A. G. (1969) *Latin America: Underdevelopment or Revolution?*, Monthly Review Press, New York.

Frankel, S. and Harrod, J. (eds.) (1993) *Industrialization and Labor Relations: Contemporary Research in Seven Countries*, ILR Press, Ithaca.

Freeman, M. (1995) 'Human Rights: Asia and the West' in Tang (1995).

Frenkel, S. (1995) 'Workplace Relations in the Global Corporation: A Comparative Analysis of Subsidiaries in Malaysia and Taiwan', in Frenkel and Harrod (1995)

Frenkel, S. (ed.) (1993) *Organized Labor in the Asia-Pacific Region*, ILR Press, Ithaca.

Frobel, F., Heinrichs, J. and Kreye, O. (1980) *The New International Division of Labour*, Cambridge University Press, New York.

Fry, H. (1977) 'The Breakdown of the American Democratic Experiment in the Philippines: An Historical Analysis of a Crisis in Modernisation', *Australian Journal of Politics and History*, vol. 23, no. 2, pp. 383–402.

Fujita, K. (1991) 'A World City and Flexible Specialization: Restructuring the Tokyo Metropolis', *Journal of Urban and Regional Research*, vol. 15, no. 2, pp. 269–84.

Gabelleno-Anthony, M. (1995) 'Human Rights, Economic Change and Political Development: a Southeast Asian Perspective', in Tang (1995).

Gale, B. (ed.) (1986) *Readings in Malaysian Politics*, Pelanduk Publications, Petaling Jaya.

Gamba, C. (1957) *Labour Law in Malaya*, Donald Moore, Singapore.

(1962) *The Origins of Trade Unionism in Malaya: A Study of Colonial Labour Unrest*, Eastern Universities Press, Singapore.

Gamboa, M. (1955) *An Introduction to Philippine Law*, The Lawyers Cooperative Publishing Company, Manila.

Garon, S. (1987) *The State and Labor in Modern Japan*, University of California Press, Berkeley.

Gatchalian, J. (1983) 'Suggested Elements of a Philippine Paradigm of Industrial Relations', *Philippine Journal of Labor and Industrial Relations*, vol. 5, nos. 1/2, pp. 83–95.

Geertz, C. (ed.) (1963) *Old Societies and New States: The Quest for Modernity in Asia and Africa*, Free Press, Glencoe.

Geiger, T. and Geiger, F. (1973) *Tales of Two City-States: The Development Progress of Hong Kong and Singapore*, National Planning Association, Washington, D. C.

George, F. J. (1992) *Successful Singapore*, SSMB Publishing Division, Singapore.

George, T. (1980) *Revolt in Mindanao: The Rise of Islam in Philippine Politics*, Oxford University Press, Kuala Lumpur.

Gereffi, G. (1992) 'New Realities of Industrial Development in East Asia and Latin America: Global, Regional, and National Trends' in Appelbaum and Henderson (1992).

(1995) 'Global Commodity Chains and Third World Development', mimeo, Department of Sociology, Duke University.

Ghai, Y. (1993) 'Derogations and Limitations in the Hong Kong Bill of Rights', in Chan and Ghai (1993).

(1994) *Human Rights and Governance: The Asia Debate*, Occasional Paper, Asia Foundation.

(1995) 'Asian Perspectives on Human Rights', in Tang (1995).

Ghazali, S. (1985) *Rukunegara: A Testament of Hope*, Creative Enterprises, Kuala Lumpur.

Ghee, L. T. (ed.) (1988) *Reflections on Development in South East Asia*, ISEAS, Singapore.

Giddens, A. (1990) *The Consequences of Modernity*, Stanford University Press, Stanford.

Gill, S. and Law, D. (1988) *Global Political Economy*, Wheatsheaf, Brighton.

Gilpin, R. (1987) *The Political Economy of International Relations*, Princeton University Press, Princeton.

Girling, J. S. (ed.) (1991) *Human Rights in the Asia-Pacific Region*, Department of International Relations, Australian National University, Canberra.

Godfried, Nathan (1987) 'Spreading American Corporatism: Trade Union Education for Third World Labour', *Review of African Political Economy*, no. 39.

Goldthorpe, J. (1964) 'Social Stratification in Industrial Society', *Sociological Review* Monograph, No. 8.

(1980) *Social Mobility and Class Structure in Modern Britain*, Oxford University Press, Oxford.

Gomez, E. T. (1991) *Money Politics in the Barisan Nasional*, Forum, Kuala Lumpur.

Goodman, R. and Neary, I. (1996) *Case Studies on Human Rights in Japan*, Curzon Press, Richmond.

Gorecho, D. (1995) 'Speeding Land Reform: Moving On, Slowly', *Philippines Free Press*, 17 June 1995.

Gramsci, A. (1971) *The Prison Notebooks*, Lawrence and Wishart, London.

Grossholtz, J. (1964) *Politics in the Philippines*, Little Brown, Boston.

Gutierrez, E. (1994) *The Ties that Bind: A Guide to Family, Business and Other*

Interests in the Ninth House of Representatives, Institute for Popular Democracy, Manila.

Gutierrez, H. (1979) 'Human Rights: An Overview', in Quisumbing (1979).

Haggard, S. (1990) *Pathways from the Periphery*, Cornell University Press, Ithaca.

Haggard, S. and Chung, T. J. (1984) *Pacific Dynamics: The International Politics of Industrial Change*, CIS–Inha University, Inchon.

Halbwachs, M. (1958) *The Psychology of Social Class*, William Heinemann Ltd., London.

Hall, J. (1986) *States in History*, Basil Blackwell, Oxford.

Haley, J. O. (1982) 'Sheathing the Sword of Justice in Japan: An Essay on Law Without Sanctions', *Journal of Japanese Studies*, vol. 8, no. 2, p. 265.

Halliday, F. (1987) 'State and Society in International Relations: A Second Agenda', *Millennium*, vol. 16, no. 2, pp. 215–29

(1989) 'Theorising the International', *Economy and Society*, vol. 18, no. 3, pp. 346–59.

(1994) *Rethinking International Relations*, Macmillan, Basingstoke.

(1995) 'Relativism and Universalism in Human Rights: The Case of the Islamic Middle East', in Beetham (1995).

Hanami, T. (1991) *Managing Japanese Workers*, Japan Institute of Labour, Tokyo.

Hannum, H. (ed.) (1992) *Guide to International Human Rights Practice*, 2nd edn, University of Pennsylvania Press, Philadelphia.

Harari, E. (1973) *The Politics of Labor Legislation*, Uinversity of California Press, Berkeley.

Harding, A. J. (1985) *The Common Law in Singapore and Malaysia*, Butterworths, Singapore.

(1991) 'Islam and Public Law in Malaysia: Some Reflections on the Aftermath of Susie Teoh's Case', *Malaya Law Journal*, no. 1, pp. xci–xcvi.

Harrison, D. (1988) *The Sociology of Modernization and Development*, Unwin Hyman, London.

Harrod, J. (1987) *Power, Production and the Unprotected Worker*, Columbia University Press, New York.

Harvey, D. (1973) *Social Justice in the City*, Edward Arnold, London.

(1985) *The Condition of Postmodernity*, Blackwell, Oxford.

Hawes, G. (1987) *The Philippine State and Marcos Regime: The Politics of Export*, Cornell University Press, Ithaca.

Haydon, E. (1962) 'Chinese Customary Law in Hong Kong's New Territories', mimeo, Department of Law, Hong Kong University.

Heinz, W. (ed.) (1993) *Regional Systems for the Protection of Human Rights in Asia, in Africa, in the Americas and in Europe*, Friedrich-Naumann-Stiftung, Brussels.

Henderson, J. (1989) *The Globalisation of High Technology Production*, Routledge, London.

Hennig, R. (1983) 'Philippines Values in Perspective: An Analytical Framework', *Philippine Sociological Review*, vol. 31, nos. 2/3, pp. 55–64.

Hepple, B. (ed.) (1986) *The Making of Labour Law in Europe*, Mansell Publishing Ltd., London.

Hickling, R. H. (1992) *Essays in Singapore Law*, Pelanduk Publications, Petaling Jaya.

Hill, M. and Lian, K.-F. (1995) *The Politics of Nation Building and Citizenship in Singapore*, Routledge, London.

Hingwan, K. (1996) 'Identity, Otherness and Human Rights in Japan' in Goodman and Neary (1996).

Hirst, P. (1979) *Law and Ideology*, Macmillan, London.

Hirst, P. and Thompson, G. (1996) *Globalisation in Question*, Polity, Oxford.

Ho, B.-M. (1989) *Hong Kong Contract Law*, Butterworths, Hong Kong.

Hobsbawm, E. and Ranger, T. (1984) *The Invention of Tradition*, Cambridge University Press, Cambridge.

Hohfeld, W. (1919) *Fundamental Legal Conceptions as Applied in Judicial Reasoning, and Other Legal Essays*, Yale University Press, New Haven.

Holland, S. (1975) *The Socialist Challenge*, Quartet, London.

Hollnsteiner, M. (1963) *The Dynamics of Power in a Philippine Municipality*, Community Development Research Council, University of the Philippines, Quezon City.

Hong Kong Labour Department (1994) *The ILO and the Application of International Labour Conventions in Hong Kong*, Hong Kong.

Hooker, M. B. (1972) *Adat Laws in Modern Malaya: Land Tenure, Traditional Government and Religion*, Oxford University Press, Singapore.

(1976) *The Personal Laws of Malaysia*, Oxford University Press, Kuala Lumpur.

(1978) *A Concise Legal History of South-East Asia*, Clarendon Press, Oxford.

Hooker, M. B. (ed.) (1986) *Malaysian Legal Essays*, Malayan Law Journal, Kuala Lumpur.

(1988) *Laws of South-East Asia: European Laws in South-East Asia*, Butterworths, Singapore.

Hopkins, K. (ed.) (1971) *Hong Kong – The Industrial Colony*, Oxford University Press, Hong Kong.

Horii, K. (1991) 'Disintegration of the Colonial Economic Legacies and Social Restructuring in Malaysia', *The Developing Economies*, vol. 29, no. 4, pp. 281–313.

Howard, R. (1993) 'Cultural Absolutism and Nostalgia for Community', *Human Rights Quarterly*, vol. 15, pp. 315–38.

Howard, R. and Donnelly, J. (1986) 'Human Dignity, Human Rights and Political Regimes', *American Political Science Review*, vol. 80, pp. 802–17.

Hsiao, M. (ed.) (1993) *Discovery of the Middle Classes in East Asia*, Institute of Ethnology, Academia Sinica, Taipai.

Hsiung, J. (ed.) (1985) *Human Rights in East Asia*, Paragon, New York.

Hsu, B. (1992) *The Common Law in Chinese Context*, University of Hong Kong Press, Hong Kong.

Hua, W.-Y. (1983) *Class and Communalism in Malaysia*, Zed Books Ltd., London.

Humana, C. (1992) *World Human Rights Guide*, 3rd. edn, Oxford University Press, New York.

Humphrey, J. (1989) *No Distant Millenium: The International Law of Human Rights*, UNESCO, Geneva.

Hunt, A. (1978) *The Sociological Movement in Law*, Macmillan, London.

Hunt, A. and Wickham, G. (1984) *Foucault and Law: Towards a Sociology of Law as Governance*, Pluto, London.

Hunt, C. L. (1978) 'Education and Economic Development in the Early American Period in the Philippines', *Philippine Studies*, vol. 36, no. 2, pp. 355–64.

Huntington, S. P. (1997) *The Clash of Civilisations and the Remaking of World Order*, Simon and Schuster, New York.

Hutchcroft, P. (1993) 'Predatory Oligarchy, Patrimonial State: The Politics of Private Domestic Commercial Banking in the Philippines', unpublished doctoral dissertation, Yale University, New Haven.

IBON (1990) 'Free Access to the Courts', *Facts and Figures*, vol. 13, no. 15, p.8.

Ibrahim, A. (1989) 'Towards a Malaysian Common Law', *Malaya Law Journal*, no. 2, pp. xlix–l.

Ileto, R. (1979) *Payson and Revolution: Popular Movements in the Philippines: 1840–1910*, Ateneo de Manila University Press, Quezon City.

ILO (1975a) *The Role of Labour Law in Developing Countries*, ILO, Geneva.
(1975b) *Industrial Relations in Asia*, ILO, Geneva.
(1987) *Labour Protection Laws in Asean*, ILO, Geneva.

Inciong, A. (1974) 'An Appraisal of the Operations of the National Labor Relations Commission' in Romero (1974).

International Industrial Relations Association (1983), 'The Viability of the Japanese Model of Industrial Relations', in *Proceedings of the Sixth World Congress*, Kyoto.

Itoh, H. and Beer, L. (eds.) (1978) *The Constitutional Case Law of Japan: Selected Supreme Court Decisions, 1961–70*, University of Washington Press, Seattle.

Jao, Y. C. (1994) 'The Development of Hong Kong's Financial Sector, 1967–92', in Leung and T. Wong (1994).

Jao, Y. C., Levin, D., Ng, S.-H. and Sinn, E. (eds.) (1988) *Labour Movement in a Changing Society*, Centre of Asian Studies, Hong Kong University.

Jarvie, I. C. (1989) *Hong Kong: A Society in Transition*, Routledge and Kegan Paul, London.

Jayakumar, S. (1971) *Constitutional Law: Cases from Malaysia and Singapore*, Malaya Law Journal, Singapore.

Jayasankaran, S. (1993) 'Made-in-Malaysia: the Proton Project', in Jomo (1993).

Jayawickarama, N. (1989) 'Protecting Civil Liberties', in Wacks (1989).

(1992) 'The Bill of Rights', in Wacks (1991).

Jessop, B. (1982) *The Capitalist State: Marxist Theories and Methods*, M. Robertson, Oxford.

(1990) *State Theory: Putting Capitalist States in their Place*, Polity, Cambridge.

Jesudason, J. V. (1989) *Ethnicity and the Economy: The State, Chinese Business, and Multinationals in Malaysia*, Oxford University Press, Singapore.

(1995) 'Statist Democracy and the Limits to Civil Society in Malaysia', *Journal of Commonwealth and Comparative Politics*, vol. 33, no. 3, pp. 335–56.

Jeyaratnam, J. B. (1989) 'The Rule of Law in Singapore', in Kehma-S (1989).

JIL (1965) *The Changing Patterns of Industrial Relations*, JIL, Tokyo.

(1967) *Labour Relations in the Asian Countries*, JIL, Tokyo.

(1969) *The Changing Patterns of Industrial Relations*, JIL, Tokyo.

(1971) *The Social and Cultural Background of Labour–Management Relations in Asian Countries*, JIL, Tokyo.

(1973) *Industrialization and Manpower Policy in Asian Countries*, JIL, Tokyo.

(1975) *Foreign Investment and Labour in Asian Countries*, JIL, Tokyo.

(1977) *Industrial Policy, Foreign Investment and Labour in Asian Countries*, JIL, Tokyo.

(1979) *Social Tensions and Industrial Relations Arising in the Industrialization Process of Asian Countries*, JIL, Tokyo.

(1981) *Agenda for Industrial Relations in Asian Development*, JIL, Tokyo.

(1985) *Toward Better Utilization of Human Resources in Asian Countries*, JIL, Tokyo.

(1990) *The Roles of Management and Managers in Industrial Relations*, JIL, Tokyo.

(1992) *Present Issues of International Migration – How Can the Sending and Receiving Countries Cooperate?*, JIL, Tokyo.

Jimenez, J. (1979) 'Civil Rights Under the New Constitution', in Quisumbing (1979).

Jocano, Landa, F. (1988) *Towards Developing a Filipino Corporate Culture: Uses of Filipino Traditional Structures and Values in Modern Management*, Punlad Research House, Manila.

(1992) 'Issues and Challenges in Filipino Value Formation', Punlad Research House, Quezon City.

Jomo, K. S. (1985) *The Sun Also Sets: Lessons in Looking East*, Insan, Kuala Lumpur.

(1986) *A Question of Class: Capital, The State and Uneven Development*, Oxford University Press, Singapore.

(1990) *Growth and Structural Change in the Malaysian Economy*, Macmillan, London.

Jomo, K.S. (ed.) (1993) *Industrialising Malaysia: Policy, Performance, Prospects*, Routledge, London.

(1994) *Japan and Malaysian Development: In the Shadow of the Rising Sun*, Routledge, London.

Jomo, K. S. and Edwards, C. (1993) 'Malaysian Industrialisation in Historical Perspective' in Jomo (1993).

Jomo, K. S. and Todd, P. (1994) *Trade Unions and the State in Peninsula Malaysia*, Oxford University Press, New York.

Jones, C. (1994a) 'Capitalism, Globalization and Rule of Law: An Alternative Trajectory of Legal Change in China', *Social and Legal Studies*, vol. 3, pp. 195–221.

(1994b) 'Women and Law in Colonial Hong Kong' in Leung and T. Wong (1994).

Jones, D. M. (1995) 'Civil Society and the Illiberal Middle Class in Pacific Asia', mimeo, Department of Political Science, University of Tasmania.

(1997) *Political Development in Pacific Asia*, Polity, Oxford.

Jones, K. (1982) *Law and Economy*, Academic Press, London.

Josephs, H. K. (1990) *Labor Law in China: Choice and Responsibility*, Butterworths, Salem.

Kahn, F. and Wah, L.-K. (eds.) (1992) *Fragmented Vision: Culture and Politics in Contemporary Malaysia*, Allen and Unwin, Sydney.

Kahn, J. (1992) 'Class, Ethnicity and Diversity in Malaysia' in Kahn et al. (1992).

Kahn-Freund, O. (1944) 'The Illegality of a Trade Union', *Modern Law Review*, vol. 7, p. 192.

(1981) *Labour Law and Politics in the Weimar Republic*, Blackwell, Oxford.

Kehma-S (1989) *The Rule of Law and Human Rights in Malaysia and Singapore*, Kehma-S Coordination, Limelette (Belgium).

Keohane, R. O. (1984) *After Hegemony: Cooperation and Discord in the World Political Economy*, Princeton University Press, Princeton.

Keohane, R. O. and Nye, R. O. (1977) *Power and Independence*, Scott, Foresman, Glenview.

Kerkvliet, B. and Mojares, R. (eds.) (1991) *From Marcos to Aquino: Local Perspectives on Political Transition in the Philippines*, Ateneo de Manila University Press, Quezon City.

Kerr, C. et al. (1973) *Industrialism and Industrial Man*, 2nd edn, Penguin, Harmondsworth.

Kessler, C. S. (1992) 'Archaism and Modernity: Contemporary Malay Political Culture' in Kahn et al. (1992).

Kettler, D. and Tackney, C. T. (1996) 'Light from a Dead Sun: The Japanese Lifetime Employment System and Weimar Labour Law', mimeo, Bard Center, New York.

Khoo, K.-J. (1992) 'The Grand Vision: Mahathir and Modernisation', in Kahn et al. (1992).

Kim, Hwang-Joe (no date) 'Industrial Relations in Korea: Issues and Perspectives', mimeo, Department of Economics, Yonsei University, South Korea.

King, A. (1975) 'Administrative Absorption of Politics: With Special Emphasis on the Grass Roots Level', *Asian Survey*, vol. 15, pp. 422–39.

(1984) 'The Informal Sector', Philippine Labour Review, vol. 8, no. 1.

King, A. and Levy, H. (1975) *The Chinese Touch in Small Industrial Organisations*, Chinese University Press, Hong Kong.

Klare, K. (1981) 'Labor Law as Ideology', *Industrial Relations Law Journal*, 4, 458–80.

Koike, K. and Inoki, T. (eds.) (1990) *Skill Formation in Japan and South East Asia*, University of Tokyo Press, Tokyo.

Kok, S.-K. (1994) *Malaysia to 2003: From Redistribution to Growth*, Economist Intelligence Unit, London.

Kossellek, R. (1985) *Futures Past: On the Semantics of Time*, MIT Press, Cambridge, MA.

Krause, L., Koh, A.-T., and Lee, T.-Y. (eds.) (1987) *The Singapore Economy Reconsidered*, Institute of Southeast Asian Studies, Singapore.

Kurihara, K. (1945) *Labor in the Philippine Economy*, Stanford University Press, Stanford.

Kuruvilla, S. (1995) 'Industrialization Strategy and Industrial Relations Policy in Malaysia', in Frenkel and Harrod (1995).

Kwan, A. Y. H. (1989) 'Social Welfare and Services in Hong Kong', in Kwan (ed.) (1989).

Kwan, A. (ed.) (1989) *Hong Kong Society*, Writers' and Publishers' Cooperative.

Kwok, K.-W. (1995) 'Singapore: Consolidating the New Political Economy', *Southeast Asian Affairs*, pp. 292–308.

Laclau, E. (1979) *Politics and Ideology in Marxist Theory*, Verso, London.

Laclau, E. and Mouffe, C. (1985) *Hegemony and Socialist Strategy*, Verso, London.

Lande, K. (1956) *Leaders, Factions and Parties: The Structure of Philippine Politics*, Yale University Press, New Haven.

Lau, A. (1991) *The Malayan Union Controversy: 1942–1948*, Oxford University Press, Singapore.

Lau, S.-K. (1982) *Society and Politics in Hong Kong*, Chinese University Press, Hong Kong.

(1987) 'Decolonisation without Independence: the Unfinished Reforms of the Hong Kong Government', Centre for Hong Kong Studies, Chinese University of Hong Kong.

Lau, S.-K. and Kuan, H.-C. (1988) *The Ethos of the Hong Kong Chinese*, Chinese University Press, Hong Kong.

Lau, S.-K., Lee, M.-K., Wan, P.-S., Wong, S.-L. (eds.) (1992) *Indicators of Social Development: Hong Kong, 1990*, Hong Kong Institute of Asia-Pacific Studies, Chinese University of Hong Kong.

(1994) *Inequalities and Development: Social Stratification in Chinese Societies*, Hong Kong Institute of Asia-Pacific Studies, Chinese University of Hong Kong.

Leader, S. (1992) *Freedom of Association: A Study in Labor Law and Political Theory*, Yale University Press, New Haven.

Leary, V .A. (1990) 'The Asian Region and the International Human Rights Movement' in Welch and Leary (1990).

Lee, C. K. (1993) 'Familial Hegemony: Gender and Production Politics on Hong Kong's Electronics Shopfloor', *Gender and Society*, vol. 7.

Lee, E. (1989) 'The Colonial Legacy', in Sandhu and Wheatley (1989).

Lee, H. P. (1995) *Constitutional Conflicts in Contemporary Malaysia*, Oxford University Press, New York.

Lee, J. (1994) 'The Emergence of Party Politics in Hong Kong, 1982–92' in Leung and T. Wong (1994).

Lee, K.-M. (1988) 'The Impact of Containerization: Work, the Wage System and Industrial Disputes' in Jao et al. (1988).

Lee, M.-P. (1994) *General Principles of Malaysian Law*, 2nd. edn, Penerbit Fajar Bakti Sdn. Bhd., Kuala Lumpur.

Lee, R. (1994) 'Modernization, Postmodernism and the Third World', *Current Sociology*, vol. 42, no. 2, pp. 1–63.

Leggett, C. (1988) 'Industrial Relations and Enterprise Unionism in Singapore', *Labour and Industry*, vol. 1, no. 2, pp. 242–57.

Lehman, C. R. and Moore, R. M. (eds.) (1992) *Multinational Culture: Social Impacts of a Global Economy*, Greenwood Press, Westport.

Leong, W. K. (1985) 'Common Law and Chinese Marriage Customs in Singapore' in Harding (1985).

Lepoer, B. (ed.) (1991) *Singapore: A Country Study*, Federal Research Division, Library of Congress, Washington, DC.

Lethbridge, D. (ed.) (1984) *The Business Environment in Hong Kong*, Oxford University Press, Hong Kong.

Lethbridge, H. J. (1970) 'Hong Kong Cadets, 1862–1941', *Journal of the Hong Kong Branch of the Royal Asiatic Society*, vol. 10, pp. 35–56.

(1985) *Hard Graft in Hong Kong: Scandal, Corruption, and the ICAC*, Oxford University Press, Oxford.

Leung, B. (1990a) 'Power and Politics: A Critical Analysis' in Leung (1990c).

(1990b) 'Political Development: Prospects and Possibilities' in Leung (1990c).

(1990c) *Social Issues in Hong Kong*, Oxford University Press, New York.

(1994) '"Class" and "Class Formation" in Hong Kong Studies' in Lau et al. (1994).

Leung, B. and Chiu, S. (1991) *A Social History of Industrial Strikes and the Labour Movement in Hong Kong*, Social Sciences Research Centre, Hong Kong University.

Leung, B. and Wong, T. (eds.) (1994) *25 years of Social and Economic Development in Hong Kong*, Centre for Asian Studies, Hong Kong.

Leung, W.-Y. (1988) *Smashing the Iron Rice Pot: Workers and Unions in China's Market Socialism*, Asia Monitor Resource Centre, Hong Kong.

Lev D. (1990) 'Human Rights NGOs in Indonesia and Malaysia' in Welch and Leary (1990).

287

Levin, D. (1990) 'Work and its Deprivations' in Leung (1990c).

Levin, D. and Chiu, S. (1995) 'The World Economy, State and Sectors in Industrial Change: Labor Relations in Hong Kong's Textile and Garment-Making Industries', in Frenkel and Harrod (1995).

Levin, D. M. (ed.) (1993) *Modernity and the Hegemony of Vision*, University of California Press, Berkeley.

Li, Z.-E. (1985) *An Introduction to Hong Kong Company Law*, Gregarian Publications Ltd., Hong Kong.

Lichauco, A. (1973) *The Lichauco Paper: Imperialism in the Philippines*, Monthly Review Press, New York.

Lim, C.-Y. (ed.) (1988) *Policy Options for the Singapore Economy*, McGraw-Hill, Singapore.

Lim, K.-S. (1986) *Malaysia: A Crisis of Identity*, Democratic Action Party, Kuala Lumpur.

Lim, L. (1989) 'Social Welfare' in Sandhu and Wheatley (1989).

Lim, M., Siang, K., Singh, K., Muzaffar, C. and Tan, P. (eds.) (n.d.) *Human Rights in Malaysia*, Democratic Action Party Human Rights Committee, no place of publication.

Liou, C. (1993) 'The Influences of Foreign Laws on the Contemporary Union Rights Policies in Taiwan', mimeo, Japan Institute of Labour, Tokyo.

Loh, C. (1995) 'The Vienna Process and the Importance of Universal Standards in Asia' in Davis (1995).

Lubis, M. (1985) 'Japan: From Economic Power to Cultural Inspiration' in Armour (1985).

Lui, T.-L. (1990) 'The Social Organisation of Outwork: The Case of Hong Kong' in Sinn (1990).

Lui, T.-L. and Wong, T. (1994) *Chinese Entrepreneurship in Context*, Occasional Paper, Hong Kong Institute of Asia-Pacific Studies, Chinese University of Hong Kong.

Lynch, F. and de Guzman II, A. (eds.) (1973) *Four Readings on Philippine Values*, 4th edn, Institute of Philippine Culture, Ateneo de Manila University, Quezon City.

Machado, K. (1987) 'Malaysian Cultural Relations with Japan and South Korea', *Asian Survey*, vol. 27, no. 6, pp. 638–60.

MacKeen, A. M. (1986) 'Islamic Fiscal and Property Laws', in Hooker, 1986.

MacNeil, W. (1992) 'Righting and Difference', in Wacks (1992).

— (1995) 'Enjoy Your Rights!: Fantasy, Symptom and Identification in the Discourse of Rights' mimeo, Department of Law, Hong Kong University.

Mahathir, M. (1970) *The Malay Dilemma*, Asia Pacific Press, Singapore.

Mahbubani, K. (1992) 'The West and the Rest', *The National Interest*, Summer 1992, pp. 1–15.

Maki, J. (ed.) (1964) *Court and Constitution in Japan*, University of Washington Press, Seattle.

Mangahas, M. (1994) *The Philippine Social Climate*, Anvil Publishing Inc., Manila.

Mann, M. (1986) *The Sources of Social Power*, vols I and II, Cambridge University Press, Cambridge.

—— (1993) 'Nation States in Europe and Other Continents: Diversifying, Developing, not Dying', *Daedalus*, Winter, pp.115–40.

Marcos, F. (1974) *The Democratic Revolution in the Philippines*, Prentice-Hall, Englewood Cliffs.

—— (1977) *The Philippine Experience: A Pespective on Human Rights and the Rule of Law*, no publisher, Manila.

Marshall, G., Newby, H., Rose, D. and Vogler, C. (1988) *Social Class in Modern Britain*, Hutchinson, London.

Marshall, T. H. (1962) *Sociology at the Crossroads*, Heinemann, London.

Martin, R. (1987) *The Law of Tort in Hong Kong*, China and Hong Kong Law Studies, Hong Kong.

Mason, A. J., (1925) *Organized Labour and the Law*, Duke University Press.

Matsushusita, K. (1984) *Not on Bread Alone: A Business Ethos*, PHP Institute, Kyoto.

Mauss, M. (1990 [1924]) *The Form and Reason for Exchange in Archaic Societies*, Routledge, London.

Mauzy, D. K. and Milne, R. S. (1984) 'The Mahathir Administration: Discipline Thru Islam', *Pacific Affairs*, vol. 56, no. 1, pp. 617–48.

—— (1986) 'The Mahathir Administration: Discipline through Islam' in Gale (1986).

McCoy, A. W. (1994) 'Rent Seeking Families and the Philippine State: A History of the Lopez Family' in McCoy (ed.) *An Anarchy of Families: State and Family in the Philippines*, Ateneo de Manila University Press, Quezon City.

McCoy, A. and de Jesus (eds.) (1982) *Philippine Social History: Global Trade and Local Transformation*, Ateneo de Manila University Press, Quezon City.

McMullan, I. J. (1987) 'Rulers or Fathers? A Casuistical Problem in Early Modern Japanese Thought', *Past & Present*, vol. 116, pp. 56–97.

Means, G. P. (1970) *Malaysian Politics*, University of London Press, London.

—— (1991) *Malaysian Politics: The Second Generation*, Oxford University Press, Singapore.

Menon, K. A. (1975) 'Malaysia: Industrial Relations in Retrospect and Prospect' in ILO (1975b).

Meron, T. (1989) *Human Rights and Humanitarian Norms as Customary Law*, Clarendon Press, Oxford.

Merrils, J. (1988) *The Development of International Law by the European Court of Human Rights*, Manchester University Press, Manchester.

Merry, S. (1996) 'Global Human Rights and Local Social Movements in a Legally Plural World', mimeo, Department of Anthropology, Wellesley College.

Milne, R. S. and Mauzy, D. K. (1978) *Politics and Government in Malaysia*, University of British Columbia, Vancouver.

Minear, R. (1980) 'Orientalism and the Far East', *Journal of Asian Studies*, vol. 39, no. 3, p. 507.

Miners, N. (1986) *The Government and Politics of Hong Kong*, Oxford University Press, Hong Kong (2nd edn 1977).

Ministry of Labor and Employment (1984) *The Bataan Export Processing Zone: Employment, Labor Relations, Working Conditions*, Manila.

Ministry of Labour (1980) *Singapore Yearbook of Labour Statistics*, Singapore. (1990) *Singapore Yearbook of Labour Statistics*, Singapore.

Minority Rights Group (1992) *The Chinese in South East Asia*, Minority Rights Group, London.

Miranda-Feliciano, E. (ed.) (1988) *All Things to All Men: An Introduction to Missions in Filipino Culture*, New Day, Quezon City.

Mirza, H. (1986) *Multinationals and the Growth of the Singapore Economy*, Croom Helm, London.

Miyoshi, M. and H. Harootunian (1989) *Postmodernism and Japan*, Duke University Press, Durham.

Mohamed, H. (1994) 'Social Welfare and the Caring Society' in National Institute of Public Administration (1994).

Mojares, R. (1983) 'Non-Revolt in the Rural Context: Some Considerations', *Philippine Studies*, vol. 31, pp. 477–82.

Monk, P. (1990) *Truth and Power: R.S. Hardie and Land Reform Debates in the Philippines: 1950–1987*, Monash Paper 20, Monash University Centre of S.E. Asian Studies.

Morgenthau, H. J. (1960) *Politics Among Nations*, Knopf, New York.

Morishima, M. (1982) *Why has Japan 'Succeeded'?* Cambridge University Press, Cambridge.

Morris, J. (ed.) (1991) *Japan and the Global Economy*, Routledge, London.

Morris-Suzuki, T. (1991) 'Reshaping the Intellectual Division of Labour: Japanese Manufacturing Investment in South East Asia' in Morris (ed.) (1991). (1992) 'Japanese Technology and the New International Division of Knowledge in Asia' in Tokunaga (ed.) (1992).

Moser, M. (1984) *Foreign Trade Investment and the Law in the Peoples Republic of China*, Oxford University Press, New York.

Mower, A. G. (1985) *International Cooperation for Social Justice*, Greenwood Press, Westport.

M.R.G. (1992) *The Chinese of Southeast Asia*, M.R.G., London.

Muego, B. (1988) *Spectator Society: The Philippines Under Martial Rule*, Ohio University Center for International Studies, Athens.

Mulhall, S. and Swift, A. (1992) *Liberals and Communitarians*, Blackwell, Oxford.

Munck, R. (1988) *The New International Labour Studies: An Introduction*, Zed Books, London.

Murakami,Y. (1984) ' "Ie" Society as a Pattern of Civilisation', *Journal of Japanese Studies*, vol. 10, no. 1.

(1987) 'The Japanese Model of Political Economy' in Yamamura and Yasuba (1987).

Murphy, C. (1994) *International Organization and Industrial Change: Global Governance since 1850*, Polity Press, Cambridge.

Muyot, A. (1992) 'The Human Rights Situation Under the Aquino Government', *Philippine Law Journal*, vol. 67, pp. 246–307.

Muzaffar, C. (1979) *Protector? An Analysis of the Concept and Practice of Leader-Led Relations within Malay Society*, Aliran, Penang.

(1988) 'Islamic Resurgence and the Question of Development in Malaysia' in Ghee (1988).

(1989) *Challenges and Choices in Malaysian Politics and Society*, Aliran, Penang.

(1990) 'Ethnicity, Ethnic Conflict and Human Rights in Malaysia', in Welch and Leary (1990).

(1993a) *Human Rights and the New World Order*, Just World Trust, Penang.

(1993b) 'Western Global Domination and Human Rights', *Third World Resurgence*, no. 33.

Myers, R. and Peattie, M. (eds.) (1984) *The Japanese Colonial Empire, 1895–1945*, Princeton University Press, Princeton.

Nakayama, I. (1975) *Industrialization and Labor–Management Relations*, Japan Institute of Labour, Tokyo.

Nathan, K. S. (1989) 'Malaysia in 1988: The Politics of Survival', *Asian Survey*, vol. 29, no. 2, pp. 129–39.

National Institute of Public Administration (ed.) (1994) *Malaysia's Development Experience*, Kuala Lumpur.

NCLB (National Conciliation and Mediation Board) (ed.) (1988) *Compilation of Voluntary Arbitration Decisions: 1988–1991*, 3 vols., Manila.

Nemenzo, F. (1995) 'People's Diplomacy and Human Rights: The Philippines Experience' in Tang (1995).

Nester, W. R. (1990) *Japan's Growing Power Over East Asia*, St. Martin's Press, New York.

Neuhaus, R. (1982) *International Trade Secretariats*, Friedrich-Ebert-Stiftung, Bonn.

Ng, F.-Y. (1989) 'Brain and Capital Drain in Hong Kong', mimeo, Faculty of Business Administration, Chinese University, Hong Kong.

Ng, I. (1992) 'Flexible Production and the Creation of Competitive Advantage in an Asian Newly Industrializing Economy: Organization and Dynamics in the Hong Kong Electronics Industry', Ph.D. Thesis, University of California, Los Angeles.

Ng, S.-H. (1991) 'Trade Union Organization and Labour Legislation' in Wacks (1992).

Ng, S.-H. and Sit, V. (1989) *Labour Relations and Labour Conditions in Hong Kong*, Macmillan, Basingstoke.

Nicholaides, P. (1987) 'How fair is fair trade?', *Journal of World Trade Law*, pp. 147–62.

Nickel, J. (1987) *Making Sense of Human Rights*, University of California Press, Berkeley.

Nield, S. (1992) *Hong Kong Land Law*, China and Hong Kong Law Studies, Hong Kong.

Nihei, Y., Levin, D. and Ohtsu, M. (1982) 'Industrialization and Employment Practices in Asia: A Comparative Study of Ten Spinning Factories in Five Asian Countries', *Economic Development and Cultural Change*, vol. 31, no. 1, pp. 145–71.

Niland, J., Lansbury, R. and Verevis, C. (eds.) (1995) *The Future of Industrial Relations: Global Changes and Challenges*, Sage, Thousand Oaks.

Noland, M. (1990) *Pacific Basin Developing Countries: Prospects for the Future*, Institute for International Economics, Washington.

Nonini, D. (1992) *British Colonial Rule and the Resistance of the Malay Peasants: 1900–1957*, Yale University Press, New Haven.

Norlund, I. et al. (eds.) (1984) *Industrialisation and the Labour Process in S.E. Asia*, Rosenborg-gade, Institute of Cultural Sociology, University of Copenhagen.

NTUC (1970) *Why Labour Must Go Modern*, NTUC, Singapore.

O'Donnell, G. (1973) *Modernization and Bureaucratic Authoritarianism*, University of California Press, Berkeley.

OECD (1977) *The Development of Industrial Relations Systems: Some Implications of the Japanese Experience*, OECD, Paris.

Ofreneo, R. (1980) *Capitalism in Philippine Agriculture*, Foundation for Nationalist Studies, Quezon City.

(1983) 'International Sub-Contracting and Philippine Industrial Relations', *Philippine Journal of Labor and Industrial Relations*, vol. 5, nos. 1/2, pp. 31– 43.

(1987) *Deregulation and the Agrarian Crisis*, Institute of Industrial Relations, Quezon City.

(1990) 'Trade Unionism and Agrarian Reform in the Philippines', *Philippine Journal of Labor and Industrial Relations*, vol. 12, no. 2, pp. 48–59.

(1993) 'Labor and the Philippine Economy', unpublished doctoral dissertation, College of Social Science and Philosophy, University of the Philippines.

Ofreneo, R. (ed.) (1992) *Labor's Vision of Development*, Karel Inc., Quezon City.

Ogle, G. (1990) *South Korea: Dissent within the Economic Miracle*, Zed Books, London.

Ohmae, K. (1990) *The Borderless World*, Collins, London.

Oppler, A. C. (1976) *Legal Reform in Occupied Japan: A Participant Looks Back*, Princeton University Press, Princeton.

Orbeta, A. and Sanchez, T. (1995) 'Philippines in the Regional Division of Labour', International Institute for Labour Studies, ILO, Geneva.

Osman, M. T. (ed.) (1985) *Malaysian Worldview*, Institute of Southeast Asian Studies, Singapore.

Othman, N. (1997) 'Cultural Reinterpretation and Mediation: Implementing Women's Human Rights in Malaysia', *Human Rights Dialogue*, vol. 9, pp. 15–17.

Pacis, V. A. (1963) *Philippine Government and Politics*, Bustamante Press, Quezon City.

Palmer, N. J. (1964) *Colonial Labor Policy and Administration: A History of Labor in the Rubber Plantation Industry in Malaya*, J. J. Augustine, New York.

Pang, E. F. (1989) 'The Management of the People' in Sandhu and Wheatley (1989).

Paredes, R. (ed.) (1989) *Philippine Colonial Democracy*, Ateneo de Manila Press, Quezon City.

Park, S. (1980) 'Dualism as a Decisive Motivation for Japanese Investment in East and South East Asia' in Park et al. (1980).

Park, S., Shin, T. and Zo, K. (eds.) (1980) *Economic Development and Social Change in Korea*, Campus Verlag.

Patrick, H. (1991) *Pacific Basin Industries in Distress*, Columbia University Press, New York.

Pearce, F. (1989) *The Radical Durkheim*, Unwin Hyman, London.

Peek, J. M. (1992) 'Japan, the United Nations and Human Rights', *Asian Survey*, vol. 32, no. 3, pp. 217–29.

Pendleton, M. (1994) *The Law of Intellectual and Industrial Property in Hong Kong*, Butterworths, Singapore.

Petersen, K. (1992) *The Maquiladora Revolution in Guatemala*, Orville H. Schell Jr. Centre for International Human Rights, New Haven.

Pettman, R. (1979) *State and Class: A Sociology of International Affairs*, Croom Helm, London.

Phang, A. (1990) *The Development of Singapore Law*, Butterworths, Singapore.

Pillai, P. and Lee, K. (1989) 'Constitutional Development' in Sandhu and Wheatley (1989).

Pinches, M. (1991) 'The Working Class Experience of Shame, Inequality, and People Power in Tatalon, Manila' in Kerkvliet and Mojares (1991).

Pineda-Ofreneo, R. (1991) *The Philippines: Debt and Poverty*, Oxfam, Oxford.

Pineda-Ofreneo, R. and del Rosario, R. (1988) 'Industrial Homeworking in the Philippines', *Philippine Labour Review*, vol. 12, 1, pp. 32–45.

Plantilla, J. (1997) 'Elusive Promise: Transitional Justice in the Philippines', *Human Rights Dialogue*, vol. 8, pp. 6–11.

Ponniah, A. and Kau, L. (1975) 'Malaysia: Industrial Relations in Retrospect and Prospect' in ILO (1975b).

Power, J. and Sicat, G. (1971) *The Philippines: Industrialization and Trade Policies*, OECD/Oxford University Press, London.

Pritt, D. N. (1970) *Law, Class and Society*, 2 vols., Lawrence and Wishart, London.

Pugh, C. (1989) 'The Political Economy of Public Housing' in Sandhu and Wheatley (1989).

Purvis, T., Hunt, A. (1993), 'Discourse, Ideology, Discourse . . .' *British Journal of Sociology*, vol. 44, no. 3, pp. 473–99.

Putti, J. (ed.) (1991) *Management: Asian Context*, McGraw-Hill Book Co., Singapore.

Quah, J. (1985) 'Statutory Boards' in Quah et al. (1985).

Quah, J. (ed.) (1990) *In Search of Singapore's National Values*, Times Academic Press, Singapore.

Quah, J. and Quah, S. (1989) 'The Limits of Government Intervention' in Sandhu and Wheatley (1989).

Quah, J., Chan, H. C. and Seah, C. M. (eds.) (1985) *Government and Politics of Singapore*, Oxford University Press, Singapore.

Quah, S., Chiew, S.-K., Ko, Y.-C., and Lee, S. (1991) *Social Class in Singapore*, Times Academic Press, Singapore.

Quirino, C. (1971) *Quezon: Paladin of Philippine Freedom*, Filipiniana Book Guild, Manila.

Quisumbing, P. (ed.) (1979) *The New Constitution and Human Rights*, University of the Philippines, Law Center, Quezon City.

Quisumbing, P., and Bonifaco, A. (eds.) (1977) *Human Rights in the Philippines: An Unassembled Symposium*, University of the Philippines Law Center.

Rachagan, S. (1992) *Consumer Law Reform*, Selangor and Federal Territory Consumers Association, Kuala Lumpur.

Radosh, R. (1969) *American Labor and United States Foreign Policy*, Random House, New York.

Rajah, A. T. (1975) 'The Role of Labour Laws in Malaysia' in ILO (1975a).

Rajah, R. (1995) 'Labour and Industrialization in Malaysia', *Journal of Contemporary Asia*, vol. 25, no. 1, pp. 73–92.

Ramlogan, R. (1994) 'The Human Rights Revolution in Japan: A Story of New Wine in Old Wine Skins?', *Emory International Law Review*, vol 8, pp. 127–213.

Ramm, T. (1986) 'Workers' Participation, the Representative of Labour and Special Labour Courts', in Hepple (1986).

Ramos, E. (1976) *Philippine Labor Movement in Transition*, New Day Publishers, Quezon City.

(1978) 'Trade Unionism, "*Kumpadre*" System and Filipino Plant Level Industrial Relations', *Philippine Journal of Labor and Industrial Relations*, vol. 1, no. 1, pp. 47–63.

(1990) *Dual Unionism and the Industial Relations System*, New Day, Quezan City.

Rancharan, B. G. (1989) *The Concept and the Present Status of the International Protection of Human Rights: Forty Years After the Universal Declaration*, Martinus Nihoff, Dordrecht.

Ratnam, K. J. (1965) *Communalism and the Political Process*, University of Malaya Press, Kuala Lumpur.

Rear, J. (1971) 'One Brand of Politics' in Hopkins, K. (1971).

Redding, S. G. (1990) *The Spirit of Chinese Capitalism*, De Gruyter, Berlin.

(1991) 'Weak Organizations and Strong Linkages: Managerial Ideology and Chinese Family Business Networks' in Hamilton (1991).

Reid, N. (1991) 'Japanese Direct Investment in the United States Manufacturing Sector' in Morris (1991).

Renner, K. (1949) *The Institutions of the Private Law and their Social Functions*, Routledge, London.

Resnick, S. and Woolf, R. (1987) *Knowledge and Class: A Marxian Critique of Political Economy*, University of Chicago Press, Chicago.

Ribeiro, R. A. (1977) *The Law and Practice of the Hong Kong Labour Tribunal*, Centre of Asian Studies, Hong Kong University.

Ricquier, W J. M. (1985) *Land Law*, Butterworths, Singapore.

Rivera, J. (1978) *The Father of the First Brown Race Civil Code*, University of the Philippines Law Center, Quezon City.

Rivera, T. (1991) 'Class, the State and Foreign Capital: The Politics of Philippine Industrialisation, 1950–1986', unpublished doctoral dissertation, Department of Political Science, University of Wisconsin.

(1994) *Landlords and Capitalists: Class, Family, and State in Philippine Manufacturing*, University of the Philippines Press, Quezon City.

Roberts, B. C. (1964) *Labour in the Tropical Territories of the Commonwealth*, Duke University Press, Durham.

Robertson, R. (1990) 'Mapping the Global Condition: Globalization as the Central Concept' in Featherstone (1990).

(1992) *Globalisation*, Sage, London.

Robinson, T. (ed.) (1991) *Democracy and Development in East Asia: Taiwan, South Korea and the Philippines*, American Enterprise Institute Press, Washington.

Robison, R. and Goodman, S. G. (eds.) (1995) *The New Rich in Asia: Mobile Phones, McDonalds and Middle-Class Revolution*, Routledge, London.

Rocamora, J. (1994) *Breaking Through*, Anvil Publishing Inc, Manila.

Rodan, G. (1989) *The Political Economy of Singapore's Industrialization: National State and International Capital*, Macmillan, Basingstoke.

(1992) 'Singapore's Leadership in Transition', *Bulletin of Concerned Asian Scholars*, 24, 3–17.

(1993) *Singapore Changes Guard*, Longman, Cheshire, Melbourne.

Rogers, M. L. (1989) 'Patterns of Change in Rural Malaysia', *Asian Survey*, vol. 29, no. 8, pp. 764–85.

Rohlen, T. (1974) *For Harmony and Strength: Japanese White Collar Organisation*, University of California Press, Berkeley.

Romero, F. (ed.) (1974) *Aspects of Philippines Labor Relations Law*, University of the Philippines Law Center, Quezon City.

Rose, N. (1996) 'The Death of the Social: Re-figuring the Territory of Government', *Economy and Society*, vol. 25, no. 3, pp. 327–56.

Rosenau, J. N. (ed.) (1969) *International Politics and Foreign Policy*, Free Press, New York.

Rouner, L. (ed.) (1988) *Human Rights and World's Religions*, University of Notre Dame Press, Notre Dame.

Rubin, B. R. (1990) 'Human Rights in Mass-Based Ethnic Conflict: South Asian Examples of Dilemmas of Definition, Monitoring and Protection' in Welch and Leary (1990).

Ruccio, D., Resnick, S. and Wolff, R. (1991) 'Class Beyond the Nation State', *Capital and Class*, no. 43, pp. 25–41.

Ruggie, C. (1983) *Antinomies of Interdependence: National Welfare and the International Division of Labour*, Columbia University Press, New York.

Rutter, M. (1989) *The Applicable Law in Singapore and Malaysia*, Malaya Law Journal Pte., Singapore.

Said, E. (1978) *Orientalism*, Vintage, New York.

(1993) *Culture and Imperialism*, Chatto and Windus, London.

Salaff, J. (1981) *Working Daughters of Hong Kong: Filial Piety or Power in the Family*, Cambridge University Press, New York.

(1992) 'Women, the Family, and the State in Hong Kong, Taiwan, and Singapore' in Appelbaum and Henderson (1992).

Salgardo, P. (1985) *The Philippine Economy: History and Analysis*, R. P. Garcia Publishers, Quezon City.

San, T. K. (1975) 'Malaysia: Industrial Relations in Retrospect and Prospect' in ILO (1975b).

Sandhu, K. S. and Wheatley, P. (eds.) (1989) *Management of Success: The Moulding of Modern Singapore*, Institute of Southeast Asian Studies, Singapore.

Santiago, L. (ed.) (1986) *Synthesis: Before and Beyond February 1986*, The Interdisciplinary Forum of the University of the Philippines, Quezon City.

Santos, E. (1976) *The Constitution of the Philippines*, The Philippine Society of Constitutional Law, Inc., Manila.

Sartorius, R. (ed.) (1983) *Paternalism*, University of Minnesota, Minneapolis.

Sassen, S. (1992) *The Global City*, New York, London, Tokyo.

(1996) *Sovreignty in an Age of Globalisation*, Columbia University Press, new York.

Scalapino, R., Sato, S. and Wanandi J. (eds.) (1985) *Asian Economic Development: Present and Future*, Institute of East Asian Studies, Berkeley.

Schirmer, D. B. and Shalom, S. R. (eds.) (1987) *The Philippines Reader: A History of Colonialism, Neocolonialism, Dictatorship, and Resistance*, South End Press, Boston.

Scholte, J. A. (1993) *International Relations of Social Change*, Open University Press, Buckingham.

Schregle, J. (1993) 'Dismissal Protection in Japan', *International Labour Review*, vol. 132, no. 4.

Scott, I. (1989) *Political Change and the Crisis of Legitimacy in Hong Kong*, Oxford University Press, Hong Kong.

Scott, J. (1976) *The Moral Economy of the Peasant: Rebellion and Subsistence in Southeast Asia*, Yale University Press, New Haven.

Seagrave, S. (1988) *The Marcos Dynasty*, Harper Row, New York.

Seah, C. M. (1985) 'Parapolitical Institutions' in Quah et al. (1985).

Segal, G. (1990) *Rethinking the Pacific*, Oxford University Press, Oxford.

Selznick, P. (1980) *Law, Society and Industrial Justice*, Transaction Books, New York.

Sengenberger, W. and Campbell, D. (eds.) (1994) *International Labour Standards and Economic Independence*, International Institute for Labour Studies, Geneva.

Serrano, M. (1992) 'The Social and Economic Dimensions of the Social Security System in the Philippines', *Philippine Journal of Labor and Industrial Relations*, vol. 14, nos. 1/2, pp. 65–81.

Shaw, W. (ed.) *Human Rights in Korea*, Harvard University Press, Cambridge.

Sheridan, L. A. and Groves, H. (1987) *The Constitution of Malaysia*, 4th edn, Malayan Law Journal, Singapore.

Shibusawa, M. (1984) *Japan and the Asia Pacific Region: Profile of Change*, St. Martins Press, New York.

Shum, C. (1989) *A Guide to Employment Law in Hong Kong*, The Commercial Press, Hong Kong.

(1994) *General Principles of Hong Kong Law*, 2nd edn, Longmans, Hong Kong.

Siegel, R. (1994) *Employment and Human Rights: The International Dimension*, University of Pennsylvania Press, Philadelphia.

Sihombing, J. (1986) 'Land Tenure in Colonial Malaya: An Historical Review' in Hooker, 1986.

Sihombing, J., Mahmood, N. and Latimer, P. (1991) *Business Law in Hong Kong, Malaysia, and Singapore*, Commerce Clearing House Asia, no place of publication.

Sinay-Aguilar, V. (1983) 'Domestic Outwork Arrangements in Footwear and Garments Industries', *Philippine Journal of Labor and Industrial Relations*, vol. 5, nos. 1/2, pp. 44–57.

Sinclair, S. (1995) *The Pacific Basin: An Economic Handbook*, Euromonitor Publications, London.

Singer, J. D. (1969) 'The Levels of Analysis Problem in International Relations' in Rosenau (1969).

Sinn, E. (ed.) (1990) *Between East and West: Aspects of Social and Political Development in Hong Kong*, Centre For Asian Studies, Hong Kong University.

Sit, V. (1983) *Made in Hong Kong*, Summerson Eastern Publishers Ltd, Hong Kong.

Sit, V. and Wong, S. L. (1989) *Small and Medium Industries in Hong Kong*, Hong Kong University Press, Hong Kong.

Sklair, L. (1991) 'Problems of Socialist Development: the Significance of Shenzen Special Economic Zone for China's Open Door Development Policy', *International Journal of Urban and Regional Research*, vol. 15, no. 2, pp. 197–215.

(1996) *Sociology of the Global System*, 2nd edn, Harvester Wheatsheaf, London.

Skocpol, T. (1978) *States and Social Revolutions*, Cambridge University Press, Cambridge.

Skocpol, T. and Evans, P. (eds.) (1985) *Bringing the State Back In*, Cambridge University Press, Cambridge.

So, A. and Chiu, S. (1995) *East Asia and the World Economy*, Sage, Thousand Oaks.

Soe, M. (1992) *Principles of Singapore Law*, Institute of Business and Finance, Singapore.

Soesastro, H. (1985) 'Japan "Teacher" – Asean Pupils: Can it Work?' in Scalapino et al. (1985).

Soja, E. (1989) *Postmodern Geographies*, Verso, London.

SOLAIR (School of Labor and Industrial Relations) (ed.) (1994) *GATT and the Social Clause: Implications for Philippine Business and Labor*, University of the Philippines.

Soysal, Y. (1994) *The Limits of Citizenship*, University of Chicago Press, Chicago.

Spooner, D. (1989) *Partners or Predators: International Trade Unionism and Asia*, Asia Monitor Resource Center.

Srithamaraks, T. (1993) 'The Influences of Foreign Law on Contemporary Union Right Policies in Thailand', mimeo, Japan Institute of Labour, Tokyo.

Standing, G. (1993) 'Labour Flexibility in the Malaysian Manufacturing Sector' in Jomo (1993).

Starr, J. B. (1988) *The United States Constitution: Its Birth, Growth and Influence in Asia*, Hong Kong University Press, Hong Kong.

Steinberg, D. (1967) *Philippine Collaboration in World War II*, Solidaridad, Manila.

Stenson, M. R. (1970) *Industrial Conflict in Malaya: Prelude to the Communist Revolt of 1948*, Oxford University Press, London.

Stephens, J. (1979) *The Transition from Capitalism to Socialism*, Macmillan, London.

Steven, R. (1990) *Japan's New Imperialism*, Macmillan, London.

Stivens, M. (1996) *Matriliny and Modernity: Sexual Politics and Social Change in Rural Malaysia*, Allen and Unwin, London.

Stone, K. (1981) 'The Postwar Paradigm in American Labor Law', *Yale Law Journal*, vol. 90, p. 1509.

Striniti, D. (1982) *Capitalism, the State and Industrial Relations*, Croom Helm, London.

Suffian, Tun M. (1988) *An Introduction to the Legal System of Malaysia*, Penerbit Fajar Bakti Sdn. Bhd., Kuala Lumpur.

Sugeno, K. (1992) *Japanese Labor Law*, University of Washington Press, Seattle.

Sum, Ngai-Ling (1994) 'Reflections on Accumulation, Regulation, the State, and Societalization: A Stylized Model of East Asian Capitalism and an Integral Economic Analysis of Hong Kong', Ph.D. Thesis, Department of Sociology, University of Lancaster.

Tan, C.-H. (1995) *Labour Management Relations in Singapore*, Prentice Hall, Singapore.

Tan, K., Yeo, T .M., and Lee, K.-S. (eds.) (1991) *Constitutional Law in Malaysia and Singapore*, Malaya Law Journal Pte., Singapore.

Tang, J. (ed.) (1995) *Human Rights and International Relations in the Asia-Pacific Region*, Pinter, London.

Taylor, J. G. and Turton, A. (eds.) *South East Asia*, Macmillan, London.

Teodosio, V., Serrano, M. and Labastilla, G. (eds.) (1990) *Labor in the Coconut Industry*, UP–Solair/Freidrich Ebert Stiftung, University of the Philippines, Quezon City.

Terami-Wada, M. (1988) 'The Sakdal Movement, 1930-1934', *Philippine Studies*, vol. 36, no. 2, pp. 131–50.

Tham, S. C. (1989) 'The Perception and Practice of Education' in Sandhu and Wheatley (1989).

Thompson, E. P. (1993) *Customs in Common*, Penguin, Harmondsworth.

Thompson, K. (ed.) (1988) *The United States Constitution and the Constitutions of Asia*, University Press of America, Lanham.

Thong, G. (1991) 'The Foundations of Human Resources Management Practice in Japanese Companies in Malaysia' in Yamashita (1991).

Thurow, L. (1992) *Head to Head: The Coming Economic Battle Among Japan, Europe and America*, Morrow, New York.

Tiongson, N., Doronila, M. L., Guillermo, A. and Mangahas, F. B. (1986) 'The Ideology and Culture of the New Society' in Santiago, 1986.

Tokunaga, S. (ed.) (1992) *Japan's Foreign Investment and Asian Economic Inter-dependence: Production, Trade and Financial Systems*, University of Tokyo Press, Tokyo.

Torres, A. (1988) *The Urban Filipino Worker in an Industrializing Economy*, University of the Philippines Press, Quezon City.

Tregonning, K. (1964) *The British in Malaya: The First Forty Years*, Association for Asian Studies, London.

Trocki, C. (1990) *Opium and Empire: Chinese Society in Colonial Singapore*, Cornell University Press, Ithica.

Tsang, S. (1988) *Democracy Shelved: Great Britain, China, and Attempts at Constitutional Reform in Hong Kong: 1945–59*, Oxford University Press, Hong Kong.

Tsang, W.-K. (1994) 'Consolidation of a Class Structure: Changes in the Class Structure in Hong Kong' in Lau et al. (1994).

Tsuda, M. (1978) 'Understanding Industrial Relations in the Philippines: The Perspective of Resident Japanese Investors', *Philippine Journal of Labor and Industrial Relations*, vol. 1, no. 1, pp. 64–83.

Tuazon, B. (ed.) (1993) *Torment and Struggle After Marcos: A Report on Human Rights Trends under Aquino*, Task Force Detainees of the Philippines, Quezon City.

Turnbull, C. M. (1989) *A History of Singapore: 1819–1988*, Oxford University Press, Singapore.

Turner, B. S. (1993) 'Outline of a Theory of Human Rights', *Sociology*, vol. 27, no. 3, pp. 489–512.

Turner, H. A., Fosh, P. Ng, S.-H. (1981) *The Last Colony: But Whose?*, Cambridge University Press, Cambridge.

(1991) *Between Two Societies: Hong Kong Labour in Transition*, Centre of Asian Studies, Hong Kong University.

Turner, M. (1991) 'Human Rights in the Philippines' in Tang (1995).

Unger, R. (1976) *Law in Modern Society*, Free Press, New York.

US Congress (1992) *Human Rights Report: Singapore*, US Congress, Washington DC.

Van Mehren, P. and Sawers, T. (1992) 'Revitalizing the Law and Development Movement', *Harvard International Law Journal*, vol. 33, no. 1.

Vasil, R. (1989) 'Trade Unions' in Sandhu and Wheatley (1989).

(1992) *Governing Singapore*, Mandarin, Singapore.

Vejerano, A. (1991) 'A Sociology of Philippine Supreme Court Decisions: 1946–1985', unpublished Ph.D. thesis, College of Social Sciences and Philosophy, University of the Philippines.

Villanueva, C. L. (1990) 'A Comparative Study of the Judicial Role and its Effect on the Theory of Judicial Precedent in the Philippines Hybrid Legal System', *Philippine Law Journal*, vol. 65, pp. 42–75.

Villegas, E. (1984) *Studies in Philippine Political Economy*, rev. edn, Silingan Publishers, Manila.

(n.d.) *The Political Economy of Philippine Labor Laws*, Foundation for Nationalist Studies, Quezon City.

Vincent, R. J. (1986) *Human Rights and International Relations*, Cambridge University Press, Cambridge.

Vogler, C. (1985) *The Nation State: the Neglected Dimension of Class*, Gower, Aldershot.

Vorys, K. von (1975) *Democracy without Consensus: Communalism and Political Stability in Malaysia*, Princeton University Press, Princeton.

Wacks, R. (ed.) (1988) *Civil Liberties in Hong Kong*, Oxford University Press, Hong Kong.

(1989) *The Future of the Law in Hong Kong*, Oxford University Press, Hong Kong.

(1992) *Human Rights in Hong Kong*, Oxford University Press, Hong Kong.

Wad, P. and Jomo, K. S. (1994) '"In-House Unions": Looking East for Industrial Relations', in Jomo, 1994.

Walker, A. (1986) *Communist Neo-Traditionalism: Work and Authority in Chinese Industry*, University of California Press, Berkeley.

Wallerstein, I. (1979) *The Capitalist World System*, Cambridge University Press, Cambridge.

Warren, B. (1973) 'Imperialism and Capitalist Industrialization', *New Left Review*, no. 81.

Weber, M. (1972) *Economy and Society*, 2 vols., University of California, Berkeley.

Wei, G. (1989) *The Law of Copyright in Singapore*, Singapore National Printers, Singapore.

Welch, C. E. Jr (1990) 'Global Change and Human Rights: Asian Perspectives in Comparative Context' in Welch and Leary (1990).

Welch, Jr, C. E. and Leary, V. A. (eds.) (1990) *Asian Perspectives on Human Rights*, Westview Press, Boulder.

Wellman, C. (1989) 'A New Conception of Human Rights' in Winston (1989).

Wesley-Smith, P. (1989) 'Understanding the Common Law' in Wacks (1989).
    (1993) *An Introduction to the Hong Kong Legal System*, 2nd edn, Oxford University Press, Hong Kong.
    (1994a) 'Anti-Chinese Legislation in Hong Kong' in Chan and Young (1994)
    (1994b) *Constitutional and Administrative Law*, 2nd edn, Longman Asia, Hong Kong.
    (1994c) *The Sources of Hong Kong Law*, Hong Kong University Press, Hong Kong.

Wessner, D. W. (1996) 'From Judge to Participant: The United States as Champion of Human Rights', *Bulletin of Concerned Asian Scholars*, vol. 28, no. 2, pp. 29–45.

Whitely, R. (1992) *Business Systems in East Asia*, Sage, London.

Wilentz, S. (1984) *Chants Democratic: New York City and the Rise of the American Working Class*, Oxford University Press, New York.

Williams, K. (1990) *An Introduction to Hong Kong Employment Law*, Oxford University Press, Hong Kong.

Williamson, H. (1991) 'Japanese Enterprise Unions in Transnational Companies', *Capital and Class*, no. 45, pp. 17–26.
    (1994) *Coping with the Miracle: Japan's Unions Explore New International Relations*, Pluto Press, London.

Wilson, R. (ed.) (1996) *Human Rights, Culture and Context*, Pluto, London.

Winkler, E. and Greenhalgh, S. (eds.) (1988) *Contending Approaches to the Political Economy of Taiwan*, M. E. Sharpe, Armonk.

Winston, M. (ed.) (1989) *The Philosophy of Human Rights*, Wadsworth Publishing Company, Belmont.

Wiseberg, L. S. (1990) *The Importance of Freedom of Association for Human Rights*

NGOs, International Centre for Human Rights and Democratic Development, Ottawa.

Wolters, W. (1984) *Politics, Patronage and Class Conflict in Central Luzon*, New Day Publishers, Quezon City.

Wong, A. and Yeh, S. (eds.) (1985) *Housing a Nation: 25 Years of Public Housing in Singapore*, Maruzen Asia, Singapore.

Wong, S.-L. (1986) 'Modernization and Chinese Culture in Hong Kong', *The China Quarterly*, June 1986.

(1988) *Emigrant Entrepreneurs: Shanghai Industrialists in Hong Kong*, Oxford University Press, Hong Kong.

(1992) *Emigration and Stability in Hong Kong*, University of California Press.

(1994) 'Business and Politics in Hong Kong during the Transition' in Leung and T. Wong (1994).

Wong, T. (1994) 'Hong Kong's Manufacturing Sector: Transformation and Prospects' in Leung and T. Wong (1994).

Wong, T. P., and Lui, T.-L. (1994) 'Class Analysis: The Relevance of Weber' in Lau, et al. (1994).

Woodiwiss, A. (1990a) *Rights v. Conspiracy: A Sociological Essay on the History of Labour Law in the United States*, Berg, Oxford.

(1990b) *Social Theory After Postmodernism: Rethinking Production, Law and Class*, Pluto, London.

(1990c) 'Rereading Japan: Capitalism, Possession and the Necessity of Hegemony' in Abercrombie et al. (1990).

(1992a) *Law, Labour and Society in Japan*, Routledge, London.

(1992b) 'The Passing of Modernism and Labour Rights: Lessons from Japan and the United States', *Social and Legal Studies*, vol. 1, no. 4, pp. 477–92.

(1993) *Postmodernity, USA: On the Crisis of Social Modernism in the Postwar United States*, Sage, London.

(1996) 'Searching for Signs of Globalisation', *Sociology*, vol. 30, no. 4, pp. 799–810.

(1997a) 'Against Modernity: A Dissident Rant', *Economy and Society*, vol. 26, no. 1, pp. 1–21.

(1997b) 'Behind Governmentality: Sociological Theory, Pacific Capitalism and Industrial Citizenship', *Citizenship Studies*, vol. 1, no. 1, pp. 87–114.

(1998) 'Globalisation, Property Relations and the History of Labour Law', in van der Linden, M. and Price, R. (1998), *The Rise and Development of Collective Labour Law*, International Institute of Social History, Amsterdam.

Woods, L. T. (1995) 'Economic Cooperation and Human Rights in the Asia-Pacific Region: The Role of Regional Institutions' in Tang (1995).

Woon, W. (1989) 'The Continuing Reception of English Commercial Law' in Woon (ed.) (1989).

(1993) 'Legal System and Human Rights Situation in Singapore' in Heinz (1993).

Woon, W. (ed.) (1989) *The Singapore Legal System*, Longman, Singapore.

World Bank (1995) *World Development Report: Workers in an Integrating World*, Oxford University Press, New York.

Woronoff, J. (1984) *Japan's Commercial Empire*, Lotus Press, Tokyo.

Wright, E. O. (1985) *Classes*, Verso, London.

Wu, M.-A. (1990) *The Malaysian Legal System*, Longman Malaysia, Petaling Jaya.

Wurfel, D. (1959) 'Trade Union Development and Labor Relations Policy in the Philippines', *Industrial and Labor Relations Review*, vol. 12, no. 4, pp. 562–608.

(1988) *Filipino Politics: Development and Decay*, Ateneo de Manila University Press, Quezon City.

Yamamura, K. and Yasuba, Y. (eds.) (1987) *The Political Economy of Japan: The Domestic Transformation*, Stanford University Press, Stanford.

Yamashita, S. (ed.) (1991) *The Transfer of Japanese Technology and Management to Asean Countries*, University of Tokyo Press, Tokyo.

Yen, C.-H. (1995) *Community and Politics: the Chinese in Colonial Singapore and Malaysia*, Times Academic Press, Singapore.

Yong, C.-F. (1991) *Chinese Leadership and Power in Colonial Singapore*, Times Academic Press, Singapore.

Yoon, D. (1990) *Law and Political Authority in South Korea*, Westview Press, Boulder.

Yoshihara, K. (1985) *Philippine Industrialization: Foreign and Domestic Capital*, Ateneo de Manila University Press, Quezon City.

Young, H. L. (1993) 'The Influence of Foreign Law on Contemporary Union Right Policies in Asian Countries', mimeo, Japan Institute of Labour, Tokyo.

Young, J. D. (1994) 'The Building Years: Maintaining a China-Hong Kong-Britain Equilibrium' in Chan and Young (1994).

Youngson, A. J. (1982) *Hong Kong: Economic Growth and Policy*, Oxford University Press, Hong Kong.

Yu, R. (1981) 'Workers' Progressive Response to Underdevelopment and Authoritarianism', unpublished Ph.D. thesis, College of Social Sciences and Philosophy, University of the Philippines.

Yue, C. S. (1987) *Export Incentives and Manufactures in Asean Countries*, Singapore University Press, Singapore.

Yusoff, M. (1992) *Consociational Politics: the Malaysian Experience*, Perikatan Pemuda Enterprises, Kuala Lumpur.

Ziskind, D. (1984) *Labor Provisions in Asian Constitutions*, Litlaw Foundation, Los Angeles.

(1990) *Labor Laws in the Middle East: Tradition in Transition*, Litlow Foundation, Los Angeles.

INDEX